TELEVISION IN
THE REAL WORLD

TELEVISION
IN THE
REAL WORLD

A Case Study Course in
Broadcast Management

Edited, with Additional Text and Notes,
by GEORGE DESSART
for
The International Radio &
Television Society

COMMUNICATION ARTS BOOKS

HASTINGS HOUSE, PUBLISHERS
New York 10016

For Nancy, Peter and Nina,
who make the real world tenable.

Library of Congress Cataloging in Publication Data

Main entry under title:

Television in the real world.

   (Communication arts books)
   Includes bibliographical references and index.
   1. Television broadcasting—Management.
I. Dessart, George.   II. International Radio
and Television Society.
HE8700.6.T44   1978   658'.91'38455   77-24415
ISBN 0-8038-7171-6
ISBN 0-8038-7172-4 pbk.

Published simultaneously in Canada by
Copp Clark, Ltd., Toronto

Printed in the United States of America

Contents

Preface

FREQUENCIES ARE SCARCE. That statement should not be news to anyone curious enough to pick up this book. Such a person will also recognize that an application to establish a broadcast facility must provide convincing evidence that the individual or group making the request is more worthy of selection than others who might wish to make use of the same frequency. Accordingly, the process of filing for a license to use a scarce frequency in the electromagnetic spectrum—and most especially in the VHF television band—really represents a demonstration of one's ability to establish and operate a superior broadcasting station. The application attests to the prospective broadcaster's financial, legal, programming, news, management, sales, and promotional abilities. If a broadcaster's success or failure in actually operating the station can be regarded as a real-world final exam, then filing a successful application is, at least, the equivalent of a stiff mid-term.

This book is essentially a text with resource materials for a course in broadcasting (or as a guide to license applicants) built around a simulation of the process of filing a license application for a new VHF television station on Channel 5 in a mythical city—Desolake, Kansouri—located in the Central Time Zone and ranking in market size with the real 75th market, Portland-Poland Spring.

The book documents in detail the results of such a simulation. Thus, in a very real sense, the book can be said to have been test-marketed. While the emphasis is on the simulation, the process set forth here has been given an added validity through an actual test-marketing in Tarrytown, New York, over a five-day period in the late Autumn of 1975.

Television in the Real World has come about as a direct result of the International Radio and Television Society's Fifth Annual Faculty-Industry Seminar held at the Tarrytown Conference Center, a converted palatial estate which rambles on a hilltop overlooking the Hudson River in the Washington Irving country, some 30 miles north of New York City. Sixty-two faculty members representing 53 institutions from all parts of the United States and from the West Indies assembled to participate in a similar simulation. In addition, 38 industry representatives, specialists in various aspects of station operation, were on hand to join the four groups into which they had been divided—called IOTA, RHO, TAU and SIGMA—as group leaders or as resource persons in programming, news, community affairs, sales and promotion. These industry representatives were from major station group management, from station representative firms and stations in New York City; Philadelphia; Boston and New Bedford, Massachusetts; Hartford and New Haven, Connecticut; Columbus and Dayton, Ohio; Baltimore; Nashville; Green Bay, Wisconsin; Rochester, New York; and Greenville, South Carolina. They were joined by a number of industry specialists—a network economist, a pay television executive, a daytime drama writer, a network news executive producer, the founder of one of the nation's leading news consultant firms, and the North American representative of a major European broadcasting system—all of whom provided additional background for their deliberations.

The results of the labors of the four groups, together with a report of their discussions, are included in this book, not so much to serve as a functional record of the event, (though some may wish to use this book for that purpose), but as a stimulus and aid to students seeking their own answers to the problem. Anyone looking merely for the minutes of the meeting may be disappointed since every effort has been made to avoid using the Tarrytown discussions to provide definitive answers. Rather, for our purpose, there is more value in setting forth a range of alternatives proposed by the discussants and some of the indications for the alternative of choice.

The final products of the group's four-and-a-half days and three long nights have been included, however, as a point of comparison for future simulators and actual applicants.

The IRTS Faculty-Industry Seminars were arranged to increase the understanding and to decrease what had been perceived as occasional friction between broadcasters and broadcasting educators. It has long been my own observation, as both a broadcaster and *quondam* academic, that each is most guilty of what he regards as characteristic of the other. Some broadcasters are highly vocal about the shortcomings of the academic, a vocalization many times more arrogant than the arrogance of which he accuses the professor. Some academics, on the other hand, are guilty of inadequate scholarship. Too often, they simply do not know the current practices of the broadcaster or, even more important, what has brought them about.

Given the shortness of the time available and the necessarily compressed nature of the experience in Tarrytown, the extent to which it served all the hoped for ends might be questioned. Some may have felt that the Seminar should have been more properly entitled the "Industry as Faculty Seminar" since a leader for each group was designated from industry ranks; in view of the task-oriented nature of the problem and its familiarity to the practicing professionals, they may have appeared to be directing rather than serving as discussion leaders. Although the industry participants were not necessarily possessed of some measure of ultimate truth, they were, nonetheless, able to add a dimension of reality by revealing how commercial broadcasters must function as businessmen, motivated not solely by profit-making, but at the same time never losing sight of its importance. Thus the industry representatives could teach what no faculty member or student who had not actually had the experience of working at the top decision-making level in broadcasting could ever otherwise have appreciated. Just watching the professionals attack the problems, was, to many, an invaluable opportunity. If nothing else, then, the exercise provided an excellent arena in which the academic might study the mentality of the commercial broadcaster, seeing how he goes about dealing with a practical, competitive problem. For the reader, it is hoped, the record of the exercise will provide a glimpse into the seldom seen world of broadcasting professionals at work, actually doing what they do.

Two things make this book possible at all. First more than a year of planning—to say nothing of the wheedling, dragooning, commandeering, cajoling, shaming, intimidating and even blackmailing on the part of the Seminar Committee to bring together the large number of experienced and seriously interested participants. Most of the material in the Appendices, essential to the simulation, was assembled or created by members of the committee. Credit for the committee's success must be laid at the feet of its co-chairmen, Gene Accas, who also somehow manages to function as Vice President for Network Relations, Leo Burnett, USA; and Aaron Cohen, then Vice President for Marketing, NBC Television Network, later promoted to Vice President for Programs, East Coast. No one who has participated in any way in these seminars could fail to appreciate the enormous personal contribution of these two leaders and of the constancy of their faith in the importance of the work they succeeded in persuading so many others to join. Under their aegis, the Annual IRTS Faculty-Industry Seminar has become an institution in broadcast education. They have also sparked the series of volumes of which this is the third. (*Broadcasting: The Critical Challenges,* edited with an introduction by Charles S. Steinberg, based on the Third Seminar, and *The Broadcast Industry: An Examination of Major Issues,* edited by Robert H. Stanley, based on the Fourth Seminar, both published by Hastings House as *Communication Arts Books,* were the earlier volumes). A complete listing of those who worked with Gene Accas and Aaron Cohen is to be found in the Appendix as is a listing of the officers of the IRTS and of its educational arm, the International Radio and Television Foundation.

The second factor, which both made this book possible and attests to its potential usefulness, is that the participants in the simulation, the faculty members and the industry resource persons in the four groups, respected the importance of the problems posed to such an extent as to fully engage themselves in working out meaningful solutions. Transcripts of the sessions, totalling 2,679 pages, are testimony to the creative energies expended and the experience applied.

As has been indicated, the transcript material has been used only selectively. The order in which some questions were taken up has been changed, few of the background addresses have been quoted at all, fewer still in their entirety. Nor, since the selection of material used reflects only the editor's emphasis on educational significance and applicability, the extent to which individual faculty members or industry representatives are quoted is not to be taken as an indication of the extent or value of their contribution to the process. In the heat of discussion, some comments went unattributed; also, some individuals are under-represented in the material quoted since they took leadership roles in working out questions in which they were particularly knowledgeable—Carl Jon Denbow and Frank M. Kearns in news; Robert K. McLaughlin in production; Lewis O'Donnell, Sherilyn K. Zeigler and Kenneth Harwood, for example. Much of the work took place in committees, after hours, and, therefore, was not recorded in the transcribed materials.

Finally, I should like to acknowledge the debt I owe to all of those upon whom I have shamelessly drawn for assistance and support: colleagues at CBS and elsewhere, members of my own staff, the CBS News Special Projects Library and many others, most especially my friend, mentor and critic, Irving Rosenthal, Professor Emeritus at City College. I should also like to express my thanks, and that of IRTS to Lou Roller and his associates at Soundscribers for the sisyphean task of producing the transcripts and to Rachel Sandberg and Abigail Myers for the unappetizing chore of turning my pages into a legible manuscript.

GEORGE DESSART

1

Introduction

Why does a station decide to begin a news broadcast at 5:30 rather than at five o'clock?

How does a radio or television station determine the needs and interests of the people in its coverage area?

What factors must be considered in putting together a program schedule?

How does a station determine how much to charge its advertisers?

THESE ARE EASILY SEEN to be important questions if one is to understand the management of a commercial broadcasting station in the United States. They are posed in a familiar, rather general form. But consider how much more compelling and challenging they become when you ask them in a slightly different form:

Should we begin our station's news at 5:30 or at five o'clock?
Should we do a children's show, a public affairs broadcast or a game show in the four o'clock time period next Monday?
How much do we charge for our late news broadcast?

The difference in the two sets of questions is the difference between this book and most standard books on broadcasting.[1*] This book tries to establish a framework in which a student can examine the problems of a broadcast station operation not in terms of assimilated generalizations, which may or may not account for all possible variables, but in confrontation with a specific problem situation as it might be encountered in the real world. This book deals, in short, with a *simulation*: all of the problems presented—e.g., community relations, programming, news, sales, promotion etc.—are seen in a specific real-life con-

---

[1*] Notes are in a separate section at the end of each Chapter of this book.

text and become the subjects of a task-oriented process. There is a specific beginning and a clearly discernible, objectivized end. The book traces the simulation of a prospective broadcast licensee applying to the Federal Communications Commission for a Construction Permit to operate a television station on Channel 5 in a mythical, but specifically described community, Desolake, Kansouri. Desolake is equal in size to the nation's 75th market and has had two VHF stations, a CBS and an NBC affiliate already in operation over the last 20 years. The city and surrounding areas are described, the programming schedule of the two older stations is given. The A. C. Nielsen Co. has provided a rating book for a typical November for the two competitors; rate cards for the other stations and a listing of available programming, syndicated programs and feature films, with the prices asked, are among the givens.

Simulations have been in use in many fields over recent years. They have long formed the backbone for graduate business education at some schools, and have been considered particularly successful in political science courses where they have been used in examining the consequences of national policy on international relations. Simulation as an educational technique is particularly useful where the learning must be primarily experiential or where complex systems are being studied as variables interact.[2]

Simulation has been little used in broadcast education. The editor has, over the past decade, developed and used a simulation entitled "Mythical Kingdom" in which students, functioning as consultants to the parliament of a mid-Atlantic island, are asked to set broad policy for a television system in a developing country. The exercise, generally conducted in a matter of a few hours, has proven invaluable with non-communications students in developing an awareness of the complex interrelationships between a society and its mass media. Broadcasting students have found it useful in learning to describe a broadcast operation, commercial or non-commercial, in terms of the functions which must be performed in order to keep it operating.

The simulation in this book, originally designed for the Fifth Annual Faculty-Industry Seminar of the International Radio and Television Society[3] represents the most extensive use of simulation in broadcast education to date. The problem posed: *Develop a viable, competitive and potentially profitable third VHF station in a traditionally two-station market.*

USING THIS BOOK

Although some readers are interested in tracing through the process on their own, most who read this chapter will be students and their instructors in a course built around this simulation. Accordingly, this section is addressed primarily to them. Simulations are effective as learning methods to the extent that they involve each and every participant. Certainly every broadcaster, and probably every teacher of broadcasting, has at one point heard a student say "I know what a program director does—but what does he really *do?* I mean what does he do on Monday morning?''

It is that kind of specificity that this simulation seeks to answer. To solve the problem posed, many tasks must be accomplished. Every student should be given a specific responsibility to the group to locate specific information or to develop a particular plan needed to complete the problem. Since the group will undoubtedly treat each problem in sequence, some students may be assigned tasks which do not seem to be on the agenda for some weeks. However, many of the questions assigned and background information to be assembled will require time to obtain. Some assignments may involve correspondence with stations in other markets and several weeks might pass before answers to letters are received. It is important that the group survey the entire task at the outset and that those with duties which will not be called into account until some future date get an early start.

Each chapter in the book is organized around a specific problem, stated at the beginning. There follows a discussion of some of the background. Next there is a list of Thought-Starter questions. These are followed by a review of the discussions which took place when the 62 faculty members and 36 industry leaders attacked the problem in Tarrytown. These discussions are presented, not to provide answers, but alternatives; to permit you to share the insights of working professionals and knowledgeable instructors in coping with the problem.

As the book progresses, these discussions are more and more summarized. They are to be used for background, to develop other insights, to suggest other ways to deal with the problem at hand. Rarely, if ever, do they present solutions. The Faculty-Industry Seminar discussions on each topic are followed by a summary and list of suggested activities and questions. Some courses will be organized with committees from the very start; others will set up specialist committees or individuals; still others will be set up with competing committees, each with subcommittees, as were the four groups in the Tarrytown simulation. Whatever your assignment, familiarize yourself with all the materials in the Appendices, whether or not they seem to bear on the responsibilities assigned to you. Each involves materials that broadcasters should be thoroughly acquainted with, no matter what their specialties. Also, the success of your group's project will depend on the extent to which you can offer informed suggestions, criticism and advice to the other members of the group. Broadcasting is always a cooperative activity—the sharing of ideas and the joint effort to reach consentual goals are always required for success.

APPROACHING THE PROBLEM

In the real world, there are two ways in which a radio or television station is established. An entrepreneur or a group of entrepreneurs decides to seek a location for a station, or alternatively, the need or desire for a station arises in a particular area and elements of the community seek out someone to establish it. In both instances, there must be an available frequency allocated to the community. The existence of an unassigned or unused VHF allocation is very unlikely. There are 523 VHF allocations for commercial use; 513 were on air as of April 30, 1976; 10 allocations had been assigned, construction permits were outstanding but the stations were not yet on air. There were, at the same time, 104 VHF allocations to Educational TV; 97 were on air and 7 CP's were not on air. The number of VHF allocations has been fixed since 1952. This represented the maximum number of stations which could be accommodated on the 12 frequencies, channels 2–13, assuming the maintenance of a separation of 55–60 miles between adjacent channels and 155–220 miles between stations using the same frequency.[4]

In 1973, the Office of Telecommunications Policy, a Presidential Agency established to study long term communications needs, proposed that as many as 83 more VHF stations might be dropped into 100 markets by reducing the standard mileage-separation restrictions previously established by the FCC.[5]

This proposal was the subject of considerable scrutiny within the industry at the time of the November 1975 Seminar. In April, 1976, as a result of a petition brought by the United Church of Christ, the FCC voted to conduct an inquiry, *Docket 20418,* into the feasibility of such so-called drop-ins. The simulation assumes that as a result of some such proposal another VHF station may be established in the mythical city of Desolake, Kansouri, "Soy Bean Capital of the Midwest." Thus, the applicants for this Construction Permit have selected an area with an unused allocation and are ready to file for a license to operate a commercial station on the frequency available.

It is important to recognize at the outset of the simulation that the license is being sought for a commercial station. True, there may very well be some public television allocations should a drop-in proposal ultimately be adopted. The problem, however, is not designed to prepare students for the eventuality of being among the handful of persons actually filing applications for those few frequency allocations which might be made available at some date in the future, whether they be commercial or public. Rather, since the information required in the filing of a license application and in the development of plans to place a station on the air embraces so many aspects of a station's operation it provides an unparalleled opportunity to examine the planning and decision-making processes central to braodcast management. Although many of those processes are common to both public and commercial stations, the exercise calls for planning a *commercial* station. Several reasons underlie that stipulation: commercial stations involve all the elements to be found in public station management, plus several not found there; there are more commercial stations than public stations and it is therefore likely that more of those involved in the simulation will find themselves employed at commercial rather than at public stations; the lessons of commercial television station management are more readily transferable to radio than are those of public television; the commercial station will remain the dominant force in American broadcasting for the predictable future as it has historically been:

> The advertiser base of broadcasting was solidified by a regulatory policy decision in the mid-1930s. Section 307 (c) of the Communications Act of 1934 directed the FCC to "study the proposal that Congress by statute allocate fixed percentages of radio broadcasting facilities to particular types or kinds of non-profit radio programs or to persons identified with particular types or kinds of non-profit activities." In 1935, the Commission recommended against the proposal observing "that the interests of non-profit organizations may be better served by the use of existing facilities, thus giving them access to costly and efficient equipment and to established audiences."[6]

During the 15 years from 1921 to 1936, there had been no fewer than 202 licenses to non-profit organizations. By 1936, only 38 were alive. Ten years later, nine of those had gone off the air and an additional nine were being operated as commercial stations. By 1964, there were 40 such non-profit organizations operating AM stations; 20 of those stations were being operated as commercial ventures.[7] Nor has the history of non-commercial television shown a different pattern—252 allocations were set aside by the FCC for educational use in 1952; within the next seven years, only 44 had managed to make it onto the air and most of them for only a few hours a day.[8] Even now, three decades after the Commission recommendation on non-profit organization broadcasting, public television is plagued by inadequate funding, often insignificant audience levels, unresolved conflict between station policy and that of national production and distribution agencies, and policies at the federal funding level which have inhibited its development into the viable force it can and should become.

Finally, it is easier to see the specific objectives to be attained in the framework of a commercial station operation. Ultimately, the value of the simulation lies largely in the process rather than in the result. Thus the learning will occur in the discipline of seeing and fulfilling tangible goals. The commercial station, with quantifyable and clearly defined means for determing the relative success of its programming, news, sales and other decisions provides a framework for determining that the simulation is proceeding toward a defined goal.

It should be apparent that the very specificity of the simulation—*i.e.* the inexorable progress toward detailed and objectivized documents setting forth programming, sales, promotion and other plans—involves following a decision-making regimen. Consonant with current scientific decision-making theory, it is possible for those engaged in the simulation to develop an *algorithm,* a sequence of steps to follow in solving all of the problems. Briefly, this can be described as:

1. Stating clear and meaningful *objectives.*

2. Examining the *context* in which they are to be considered and assigning values to *criteria* whenever possible.

3. Determining *constraints*.

4. Considering *alternatives* and developing a strategy which will op-
timize criteria within the constraints.[9]

Let us take a deliberately far-fetched example. KIRT is considering the use
of a symphonic orchestral sound. If we state our objective in terms of establishing the KIRT Symphonic Orchestra or even the KIRT Chamber Orchestra, we have stated meaningless objectives since they carry with them the consideration of only one set of alternatives and thus beg the answer. What we are
really trying to do is discover alternatives which would give KIRT a distinctive
on-air sound. Once the objective is stated in those terms we must ask what we
need to know in order to solve the problem. The *context* in which we examine
the problem would thus include the nature of the audience we will be serving;
the various objectives of the station; the activities of the competing stations; the
practices of all the radio stations in the community; the resources available; the
experience of other stations both live and on record, locally and elsewhere, in
the past and present; probable developments in programming in the foreseeable
future; etc. It should be clear that gathering this information will involve considerable research beyond the scope of this or any other single book. The activity sections at the conclusion of each chapter will suggest some of the sources
for the information needed and some ways to tap various sources. Obviously,
those lists are not exhaustive, but are merely intended to stimulate thought.

The *criteria*, in this case, will be self-imposed. A distinctive sound, a
promotable broadcast element which will distinguish this station from the others, prestige in the community, support of community institutions, are some of
the criteria which the station's management might, to some extent or other,
wish to consider. On the other hand, the *constraints* would include the budget
available, the cost of live musicians, the availability of a suitable recording facility, the cost of recorded music, the cost of orignal compositions, the quality
of pre-packaged materials and the comparative quality of the competition's
musical signature against which KIRT's would inevitably be compared. The
term *constraint* may be understood as "the region within which we should look
for a solution."[10]

One last point should be made about the decision-making process. Any
decision involves risk. It is popularly assumed that a decision can be judged,
after the fact, as right or wrong depending on whether the outcome can be seen
to be pleasing or profitable or good as measured in some other fashion. It is
certainly desirable that every decision, in this simulation or in real life, result in
achieving the objectives stated. But to judge decisions solely on their outcome
is to insist that all decision makers accurately foretell the future. Far more important criteria for judgment are the two related questions.

1. Did the decision-maker seek out all the information which could be
made available to inform that decision?

2. Did the decision-maker consider the information available?

A right or wrong decision is right or wrong depending solely on the information available. One authority in the developing field of decision analysis, Morton Tribus, offers the following illustration:

> . . . suppose a person whom you know to be both wealthy and honest comes up to you and offers the following wager: You pick a coin out of your pocket and toss it ten times. If you get at least one head, he will pay you $2,000. If not, you pay him $1.00. Suppose you accept the bet and lose, was it a *wrong* decision? Given the chance, would you make the same *wrong* decision again? Of course you would! The odds in your favor are roughly 1024 to 1. A fairer bet would have been to offer $1,000 to his $1. What we may more properly conclude is that you made a good DECISION but had a bad OUTCOME. If a decision involves risk, it is always possible that a good decision can lead to a bad outcome and that a bad decision can lead to a good outcome. This is what is meant by *risk*. [11]

There are risks involved in the process upon which you are about to embark. The history of broadcasting is testament enough to that. More important, there are rewards. Those rewards will go to the best informed and most involved.

NOTES

1. Among the sources cited in this volume are several which serious students will find particularly helpful in connection with the central problem considered. These include:

Ward A. Quaal and James A. Brown, *Broadcast Management: Radio-Television*. Second Edition Revised and Enlarged, New York, 1976, Hastings House. The particularly generous citations make this volume an essential in any broadcasting library.

Yale Roe, editor, *Television Station Management; the Business of Broadcasting*, New York, 1964, Hastings House. A somewhat older book but a helpful overview of the functions of various station departments;

Sydney W. Head, *Broadcasting in America: A Survey of Television and Radio*, Third Edition, Boston, 1976, Houghton Mifflin Company. Extensively revised, this edition again demonstrates why the book has long been the standard one-volume introduction to the field;

Martin Mayer, *About Television*, New York, 1972, Harper & Row. A readable journalistic account of the industry and its problems.

Les Brown, *Television: The Business Behind the Box*, New York, 1971, Harcourt Brace Jovanovich. The former television editor of *Variety* now the broadcasting reporter for *The New York Times*, uses a calendar year in American television to develop considerable insights into the relationship between the network schedules and the business interests of the industry.

Broadcasting Yearbook, 1977, Washington, Broadcasting Publications Inc. Published by the one indispensible trade journal in the industry, this annual compendium includes data on every radio and television station licensed or authorized in the United States; on the nation's top 207 markets; on equipment manufacturers, consultants, representatives, owners, brokers, engineers; on the FCC, its regulations, its history and its bureaucracy. An incredibly helpful volume.

2. *Vide* James A. Robinson, "Simulation and Games" in Peter H. Rossi and Bruce J. Biddle (eds.), *The New Media and Education: Their Impact on Society,* Garden City, New York, 1966, Doubleday. A brief but perceptive description of games and simulation is given by Fred Guggenheim, "Educational Technology" in Monroe C. Gottsegen and Gloria B. Gottsegen (eds.), *Professional School Psychology,* Volume III, New York, 1969, Grune and Stratton. The classic work in simulation remains that of Guetzkow. Those who wish to explore the subject more fully should examine H. Guetzkow (ed.), *Simulation in Social Science: Readings,* Englewood Cliffs, New Jersey, 1962, Prentice-Hall and *Simulation in International Relations: Developments for Research and Teaching,* 1963.

3. Two previous Communication Arts Books from Hastings House record the Third and Fourth Annual Faculty Industry Seminars: Charles S. Steinberg (ed.), *Broadcasting: The Critical Challenges,* 1974 and Robert H. Stanley (ed.), *The Broadcast Industry: An Examination of Major Issues,* 1975.

4. *Rules Regulating Radio and TV* Volume 3, Washington, D.C., March 1968, Federal Communications Commission, S 73.610. Also available in *Broadcasting Yearbook, op. cit.* p. A-14. See also pp. A5–6.

5. ———, "Technical Analysis of VHF Television Broadcasting Frequency Assignment Criteria" and *The Radio Frequency Spectrum: United States Use and Management,* Washington, D.C., 1973, Office of Telecommunications Policy.

In April, 1975, the FCC adopted (Docket 20418) an inquiry into the feasibility of drop-ins into top 100 markets as a result of the United Church of Christ petition based on the OTP study. The Department of Commerce's Institute for Telecommunications will conduct a study of feasibility based on Knoxville, Tenn. "Where Things Stand," *Broadcasting,* Sept. 26, 1976, p. 13.

6. William K. Jones, *Cases and Materials on Regulated Industries,* University Casebook Series, Brooklyn, New York, 1967, The Foundation Press, p. 1037.

7. *Ibid.*

8. Mayer, *op. cit.,* p. 314.

9. Engineering Concepts Curriculum Project, Polytechnic Institute of Brooklyn, E. E. David Jr., J. G. Truxal, Co-Director, E. J. Piel, Executive Director, *The Man-Made World,* New York, 1971, McGraw-Hill Book Company, Chapter 2 *passim.*

10. *Ibid.* p. 49.

11. Martin Tribus, *Rational Descriptions, Decisions and Designs,* New York, 1969, Pergamon Press, p. 2.

2

FCC License Application

The replies to the following questions constitute representations on which the Commission will rely in considering this application. Thus time and care should be devoted to the replies so that they will reflect accurately applicant's responsible consideration of the questions asked.

Replies relating to future operations constitute representations against which the subsequent operation of the station will be measured.

—Instructions, General Information and Definitions for TV Broadcast Application, *Federal Communications Commission*, Form 301, Section IV-B, Page 7.

EVERY BEGINNING IS, as T. S. Eliot inferred, a presumption. So it was for the 62 faculty members assembled at Tarrytown; so it has been for every group of students to whom I have presented the simulation problem in the Mythical Kingdom; so it will be for you as you set out on your own examination of the problem this book addresses. How does one presume? How does one begin?

Fortunately, in this instance, we have the FCC License Application as a framework for our deliberations. Since the problem is to develop a series of plans and proposals which would result in a compelling showing before the Commission and which would result in your application being given favor over all other contenders, you can at all times use the demands of the license application itself to set parameters, establish priorities, and chart a course for the problem.

The requirement that a federal license be prerequisite to every "transmission of energy or communications or signals by radio"[1] derives from the commerce clause of the United States Constitution (Section 8) which asserts federal government jurisdiction over "Commerce with foreign nations, among the several States, and with the Indian tribes." The application of the principle to radio was first enunciated in the Radio Act of 1912.[2] By 1934, when the present Communications Act became the operable law, the license itself had become not only a means for the allocation of scarce resources, but also the basic tool by which the then established Federal Communications Commission would exercise its supervision over the industry it had been mandated to supervise. Thus the License Application is more than a mere formal prerequisite. Its questions convey to the broadcaster the Commission's jurisdiction over certain areas of concern and the sense of urgency with which it views particular aspects of a broadcaster's operation. The broadcaster's own responses to the questions posed in the License Application become the standard by which the licensee himself is judged in having operated in the "public interest, convenience and necessity."

In establishing a new station, a potential licensee has one of two courses open. The applicant may seek an unused channel on the existing Table of Assignments (the situation assumed in the present simulation) or may, in certain circumstances, petition the FCC to modify the Assignments Table in order to accommodate the use of a particular frequency in the desired location. In either case, the procedure is the same in that the law requires that the first step is to obtain a Construction Permit. To obtain the Construction Permit, the following steps must be followed:

1. An application must be filed on Form 301 (See Appendix 1).

2. Public notice of the Commission's acceptance of such an application must be made in the community affected (the proposed City of License and the immediate surrounding area).

3. A period of time—generally 30 days, although it may be longer at the Commission's discretion—must be allowed for Petitions to Deny to be filed with the Commission.

Petitions to Deny are precisely what their name implies. They ask the FCC to deny the application for any one of a number of reasons. An existing station, for example may object to anticipated signal interference within its licensed contour. Other parties may object to assumed economic interference.[3] Still others—representatives of various community interests—may present objections to the proposed station or to its plans of operation. Petitions may be filed on behalf of any recognized "Party in Interest." Should a Petition to Deny be filed, the Commission has, under law, a number of alternatives. The Petition may be dismissed as lacking in standing or in substance, an Evidentiary Hearing may be set for the parties involved—the applicant, the petitioner and others who may feel impelled to come forward—or the Commission may approve the

Petition and deny the application. This action would be subject to an appeal procedure, initially a petition for rehearing and, ultimately, recourse to the federal courts. Indeed, any ruling by the Commission would be subject to appeal on the part of the denied party.[4]

Once a Construction Permit is granted—either in the absence of any Petitions to Deny, after the FCC has dismissed Petitions which have been filed, or after petitioning groups or individuals have accepted the applicant's assurances and chosen to withdraw their petitions—the applicant is given a limited period in which to construct broadcasting facilities and make ready for operation. Once this is done, and only then, a License is granted, assuming that

> "all the terms, conditions and obligations set forth in the application and permit have been fully met, and . . . no cause or circumstance arising or first coming to the knowledge of the Commission since the granting of the permit would, in the judgment of the Commission, make the operation of such station against the public interest."[5]

The "terms, conditions and obligations" are set forth by the applicant, under oath[6] on FCC Form 301, as revised in January 1971, the appropriate form for all Construction Permits. The titles of the Form's seven sections describe the scope of the FCC's inquiry in determining whether the public interest, convenience and necessity would be served by granting the application. They also serve to establish the limits of our problem in the simulation:

> SECTION I. Identifies the applicant, the purpose of the application, the requested facilities and their location, the identity of the responsible persons as well as the identity of the organization for whom the application is made.
>
> SECTION II. Legal Qualifications of the Applicant
>
> SECTION III. Financial Qualifications of the Applicant
>
> SECTION IV-B. Statement of Program Service of Broadcast Applicant (TV)*
>
> SECTION V-C. Television Broadcast Engineering Data.**
>
> SECTION V-G. Antenna and Site Information.
>
> SECTION VI. Equal Employment Opportunity Program.

LEGAL QUALIFICATIONS

The Communications Act of 1934 permits the Commission to determine what criteria for the "citizenship, character, and financial, technical, and other qualifications of the applicant to operate the station" it shall by regulation prescribe. What is not left to the discretion of the Commission, however, are

---

* Section IV-A is the corresponding section for AM and FM Station Applications.
** Section IV-A is for Standard (AM) Engineering Data, Section IV-B for FM.

certain requirements concerning citizenship. Citizenship is perhaps the single most clearly specified requirement for licensees in the entire Communications Act. In Section 310(a) the law clearly states that licenses can neither be granted to nor held by aliens or representatives of aliens. Further, foreign governments or their representatives are barred from holding licenses. So are corporations organized under the laws of any foreign government or American corporations in which any officer or director is an alien. No more than 20 per cent of the stock of any corporation holding a license may be owned or voted by foreign governments or by foreign nationals. Nor may a license be granted to any corporation which is controlled by another corporation one-fourth of whose directors or owners are not citizens.

Citizenship is, of course, an absolute. One is or is not a citizen, a fact which can be readily established, in most cases, by objective criteria. But what of "facts concerning the . . . character of the applicant?" What objective criteria could be set here and why should the Commission even attempt to? Government regulation in this country was initially prompted by the problem of interference. When Admiral Evans, making for a landfall at Portsmouth, New Hampshire aboard the flagship of a fleet which had just completed a successful world tour, could not get through to the Portsmouth Navy Yard because of interference from ham operators, some of whom did not hesitate to broadcast fake orders to ships of the fleet, the United States Navy set up a demand for regulation which resulted in the Radio Act of 1912.[7] By 1925, however, it was apparent that the real question was more than simply frequency regulation. On November 9, then Secretary of Commerce Herbert Hoover told the Fourth National Radio Conference:

> It is a simple fact that we have no more channels. It is not possible to furnish them under the present state of technical development. It takes no argument to demonstrate that 89 wave lengths (and no more are available) cannot be made to serve innumerable stations, no matter how ingenious we may be in arranging time divisions and geographical separations. It is not a question of what we would like to do but of what we must do.[8]

The issue was really one of scarcity of what was now becoming an increasingly attractive resource. Many wanted call letters but few could be chosen. Under such circumstances, it was clearly in the public interest to assure that brigands and mountebanks were not among the chosen few.[9] Accordingly, the Radio Act of 1927 which came into being as a result of the conference, permitted the newly formed Radio Commission to "prescribe the qualifications of station operators"[10] and to require that all applications filed with the Secretary of Commerce set forth "facts as to . . . character."[11] If the law itself demurred in describing what would be considered an acceptable definition of good character, the case law arising from the comparative hearing process is replete with examples of what the Commission would consider earnest of poor character.

Applicants have been questioned concerning such things as misrepresentations before the Commission in previous as well as present dealings; "trafficking" in licenses (establishing stations with the express purpose of selling the going concern to the highest bidder); misuse of frequencies in the past; convictions for such matters as conducting lotteries; unfair or anti-competitive practices.[12]

Indeed, the caution concerning anti-trust runs deep in the history of broadcast regulation. As Joel Rosenbloom describes it:

> . . . the belief "that certain companies and interests have been endeavoring to establish a monopoly in wireless communication . . ." (H.R. Rep. No. 1416, 67th Cong., 4th Sess., p. 4) lent urgency to the demand that Congress act before rights which the courts might construe as vested and immune to governmental action could be established.[13]

It was that caution which has been largely responsible for the limitation of license terms to three years.

FINANCIAL QUALIFICATIONS

If brigands and mountebanks are to be eliminated as contenders for scarce resources, so too are bumblers. Of course, obtaining information necessary to allay concerns about monopolistic intent or practices is one reason for requiring financial data. But another, and perhaps even more important reason, is that the public interest can hardly be served if the frequency remains unused or goes off the air because of the licensee's lack of resources or failure to use wisely what resources are available. Further, the history of broadcasting in the United States provides many examples of failure due to the inability of a new licensee to sustain unexpected construction delays, lack of advertiser interest or the inability to break pre-existing viewer patterns. Every FCC Annual Financial Data Report records the surrender of some licenses.[14] Accordingly, the Construction Permit application must contain information which will assure the Commission that there is enough money available to complete the construction, get the station on the air and keep it going. The current rule of thumb is that there must be sufficient funds to enable operation for a full year.[15]

The Commission's instructions on Section III make it clear that the intent is to elicit complete information on any agreements, written or oral, which bear on the present or future financing of the station. Four questions are asked. Question 1 asks for a balance sheet detailing the projected costs for land, buildings and equipment including whatever freight, labor or other costs will be incurred in getting equipment in place and functioning. Estimates of first year operating costs and revenues are also asked for, and the applicant is required to append a detailed breakdown, including programming costs, of the projected first year's operation. Details of financing, bank loans, deferred credit from suppliers, profit from existing operations, must also be included.

Questions 2, 3, 4 speak to the resources of the applicant and his backers. Question 2 requires a balance sheet for the applicant together with details on net income over the previous two years. Question 3 requires details on all bank accounts held by applicant. Question 4 deals with all partners, shareholders and subscribers who have furnished or will furnish "funds, property, credit, loans, assurances, donations or other things of value, or will assist in any other manner in financing the station." Copies of all agreements and their terms must be filed. Additionally, financial statements and details on net income during the previous two years must be filed for all prospective sources of funds or assistance (except banks and equipment manufacturers). Proof of bank loans or equipment financing must be provided together with details of the agreements.

Like other information in the application, the financial data become part of the public file, which must also include supplemental reports within 30 days of any changes in capitalization, organization, officers and directors or of any transaction affecting ownership or voting rights of stockholders throughout the license term. Corporations with more than 50 stockholders need report only those transactions involving officers or directors or involving those who own more than one per cent of licensee's stock.[16] One consequence of the public nature of such information is, as Sydney Head points out, that accurate financial data concerning broadcasting, unlike the case in motion pictures or other media, is always readily available.[17]

Section IV-A and IV-B are the sections of greatest interest to most communications students. Section IV-A is entitled: *Statement of AM or FM Program Service*. Section IV-B, with which we shall be concerned, is the *Statement of Television Program Service*. In this section are questions about the percentages of the broadcast day which the applicant proposes to devote to News, Public Affairs and other programming exclusive of Entertainment and Sports as well as information concerning commercial practices, Public Service Announcements, and the Ascertainment of Community Needs. This section and the issues it addresses will be discussed in full in the Chapters on the Composition of City of License, Ascertainment and Programming.

ENGINEERING DATA

Section 303 (e) of the Communications Act of 1934 requires that the FCC, in addition to assigning frequencies and determining the power for individual stations:

Regulate the kind of apparatus to be used with respect to its external effects and the purity and sharpness of the emissions from each station and from the apparatus therein.

A system of private broadcasting—specifically, for our purposes, of private television—might have been established in the United States. That is to say, it was and is at least theoretically possible to envision a system requiring us as viewers to have separate receivers for the broadcasts of the American Broadcasting Companies, CBS, the National Broadcasting Company and any other station-owning company we might choose to name. That we can receive the broadcasts of all the competing companies on the same receiver is, at least in great part, due to the initial use of radio for the sending and receiving of distress signals. The fact that radio was initially perceived as a system for disseminating signals immediately involved with the saving of human life gave rise to the Intercommunication section, Regulation 11, of the Radio Act of 1912. This specified that interchange of signals was required of licensees "without distinction of the radio systems adopted by each station, respectively."[18]

This principle has been reaffirmed on several occasions, most notably with respect to the determination as to whether VHF or UHF would be the dominant television service and as to whether the CBS mechanical system or the RCA system of compatible color broadcasting would prevail. In other words, it has long been established that problems of interference are not the only technical considerations involving FCC determination. Setting aside the myriad possible variations by which a system for distributing 6,000,000 bits of information per second might function, with the consequent negative impact on the consumer, the desirability, if not the necessity to maximize broadcasting's potential emergency service role, has operated to insist upon a uniform, interchangeable transmission and reception system. Accordingly, the FCC has become very much involved in engineering questions. The Commission specifies general criteria of the broadcast system[19] and specific regulations for assuring that these standards are met.[20] Thus the applicant must assure, not only that assigned frequency and power limitation requirements will be met, but also that all equipment selected will meet the criteria for intercommunication. Further, the applicant should be aware that FCC Regulations stipulate periodic inspection of equipment and its operation.[21] An NAB study of the most frequent violations cited by the FCC during the six-month period from July 1 to December 1, 1965, for example, shows that FCC inspections revealed violations by TV stations of various sections of the Regulations. Those most frequently violated included Section 73.39 on calibration of remote ammemeters; Section 73.47 on Equipment Performance Measurements; Section 73.57 on Maintenance of Operating Power, etc.[22]

Specifically, Section V-C asks for location of station, transmitter and studio. The make and type of transmitter as well as its power must be given. Some transmitters, as well as some examples of various other types of equipment, have already been accepted by the FCC as meeting its criteria. If the particular transmitter the station plans to install is not one of those accepted, details including schematic diagrams must also be filed. In addition, the applicant must indicate how operating power is to be determined and how maintained. Similarly, details on multiplexers—those devices which permit two or more signals (black and white as well as color, for example) to be sent over the same channel. The exact location of the tower must be listed giving its latitude and longitude to the nearest second. So must its height, plan, make and type. Information as to lines from transmitter to antenna must also be set forth. Other questions deal with details of operation, power loss and monitors. The location of the transmitter and of other stations' transmitters must be plotted on a U.S. Geological Survey map. Charts must be prepared which show the effective radiated power and other measurements at 45 degree intervals around the compass.

Section V-G deals with the antenna tower details. A plan of the tower and associated buildings must be filed as must considerable data on the possible impact of the proposed tower on aviation traffic. The distance from the tower to airways as well as details on any landing strips must be specified. An Instrument Approach Chart or Sectional Aeronautical Chart showing the tower must be plotted and filed.

In the interests of time, certain sections of the application were not considered at the IRTS Faculty Industry Seminar. After all, it was reasoned, the participants had less than one full working week in which to plan their four versions of the Desolake station and could only concern themselves with so much. There were other reasons, too. Some of the requirements for license holders do not involve the same critical examination as do others. Programming depends on the decisions of the putative licensee. On the other hand, the citizenship of the applicant is a given, and he either is or is not a person of character. Further, except insofar as they may be important to consider in connection with a discussion of what has historically been given weight in comparative hearing procedures, there is little to be learned, for the communications student, in detailing answers to legal and character qualifications questions.

Similarly, for practical reasons, the engineering section was not examined except in a cursory fashion. As can be seen (Appendix 15), a Building, Transmitter and Equipment Package description was provided to participants. Thus, the results of deliberations as to how to assemble and finance the physical properties of the proposed station become a given. In this model prepared under the direction of Robert J. Wormington, President of Westport Television, Inc., a prefab building was postulated adjacent to the transmitter. Given the option of either building a tower for the exclusive use of the station or sharing one with an existing station in the market, the planners chose the latter course, assuming that they would be able to interest an already operating station to join in such a venture and that a buyer could be found for a build, buy-back and lease arrangement. Similarly, the planners indicated that they were faced with the choice of a turnkey single supplier contract for start up equipment or developing a two-phase equipment priority list and constructing with various suppliers, in this case RCA, General Electric and Ampex. There are, of course, certain built-in assumptions underlying any plan. These assumptions will reflect the judgment of the planners as to the needs of the station over the next few years and will, in turn, dictate certain production choices in news and programming. They will also determine, to a large extent, the look of the station—the visible image and embodiment of its attitudes toward programming and toward the community.

Obviously, other decisions might have been made with respect to the physical conditions under which the station would be built and the kind of equipment it would buy in order to get on the air. Those using this book as the basis of a course in broadcast management may wish to adopt the package as a given. Others may wish to completely discard it and have the problem considered anew by the class or an engineering committee. Alternatively, the given package may be compared to another model developed, one group in the simulation using the package and another developing its own facilities and engineering plans.

It might be argued by some that the financial qualifications section falls outside the scope of the broadcasting course. Such matters as statements of assets and consolidated balance sheets are, of course common to all business enterprises. Successful completion of that section might appear to depend more on the business acumen of those involved than on their skills as communicators. And yet, in the real world the simulation attempts to replicate, the ability to use one's communications skills depends absolutely upon the success with which business judgments have been made. Every practitioner of television has had to come to grips with the financial realities of the industry. Familiarity with the considerations embraced by Section III is essential for the broadcasting student who wishes to understand the context in which programming decisions are most frequently made and who would learn to control a significant portion of a station's operation. Further, the Section represents an important result of the entire simulation problem. The cost of equipment is dependent upon the engineering decisions made; the other cost estimates are dependent upon the kind of programming chosen. Revenue estimates can only be arrived at in the light of the station's news philosophy, programming, commercial policies and sales strategies as Chapter 9 will show. However, although it cannot be completed until all other decisions have beem made, Section III should be carefully examined at this point so that the interrelationship of the various decisions can be kept in mind throughout the simulation.

No discussion of license applications can stand without reference to the Comparative Hearing process. As has been pointed out,[23] the scarce resource which a frequency capable of carrying broadcast signals represents may ultimately have to be given to one of two or more competing applicants. Thus, it is never enough to consider the proposals in an application *in vacuo;* the prudent applicant always considers how they might hold up in a hearing. For, as the U.S. Appellate Court for the District of Columbia put it in a 1949 decision:

> . . . a choice between two applicants involves more than the basic qualifications of each applicant. It involves a comparison of character-

istics. Both A and B may be qualified, but if a choice must be made, the question is which is the better qualified. Both might be ready, able and willing to serve the public interest. But in choosing between them the inquiry must reveal which would better serve that interest . . . Comparative qualities and not mere positive characteristics must then be considered.[24]

William K. Jones lists 15 "traditional areas of comparative consideration applied alike in AM, FM and television cases": 1. Local ownership. 2. Integration of ownership and management (a resident owner being assumed to be more likely to attend to local issues). 3. Diversification of backgrounds of owners. 4. Participation in civic affairs. 5. Proposed programming. 6. Proposed program policies. 7. Carefulness of operational planning. 8. Relative likelihood of effectuation of proposals. 9. Broadcast experience. 10. Past broadcast record. 11. Technical facilities. 12. Staffing. 13. Violations of law and other reflections of character. 14. Areas and populations to be served. 15. Diversification of control of the media of mass communications.[25]

The important point to remember is that although the FCC might not think twice about the residence of the proposed General Manager or the extent to which the engineering staff of the proposed station was drawn from the city in which the station proposed to operate as long as there were no competing applications, once there are two qualified applicants even the most insignificant point becomes a possible advantage for one of the competing applicants.

When the minimum qualifications of both applicants have been established, the public interest will be protected no matter which applicant is chosen. From there on the public interest is served by the selection of the better qualified applicant, and the private interest of each applicant comes into play upon that question. Thus, the comparative hearing is an adversary proceeding. The applicants are hostile, and their respective interests depend not only upon their own virtues but upon the relative shortcomings of their adversaries.[26]

In such an arena, it is not surprising that even such tangential questions as the comparative adequacy of studio toilet facilities or parking lots may come under close judicial scrutiny.[27]

NOTES

1. William K. Jones, *Cases and Materials on Regulated Industries*, University Casebook Series, Brooklyn, the Foundation Press, 1967, p. 1024.
2. *Ibid.*, p. 1022, or see 37 Stat. 302 (1912), repealed, 44 Stat. 1174 (1927).
3. *Ibid.*, p. 1065. Jones discusses the fact that there has been considerable litigation regarding the question of who is a legitimate "party in interest" and cites numerous instances accepted in the case law under two general categories: existing licensees expecting interference, and

others who can establish "reasonably identifiable economic injury." Included in the latter category have been broadcasters expecting "loss of audience beyond their normally protected contours," broadcasters with whom the station will not interfere but who expect diversion of advertisers, newspapers complaining of the same kind of loss of advertising revenue, and "even a manufacturer complaining of a station's practices in advertising the competing products of the station's manufacturing affiliate."

4. Federal Communications Commission, "Broadcast Procedure Manual," FCC 74-942, Federal Register, Vol. 39, No. 173, Thursday, September 5, 1974. Much of the material is also available as Appendix B in Robert H. Stanley, *The Broadcast Industry: an Examination of Major Issues,* for the IRTS, New York, 1975. Hastings House.

5. 47 U.S.C.A. Section 319 (c). *The Communications Act of 1934, as Amended,* may be obtained from the Superintendent of Documents U.S. Government Printing Office, Washington, D.C., 20402. Those sections dealing with broadcasting may also be found in Walter B. Emery, *Broadcasting and Government: Responsibilities and Regulations,* East Lansing, Michigan, Michigan State University Press, 1971, Appendix I, p. 407ff.

6. *Ibid.,* Section 308 (c).

7. Erik Barnouw, *A Tower in Babel,* A History of Broadcasting in the United States, Volume 1-to 1933, New York, Oxford University Press, 1966, p. 31.

8. *Proceedings of the Fourth National Radio Conference* (Government Printing Office, 1926) cited by Joel Rosenbloom, "Authority of the Federal Communications Commission", Appendix I in John E. Coons (ed.), *Freedom and Responsibility in Broadcasting,* Evanston, Northwestern University Press, 1961, p. 109.

9. *Independent Broadcasting Company v. FCC,* 89 U.S. App. D.C. 396, 193 F.2nd, 900 cited by Rosenbloom, *loc. cit.,* p. 165–6.

10. Public Law No. 632, February 23, 1927, 69th Congress. *An Act* For The Regulation of Radio Communications and for Other Purposes, SEC. 5, Barnouw, *loc. cit.,* p. 303.

11. *Ibid.,* SEC. 10, p. 305.

12. Jones, *op. cit.,* p. 1975

13. Rosenbloom, *loc. cit.,* p. 106.

14. ———. *39th Annual Report/Fiscal Year 1973,* Federal Communications Commission. p. 197. "Tables on Broadcasting Since 1949, Commercial TV." lists 18 stations as "deleted" in 1973, 34 in 1972 and 42 in 1971. No fewer than 573 such deletions are listed for the 25-year period.

15. Jones, *op. cit.,* p. 1976.

16. Emery, *op. cit.,* pp. 345–6. FCC's interest in these matters stems from its concern with respect to the possible transfer of ownership or control of a license. Chapter 20 in Emery discusses this concern in detail and lists those instances in which prior written permission for a transaction must be obtained.

17. Sydney W. Head, *Broadcasting in America: A Survey of Television and Radio,* Boston, Houghton Mifflin Company, 1956, p. 268.

18. Appendix B in Barnouw, *op. cit.,* p. 295.

19. ———, "Standards of Good Engineering Practice Concerning Television Broadcasting Stations," effective December 19, 1945, as amended October 10, 1950, Federal Communications Commission, Table I-1, quoted in Howard A. Chinn, *Television Broadcasting,* New York, 1953, McGraw Hill Book Company, p. 4.

20. For a complete list of publications available from the FCC see Appendix, 39th Annual Report, *op. cit.,* pp. 189–191.

21. *Rules Regulating Radio and TV* Volume 3, Washington, D.C., March 1968, Federal Communications Commission, S 0.121.

22. Ward L. Quaal and Leo A. Martin, *Broadcast Management,* New York, ———, Hastings House, p. 129, The second edition, Revised and Enlarged and by Quaal, and James A. Brown lists p. 318, unranked violations for 1975.

23. *supra,* p. II-4.

24. *Johnson Broadcasting Company v. FCC*, 85 U.S. App. D.C. 40, 175 F. (2d) 351,4 RR 2138 (1949), quoted in Emery, *op. cit.*, p. 244.
25. *Op. cit.*, p. 1801ff.
26. *Ibid.*, p. 1078.
27. *Ibid.*, p. 1983.

FOR THE STUDENT

1. With the advice of local bankers or appropriate business administration faculty, develop a financial plan for the new station which will assure adequate capitalization and minimal cash flow problems during the initial license term.
2. In Appendix 15, the equipment, engineering and facilities package presented to the IRTS Seminar participants, several alternatives are mentioned, one is chosen. Develop a second alternative plan.
3. Solicit one or more equipment proposals from other suppliers for comparison.
4. Inventory the major equipment available at a local station and/or of one of a market size comparable to that of the proposed KIRT-TV. Evaluate and update in terms of current state-of-the-art.
5. Prepare alternative plans for equipping the station making maximum see of ENG, using portable remote control equipment and using conventional studio and news film equipment.

3

Ascertainment of Community Needs

3. QUESTION: What is the General purpose of Part I, Section IV-A or IV-B?

ANSWER: To show what the applicant has done to ascertain the problems, needs and interests of the residents of his community of license and other areas he undertakes to serve . . . .[1]

IN 1968, THE FCC brought forward its long awaited statement on determining how broadcasters might establish that they were programming to meet the needs of their communities. Entitled *Primer on Part I, Section IV-A and IV-B of Application Forms Concerning Ascertainment of Community Problems and Broadcast Matter to Deal with Those Problems,* its message was simple. Salesmen had been tapping their order pads to the same message for generations. They had been tapping their feet to it since Robert Preston took to the stage in the 1957 Broadway hit, *The Music Man,* fervently advising drummers on The Rock Island, "You gotta know the territory!"

Broadcasters had always been presumed to know the territory. How else, it was argued, could they succeed as local businessmen? Yet, in 1964, the Communications Department of the United Church of Christ was able to initiate a procedure which by 1969 would establish, to the satisfaction of Judge Warren Burger, then of the Circuit Court for the District of Columbia,[2] that at least some Jackson, Mississippi broadcasters did not know the territory. WLBT-TV's management seemed to know, the Church of Christ contended in its brief, that small portion of territory which contained the golf course and that portion which contained the shops and offices of the principal merchants. They did not seem to know, it was charged, the territory inhabited by the majority of the area's citizens, most of whom were black. No blacks worked at the station in

21

any but the most menial of positions. More importantly, no blacks had been asked by the station's management to set forth what they believed to be the community problems most in need of discussion, explication, and amelioration. As a result, the station's programming, especially in the elements which addressed themselves to public affairs and other service interests, was out of touch with the community.

Largely as a result of the Jackson case and a growing sense of unease on the part of the Commission staff that the basis for determining who was sufficiently aware of the community to warrant being given a license to operate a station in the public interest was, at best, ill-defined, the *Primer* was adopted to set up a protocol for future applicants. It was also felt that some procedure should be established to assure that renewal applicants were still substantially in touch with the communities they undertook to serve. Accordingly, the procedures for new applicants were applied to renewal applicants on an interim basis until a permanent procedure for renewals could be arrived at.

Such a procedure has now, as of January 7, 1976, been instituted.[3] But for several years, the 36 catechistic questions and answers of the *Primer on the Ascertainment of Community Needs* dictated how broadcasters throughout the country were to determine and act upon community problems. The term "ascertainment," synecdochically used for the entire process, entered the language of broadcasters and harried community leaders alike. Under the provisions of the FCC's Public Notice of August 22, 1968 (68-847) and the explanatory primer, every broadcaster in the market, in the six months immediately preceding the filing of a license renewal application, was to assign principals or policy-making management to conduct face-to-face interviews with all the significant leaders of the community in 13 specified subject areas.[4] It was estimated that if all the broadcasters in New York State followed the procedures to the letter, six full working weeks of the Governor's time would be given over to answering the same solemn questions on problems facing the community. The Mayor of the City of New York and his top aides might be required to devote three-and-a-half weeks to the process. Little wonder that public officials and other community leaders came to consider the process somewhat cynically and, in many cases, to actually refuse to participate or to insist that any participation be jointly undertaken by several stations at once.[5]

The *Primer* was particularly careful to encourage stations to be attentive to minority and other interest groups which might be underserved by established community institutions, public and private. Accordingly, considerable suspicion was aroused in the minority communities throughout the country when their representatives, with no previous history of contact with broadcasting, were sought after to participate in the ascertainment process. Some minority group spokesmen expecting immediate and obvious results, were once again disappointed in media they had long since come to regard as remote from their communities and their needs. Others saw the entire process as a cynical attempt to get them to ratify existing programming. In at least one instance, a group advised its members that "being 'ascertained' is less violent but just as devastating" as being mugged or raped.[6]

The 36 questions in the *Primer* describe a six-fold process designed essentially to assist the Commission in determining to what extent the public interest is being or is likely to be served by a particular applicant: 1. Determining the Composition of the City of License. 2. Consultation with Community Leaders. 3. Surveying the General Public. 4. Setting Forth the Problems Perceived. 5. Evaluating the problems. 6. Broadcasting to Meet the Problems.

> 4. QUESTION: How should ascertainment of community problems be made?
>
> ANSWER: By consultation with leaders of the significant groups in the community to be served and surrounding areas the applicant has undertaken to serve, and by consultations with members of the general public. In order to know what significant groups are found in a particular community, its composition must be determined.[7]

A sociometric map of the territory is thus seen to be the key to the process of determining how to serve the community. As can be seen from the description of Desolake, Kansouri furnished the Seminar participants[8], it can also be a most helpful business tool. The Desolake material sets forth a description of the city government; the three Metro Counties[9]; their size, agriculture, and other industry; population and population characteristics; growth and development during the past decade; economic data such as consumer spendable income and retail sales data; 1974 employment data and characteristics; higher education; cultural and recreational facilities; and the various communications media, their circulation and advertising rates.

Comprehensive though this listing might appear to be, it would not seem to satisfy the specific requirements of the FCC *Primer*. The *Primer* mentions, for example, a number of categories in which significant community leaders to be consulted can be found: 1. Agriculture. 2. Business. 3. Culture. 4. Education. 5. Eleemosynary Organizations. 6. Government. 7. Labor. 8. Politics. 9. The Professions. 10. Racial and/or Ethnic Groups. 11. Civic Organizations. 12. Health. 13. Religion.

However, this list is not to be considered comprehensive. The *Primer,* in Question 13a, cautions the applicant that:

> Groups with the greatest problems may be the least organized and have the fewest recognized spokesmen. Therefore, additional efforts may be necessary to identify their leaders so as to better establish a dialogue with such groups and better ascertain their problems.[10]

Further, applicants are cautioned that applications may be challenged on the grounds that a significant group has not been consulted. And how is the applicant to know which groups are significant?

The "significance" of a group may rest on several criteria, including its size, its influence, or its lack of influence in the community.[11]

Joseph Heller could scarcely improve on that statement as a prototypic bureaucratic obfuscation. Little wonder that broadcasters and applicants have chosen to broaden their inquiries to include virtually every one who claims a constituency, no matter how small. Indeed, a subsequent FCC Report and Order[12] indicates that significant groups may include, if they "comprise a significant segment of the community:"

Voluntary associations and agencies dealing with the needs of the elderly, the indigent and the handicapped, with welfare associations, tenant groups, property owners associations, and other groups organized for the express purpose of protecting particular needs and interests.

The January 7, 1976 *First Report and Order,* although it is directed to the renewal process rather than to the application for a construction permit, further refines the Commission's attempts to produce a sociometric matrix. This document provides the following categories: 1. Agriculture. 2. Business. 3. Charities. 4. Civic, Neighborhood and Fraternal Organizations. 5. Consumer Services. 6. Culture. 7. Education. 8. Environment. 9. Government (local, county, state and federal). 10. Labor. 11. Military. 12. Minority and Ethnic Groups. 13. Organizations of and for the Elderly. 14. Organizations of and for Women. 15. Organizations of and for Youth (including children) and Students. 16. Professions. 17. Public Safety, Health and Welfare. 18. Recreation. 19. Religion. 20. Other.[13]

Korzybski's basic tenet in general semantics—"the map is not the territory"[14]—may be beyond question. Equally true, however, given the nature of television in our society, maybe the suspicion that the map can *become* the territory and that by singling out certain groups for particular attention the broadcaster, seeking only to fulfill the mandate of the licensing authority, may succeed in enfranchizing an otherwise powerless movement. For the Commission's intent with respect to the Composition of the City of License is clear:

The purpose requiring a determination of the community is to inform the applicant and the Commission what groups comprise the community. The applicant must use that information to select those who are to be consulted as representatives of those groups.[15]

Clearly, the description of Desolake would be insufficient for an applicant preparing to ascertain the community needs. There is no description of public service organizations, for example, one of the specific requirements mentioned in the *Primer*. By comparison, the following Table of Contents for "the Brief Description of the City of License" filed by KMOX-TV, the CBS Owned station in St. Louis in connection with its 1974 Renewal Application, and typical of those of major market stations, indicates considerable detail with respect to the significance of various data and of the groups which the data describe:

COMPOSITION OF THE CITY OF LICENSE

TABLE OF CONTENTS

I.	Introduction	
II.	History	
III.	Government	

     A.   Local

          1.   Executive
          2.   Legislative
          3.   Judicial

     B.   State Rpresentation

     C.   Representation in U.S. Congress

     D.   Black Progress in Politics

IV.   Characteristics of the Population of St. Louis and the St. Louis Area .

     A.   Introduction

     B.   Ethnic Composition (Including Black/ Other Minorities) and Sex

     C.   Foreign Background

     D.   Age

          1.   General
          2.   Youth
          3.   Elderly

     E.   Religious Affiliation

     F.   Marital Status

     G.   Composition of Families

     H.   Education

     I.   Economic Characteristics

          1.   Income Levels By Ethnic Composition
          2.   Poverty Status
          3.   Employment Status

J.   Business and Industry

        1.   Manufacturing
        2.   Trade
        3.   Transportation
            a.   Place of Work and Mode of Travel
            b.   Bi-State Development Agency
            c.   Airport Controversy
        4.   Labor Unions

K.   Occupational Data

V.   Characteristics of St. Louis in the Areas of
      Housing, Model Cities, Education, Crime, Law
      Enforcement and Justice, Health Care, Welfare
      Ecology and the Environment, Culture and Re-
      creation.

A.   Housing

        1.   General
        2.   Urban Renewal
        3.   Public Housing

B.   Model Cities

C.   Crime, Law Enforcement and Justice

        1.   Crime
        2.   Police
        3.   Juvenile Justice System
        4.   Prisons

D.   Health Care

E.   Welfare

F.   Ecology and the Environment

G.   Culture and Recreation

VI.   Funded Agencies

VII.   Bibliography

    You will note that the last entry in the St. Louis Table of Contents is a bibliography. Again, the *Primer* cautions that specificity is required and that "guesswork or estimates based upon alleged area familiarity are inadequate."[16] The *Primer* suggests gathering data from the U.S. Census Bureau, the Chamber of Commerce and other reliable sources. It also states that an applicant might make use of a professional service to provide background data and prepare information concerning the Composition of the City of License although it warns that the applicant will be responsible for the reliability of such a service.[17]

There is another and more compelling reason, however, for an applicant to wish to develop the data without the intervention of a professional service. That is, of course, the additional familiarity with the territory which preparing the submission will develop.

Despite the charges of inaccuracy, particularly in respect to minority communities,[18] census data is the most reliable available information on population and certain other characteristics of the region under study. The Census Bureau's 1970 Census of Population, for example, contains tables listing for each state—by SMSA—by place of more than 10,000 population, and by county, numbers of persons by race, by sex, and by age—19 separate age groups from under five years to 75 years and over. Other tables list the relationship of persons to head of household broken down by race and by sex. Inmates of institution, by race, are also listed.[19] A companion series of tables, state by state as are the population characteristics, is found in the *1970 Census of Housing*. These include, again for each SMSA, for each locality of more than 10,000 persons and for each county, numbers of owner and renter units; numbers of vacancies; numbers of units by number of rooms; numbers of units in structures; data on plumbing facilities; persons per unit and persons per room; value per unit of housing, were it then for sale; units per contract rental amount; and numbers of mobile homes.[20]

Obviously, the Bureau of the Census is not the only source to be consulted. Some counties publish, through their planning boards, a description of the county. Many of these have come about as a result of studies funded under §1701 of the Housing Act of 1954 as amended; often they have been published in several volumes over the course of a number of years. The *Population and Economic Base Study of Morris County, New Jersey,* for example, runs to 61 pages and covers population, employment and land use. Prepared by a marketing and opinion research firm, Sidney Hollander Associates, it includes a description of the history of the county, regional population and housing characteristics, and considerable data on the population, employment, land use and investment growth projected to 1985.[21] Monmouth County, New Jersey's *Economic and Social Survey* is the third in a series of five volumes which also cover land use and physical characteristics, population and housing, circulation and transportation and general development.[22] The Orange County, New York, Planning Department publishes a single volume *Data Book* which includes listings and descriptions of such diverse locations and activities as places of worship, retail and wholesale trade, motor freight forwarding companies, savings and loan services, fire insurance, private and parochial schools, industrial establishments and utility companies and their rates.[23]

Although neither the American Association of County Executives nor the Department of Housing and Urban Development has any definitive idea as to how many of the 3,000 counties in the United States publish compendia of this kind, it is a safe assumption that county offices, particularly planning boards or departments, are sources of valuable information.

A prospective broadcaster coming in cold to a new community would obviously read the local papers to get some feel of the territory and would almost certainly visit the local library. Even the telephone directory can be a valuable source of information. City, County, State and Federal offices located in the area are, of course, listed in the white pages. But the Yellow Pages are an even more fertile source of information. Consider what 30 minutes with one directory yielded. The Rockland County, New York, Yellow Pages included 28 listings under "Associations" with a cross reference to "Social Service Association" (32 listings) which in turn instructed the reader to consult "Club" (49 listings) "Home-Institutional," (5), and "Missions," (2 listing). More important than the number of listings, although that information alone may tell us something about the way a community is organized, is the kind of organization listed in each category. For example, in addition to the expected Heart, Cancer, and Boy Scout listings there were listings for a "Duffer's Association" and a Fish Club under Associations. There were also listings for a Haitian Center and a Ukrainian Hall Association. There was a Women's American ORT listing and listings for B'nai B'rith and Bikur Cholim. Does this county have a significant Ukrainian-American, Haitian, or Jewish population? Under "Social Service Organizations" are listed the Catholic Charities and United Way, probably good sources for information on the county's makeup. There also is a listing for a "Tolstoy Farm." The 49 clubs include several country clubs and some purely commercial ventures such as a dating service. But the heading also includes three Italo-American organizations and one Women's Center. The 10 "Fraternal Organizations" listed include the Knights of Columbus, Knights of Pythias, American Legion, two Elks halls and four Masonic Temples. "Chambers of Commerce" directs us to "See Business and Trade Organizations." There is no such listing. Can this be a bedroom community? Is there some other reason to account for the lack of Business and Trade organizations? Thirty-one "Labor Organizations," however, are listed. The Building and Construction Trades Council has a large display ad. Is this significant? Does this group of labor organizations represent commensurate power or influence in the county? There is one listing, located in the county seat, under "Labor Relations Consultants." If one gave him a call—never underestimate the flattery of calling on someone as an expert—he might be able to shed some light on that question. There are 14 Religious Organization entries under "Churches," with 31 separate denominations listed. There are also 4 numbers listed under Non-Denominational. Among the denominations are Baha'i and three "Eastern Orthodox," including one Greek Orthodox and two Russian Orthodox churches. Does that fact shed some light on the Tolstoy Farm listing? The "Synagogues" listing confirms the presence of a sizable Jewish population. There are no fewer than 33 Centers, Congregations and Temples listed.

Drawing conclusions on the basis of telephone listings is no less dangerous and misleading than it was when *The Literary Digest* predicted a Hoover landslide over Roosevelt on the basis of a poll of telephone subscribers. But such an examination of the Yellow Pages does give an investigator some place to start, a number of questions to pose, and some indication of where the answers might be sought.

In preparing a description of the Composition of City of License, there is no substitute for the classic journalistic adjuration ascribed to Joseph Pulitzer: "Accuracy, brevity and especially accuracy."

It is now appropriate to address the simulation problem as did the Faculty-Industry Seminar members.

IRTS SEMINAR—Thought-Starter Questions:

COMMUNITY AFFAIRS/ASCERTAINMENT

Problem C: Develop a Community Relations and Ascertainment program for *your* station in Desolake.

1. Are there any special characteristics of the station's audience which should affect the ascertainment process?
2. What mechanism will be set up for pre-license and for on-going ascertainment?
3. What mechanisms will be set up to assure that ascertainment efforts are reflected in programming?
4. Of the community's needs and problems that were discovered in the station's ascertainment process, which one(s) will the station attempt to deal with?
5. What "other" programming (religious, agricultural, etc.) will the station offer and when will it be offered?
6. Will the station program to specific minority audiences?
7. If not, how will the needs of various groups be served?
8. What record keeping procedures will be set up to gauge promise versus performance?
9. Is there a relationship between the station's EEO practices (recruiting and employing women and minority-group members) and its on-the-air product (programming)?
10. What is the station's policy, if any, toward organized public interest groups?
11. Should the station make any provision for public access?
12. What policy will the station adopt regarding the acceptance and/or production of Public Service Announcements?

*   *   *   *

In light of these questions, and others generated in the Workshop and the Group's discussion/decisions on them—*what is the station's Community Relations and Ascertainment posture and policy to be?*

FACULTY-INDUSTRY SEMINAR DISCUSSION

At the conclusion of the Tarrytown sessions, each of the participants was asked to fill in a Seminar Evaluation Questionnaire. Question 2 asked: "Of all the session scheduled, which one did you find most valuable? least valuable?" Three of the 63 responses received, listed ascertainment as the most valuable; 10 responses, 31.5% listed the ascertainment session as the least valuable. Since the ascertainment process involves both primary and secondary source research, contact with a wide variety of people engaged in interesting pursuits, and the development of issue-oriented local programming, the possibility that the subject itself would be uninteresting to the group must be ruled out. However, the severe time constraints under which the Seminar was held had prompted the prior development of a tabulated list of community problems as they might be perceived by residents of Desolake, and a public affairs program schedule based upon the list. Little seemed to remain to be done. Unlike the other sessions which were clearly seen to be task oriented, this session appeared to some to be merely an opportunity for presentation of views and, in two of the groups at least, was dominated by the industry leader or resource person. With less opportunity to participate in meaningful problem solving, many apparently felt that the hour alloted to ascertainment did not permit the development of sufficient information which was new to them.

The material included in Exhibits 1 through 4 in answers to Section IV-B, PART 1, Question 1 (A,B,C,D) which was made available to the IRTS Seminar participants, match the process (determination of composition of city of license, interviews and surveys, listing of problems described, evaluation and detailing of programming proposed to meet ascertained needs), described above. They are included in Appendix (4) to serve as a background for the discussion which follows and to provide an example of a format used by some stations, and not to substitute for the process of developing public affairs and other non-entertainment programming. Exhibit 1 only refers to the Description of Composition of City of License. In an actual filing, material included in the description of Desolake, Appendix (2), as well as other material would be included as part of that exhibit.

Similarly, a description of the methods used to select members of the audience for the general public survey would be included. An excerpt from an NAB publication, *Ascertainment of Community Needs: Suggestions for the Survey of the General Public,* which includes tables of random numbers and instructions for their use is in Appendix (5). Exhibit 2's listing of ascertained needs includes examples of the perceptions which the *Primer* requires be listed.

Even with the results of a purported ascertainment effort and with a proposed non-entertainment program schedule in hand, there remained several tasks to be performed, as an examination of the Thought-Starter Questions shows. Questions 1–3, for example, dealt with ongoing ascertainment mechanisms, 4–7 with programming, 8–10 with record keeping, and the other questions with miscellaneous means for serving potentially disaffected groups.

In commencing their discussions, almost all groups observed the problem inherent in conducting the session at the point in the week where it appeared, on the afternoon of the second full day and only after the programming and news sessions. The ascertainment resource persons each observed, ruefully, the similarity between that scheduling and what too often happens in the station situation. In IOTA, the group was told that "art had once again imitated life. After having determined how the news is to be done, whether or not there are to be editorials, what kind of programming there will be, you now examine the needs and interests of the community." JON MILLER (Director of Public Affairs, WPVI-TV, Philadelphia, Pa.), told the SIGMA Group: "This would be the grossest possible error in programming at a station. Ascertainment is the key to programming." In point of fact, most of the discussions in each of the groups centered on finding ways to assure that the ascertainment process was given sufficient priority in the day-to-day operation of proposed new station. "Ascertainment is time consuming and a chore," Industry Discussion Leader GEORGE MITCHELL (Vice President & General Manager, WKEF, Dayton, Ohio) told the TAU Group: "However, having gone through the last one and having realized that we have indeed in the last three years used the ascertainment as a basis for some of our community affairs programs and some of our news and some of our specials and special events, I am now convinced that it is a good process." JOSEPH DOUGHERTY (President, Broadcast Division) described having worked on the transfer application Capital Cities filed for their Fort Worth and Houston stations: "When I got through, I frankly knew more than the manager of that station had known about the community. It's a small price to pay for a license." ANDY POTOS (Vice President and General Sales Manager of Storer Television Sales), SIGMA Industry Discussion Leader, agreed: "The process is very important. I think the FCC would want you to go through the process for what it does for the management of a television station. The act of contacting the community leader directly and personally making an appointment, going to his or her turf and conducting the hearing there gets the management in touch with the community."

RHO addressed the problem in terms of who would serve as watchdog over the entire process. "The general manager, whoever he is, is going to be a very very busy guy, especially his first few months," Discussion Leader RICK LEVY (General Sales Manager, WLWC, Columbus, Ohio) reminded the group. "He will probably not be able to pay it attention. The problem then is, how do we maintain a really open line between those in our community and those in management at the station. We want to be as open as possible to the community. How do you direct this so that you don't get a thousand groups coming in with the lettuce workers alone demanding four hours?"

C. A. KELLNER (Marshall University) suggested a community affairs director, reporting directly to the general manager, "able to analyze the ascertainments, knowing the areas of particular concern to the community, helping the general manager write the editorial, and having a close working relationship to the news team." The suggestion was advanced that the function should be in the hands of the news department. But WESLEY WALLACE (University of North Carolina) reminded the group that they had gone to great lengths to remove the news director from handling editorials:

> You took that responsibility out of his hands for a very good reason. Those are advocacy matters. Community affairs involves advocacy. If you require a news director to do community affairs, you have bound his hands with respect to his function as a news director. His function is to go after the news wherever it is and under whatever circumstances. That is antagonistic to the function of community affairs.

RAY STEELE (University of Pittsburgh) saw the function as very broad:

> He is your PR man, he is going to cover some of your in-house problems, he is a customer relations man, and he has this constant ascertainment problem. You are going to work him in a lot of different ways. He will attend a lot of evening functions and eat a lot of rubber chicken. He should be able to fight with the news director, with the sales manager, with everybody. The general manager can decide who provides what programming for whom. That's what he is paid big bucks to do.

RICK LEVY described how it worked at his station:

> Our community affairs director attends weekly staff meetings with all the other department heads. If she sees a problem in the community and feels we are not paying attention or if we have had a group come in with a complaint, she makes a suggestion. At that point the general manager decides whether it can be handled by the news department, possibly in a mini-doc, or whether it requires a special half-hour by the program department. Practically speaking, that is the way it works at many stations.

But ANDREW JACKSON (Vice President of Capital Cities Communications Inc.), the RHO Group Ascertainment Resource person, struck a note of caution:

> I have seen situations where I believe the fact that there was a community affairs director was a disadvantage. He is a guy without any real authority and he goes back to the station and sometimes he is listened to and sometimes he is not. But always, he tends to insulate the general manager from the things the general manager and all the department heads should be exposed to. The community affairs director sees them every day but the general manager does not.

Consultants from the local universities were suggested, as was putting a special assistant to the general manager on the staff temporarily until the station was established. Another means suggested to assure continual consideration of the problem and a flow of information was a committee.

To that, JEFFREY LOWENHAR (Temple University) observed:

> There is about 300,000 years of history to suggest that committees never do anything very well, whether those committees are in the broadcasting industry, the petroleum industry or the educational industry.

Once the responsibility for monitoring the ascertainment efforts and assuring that they provide input into the station's programming is determined, a mechanism must be decided upon to facilitate the face-to-face interchange between station and community leaders and for keeping track of each meeting and its possible consequences, if any. IOTA was concerned about the selection of community leaders. Since the Commission has now specified the approximate number of leaders to be consulted in various sized markets, ([24]) how can the station make the selection? "Ask yourselves who, if you were members of a particular interest group, you would feel the station would absolutely have to consult in order to have begun to examine the field," the IOTA Group was advised: "Ask for referrals, consult other organizations. A church serving a particular ethnic group can suggest secular leaders. Ask members of the group." JON MILLER warned the SIGMA Group of the dangers of relying on secondary research. "Black people in Philadelphia have told me, 'Those survey people never even came into our neighborhood, they'd be scared.' It seemed a reasonable premise, so we set out to do our own survey of the leadership and we met with the groups." Citing the *Primer*'s caution about the elusive nature of leadership in disaffected areas, DOUGHERTY recounted the Capital Cities experience from Philadelphia, New Haven and Fresno after the transfer of licenses from Triangle and the challenge by and settlement with the groups represented by the Citizens Communications Center:

> The group keeps changing all the time. We put a million dollars up front for programming by these groups over a three-year period of time. What happened was that everybody who wanted to rip something off, showed up. We dramatically changed the lives of our general managers during that period. Fortunately, there were no heart attacks and they all survived to say the same thing: whatever we do next time, don't put the money up front. So, we didn't. We had lived with the agreements with all three community groups for three years and we by then had established some rapport with them and they saw us in quite a different light because we had a good track record. We met some fine people from community groups who really helped us. Over the three-year period we had some 56 programs the minority community did. Some were terrible by our standards but some of them were

very good. In Fresno, with the Indians, the Blacks and the Chicanos, they did even more programs. We lost a car in Wounded Knee—it was ripped off—but the programming was good. We were really pleased with it and so were they.

HAYES ANDERSON (San Diego State University) reported to the RHO Group on the effectiveness of minority affairs panels in the San Diego area, in terms of ascertainment, ongoing input from the minority communities and assistance in programming to those areas. ANDY JACKSON supported the idea of regular meetings with such panels, calling them effective in keeping in touch. "The key to it," he advised, "is in meeting with sub-committees. If you can expose department heads to the process it really can work." He cautioned, however, that a station has to be sure it is not just meeting with a small segment of the minority community, to the exclusion of those who might really represent the community as a whole, an experience which he acknowledged one Capital Cities station had had at the time of the transfer.

LARRY JOHNSON (Director of Community Affairs for WNBC-TV, New York), laid out the broadcast ascertainment problem for the TAU Group:

Consider, month in and month out, inviting in a dozen people from a broad cross-section of your community to build up your record. You might have a weekly or monthly community leader luncheon. The questions should be structured, and notes taken. If you plan these meetings properly, they can be very effective.

JOHNSON also advocated the development of a simple form so that all department heads at formal meetings or production people meeting leaders in connection with developing a show, could keep adequate records. The problem of record keeping was acknowledged by a number of participants to be one of the critical areas in the ascertainment process. One resource person cited the fact that records had been challenged at several stations; another industry leader talked of missing opportunities to claim ascertainment interviews because records were not inserted in the file. BERTRAM BARER (California State University, Northridge) shared the perception with his colleagues that much of the ascertainment process for a station is defensive: "It's carefully designed so that you can respond to petitions to deny."

Both MITCHELL and JOHNSON told their group of the quarterly review process their stations conducted, JOHNSON pointing out that they went so far as to produce what amounted to a quarterly composite week review of the station's logs for each of the NBC Owned stations.[25]

Some discussion was devoted to the conducting of the general public survey. Since the *Primer* specifies that such a survey must be representative if conducted by an outside surveying organization but need only be random if conducted by the station staff itself, it can be seen to be less costly if done in-house. Various alternative methods—computer generated phone numbers, random mailings of questionaires, the use of random number tables and a method used by a Lexington, Kentucky station—were considered. JAMES HARRIS, (Eastern Kentucky University) described the Lexington procedure for his colleagues in SIGMA as completely automated. The telephone automatically dials a number obtained by computer generation and plays a pre-taped message. The answer to the questions posed are recorded and the unit goes on to call the next number. HARRIS reported that the method would permit the station to greatly increase its general public survey from 250 to 1,400 automated calls for the next ascertainment period.

The purpose of the ascertainment process, and its end product, is the production of programming to meet the expressed need of the area served as perceived by community leaders and members of the public and as evaluated by the station. Even were programming to meet the needs not mandated by the *Primer,* few broadcasters would go through a lengthy process such as ascertainment without finding a programming pay out.

A thoughtful analysis of the perceptions noted and a consideration of how the new Desolake station might bring its resources to bear on meeting the problem, had presumably occurred after the purported ascertainment interviews. The results of this analysis and planning are filed in Exhibit 2. Several of the participants in the Tarrytown seminar, however, were notably dissatisfied with the material thus furnished. HARRIS cited the enormous in-migration rate given for the Desolake area and compared this rate to other areas he had personally known. Such an in-migration, he reminded his colleagues, generally results in an identifiable cluster of needs and problems, especially those associated with anomie and alienation among the migrant group. The ascertainment of Desolake revealed none of these problems.

Admittedly, the material developed with respect to Desolake was put together from whole cloth to serve as materials with which those engaged in the simulation might work. But the attack, to which the results of the survey was subjected, is, if less than justified, certainly instructive for students of the process. Ascertainment results become part of the station's record. They are placed in the Public File, that collection of documents which must be made available to any member of the audience upon demand.[26] On the date on which the anniversary of a station's filing falls in 1976 and on each anniversary thereafter, notes on the individual interviews with community leaders must also be in the file. Accordingly, the station must be prepared to defend not only the programming devised to meet the ascertained needs of its audience, but also, particularly in a Petition to Deny or other license challenge procedure, the ascertainment material itself. Other participants objected to the programming, not only on its own terms, that is to say, the presumed effectiveness of the programs as programs, but also with respect to the extent to which they might actually serve to ameliorate or solve the problems developed and the extent to which they represented reasonable choices of problems in service to which the station's limited resources of air-time, money and energy should be devoted.

MARY JEAN THOMAS (Loyola University of Chicago) summarized the views of several in the SIGMA Group:

> The more I read the promises that were made in our names about our community service programming, the more I get the feeling that we have been led down the garden path and, as a friend of mine used to say, these are filled with fraught. First we have three programs where we are assigning the burden to the groups themselves, to the old people, to the community neighborhood organizations, and to CORE. Second, CORE is not necessarily the voice of the Black community and that might cause us more problems than we know how to deal with. Third, we are giving access with no real commitment to help these groups do the kind of programming required. I think they will be coming back to us at the end of the first period complaining that we are expecting too much and giving too little support. Fourth, we have one program listed as RECREATION TODAY. I looked through the ascertainment phrases and where those about the need for recreation came from were the small towns. Now if you have to drive 40 miles to a movie and there's no decent restaurant, you have a recreation problem. I don't see how in the world the television station is going to meet that problem, especially with the tack it has taken here, a proposed program publicizing public recreational facilities. If somebody comes to us and asked what the heck that is all about, what community problems we are trying to deal with, what the need for recreational facilities really means and how that program could possibly meet that need, I don't know what we could say. It is dangerous to promise programs without thinking them through.

> JAMES FLETCHER (University of Georgia): The program essentially institutionalizes the very people who have led us down the path of no recreation in the past.

Much of the discussion on the proposed programming turned on the question of access. To what extent and how should a station consider providing a forum for special interest groups, minority groups, or others to express their point of view? To what extent should the control of public affairs and other informational programming be relinquished to other than its staff professionals? Is the control of content by minority groups any different from the control of religious programming by the Council of Churches or other religious groups that has become institutionalized in many stations? JON MILLER cautioned that access must be thought of in several senses:

> Access should not mean giving someone time to do whatever they want. Access should mean providing an opportunity to people in the community you are trying to serve. Access, in terms of what happens between 7 and 8:00 P.M. in prime time, means the opportunity for producers of syndicated materials to get a shot at air time; community

organizations can be given access to air time in the form of public service announcements; individuals can be given access to reply to editorials; others can come to you with a point of view that is not generally
being heard, and you can help develop that for broadcast and thus give
them access. But, beyond the access of people to television, there is
also the access of ideas. When someone comes to describe a problem
not being met, find ways to respond. Access is not just allocating time
and having people do whatever they want or whatever they can.

SUMMARY

The value to a broadcaster of a certain knowledge of the fabric of the community, all of its established groups, all of its leaders, all of its disaffected,
should be apparent. It has always been presumed; with the Primer on the Ascertainment of Community Needs, it is now mandated. Further, the method by
which a broadcaster can and should obtain and update that knowledge is also
mandated. Successful broadcasters find mechanisms for remaining in touch
with all elements of the community, meeting with its leadership, surveying its
people, engaging in an ongoing dialogue with its dissidents. The results of this
ongoing effort are subject to scrutiny, not only by the FCC at license renewal
time, but also by community groups, by students and critics of the media and
by those who believe themselves to have been wronged and are in search of
redress. Meticulous record keeping which documents superior continuous ascertainment is required. Analysis of perceptions of community problems leads a
station to consider which problem areas to address and in what form, thereby
giving rise to editorial campaigns, public service announcements, investigations
or features on news broadcasts, discussions of public issues or other programs
to meet the ascertained needs and interests of the area served.

NOTES

1. Primer on Ascertainment of Community Problems, 27 FCC 2d 650 (1971) The *Primer* is included as Appendix 3 of this volume.
2. Office of Communications of the United Church of Christ v. Federal Communications Commission,—F. 2nd—(D.C. Dir. 1969), 16 P&F Radio Reg 2d 2095 (1969).
3. First Report and Order in Docket 19715, 35 P&F 2d 1555 57 FCC 2nd 418 released January
   7, 1976.
4. *Primer, op. cit.,* p. 10.
5. The Commission has authorized joint ascertainment under certain specified conditions.
6. Humberto Cintron, "View From 'El Barrio,' " newsletter of the Puerto Rican Media Action
   and Education Council, Julio Rodriguez, ed., New York, May 24, 1974.
7. *Primer, op. cit.*
8. Appendix 3.
9. Metro area is a term used by the A.C. Nielsen Co. to designate those counties, 50% of whose
   population falls within the SMSA. SMSA, Standard Metropolitan Statistical Area, is a term
   defined and named in the Bureau of the Budget publication, *Standard Metropolitan Statistical*

Areas: 1967, Washington D.C., 1967, U.S. Government Printing Office. "Except in the New England states, a standard metropolitan statistical area is a county or group of contiguous counties which contains at least one city of 50,000 inhabitants or more, or "twin cities" with a combined population of at least 50,000. In addition to the county, or counties, containing such a city or cities, contiguous counties are included in an SMSA if, according to certain criteria, they are socially and economically integrated with a central city." *1970 Census of Housing HC (V1)-34, New York,* February, 1971, Washington, D.C., U.S. Department of Commerce, Bureau of the Census.

10. *Primer, op. cit.*
11. *Ibid.,* Q. 10.
12. FCC 71-176; Section 31.
13. *loc. cit.,*
14. Alfred Korzybski, *Science and Sanity; An Introduction to Non-Aristotelian Systems and General Semantics* (Third edition with new preface) Lakeville, Ct., 1946, International Non-Aristotelian Library Publishing Company, *passim.*
15. *Primer, op. cit.,* Q 10.
16. *Ibid.,* Q. 9.
17. *Ibid.,* Q. 12.
18. See especially the United States Civil Rights Commission report, *Counting the Forgotten, The 1970 Census Count of Persons of Spanish Background in the United States,* Washington, April, 1974.
19. *PC (V2),* February 1971, Washington, D.C., U.S. Department of Commerce, Bureau of the Census. 52 reports were issued, number one for the United States and numbers two through 52 for the various states and the District of Columbia in alphabetical order. They are for sale by the Bureau, Washington, D.C. 20233 or at U.S. Department of Commerce field office for 30 cents each.
20. *op. cit., HC (V2)* volumes are numbered and sold as are the *PC (V2)* reports.
21. The publication specifies as additional sources of copies the Clearinghouse for Federal Scientific and Technical Information, Washington, D.C., and the HUD Regional Office Library, Region II, 630 Widener Building, Philadelphia, Pa., as well as the Morris County Planning Board in Morristown, N.J.
22. Prepared and published by the Monmouth County Planning Board, Freehold, N.J., January, 1969.
23. Revised and published annually by the Orange County Planning Department, County Building, Goshen, New York.
24. *Population of City of License　Number of Consultations*

Population of City of License	Number of Consultations
10,001 to 25,000	60
25,001 to 50,000	100
50,001 to 200,000	140
200,001 to 500,000	180
Over 500,001	220

First Report & Order Docket 19715, *loc. cit.*

25. Composite weeks are those seven days, selected at random, for which the FCC requests logs in connection with license renewal every three years and the filing of the Problems/Programming Report Form 303A, annually. For 1975, for example, the sample week consisted of:

Sunday	September 7
Monday	March 10
Tuesday	July 29
Wednesday	October 29
Thursday	January 9
Friday	April 4
Saturday	June 21.

26. S 1.526, FCC Broadcast Rules lists items which must be specifically in a public file "maintained for public inspection." These include:

   1. Copies of application with all correspondence with the FCC and other documents pertaining to them; notices of any petitions to deny filed.
   2. Information on changes in broadcast service or in the ownership of the station; requests for extension of construction time.
   3. Ownership reports
   4. Information on broadcasts by or on behalf of political candidates.
   5. Annual employment reports.
   6. A copy of the FCC *Public and Broadcasting Procedure Manual*.
   7. Letters received from the general public concerning the station's operations and programming.
   8. Copies of Annual Programming Reports.
   9. A copy of the "current annual listing of what the licensee believes to have been significant problems and needs of the areas served by the station," quoted in *Broadcasting Yearbook 1975*, pp. A-23-23. See also *The Public and Broadcasting Manual*, FCC74-942, 39 FR 32288, September 5, 1974.

FOR THE STUDENT

1. In consultation with local planners, members of the architecture or planning departments, civic groups, determine what sources are available in your locality from which to develop a community profile.
2. Develop an inventory of the community leadership of your own community determining which leaders in each category of the FCC checklist should be interviewed to ascertain community needs.
3. Following the protocol for random number selection, conduct phone interviews of members of the general public. Prepare a list of perceptions discovered.
4. Conduct and report on an actual ascertainment interview.
5. It has been said that any professional broadcaster should know the results of an ascertainment process before it is conducted. Test this assumption and compare the results actually obtained by a local station with what might have been predicted.
6. What are the PSA policies of local radio and television stations? How can they be improved upon in proposals for KIRT-TV?

4

Programming: The Affiliate Question

The ether is a public medium, and its use must be for public benefit. The dominant elements for consideration in the radio field is, and always will be, the great body of the listening public.

We simply must say that conditions absolutely preclude increasing the total number of stations in congested areas. It is a condition, not an emotion; but this implies a determination of who shall occupy these channels, in what manner, and under what test.

HERBERT HOOVER, Secretary of Commerce.
Address to the Fourth National Radio
Conference, September 9, 1925.

THE SIMULATION EXERCISE began with the CP, the Construction Permit Application, which is prerequisite to obtaining an FCC license for the proposed new station. This was the appropriate starting point, not only because of its chronological primacy in the license process, but also because of its ongoing importance as the standard against which the station's performance must be measured. Of all of the assets of the new station, the license is the *sine qua non*.

In the previous chapter we considered the process by which the station will fulfill its mandate to discover the changing needs and interests of its community. It is appropriate, therefore, to begin thinking about the problem of programming the new station by examining the FCC's expressed interest in the broadcast schedule.

Section IV-B of FCC Form 301, the *Application for Authority to Construct a New Broadcast Station or Make Changes in an Existing Broadcasting Station,* the application for a construction permit, and Section IV-B in Form 303, the License Renewal Application, are entitled "Statement of Television Program Service." They contain questions relating to the licensee's proposed programming as well as, where applicable, to past programming.

Joel Rosenbloom, formerly legal assistant to Chairman Newton N. Minow, of the Federal Communications Commission, in a lengthy and detailed monograph has traced the Authority of the FCC in posing such questions. Rosenbloom sets forth as settled law that:

1. . . . the Communications Act authorizes the Commission "to classify broadcast stations" as to the type of programming they carry; "to make reasonable judgments as to the public interest served by the programs offered by each class; and to assign radio frequencies on the basis of those judgments.

2. The Act authorizes the Commission "to consider the nature and content of the programs proposed in deciding whether to grant construction permits or station licenses.

3. The Act "forbids the Commission to censor, i.e. to prevent the broadcasting of any individual program on the ground that its content is objectionable."

4. The Communications Act is fully compatible with the First Amendment.[1]

He then follows the development of Commission policy through the legislative history of the Radio Act of 1927 to the time of writing, 1961. Rosenbloom notes that a report to the Committee on Merchant Marine and Fisheries, House of Representatives, 70th Congress, in January 1928, shows that the Commission was already requiring applicants to provide "such information as the average amount of time per week devoted to 'Entertainment,' 'Religious,' 'Educational,' 'Agricultural,' etc. programs, and whether or not direct advertising, including the quotation of merchandise prices was conducted."[2] These questions had been developed under the Commission's General Order 32 which "took the position that too much duplication of programs and types of programs in a particular area should be avoided."[3]

At various times, the Commission has attempted to specify those types of broadcasts which should be included in a schedule so that "the tastes, needs, and desires of all substantial groups among the listening public should be met, in some fair proportion, by a well rounded program in which . . . matters of interest to all members of the family find a place."[4] By 1960, there had emerged a check list of 14 categories:

1. Opportunity for local self expression. 2. Development of local talent. 3. Editorializing. 4. Service to minority groups. 5. Children's

programming. 6. Religion. 7. Education. 8. Agriculture. 9. Sports.
10. Entertainment. 11. News. 12. Public Affairs. 13. Weather and
market reports. 14. Political broadcasts.

Currently, Form 301 and Form 303 call for reporting the amount of time
devoted to all programs and to those programs which fall into three categories:
1. News. 2. Public Affairs. 3. All other programs, exclusive of Entertainment
and Sports.

The licensee must also indicate how much of each type was locally produced. Data is broken down into three time periods, 6:00 AM to Midnight,
Midnight to 6:00 AM and, because of the importance of prime time, 6:00 PM
to 11:00 PM.

As can be seen from the copy of Form 301 in Appendix (1), definitions of
these categories appear on pages 7 and 8. One such definition bears examination because it has been particularly troublesome. The definition for Public Affairs programs states:

> Public Affairs programs (PA) include talks, commentaries, discus-
> sions, speeches, editorials, political programs, documentaries, forums,
> panels, round tables, and similar programs primarily concerning local,
> national and international public affairs.

Circular definitions of this character are less than helpful particularly in
reconciling the views of a producer who may have read Jose Ortega y Gassett
and a communications lawyer who had not. Ortega y Gassett wrote:

> Public life is not solely political, but equally, and even primarily, in-
> tellectual, moral, economic, religious; it comprises all our collective
> habits, including our fashions both of dress and amusement.[5]

A recent Report and Order, Docket 19861, which dealt with non-commercial stations' requirements to retain audio recordings of discussions involving
issues of public importance, included what many hoped would be the new definition of public affairs:

> Thus we believe that compliance with the provisions of Section 399
> (b) will be achieved by the recording and retention of those programs
> which consist of talks, commentaries, discussions, speeches, edito-
> rials, political programs, documentaries, forums, panels, round tables,
> and similar programs primarily concerning local, national and interna-
> tional public affairs where the licensee, on the basis of a subjective
> good faith judgment, determines that the program in question involves
> an issue or issues that are likely to have an impact upon the commu-
> nity at large, society, or its institutions.[6]

Viewing content in terms of the impact of an issue on the community at
large, society or its institutions may help to bridge the gap between Ortega y

Gassett and what the responsible broadcaster would believe to be a defensible classification.

Although the concept may remain helpful to the broadcaster, the specific language on an issue's being likely to have "an impact upon the community at large, society, or its institutions" did not survive in the Commission's long-awaited redefinition. Since April of 1972, the Commission had been engaged in a comprehensive review of its rules. Many reforms had already been made as a result of this study, among them the revisions in the ascertainment procedures discussed in Chapter 3. On March 19, 1976, the Commission adopted a *Report and Order In the Matter of Revision of FCC Form 303, Application for the Renewal of Broadcast Station License and Certain Rules Relating Thereto* (Docket No. 20419) FCC 76-264, released May 3, 1976. Although designed to develop a new, shorter renewal application form for radio stations, the Report and Order produced several changes, particularly in respect to programming, which apply to television stations. Comments had been solicited, for example, on such matters as whether to combine news and public affairs into a single program category, whether to develop a broad category entitled "community service" to embrace all three present non-entertainment and non-sports broadcasting, and, most important for the present discussion, a new definition of "public affairs." Combined or new categories were rejected. In Paragraph 46, discussing the inadequacy of the present circular definition and the lack of consensus on proposed changes, the Commission also rejected the notion "that public affairs programming should be devoted only to those issues uncovered by the licensee during his ascertainment process" as too restrictive (many national and international issues, it declared, would not emerge in the ascertainment process):

> As in many programming areas, the Commission intends to rely on the good faith judgment of the licensee as to what programs should be categorized as public affairs. We recognize that distinctions between news, public affairs and all other programming may at times be quite subjective. We believe that the broadcasting licensee can and should make these judgments and, absent a pattern of abuse of discretion on the part of the licensee, we intend to accept the licensee's judgment.

The Commission then set forth its new definition:

> Public Affairs programs are programs dealing with local, state, regional, national or international issues or problems, including, but not limited to, talks, commentaries, discussions, speeches, editorials, political programs, documentaries, mini-documentaries, panels, roundtables, vignettes, and extended coverage (whether live or recorded) of public events or proceedings, such as local council meetings, Congressional hearings, and the like.

With this definition, the element of a program that is relevant to
defining it as a public affairs program is the subject matter involved,
not the format, length or other technical aspects of the program.

Thus, the impact on the community is not to be the test; rather, the broadcaster may, apparently, use his discretion to determine whether "our fashions
both of dress and amusement" can properly be described as local, state,
regional, national or international issues or problems.

One other point must be made concerning classification. There are three
concepts which are frequently confused by experienced broadcasters and distinguished educators as well as by students and members of the general public.
There is a discernible difference among the terms "public interest," "public
service" and "public affairs." If a preponderant majority of American television viewers choose to watch the Motion Picture Academy's annual Oscar rit-
ual, is that broadcast not in the public interest? The Commission would seem to
have said so. Since the very earliest statements on program types it has recognized entertainment as one of those categories of broadcasts which serve the
public interest. A Hollywood starlet recounting her personal history of
alchoholism may be of genuine benefit to a particular viewer who might learn
how to cope with her own, similar problems. Such a broadcast would surely be
in the public interest. It would also, in helping that viewer and possibly others,
be providing a public service. It would not appear to be a public affairs broadcast. Conversely, a broadcast on the extent of alcoholism and the cost to the
taxpayers in hospital facilities, absenteeism or traffic accident consequences,
might fail to make any change in anyone's life and thus be of far less ultimate
consequence. It would, however, be classified as "public affairs"!

How much of each category should a station produce? So far, no firm percentages have been set. Periodically, efforts have been made by Commissioners, members of the staff or citizen groups to stimulate the Commission to
establish minimum figures. In 1971, the FCC proposed, in a proceeding still
pending, 15% local programming, and 15% news and public affairs in the top
50 markets. In smaller markets, stations would be expected to present 10%
local programming, 5–8% news, and 3% public affairs.[7] Nicholas Johnson, a
former Commissioner, is currently Executive Director of the National Citizens
Committee for Broadcasting which has announced the development of a coali-
tion of groups (among them NOW, the League of Women Voters, and the
ACLU) and at least one broadcaster whose ultimate aim is the setting
of much higher percentages. Their announced short term goal is to require,
through negotiation or through the Petition to Deny process, that all stations
carry one hour of network and one hour of local public affairs programming in
prime time each week.[8]

Stations must file their percentage figures each year and again on the oc-
casion of their license renewal applications. These are also placed in the sta-

tion's Public File and are thus available to any who would seek them out. The FCC publishes an annual summary of reported figures by market. A manager may, therefore, compare his proposed figures with the national figures or with those in his market. In 1974, for example, the latest figures available,[9] the national averages (699 stations reporting) were as follows:

	6 A.M. – Midnight (100%)	6 P.M. – 11 P.M. (100%) / 5 P.M. – 10 P.M. (Central & Mountain)
All Programs		
1. News	8.9	11.7
2. Public Affairs	4.1	2.5
3. Other Non-Enter-tainment, Non-Sports	8.7	2.4
Total	21.7	16.6
Locally Produced Programs		
1. News	4.8	6.1
2. Public Affairs	1.8	1.2
3. Other Non-Enter-tainment, Non-Sports	2.0	0.7
Total	8.6	8.0

For the nation's actual 75th market, Portland-Poland Spring Maine, they were:

All Programs		
1. News	7.3	11.2
2. Public Affairs	3.2	2.5
3. Other	11.8	1.7
Total	22.3	15.4

Both the national and local figures serve to confirm our own common sense observation that the American people look to television for more than news, public affairs and "other" broadcasting. No matter what is on the television menu, for most of the audience the staple of their viewing diet will be entertainment.[10] The IRTS Seminar Thought-Starter Questions for considering programming reflect this fact:

IRTS SEMINAR—Thought-Starter Questions

—PROGRAMMING

PROBLEM A Develop a viable, audience-appealing competitive program schedule for *your* station.

1. Basic question (applicable not only to Programming, but to entire station's operation): Will you seek an ABC network affiliation, or remain independent?
2. What *Promises* were made in the license application, relative to local live origination, public affairs and news programming?
3. In the two key day-parts for local programming decisions, (so-called early fringe: 3–5 P.M. Desolake time; and prime access 6:30–7 P.M.) what will the station's program targets be—kids? adults, "kid-ults"?
4. Is the station wise in trying to develop a programming "look"—i.e., the "young adults' station" . . . "the something-for-everyone station" . . . etc? Is this desirable, is it achievable?
5. What syndicated programs and feature films are available to the station, and what are general price ranges for these?
6. What is the station's physical capability for local live production?
7. What is the importance in Desolake of local commercial production to local sales?
8. Will the station clear for broadcast all network programming that ABC offers (presume a "Yes" response to Question 1); or will there be selective non-clearance of certain series, day-parts, etc., to permit local or syndicated programming?
9. Should the station seek out non-network, local or regional sports programming?
10. What budget and effort can or should be invested in local programming or talent?
11. In the late fringe period (post late news to sign-off), will the station take the network feed, or originate its programming locally, with syndicated properties?

In light of these questions, and others generated in discussions and the decision process, *what is the program schedule for your station?*

There are 168 hours in a week. Every week. That is the central programming problem for KIRT or for any other station: how many of those hours will your station be on the air and what will you present in that time?

A significant given in the problem we are considering is that there are two other VHF television stations operating in the city of Desolake. One, KNAC, is affiliated with NBC; KBGA is affiliated with CBS. Neither of the stations already operating has a secondary affiliation with ABC.[11] It is, therefore, possible for KIRT to affiliate with ABC. The problem assumes (with considerable justification) that ABC would welcome such a proposal.

Is an affiliation desirable for the new station or should it remain independent? This is the first decision which any group working on this problem must make. Not only is affiliation an important consideration in setting up a program schedule, it may underlie virtually any decision which the station makes. Preliminary plans might be made, for example, with respect to KIRT's news staff and its news gathering facilities. But without knowing whether it will have ABC News' network broadcasts available to its audience or whether DEF, the ABC news syndication service, is the logical choice, and whether any KIRT early news broadcast would be adjacent to a network newscast, anything but the most generalized planning is out of the question. Similarly, it is impossible to develop a promotion strategy for the station without knowing whether or not the station is to be promoted as the new source of ABC entertainment programs, sports, news and information or as the new all-local voice in Desolake. In short, as indicated in the list of Thought-Starter Questions, the basic decision to be made is whether or not to affiliate.

In order to make such a decision it is essential, first of all, to understand exactly what is involved. Affiliation means that the station becomes, on those occasions when it chooses to, part of an interconnection of stations, coast to coast, presenting the same program. The network itself, the company which puts together that combine of stations, provides the programming and purchases the time from the individual stations. The network then resells the time to a national advertiser at a rate sufficient to cover the costs of producing the program and purchasing the air-time from the affiliated stations while still making a profit for itself.

The sample affiliation contract for the mythic Universal Broadcasting Company (Appendix 6) is derived from and typical of those used by ABC, CBS and NBC.[12] It specifies that KIRT will have to pay the installation costs but that the network will pay all other interconnection costs, generally referred to as line charges. KIRT is given first refusal on any network program. If the station so refuses, the network, to satisfy its contracts or to discharge its public interest responsibilities, may make that program available to another station in the market. The contract then goes on to spell out the rather elaborate compensation formula typical of such contracts. Essentially, this formula works as follows: For each station, a rate of compensation is set by the network, various time periods throughout the day—day parts as they are called—being assigned

a percentage of the prime time rate. Thus early fringe, here defined as 5–6
P.M., and late fringe, 11 P.M.–1 A.M. are computed at 50% of Full-Rate. Full
Rate is paid for time from 6–11 P.M., Monday through Sunday. Other time
periods are computed at 35%, 26¼% or 20%. At the end of the month, all of
the network programming carried by the station is tabulated and converted into
so-called equivalent hours. For this purpose, each hour of prime time is equal
to one hour; each hour of Early Fringe is equal to ½ hour. Five hours of the
early morning time, 7–9 A.M., computed at 20% of full rate, equal one hour of
equivalent time. From the total equivalent time for the month, the first 24 hours
are deducted "as a means of sharing overhead cost." The network then pays
the station an amount equal to the full rate times the number of equivalent
hours. Special programming, such as sports and special events, is covered by
separate agreements and there are provisions for such items as print costs on
unsponsored programs. Restrictions are placed upon the use of programs, the
sale of unsponsored network programs by the station, and the deletion of commercials, credits or promotional announcements. The contract also has a 30-day
cancellation clause.

FACULTY SEMINAR DISCUSSION

All four of the groups dealt with the problem near the very beginning of
their deliberations and approached it from the same perspective. WES WALLACE,
a member of the RHO Group, put it as follows:

> With a viable network available, I don't think there is very much
> choice. Anyone who has had to program 18 to 20 hours a day from
> scratch would not put up with it long if there were a network available
> and especially if that network were ABC looking the way it has re-
> cently. In this particular market, you have to compete with two other
> V's—VHF stations.

This economic argument was echoed elsewhere. BERT BARER warned the
SIGMA group that he would be loath to try to attract six other investors to join
him in going into the 75th market against two already established V's, "particularly in today's tight money market" unless he had every advantage including
a network affiliation. In the IOTA group, REY BARNES was telling his colleagues: ". . . it would be sheer idiocy to consider an independent operation
unless we knew what kind of angel we have backing us since we are starting up
in a limited budget situation."

ROYAL COLLE (Cornell) made the same point in the TAU group: "It would
be different if we were to assume that we were Westinghouse starting up this
station than it would be if we were a group of citizens without Westinghouse's
resources."

GEORGE MITCHELL, the Industry Discussion Leader, commented on this point: "I've noted over the last 20 years in broadcasting people who came in with piles of gold and are now trying desperately to get out of the broadcasting business—Kaiser, U.S. Communications backed by American Viscose Corp, United Artists Broadcasting. No matter how much capitalization you have, a day of reckoning comes."

Most agreed that the new station, as JOHN GOLDHAMMER (Program Director, WTOP-TV, Washington, D.C.) resource person for the RHO group, put it, "could not afford to buy all the programming necessary." GOLDHAMMER, however, continued with a note of sadness that struck a responsive chord among many others, "It's too bad. I'd love to toy with an independent station."

Although many seemed swayed by the uncertainties attendant to putting a new station on the air, not all were ready to adopt the network affiliation. K. R. GREENWOOD (University of Tulsa) cautioned the RHO group:

> You'll have to take a look at what you'll be able to sell against two strongly entrenched news blocks. I think we have to be careful that we don't get so locked in to the network that we can't look for the counterprogramming opportunities that will be necessary to get the audience that will make the station competitive in the market.

Meanwhile, JIM FLETCHER also cautioning against too close a tie to the network—a tie which would result "in taking some of the bombs that are on ABC"—nevertheless suggested to SIGMA group: "If we can't afford some competitive programming in prime time in this market then there's no sense in trying to be an independent."

ANDY POTOS, the Industry Discussion leader of the group, reinforced the point:

> We have an independent station in Boston which grosses close to $10 million dollars a year. Yet our profit is about zilch. It will be a long time before we get the station to a profitable point.

Bringing the example back to the Desolake station POTOS continued:

> When you have to buy programming that's very expensive to be competitive and you have to program from sign-on to sign-off you are talking about untold hundreds of thousands of dollars. I don't know whether the bank or the individuals who are bankrolling this station would feel that that kind of expenditure was warranted at this point.

ELIZABETH BAIN of yet another station rep firm, Katz Television, serving as a program resource person for the SIGMA group, seconded POTOS:

> Out of the 53 stations that Katz represents, about ten are independents. I can tell you that there are very few of those ten that are operating in the black and those few are just doing so this year. Although those sta-

tions which have major corporations in the background or have other businesses to depend on aren't too worried, the ones that are truly independent are concerned.

BAIN went on to advise the group:

How long those stations can go on is questionable. There comes a time when you have to assess your business and bring yourself to a point of decision. So I think you are very fortunate in having an opportunity to affiliate in the 75th market, Desolake.

Participants in all four groups had been given the latest available annual NAB Television Financial Reports, excerpts of the 1975 edition of which appear in Appendix 7. These data show that 295 (85%) of the 346 VHF stations which are affiliated with a network showed a profit while only 27 of 39 (69%) of the tabulated independents were profitable. Those figures are comparable to the broader based *FCC 39th Annual Report, Fiscal Year 1973*, the latest available at the time, which detailed the Revenues, Expenses and Incomes of Independent stations for 1970–1972.[13] These data show that while 87.1% of all network affiliated VHF stations reported making a profit, only 66.7% of the Independent V's did so. Further, the data also show that programming expenses for independents represented 49.1% of total revenue net of all cash discounts and commissions paid to agencies, representatives and brokers. Programming expenses for affiliated V's were reported to be 30.1%.[14] Not surprisingly, LIZ BAIN struck a responsive chord.

Even so, there were arguments advanced against affiliation. WILLIAM HAWES (University of Houston), for example, worried in the SIGMA group that not enough consideration was being given to the other side and asked for some counter arguments. In response, LORIN ROBINSON (University of Wisconsin), reminded the group that:

. . . there is talk this season of audience apathy directed toward network programming. It's possible, therefore, that a different approach, a strong local orientation in contrast to the network fare being offered on the two affiliates in the market might have more impact. It might make a bigger impression in this small market than more of the same, which is what ABC offers.

One member of the group, picking up on this idea, suggested that Desolake seemed a very community-minded area and that a locally oriented station could capitalize on that feeling, attracting support from many local organizations and coming on the air with a "big burst of publicity." This argument failed to persuade RAY STEELE:

I don't think that we can get enough impact and real momentum going to stimulate the kind of resources we need to keep ourselves from going into the scarlet red in a very short time.

Others agreed, contending that apart from news, local programming historically had had little impact. ROD CLEFTON (Gonzaga University) added some further notes of caution:

First of all, local programming is the most expensive programming you can do. Second, it does not sell. Third, we are going to have to have some local programming anyway in order to get a license.

The same discussion in the RHO group prompted WES WALLACE to observe:

If you examine the local programming any station does, you see that most of it is syndicated. And syndicated programming looks like the network. So local programming isn't going to make a big splash. Neither is the public affairs and community programming. If we are strong in news, that's where we'll make our local impact, even if we are an independent, because the rest of our programming will be stuff that is brought out of a can and will look just like the network when it rolls.

From the back of the room came the following assent:

There's an old adage that says, "as local news goes, so goes the station."

Members of each group, on the other hand, spoke to the impact in the community the new ABC affiliation might develop. As JAMES FLETCHER put it to SIGMA:

With the affiliation we not only get a consistent personality for our station, we also get a promotional package that has been a long time in the building. Many of the ABC programs that have not been shown in the market have still been written about and they show up in *TV Guide*. Our audience knows the names of the stars and they see them on the talk shows of the other networks. So they're already looking forward to the opportunity to see these network personalities they've been waiting for. Besides, ABC has an excellent reputation for helping stations with their own promotion.

In a similar vein, PETER WEINER (Castleton State) was reminding his associates in TAU:

I think it's important for us to remember what year we are talking about. We're not talking about 1973 or 1978 but 1976. It's not only a national election year but also a year of the Olympics. How can we pass up the opportunity to get the election coverage as well as, in the very beginning of the year, getting the consumers used to tuning into our station? We can have the Winter Olympics coming on in January. We have an audience that's just waiting to be served.

Meanwhile, the SIGMA group was also citing ABC Sports as an important factor in weighing the decision to affiliate. ROD CLEFTON saw ABC Sports as "getting out and talking to the folks—young programming to get to the college crowd which certainly isn't being done by the CBS station." CLEFTON went on to suggest that KIRT could quickly develop its identity with the community by following the local football team, "as a loss leader, if necessary." BRUCE LINTON (University of Kansas) pointed out that the equipment package seemed to anticipate just such programming with its emphasis on remote equipment. "Many midwestern stations are kept going by their sports programming," CHARLES PHILLIPS (Emerson College) noted, adding:

> It's different there than anywhere else in the country. In the Midwest, I believe, they go crazy about sports. What bothers me, though, is how can we accommodate a fairly heavy commitment to local sports and still satisfy ABC?

Not everyone agreed that the sports activities in Desolake were attractive enough to sustain an audience. JAMES HARRIS observed:

> You can't put the college football games on; the NCAA restrictions will prevent that. You wouldn't want to put the college basketball games on; the team just isn't that good. Its record isn't good. Triple A Baseball? Even the best team isn't going to draw. If they get 2500 people out to see a home game they're doing very well. So you're not going to put them on television. That leaves you with ABA Basketball. We aren't going to make money with ABA Basketball. As we all know, even the ABA Championship games have a difficult time selling . . .

ANDREW POTOS, the SIGMA discussion leader amplified from the vantage point of Storer Television Sales:

> The market is glutted. The network sports programming has increased almost 200%. That means the national advertiser has plenty of opportunity to buy network if he needs sports programming to reach his market. And he can buy network much more cheaply than he can buy national spot. That's another reason for the networks to produce sports shows and for the local station to fail to make money on local sports. Our independent station in Boston broadcasts the Boston Bruins, probably the hottest hockey team in the country, and the Boston Red Soxs who had a phenomenal year. And even with those two hits we had a hell of a hassle to make a buck.

MARY JEAN THOMAS summed up the prospects for an independent in Desolake:

> That ABA Basketball team is about all we've got. Even if we develop the best film library of any station in the area we still aren't going to

cut into the network ratings. It doesn't work in Chicago. WGN coun-
terprograms against those early morning quiz shows with the best film
library you could imagine. They hardly show up in the ratings. I think
we have to go with ABC. And let's start with the new season so we
can ride the coattails of all that ABC publicity.

All four groups were moving toward a decision. But not without some res-
ervations. In the SIGMA group, CLAUDE SUMERLIN (Henderson State University) expressed concern about the contract KIRT would have to sign:

Is this standard procedure for the network to reserve the rights to set
the rate? And to cancel if they don't find the station profitable enough?
I find that co-optative. The station should have the right to cancel the
network if we don't find the network profitable. Is this contract negotiable or is it take it or leave it?

BARER: "They protect you for a certain number of days and compensate you
on the basis of your previous ratings. So it isn't a free for all. If the audience
goes up during that period, we can renegotiate."

But HARVEY SESLOWSKY, of Film Service Corporation, one of the programming resource people in the group, pointed out:

I was with ABC affiliate relations for a couple of years and I can tell
you that the rate of compensation is what you have to be concerned
with. The usual rate is around 30% for a primary affiliate. But ABC
could go higher. As a practical matter, to obtain affiliation with the
maximum rate it would be wise, at least to begin with, to clear the entire schedule.

However, in the RHO group, JOHN GOLDHAMMER was proposing what he
described as "selective affiliation" as an alternative to either independent
operation or full affiliation:

You go ABC network but you don't clear all the shows. You are
selective. There is something unusual in this market that has to be considered. ABC traditionally has done well in young demographics—it
has appealed to men 18 to 49 and to women 18 to 49. Desolake is a
market that has over 50% of its men in the 18 to 49 age group but less
than 50% of the women are 18 to 49. It's an interesting market. It's
also an NBC powerhouse, judging from the ratings. A strong NBC
market is automatically an old-skewing market. You have to take this
into consideration when you decide whether or how to affiliate with
ABC.

KEN GREENWOOD, to the contrary, felt that there were sales considerations
which should prompt RHO to adopt a full affiliation:

We will have to rely on network revenues just to pay the bills. Our
station is going to have problems with national advertising no matter

what we do. And national advertising is going to be more familiar with ABC's shows than with any syndicated or other programming we put on.

When the question of accepting the entire ABC schedule came up in the TAU group discussions, several expressed concern. JOHN STANTON (Temple University) felt that the alternatives had not been sufficiently explored. JAMES BROWN (Loyola University at Los Angeles), like his colleagues in other groups, suggested something less than automatic full clearance:

> There is an underlying assumption that we are running a business and we must attract an audience and see a fast return on our investment. I think we are going along with that assumption quite properly. But we are not just economists here. We are broadcasters and persons who have personal values. I think we all want to make broadcasting better as well as to get strong profits. If that is a consideration, I think we must give ourselves more options in prime time than just taking the network, even if that means some little loss.

MITCHELL:

> I think there are two basic principles we must remember: One, we must become economically viable because we can't serve anyone if we are dark and two, we cannot serve people who will not watch.

BROWN:

> Those are cautions, to be sure. But they do not mean that we have to go for every single dollar. We can't be too anxious and we can't leave outselves open to formal criticism.

Al Korn, Vice President of Programming, RKO General Television, and the programming resource person for the group, interjected the reminder that pre-emptive programming could be competitive:

> We could put in a good movie which certainly could attract audiences from the CBS and NBC stations, and there's a very good show which is attracting considerable interest, *Space 1999*. But it makes no sense at all to pre-empt a really strong show. You would just be cutting down on your audience levels. Any pre-emptions of ABC should take place in the first hour. That's where the weaker shows are. That kind of decision—*when* to pre-empt—should be made on the basis of the strength of the show and not on the basis of strong personal values.

LOUIS A. DAY (Central Michigan University) suggested a calm pragmatism:

> If we don't do well in the March ratings, we pre-empt. If we do do well, we go to the network and say ''what about increasing our rate?''

(We also increase our own rate adjacent to the network.) In other words, either way, we increase the revenue coming in without having risked a great deal up front.

CAROL REUSS (Loyola University of New Orleans) thought the determining factor should be that the station was just coming on the air:

If the station opts for more flexibility in the schedule, for more creativity, aren't we going to have to devote more money to promote it? Wouldn't it be wiser, for a brand new station, to run with the network in this first year? To go with what we know is coming up rather than invest the time and budget on our own programming?

IOTA had explored the notion of starting independent and then, at a later date, affiliating. The group moved away from this idea as it became apparent that the independent would have more difficulty in becoming economically sound and might not, without the bottomless bankroll they had discussed earlier, be able to survive until that time. But still, some wished to hold out. As WALTER BUNGE (Kansas State University) put it:

In the short haul, I would affiliate. But in the long haul, we're going to have cable in this market. Once cable is in there, the alternative to network programming is going to be such that a network affiliation will no longer have a particular attraction to the viewer. As an independent, we could buy from other sources, sources which, in ten years or so, are going to meet the competition from the networks and maybe even beat them. Networks are going to lose some of their power in controlling programming and that will make it much more attractive, in the long haul, to be independent.

JIM COPPERSMITH, General Manager of WNAC-TV, Boston, and Industry Discussion Leader of the group, objected that we have to program for the 70's and 80's rather than the 90's:

We've got a healthy line of credit, but the banks are not going to sit still for ten years of operating losses so that we can realize the dream.

BUNGE:

The independent is not going to be a loss operation. All I'm saying is that it will not be as profitable as the affiliate.

The group disagreed. REY BARNES questioned the basic premise:

I'm going to present another view of cable. I don't know if you've been noticing but the cable people themselves are becoming cautious in the materials they send out because of the increased cost per mile of the initial plant. It's going up at a terrific rate—in some places to as much as $50,000 a mile. I know of one large installation in Salt Lake

City for which the initial estimate was $4,500. By the time they got through, they were talking about $15,000 a mile. We have a very small plant investment for our station here in Desolake. But this kind of large scale investment which cable requires is going to retard cableization at least until there is a technological breakthrough. We are safer going into our station assuming no cable.

Besides, as EDWIN L. GLICK (North Texas State) said:

I wouldn't be so sure it would not be a losing operation. I live in a market with three network affiliates and one of the most successful independents in the country, Channel 11, Dallas. But there is no question, even though they are successful financially, that the prestige and the good advertisers are going to the network affiliates. As a new station, you are building up a reputation. Later you might want to cast off the network affiliation because you are in a cableized city. But, by then you have built that reputation as a network affiliate. Dallas is a real life situation where the independent has the least prestige.

HOWARD STEVENS (Suffolk County Community College) agreed:

I think we have to concern ourselves with the short haul. If the market ever does become highly cableized then we can turn over our affiliation. We've got to get in there and start our operation and put off investigation of cable to some later day.

In the end, IOTA, like the other groups, was swayed by arguments such as those. They were also impressed with the laundry list of affiliation advantages JIM COPPERSMITH gave in response to an inquiry:

Let me set out a couple of givens in the market place. Number one, the affiliate gets a higher unit rate, and a higher cost per thousand for what I perceive to be the following reasons. A network affiliate produces what the buyers call "big reach" announcements—higher rated units. There's a romance, apparently, in the minds of the buyers which attaches to a 20 rated spot or to a 30 rated spot as opposed to building a reach, having the announcement seen by the same gross numbers of people, through a series of lower rated announcements. This is what the independents must do.

Number two, because the affiliate does not have the tremendous program costs that an independent does, it can make a greater commitment to its news operation. Ideally, though not always, this produces a better news product.[15] And there is a romance in the advertisers' minds about news. There is the availability of sports programming delivered by the networks. Lower start up costs for programming; the availability of more first run programming; compensation for programming car-

ried; network news gathering; and the availability of most of the pre-
mier sports attractions. These are the advantages of affiliation.

All four groups voted to affiliate with ABC.

NOTES

1. Joel Rosenbloom, "Authority of the Federal Communications Commission," Appendix I in John E. Coons, ed., *Freedom and Responsibility in Broadcasting,* Evanston, Ill., 1961, North-western University Press, p. 96.
2. *Ibid.*, note 21, p. 131.
3. *Ibid.*, p. 132.
4. Federal Radio Commission "Third Annual Report" quoted in Ward L. Quaal and James A. Brown, *Broadcast Management: Radio-Television,* Second Edition Revised and Enlarged, New York, 1976, Hastings House, p. 369.
5. Jose Ortega y Gasset, *The Revolt of the Masses,* New York, 1932, W. Norton and Co. The passage is also to be found reprinted as "The Coming of the Masses" in Bernard Rosenberg and David Manning White, *Mass Culture: The Popular Arts in America,* New York, 1957, The Free Press, p. 41.
6. Docket 19861, 57 FCC 2nd 19, 1975, 35RR 2nd 1154; see also 57 FCC 2nd 1177, 36RR 2nd 372.
7. Quaal and Brown, *op. cit.*, p. 368.
8. *Broadcasting,* January 19, 1976, p. 26.
9. FCC News Release, Mimeograph NO. 53027, August 11, 1975.
10. The concept of menu and diet applied to television viewing was first developed by Gary A. Steiner in his pioneering study at the Bureau of Applied Research of Columbia University, *The People Look at Television: A Study of Audience Attitudes,* New York, 1963, Alfred A. Knopf. A decade later Robert T. Bower updated the study in *Television and the Public,* New York, 1973, Holt, Rinehart and Winston. Bower found news and public affairs making up 17 percent of the weekly viewing diet during his sample week. He and Steiner also found "reasonable similarity" in the viewing habits of people with different backgrounds (level of education, sex, age), although they expressed very different attitudes toward television.
11. In 1975 there were in addition to the 185 primary affiliates, 67 stations with secondary ABC affiliations. Secondary affiliations are most frequently found in two-station markets. A station with two affiliations relies most heavily on its first network with which it is affiliated but carries some of the programming of the second.
12. Copies of actual ABC, CBS and NBC affiliation contracts may be found in *Legal and Business Problems of Television and Radio,* Course Handbook, New York, 1976, Practicing Law Institute. $20.
13. *loc. cit.*, pp. 228–9.
14. *Ibid.*
15. Coopersmith cited WNEW-TV, New York; WTTG, Washington; KTTV in Los Angeles; three Metromedia stations and WGN-TV in Chicago as among the exceptions. "They devote a tremendous amount of their resources to news, but most independents, especially those not in the large markets, just cannot do that."

FOR THE STUDENT

1. Prepare an analysis of stations in the 50th to 100th market range comparing independent and affiliated stations for various cost items and for profitability.
2. Compare the several networks' affiliation contracts. Does comparison suggest any room for negotiation in a KIRT-TV affiliation agreement?
3. Obtain from *TV Guide,* newspaper listings or other sources, program schedules for independent stations in various sized markets.
4. Cost out alternative program schedules for an independent KIRT-TV.

Programming:
Local Origination

Pursuant to the Communications Act of 1934, as amended, the Commission cannot grant, renew or modify a broadcast authorization unless it makes an affirmative finding that the operation of the station, as proposed, will serve the public interest, convenience and necessity. Programming is of the essence of broadcasting.

ATTACHMENT A, Instructions, General Information and Definitions for TV Broadcast Application, *Federal Communications Commission, Form 301,* Section I V-B, Page 9

SINCE THE PROBLEM calls for the establishment of a commercially viable station, the decision to affiliate with ABC has to represent a major step toward the accomplishment of the desired end. With that decision as much as 40% of the program day may be scheduled at no cost to the station. Not only will the new station be able to compete on a generally equitable basis for the available audience, an even greater audience may be attracted. If past performance elsewhere is to be any sort of guide, the number of persons watching television in Desolake will actually increase.

Narrowly viewed, the affiliation contract permits KIRT to exercise first refusal rights to ABC programming. If KIRT elects to take a particular show, ABC will actually pay the station to do so. FCC rules dictate that this arrangement can be in effect for only two years. However, the rules permit and custom encourages both sides to expect almost automatic renewal of the contract for successive two year terms. And during each of those terms, the station may identify itself in the marketplace as the ABC affiliate. Usually, that is expressed and understood as the station actually being ABC in Desolake, one and indivisible with David Hartman, Harry Reasoner, Howard Cossell and "the Fonz." Signing an affiliation contract means much more than merely accepting a network programming service. For better or worse, affiliation for the local station involves identification with the national public relations objectives, the news policies and the public perception of the network with which the station signs. For its part, the public does not know what the relation of the affiliate with the network really is, nor should it be expected to know.

Important though the decision to affiliate may be, it by no means settles all of the station's programming problems. Admittedly, some 40% of the schedule is taken care of. But the amount of money coming in for the sale of that portion of the broadcast day, exclusive of returns from the sale of station breaks adjacent to the network, will come nowhere near meeting 40% of the station's costs. In 1972, the nation's 428 network affiliated VHF stations reported to the FCC that network payments amounted to 11.5% of total revenues and offset 18.9% of total costs.[1] What this means to a station in Desolake can be seen by examining the expenses in the nation's actual 75th market, Portland-Poland Spring. In 1972, the three stations in this market reported time sales to the networks which covered 23.7% of total expenses, a figure somewhat higher than the national average.[2] Nevertheless, these sales left each of the stations with an average of $1,058,469 in expenses to be made up elsewhere. Even applying the rule of thumb, that every $100 in network base rate compensation means $50,000 a year in revenues to the station[3], it is apparent that a significant return must accrue from the locally scheduled portion of the broadcast day. In turn, KIRT must seek to be and succeed in becoming highly competitive in order to survive. This is the rubric under which the rest of the problem must be solved.

Two kinds of information are required to accomplish the task, information about the competition in the market and information about the options open to the new station's programmers. In the real life situation, the competition's schedule can be obtained from *TV Guide* or the newspapers and, most important, from watching those programs which are unfamiliar. Here, a schedule is given in Appendix 8. Note that times given on this schedule are New York times. Thus 9:00 P.M. on the schedule must be read as 8:00 P.M. for Desolake and the rest of the country except for areas in the Eastern time zone.

Television schedules, we all know, change season by season. Lately, they have been changing three times a year. By the time you read this, some of the programs listed in Appendix 8, particularly in prime time, will have changed. This fact, it is important to note, does not affect, in any way, the value of the material in the appendices, this simulation or the role the Fifth Faculty-Industry Seminar participants can play in assisting students now or in the future. The names of the broadcasts they thought about may be forgotten but the principles are not. Anyone troubled by the presumed dating of the materials in this volume will simply change the names of the programs. The problems underlying both the simulation and American broadcasting will remain the same.

Data on the effectiveness of the competition is, of course, more important than the mere schedule. It is the effectiveness of the other two stations in attracting audiences against which KIRT will have to compete. The A. C. Nielsen Company, perhaps the best known and certainly the most widely used of the professional firms engaged in continuous audience measurement studies, has compiled and presented such data for Desolake exactly as it would be provided for any other market. Nielsen prepares two sets of reports, the Nielsen Television Index, NTI, which reports national ratings and the Nielsen Station Index, NSI, which reports on an individual market. This NSI report, or "book" as it is known in the trade, is for November 1975, the period of the Tarrytown Seminar, and contains all the information which characteristically appears in such a report. The report constitutes Appendix 8.

Those who have not previously worked with rating books will find it essential to study the Market Data given at the beginning of the book.[4] First of all, there is a map showing the counties in the area indicating which fall into the DMA (the designated market area) which the data in the report measure. Figures are given in Table I on the number of total households and households with television. Obviously, it is the latter group in which we are interested. It is important, however, to realize that percentages given are not percentages of the entire population but only of that 98% of households which have television sets. Table II details how many of the households in the DMA have more than one set, how many have color, how many can receive UHF signals (a less important figure nowadays as the overwhelming majority of sets ever made have been manufactured since 1964 when the law requiring all-channel reception capability went into effect) and how many can receive cable. This figure is of growing importance to the broadcaster and to the advertiser.

Table III provides estimates of the demographic breakdown of the DMA figure. Nielsen data, like that of any other market research organization, is based on sampling. Table IV and its notes indicate the statistical reliability of the information. Finally, the note beneath Table V cautions that the data are provided only on the DMA and not on the larger NSI area.

Within the body of the book, two sets of schedules are included. On pages 1 through 5 there appears a summary of so-called across-the-board or strip programming. By consulting this schedule one can see the average performance of programs which appear every day, Monday through Friday. Beginning with page 6 each day is taken up separately, the figures given representing, for example, the average of all Mondays during the month.

To understand what the figures given represent, it may be helpful to look at one time period. At 9:00 A.M. Monday through Friday, the schedule on page one tells us, KNAC broadcasts *Celebrity Sweepstakes* while KBGA is broadcasting another game show, *Spin Off*. HUT, pronounced "hut" and standing for "homes using television," is listed under HH or "household" Rating in the Program column, as 20. This HUT level, sometimes also called "sets in use," represents a percentage of the total television households. Since Table I had listed 258,000 as the total number of television households in the DMA, we can read from the rating book that on the average weekday in Desolake, Kansouri, during November, 1975, 51,600 households—20% of all those owning television sets—had sets in use.

The *rating* is always a percentage of the number of television households in the market. Thus, at 9:00, we can see that 9% of all households were tuned to *Celebrity Sweepstakes,* while 11% were tuned to *Spin Off.* Since the HUT level varies considerably from one time of day to another, a rating at one time of the day cannot be compared to a rating at another time of day and is, therefore, of less importance to the local station management than is the next set of figures, the Share of Audience. In our example, these figures show that at 9:00, 49% of all the sets in use—49% of the available audience, were tuned to KBGA, while KNAC attracted only 42%. The remaining 9% may be assumed to be watching the Public Television station in the market, figures for which are not given but can be seen not to be significant, or are watching cable. It is important, in thinking about the comparative performance of television programming, to bear in mind that *Ratings measure percentages of the total audience in the market* while *shares measure percentages of the available audience at that time.*[5]

The other figures represent audience composition data and provide a breakdown of the numbers of persons in the respective categories. Thus, at 6:00 P.M. on the average weekday in November 1975, for example, 19% of all men in Desolake and 21% of all women were watching KNAC's Evening Report, 10% of all men in the 18–49 age group were watching. Since each of these figures represents a percentage of a different universe, care must be exercised in attempting to average or perform other arithmetic functions with the data.[6]

In addition to information about the other stations in the market which is supplied by the rating and share data, the programmer, in order to compete, must also know what programming options are open. Essentially, there are three categories into which non-network programming falls: locally produced programming; feature films, most originally made for showing in motion picture theaters; and syndicated programming, on tape or film, whether off-network programming comprised of broadcasts originally shown on one of the networks, or syndicated programming developed specifically for distribution to stations, especially for their prime time access periods.

Included in Appendix 9 is material on feature films available. This consists of a note on feature film pricing, and a description of four packages available. This material has been supplied by the actual film distributors and contains the basic information stations would need. The packages listed are *Premium Package 2,* 12 films available from Metromedia Producers Corp.; *Universal 49,* 49 films available from MCA; Volume 19, containing 30 films distributed by Warner-Brothers Television; and *Viacom II,* a package of 21 features which Viacom Enterprises distributes. For each package, titles, stars, dates of release and previous network broadcast history, if any, are provided as are running times and availability dates. In some cases a package includes features which may not be broadcast until some specified future time.

Appendix 10 includes a list of 44 series not already under contract to KNAC or KGBA and therefore available for syndication, the length of their episodes, their price per broadcast, and whether or not the series has sufficient episodes for stripping or must be scheduled on a once a week basis. Any scheduling restrictions are also shown. Following that listing, in Appendix 11, is a summary of the syndication history of no less than 229 different series. Grouped by program type, (situation comedy, adventure, mystery and suspense, variety, sports, western etc.), each series is analyzed in terms of the demographics of its previous audiences. Figures given are the numbers of women, men and total adults per viewing household. Number of viewers in the 18–49 age bracket are also given.

Decisions about locally produced programming do not for the most part, require reference material. Admittedly, the variables in programming cost are so great as to make it impossible to set down any average figure. In New York City, for example, an O & O producing a daily half-hour talk show may well find itself incurring costs in the neighborhood of $15,000 per week, even without having to pay guests. A similar format, in a market where there are few union contracts, where wage scales are lower and where the audience might not expect the same level of technical quality could be turned out for a fraction of the cost. Most of the decisions which will affect costs in the market, the selection of formats, union contract provisions, the availability of technical resources and the selection and scheduling of talent are within the control of the simulation exercise itself. Wage scales for broadcasters in the 76th to 100th markets are provided in Appendix 12.

With this information at hand it is possible to develop answers to the remaining Programming Thought-Starter Questions and to produce a program schedule.

IRTS SEMINAR—Thought-Starter Questions

—PROGRAMMING

PROBLEM A: Develop a viable, audience-appealing competitive program schedule for *your* station.

1. Basic question (applicable not only to Programming, but to entire station's operation): Will you seek an ABC network affiliation or remain independent?

2. What *Promises* were made in the license application, relative to local live origination, public affairs and news programming?

3. In the two key day-parts for local programming decisions, (so-called early fringe: 3–5 P.M. Desolake time;

and prime access: 6:30–7 P.M.) what will the station's program targets be—kids? adults, "kid-ults"?

4. Is the station wise in trying to develop a programming "look"—i.e. the "young adults' station" . . . "the something-for-everyone station" . . . etc? If this is desirable, is it achievable?

5. What syndicated programs and feature films are available to the station, and what are general price ranges for these?

6. What is the station's physical capability for local live production?

7. What is the importance in Desolake of local commercial production to local sales?

8. Will the station clear all network programming that ABC offers (presume a "Yes" response to Question 1); or will there be selective non-clearance of certain series, day-parts, etc., to permit local or syndicated programming?

9. Should the station seek out non-network, local or regional sports programming?

10. What budget and effort can or should be invested in local programming or talent?

11. In the late-fringe period (post late news to sign-off), will the station take the network fee, or originate its programming locally with syndicated properties?

In light of these questions, and others generated in discussion and decision process, *what is the program schedule for your station?*

FACULTY SEMINAR DISCUSSION

The task is to devise a program schedule for the 126 hours a week KIRT, Desolake, is to be on the air. Having decided that the station will seek, and presumably obtain, an affiliation with ABC, programming for a certain number of those hours—perhaps as much as 40% to 60%—is available from the network. In deciding how much of the network to clear and in planning how to program the rest of the broadcast day, the first thing any group must do is clarify its objectives. Then the group must decide upon a protocol for reaching those objectives, a plan of action which permits breaking down the task into components and dealing with them in a logical sequence.

The four groups in Tarrytown spent much of their first full day in discussing their objectives. In fact, this was to become a leitmotif recurring through-out the entire seminar. All accepted, implicitly, that the station they would design should be economically viable. In meeting that general objective, a given for a commercial station under a free enterprise system, a number of spe-cific alternatives are open. JIM COPPERSMITH set out a list for the IOTA discus-sions:

Are we looking for ratings dominance? Are we looking for profit—the speediest possible profit acceleration? Or are we looking for slower, healthier, long-term growth opportunities? Are we concerned about demographics? Do we want to be the station which best serves the community? These questions speak directly to one thing—how you program your station. Bear in mind that it is axiomatic in this business that revenue follows audience.

Each of the four groups followed a different procedure in looking at the broadcast day. RHO reasoned that the most logical approach was to start with the station's commitments to the FCC with respect to news, public affairs and other non-entertainment programs, allocate times for those broadcasts and fill in the remainder of the schedule. SIGMA was impressed by the argument that most of the station's profits will come from Early Fringe, that period from the end of the network's daytime schedule to the network evening news. Accord-ingly, the SIGMA group concentrated on the placement of the station's Early News, as the keystone to early fringe, attacked that portion of the broadcast day first, and then programmed around it. TAU began with sign-on and proceeded hour by hour though the day. IOTA, however, took another course:

F. DENNIS LYNCH (Cleveland State University): When you were outlining initial options, Jim, you suggested that we might go after maximum ratings and profits or we might seek long-term growth op-tions. What practical difference would selecting that option make to programming?

COPPERSMITH: You can, I believe, put a new station on the air and make very dramatic inroads in terms of ratings, homes and shares, through skillful counter-programming, putting different formats, kids programming, kid-adult programming, against the established formats on the competition. You'll get big ratings—a lot of homes. But not the most desirable demographics. You could also put on programming that would do well in terms of number of homes but will produce heavily weighted older demographics. You can build circulation fast *or* you can program similar to your competition and try to build an audience with well balanced demographics in the hope that your programming will be better. Do I put news at noon right opposite two established newscasts, knowing full well that I'm not immediately going to have the highest rated Noon News in the market? Because I have faith in the quality of my product, because I think I know a little more about the news, about pacing, about format, I do and ultimately I'm going to have a competitive news and hopefully I'll win.

KENNETH HARWOOD (Temple): Another partial response to Dennis Lynch—look at the description of the building, transmitter and equipment package furnished. (Appendix 13) A million and a quarter worth of equipment. And notice Item B on page 2. This company is going to arrange with another station to build a television tower, sell it to the financier and then lease it back on a long term lease. Now, what this suggests is that this company is not putting down a lot of capital to invest in that land or in building the tower. They are neither well financed nor do they seem to be prepared to stay there a long time. Now, let's assume they are planning to sell out in three to six years. That would have a very important effect on how we plan to program.

COPPERSMITH: Well, what are we planning to do? Do we want to put down for a lifetime and become part of this community or do we want to be, as you suggest, trafficking that license?

HARWOOD: You either need better financing or you need a plan to get out.

COPPERSMITH: What's wrong with the financing?

HARWOOD: The financing is capital short. You either cannot or choose not to buy or rent a building. If we go into that community to stay there, and if we have our own land and building, we can go into auxiliary enterprises, such as data transmission, paging services, and other uses for a tower from which we can get revenue. This is probably a fly-by-night operation.

REY BARNES: There's something else which makes me feel as Ken does. They didn't choose a turnkey alternative. With a turnkey operation, we would have had our entire facility right at the beginning. It would show they were willing to make a commitment. Instead, they chose the B alternative (they said it was recommended by the chief engineer), which is an item by item buying procedure. Either you make an initial buy which involves all your capital outlay for equipment or you build your inventory as you go along, over a period of time. Now that may be a good, conservative way to . . .

HARWOOD: But it suggests they're underfinanced.

COPPERSMITH: Then the question is, if you are under-financed, how do you build your business so that when you go into the banks you can impress them with the money you are making and with the impact you have made on the market?

BARNES: This has got to be a black line operation. Let's face it. If we're going to operate in the public interest, convenience and necessity we've got to make money out of this operation so we can look at increasing our service sometime down the road.

COPPERSMITH: I think the first thing we need to know then is how many dollars are coming into this market. Then depending on our station's philosophy we can decide what share of that dollar we can realistically get in year one and start spending money on our programming based on that realistic share.

HARWOOD: There can't be much money in that market. I give you again that same terrible document, page one near the bottom. They can't even afford to build and retain on their budget a $67,000 building!

LEE EDEN, Director of Programming, Corinthian Broadcasting Corp: Ken, I don't think you can assume that it isn't much of a market. Based on this information, you can assume that your backers are kind of cheap. Corinthian has a small station in Indiana, in the 90th market, and it has a $5 million operating budget.

LYNCH: We have to get to some decisions. I suggest appointing subcommittees. One to bring in some kind of budget, and two groups to bring in specific proposals. One will bring in a proposed schedule for the quick impact mentioned. The other group, also trying to make a big splash, will try to do it with long range growth in mind. In other words, we will have two programming approaches—a counter-programming quick impact approach and a more conservative, long-term growth approach.

Counter programming occupied the attention of each of the groups at one point or another. It was one of several strategic questions considered. In RHO, counter-programming came up early on as they discussed when to schedule early news:

JOHN GOLDHAMMER: Traditionally, the weakest station in the market assumes a position of counter-programming to news. We have to believe that our station will be the weakest, at least in the very beginning. In our case, the counter-programming would be to go on with local news before the other stations so as not to compete with their local news. Then we would place network news against their local news.

CARL WINDSOR (John Brown University): One of the Tulsa stations was quite successful putting entertainment programming against the competitor's news. Up until a year ago, they had ABC News from five-thirty to six, followed by *Truth Or Consequences,* followed by a half hour of local news. It was rather unusual but it worked. They felt they gave people an alternative.

GOLDHAMMER: Here we have to compete with network news at five thirty and the local news at six. That's rough. That's very rough. What we don't want to do is pit network against network and local against local. Especially with NBC. NBC is a real powerhouse in this market with a 53 share out of a 41 HUT.

WES WALLACE: I've come to the conclusion we ought to go at five o'clock. That's assuming we have people getting home by then. We don't really know what the employment patterns are in Desolake. Five o'clock would certainly do what you suggest. It would put our network news up against their local. But aren't we a little out of order? Shouldn't we discuss news policy before we decide on when to do an early news?

ACE KELLNER: Before that decision is made, we should decide whether we are going to have an early news. One of the most expensive operations is the launching of a news program. I believe we should have to do it eventually, but we should examine whether or not at the outset, as a new station going on the air, we should have an early as well as a late news. Perhaps we should simply carry network news until we are competitive.

RAY STEELE: We may need to answer a basic question about how much value we place on local news. Our application commits us to 65% of our news devoted to local. After we decide on what value news has to us, then we can decide whether to go big with local news.

WILLIAM PARSONS (Northern Kentucky State College): May I point out the needs and problems enumerated in our license application? I assume they are going to be met, to a certain extent through our news coverage. If that is the case, then local news is essential.

RICK LEVY: It is not only essential, it is preferred. We can turn it to our advantage. This market is growing enormously—thirty percent growth in ten years. That means a lot of new people. And theoretically young people coming in to the market. NBC and CBS both have an older skew to their news. We can try to hit that younger audience, that newer audience just coming into the market.

KEN GREENWOOD: When I look at this market I see a lot of factors pertinent to a discussion of news. For instance, I see three metropolitan newspapers in a small town of two hundred thousand. That says something to me. I see six commercial FM, seven AM stations, a public television station and eleven suburban newspapers. That indicates to me that somebody is doing a fair job of covering the news. At least collectively, there's a lot of competition for news in this market. Furthermore, it's a high circulation market and although AM rates are low for the size market, FM, the newspapers and billboards all get good rates. To me, this is a very competitive media market. That raises a logical question: do we want to schedule as much news as we possibly can and build our schedule around that? It would make for a heavily promotable station.

The other groups were also weighing strategies for attracting an audience to the new station. AL KORN told the TAU group:

The most important thing is to get a strong enough lead-in so that people will sample your news. The station that has a successful newscast will be the successful station. Amusement shows come and go but people know their stations by the public affairs, the public service and the news they bring to their communities.

GEORGE MITCHELL: Let me throw this out for your consideration: What service does the third redundant newscast in a market provide? What service is there in a third guy standing up and saying the same thing the other two guys are saying? Who says you have to have news, anyway? This was a problem I had to face in Dayton, Ohio where WHIO dominated the market just as the NBC station does in Desolake. I have eliminated our news department and evolved a community affairs and special events department. We have community affairs 7:00–8:00 P.M. on Saturdays, 6:00–7:00 P.M. on Sundays and whenever else a community problem arises. We had a recent election with four very complicated issues that the League of Women Voters opposed and we had a prime time special with supporters and opponents. Before we made the change, our news hour had brought about a degradation of our audience for 90 minutes before and 90 minutes after. We had 28,000 people watching the *ABC Evening News* at the time we dropped it. Now we have 127,000 people watching *Wild Wild West*. Here in Desolake, we're the new kid on the block. The other two stations have a 20-year lead on us. They have tremendous loyalty. We're not even going to get sampled. People aren't even going to try to see if you have a better product. That's the worst of it. You won't even get sampled.

JOSEPH S. JOHNSON (San Diego State University): That's a very useful caution. But we might just play it a different way. I have experience with a station that had been doing a lot to make inroads into the market and it had never become an important station in the market. The thing that did it, that made them important, was that they did ex-

actly the opposite—they cut out all of the nice public affairs programming and the other things they were doing and concentrated all
their attention in the news area. They told the local people we're one
of you and we really care about you. All those important issues that
are talked about in ascertainment they covered in the body of their
newscasts. And with that kind of effort they became the dominant
news station in the market. With an ABC affiliation. Their audience
for programming on both sides of their news increased dramatically
and their image in the community is incredibly high. Can we come in
and do the same thing here in Desolake? Is NBC doing well because
these guys are really good? Is it because the CBS guys are half-
hearted? Can we come in with an exciting news effort and really clean
up on these guys? Can we go after the local issues that haven't been
done?

H. EUGENE DYBVIG (Southern Illinois University): I was in a two
station market where the NBC station had a solid news operation but
we were doing a very prosaic job with our news. A new station came
in with a big news budget and made a big splash and that new kid on
the block just walked away with the news in the first book. They made
their news exciting and they made it different. It was so bad—they
walked away so far that we threw out our news and went to straight
programming. In the next book we won the time period.

ROBERT ARNOLD (Florida Technological University): The philosophy I followed and maybe we should follow here, is that every percentage point you can gain in a rating is a good thing. I used to start
our station half an hour before any other station came on the air. It
was economically feasible all those many years ago. If we can do it
now, maybe we can pick up that one percentage point with the rural
audience.

DONALD AGOSTINO (Indiana University): Look at the demographics: even though this is an agricultural market, most of the people
are not in agriculture. They are either in the professions, construction
or the semi-skilled trades. If you look at the ratings, the Monday night
movie is out-polling *All In The Family* two to one. The Sunday night
Movie Mystery and other films are running strong. Perhaps we should
buy a strong film package and build a film source image.

MITCHELL: When I was trying to put a new UHF on the air and
had to stimulate UHF conversion as well as tuning, my first year motion picture budget would not allow me to buy first run blockbusters.
So I bought contemporary European product rather than American film
because I knew that in the papers I would be the only station day after

day with "four star double A" ratings. Just the frustration of missing excellent movies would inspire people to convert and to tune in.

AGOSTINO: Perhaps we could counter program in the afternoon with a film, give it a second run in the mornings, develop a staggered schedule with a lot of film. That's an untapped audience.

In the SIGMA discussions, LIZ BAIN was suggesting much the same kind of approach:

I have found that one audience which stations seem to neglect is the blue collar worker between 4:00 and 6:00 P.M. That's an untapped audience. I have found a very successful strategy is to pick a narrow, special audience such as men and then figure out how to do the kind of programming that will pick them up as a bonus. Program to kids and pick up the men, for example.

That's one of several strategies we should consider. Another is jumping the gun on the other news shows giving us the advantage of a lead in. We have to decide whether local or network is the better jumping board to beat them to the draw. The other strategy is placement of the news—network against their local, network against network, entertainment against their news—all these are factors we should consider.

BERT BARER: Why not news as entertainment? Why do we have to separate them? I don't mean a song and dance act. I mean presenting news that will attract attention. There are a variety of ways news can be made interesting and attractive. Get first rate reporters to do a lot of good digging, get into a lot of controversial areas, spend a lot of time at City Hall asking the kind of questions that are painful to answer. That's entertaining. It's attention getting and extremely important. The public will tune that in.

HARVEY SESLOWSKY: Taking into consideration what you have suggested and also what Liz Bain said about coming in first, do you think it would be a good idea to run a local newscast at 5:00? KNAC is running *Truth Or Consequences* and KBGA is running *Dialing For Dollars*. Assuming it's the kind of news you are talking about—a great news, and the first news in town?

CLAUDE SUMERLIN: Wouldn't 5:00 be a little early for people coming home from work?[7]

LIZ BAIN: This is a large blue collar market and the chances of people getting home early are fairly good. A large composition of news audiences is women. Women watch news more than any other single kind of show. You have the men available, the kids will not tune in news, from an audience composition standpoint, 5:00 may be a beautiful place to put the news.

WILLIAM HAWES: Isn't it important to consider that the PBS station is probably running *Electric Company* and *Sesame Street* and the kids are going to fight you for the TV set?

ROD CLEFTON: If the PBS station is, they are probably getting a five or six share. That's what they got in our market—Spokane—which as you know is pretty close to being the nation's 75th.

MARY JEAN THOMAS: I'd like to promote a news show with "first in the news and last in the news!"

BRUCE LINTON (University of Kansas): I'm not sure how close the demographics of Desolake are to Kansas City, but the third station in Kansas City, in terms of news, has just gone to 5:00. Trying everything they can to get back. So far, it hasn't been successful. I don't know if this means that Kansas City is too large, or the people aren't getting home in time, or what. But the strategy hasn't worked.

JIM HARRIS: From a programming point of view, is there any advantage in going to an hour local news in addition to the network half hour? I know they are doing this in many markets including mine. But nobody else is doing this in Desolake. They're all sticking to the half hour.

LIZ BAIN: According to a study we did at Katz in markets 51 through 100 in the Fall of 1975, 42 CBS affiliates are doing a half hour, 47 NBC affiliates are doing a half hour, and 40 ABC stations are doing a half hour news. Nine CBS stations were doing an hour, five NBC affiliates were doing an hour, and only four ABC affiliates are doing an hour.

ROD CLEFTON: I can speak from experience. We were the leading news station in the 75th market and I put an hour news on the air. We expanded our already existing half hour. We continued to win the first half hour but we were in trouble with the second half hour. In a market of this size, it's very very difficult. We have a small staff and an hour is again just that much more expensive to produce. In Los Angeles you have a sufficient audience turnover to make this thing work. You can go 90 minutes, 120. Just like a newsreel.

LIZ BAIN: You know, there's another contingency that we haven't discussed yet. A personal theory of mine is that a show that follows the news often determines the news viewing. If you have a strong show following your network news, the laziness of the dial-turner might keep him with local news, and then with network news until your very strong 6:00 show. Which I think should be entertainment.

SESLOWSKY: I think we ought to strip an hour five days a week, from 6:00 to 7:00. At 6:00 we have a classic counter-programming situation. There are two news programs running against us. Now if we make some assumptions about what we've already set up, we can assume that 3:30 to 6:00 is going to work for us. We're going to bring in the kids, then we're going to broaden our audience from 4:00 to 5:00. We're going to come on with a fantastic news from 5:00 to 5:30. We are going to get all the local people to look at it and they're going to lead-in to our ABC news. My assumption as a programmer is that people in Desolake won't want to see local news at 6:00 as much as they did before our station went on the air because we've done the job. They've already seen the local news on our station. So we have a classic situation here, an opportunity to grab a tremendous amount of tune in. In addition to the people who've already seen the news, we can get those who don't want to watch news. We can get the kids. Grab a lot of people with the right counter-programming, something that has a track record and has buyer acceptance.

Track record and buyer acceptance, looking for appeals to the audience available in the day part, evaluating the demographics, building audience flow, and assessing the peculiarities of the market, all must be taken into consideration in making programming decisions. So, too, must certain business practices. In Tarrytown, the resource persons and discussion leaders shared insights which they had developed as professional programmers and station managers. LEE EDEN, for example, warned about "checkerboarding", programming a different show each night in a time period, particularly when hours of off-network product were involved. One proposal before the IOTA group called for scheduling *The Fugitive, Mayberry RFD, Here Come The Brides* and *The Honeymooners*. EDEN noted that *Mayberry RFD* alone had more than a hundred episodes and *The Honeymooners* not many less. "There is eight years worth of product we are committing ourselves for just for five hours a week of programming. If we could be totally sure that everything we chose was good it would be one thing, but we are talking about a market where two stations have already picked over the list." EDEN cautioned that with seven individual series in a time period, a station would be lucky if two nights worked.

JOHN GOLDHAMMER also cautioned against buying too many off-network shows. Those series made for prime time access, he pointed out, are offered on a one-year basis and a station can frequently make a six-month deal. But a series like *Mod Squad*, GOLDHAMMER told the RHO group, is sold on the basis of six runs over five years: "That's a major financial commitment." GOLD-HAMMER also reminded the group that a disadvantage to stripping was that a wrong choice would affect four or five nights while a wrong choice in a checkerboard period would only be a wrong choice for that one day.

GEORGE MITCHELL spoke in the TAU session of how the ratings were differently affected by shows which were stripped and by shows which were checkerboarded. "There is an overstatement of strippped programs and an understatement of checkerboard programs. And the reason for this is quite simple. People don't follow instructions in keeping diaries. They don't always fill them out religiously while they're viewing. They leave them to the end. And then it's 'Oh my God, tonight's Tuesday, I'd better fill this out because it has to be in the mail by tomorrow. Now what did I watch last week?' It's easy to remember Carson—he's on five days a week. But one night a week shows are easily forgotten. That's one reason why ABC is trying to group a number of different shows—a checkerboard—under the umbrella title, *Wide World of Entertainment.*"

Several syndicated series, *Animal World, The Protectors,* for example, were listed as available for barter. A note accompanying the schedule in Appendix 10 properly describes bartered programs as available at no cost to the station. Of the five commercial minutes for which the show is cut, two are available for the station to sell while three are sold by the syndicator. Discussion leaders and program resource people alike warned against embracing barter too warmly. "Because there is no capital outlay, it doesn't cost anything—on paper," GOLDHAMMER put it to the RHO group, "but it may also be the most expensive programming you can buy. In a sense, you are betting against yourself. If the show is successful, the value of those spots you have given away increases."

AL KORN and GEORGE MITCHELL echoed this view in the TAU discussions. MITCHELL pointed out that barter negotiations frequently turned on the syndicator's or agency's desire to see the show, and the commercials they were supplying, in a particular time period. He described a negotiation process which might result in some or all of the spots being spun out of the show itself then left entirely up to the station. KORN went on to explain that the number of spots, and thus the payment in kind for the show, was also frequently negotiable: "That's how purchasing goes, in the broadcasting business. A man can come in your office with a $1000 price for a series and walk out with $200 and a deal. Supply and demand. In the major markets, New York and Los Angeles, the syndicator is in control. But somewhere down the line, he's going to take less of a price than he asked for just because he isn't in that market. And that's how simple the purchase of programming is." MITCHELL continued, "They came in with a $2400 per episode price for the *Mary Tyler Moore Show.* In our market we have never paid more than $900 for anything before. All three stations made offers and the show was sold in the neighborhood of $1200. The question is, how much inventory do you have to give up from that program just to pay for it?" KORN suggested: "A good rule of thumb for judging programming expenditures is the station rate for that particular time period."

Purchasing syndicated programming involves making commitments of large sums over relatively long periods of time. All the professional programmers stressed the necessity to develop as much information in advance as possible. Several pointed out that the unwary had been duped in the past because of their acceptance of the demonstration reel and their failure to screen enough of the series to assure that it was representative. Obviously, the reel the salesman proudly shows his prospects contains the most appealing samples of the series. Sometimes the samples are not typical. Others spoke of the fact that unlike feature films which are known to do well in any time period, some series do not seem to do well in particular day parts. "Each day-part represents a different theater with different demographics and somewhat different appetites," JIM COPPERSMITH told the IOTA group, "Analyze the performance of different programs in the marketplace in different day parts. For example, one of the things that comes out of the Desolake rating book is that game shows do damn well in prime time access but in daytime they don't do as well as soap operas." If the station is to avoid taking a loss on a significant portion of its programming inventory, it must consciously strive for flexibility in its purchases. There should be another time period into which a show can be moved if it proves not to do well in the time period for which it is bought.

GEORGE MITCHELL cited his concept of "parallel markets" as helpful in this regard. Audiences in ten cities have been found to behave very much as those of Dayton, Ohio, in their reaction to programs and program types at particular times of day. Much of the popularity of *Dinah!* and of *Gilligan's Island* with professional programmers was ascribed to their demonstrated ability to attract audiences in various time periods. Another, though more elusive, benefit these series were said to enjoy is favor in the eyes of time buyers. This was felt to be particularly important in smaller markets. With 80 percent of the nation's viewers concentrated in the top 50 markets, there is understandable reluctance on the part of time buyers to buy 65 additional markets in order to reach the remaining 20 percent. Because of the vagaries of buyer preference, the programmers cited the importance of input from the sales manager at some point in the decision making process.[8]

Each of the four groups expressed interest in feature film, some for scheduling during the day, some for the weekend and, in at least one case, with an eye to pre-empting *Wide World of Entertainment* as many ABC affiliates do, a particularly attractive option in the Central Time Zone where HUT levels remain high after the late news. With an estimated 20,000 features available for television, and with at least one film available each night on network television in many markets, the difficulty of establishing a film series is apparent. As can be seen from Appendix 9 materials, feature films are sold in packages and, although each package contains at least some particularly attractive titles, not all the films in every package can, by any stretch of the imagination, be considered blockbusters. Therefore, some programmers reason, a station has to find a gimmick in order to promote its film offerings. Other programmers ascribe the need for a gimmick solely to the extent of the competition and to the fact that the viewer needs to identify a time period so that his weekly viewing can become habitual. Still others contend that such film series as Western Theater, Classics of Suspense and Action Features merely mask an inordinate number of westerns, grade B mysteries or crime films in particular feature packages. Whatever the ultimate cause, the fact remains that such series titles and the attendant promotion can attract many more viewers than the same films as part of a generalized feature scheduling might hope to lure.

Examples from participants and programmers alike of successful special series included holiday film promotions, historical series, the presentation of classics, special star weeks, a series of features for adult viewers which swept its time period in Iowa, and an Academy Award Theater. The reporter of that successful promotion astounded his colleagues by recounting how many Oscar winners for such accomplishments as lighting, music, costume and special effects might be found in even the most seemingly pedestrian package.

Almost all of the programmers advocated a large library if feature film programming was to be scheduled at all. A regularly scheduled Monday through Friday series, they reminded the participants, means 260 showings a year. Ideally, AL KORN contended, no title would appear more often than twice a year in the same time slot. LIZ BAIN went further. Scheduling feature film effectively, she claimed, should involve two primary time periods and one lesser, throw-away time period a week. All cautioned that packages should be examined not only in terms of the freshness of the product, the titles, the stars and the proportion of color film, but also in terms of length, the longer the film, in general, the more desirable. In any event, films less than 75 to 80 minutes, they felt, posed problems in that the story line would have to be chopped excessively. HARVEY SESLOWSKY warned that a film library in a market of the size of Desolake should include at least 300 titles; AL KORN introduced the sobering realities of investment which building a film library involved. In Desolake, at the given book value of $1000 a title, such a library could mean a long term investment of $300,000; in New York, packages of 20 or so films are often sold at $35,000 to $40,000 per title.

Most of the discussion, as can be seen, turned on the selection and purchase of recorded programming, syndicated series and feature film packages. Little of the time was given over to planning of locally produced programming. This was almost undoubtedly pre-determined by the fact that a description of Public Affairs programs, said to include: *Editorials Big 5 Depth Report, Senior Citizens Forum, Core Soul Den* and *Televised Meetings,* together with *Romper Room,* classified as Other (Instructional); *Recreational Today;* etc., had been furnished to the participants as Exhibit 3 to the Construction Permit Application. (Appendix 4) This had been done by the planners of the seminar in the belief that the limited time available could be better used by giving the participants access to persons and ideas in areas with which they might be less familiar.

Each of the groups soon appeared to be operating on the assumption that it would, in any case, be impossible to program their local station for 50 to 55 hours a week with locally produced programming alone and they sought to learn from the skills the working professionals put at their disposal. The results bore a striking though unsurprising similarity to one another, from group to group, both in the kind of decisions arrived at and in the nature of the discussions which led up to them. To some extent, it might be argued, this came about as a result of the fact that the managers and resource persons in the four groups had developed a common mind set with respect to those problems of commercial operation which had occupied their attention over the last decade or two. This factor was undoubtedly abetted by the significant commercial broadcasting experience which more than half of the faculty participants reported in their *curricula vitae*. In large measure, however, the similarities from group to group must be seen as reflecting a common set of conclusions derived from the same body of data under the same given circumstances. All the participants may have responded to what they perceived as systemic imperatives.[9]

If the groups perceived the imperatives clearly, they did not accept them quietly. Late in the afternoon, GENE DYBVIG might have been voicing the malaise of many in any one of the four groups:

I would like to make a comment about the program schedule we have developed. It's the same kind of program schedule I developed when I was in the business; it's the same kind of program schedule that I would tell my students to develop. We have done nothing today to distinguish ourselves as a station from any other station. We have played right down the middle—right down that old line. We said, "We can't do this, we can't do that. This is axiomatic, that is axiomatic." Does this mean that television is now committed forever to do the same thing?

Another member of the TAU group, ROYAL COLLE, agreed:

We went the Kraft commercial way. We elected to do nothing but make money. None of us came up with anything creative.

In IOTA, HOWARD STEVENS asked:

Is there a possibility for creative programming to succeed? We atarted out by thinking in terms of what would be "good programming for our audience." We've come up with programming to the least common denominator. We as educators should be able to inspire the audience to be greater. Taking into consideration our scheduling factors, cost, and the least common denominator audience, isn't there some possibility for creative programming?

COPPERSMITH: Did you ever take a close look at the ratings of educational stations? They do marvelous, beautiful, sensitive things and they have a right to serve that small audience. But even in Boston where the educational station is on Channel 2, they don't make a dent in the market. We have an obligation to serve, we have a public license, and we can and do do beautiful things—*The Autobiography of Miss Jane Pittman, The Pueblo, Fear on Trial.* Many examples. But they generally fall into the range of network budgets, network production budgets and network promotion budgets. Magnificent performers and incredibly expensive promotion campaigns. On those rare occasions when we as broadcasters reach for the stars, we're reaching with hands laden with money bags. A television station must compete in the marketplace in terms of its need to appeal to a mass audience.

BUNGE: The exercise calls for putting a station on the air, not for creating an ideal station.

LYNCH: We may have to put on a station which some of us, perhaps, are not interested in watching. I don't see how we can get away from this schedule and still be on the air at the end of the year.

BARNES: A program manager of KPIX once talked about the proliferation of shows which are alike. He said it was a kind of strawberry jam concept of programming—the more you spread it, the thinner it gets, until finally, it becomes tasteless. I think maybe we're faced with that problem right now.

CHARLES RUSSEL (Cornell University): Can't we compete without repeating what the other stations are doing? I showed the background material to some students prior to coming down here. Their response was a little sophomoric but it may have some validity. They looked at this station as a quick and dirty operation. They compared it to a discount house coming into a community, working off the gravy and running. And they said that John Q. Citizen is not going to continue to put up with the pap that television is putting out today, and Desolake is no exception. We're not giving the viewing audience enough opportunity to sample the variety it deserves.

BUNGE: It may be possible that if we put on alternative programming we might lead some people into new programs that aren't now on the air. The question is, would they be led into that programming before we were broke? I don't know that many people who have tried that.

PETER LONGINI (Brooklyn College): The kind of quality we were talking about is not limited to educational materials. We don't see ourselves as a version of a PBS station. We see ourselves as a quality shop, putting out the best we know how in both news and entertainment, selecting for local use programs which have more interesting scripting, more interesting production. The level of writing and sophistication of *All in the Family* in contrast to *Big Eddy* or something like that . . .

LEE EDEN: None of that kind of material is available to you as a local broadcaster.

GLICK: My job is to educate students for the real world. And I'm concerned about a certain arrogance among educators. The feeling that what *I* like—PBS or the BBC *Third Program* or whatever—is what everybody should like. The feeling that anybody who likes, God forbid, the *Beverly Hillbillies* is to be—what's the word? . . .

. . . *Sterilized.*

GLICK: . . . not programmed to. There is nothing wrong with providing a service to those people and making a profit providing you can also do the other things that allow you to hold up your head.

HARWOOD: It is the function of a local programmer to select the very best quality from what is available that will be acceptable to his audiences and financially viable. That is a positive function and it is really worthwhile. I think we have made a good run at it.

HOWARD STEVENS: I think we are faced today with what broadcasters are continually being faced with in their selection of programs. We are backed into a choice of what's available. I agree that Tandem[10] gives us the kind of productions we are looking for. But if that's the state of the art, why can't we get that level of script and acting. Why has the audience no choice but this other stuff?

COPPERSMITH: Norman Lear, the producer of *All In The Family* and *Mary Hartman, Mary Hartman* sat in my office not six weeks ago and talked about that very subject. He is suggesting a move toward a co-operative venture amongst stations throughout the country which would provide their collective resources to produce high quality syndicated programming. I suggested that a good place to start this movement would be with the rep companies.

TILL CURRY (West Virginia State College): I think the uneasiness many of us feel today comes from the thought, the hope that through some process we in this room today could come up with original thinking about what can be done with television. Out of this group and the others there should be ideas coming up that might be adaptable to the marketplace.

The TAU group had been concerned about a search for creativity, IOTA had been virtually obsessed with the topic. In the room where RHO met, the group was divided. BILL PARSON was apologetic:

Maybe it's because I'm almost an interloper here. In my institution I'm in charge of all the arts and my own field is the theater. But when I look at the television station we are planning to put on the air here, I must confess I am a little disappointed. We didn't talk about anything that was innovative. If we're starting a new station and planning to attract an audience from the existing stations, shouldn't we be doing our own programming?

JAMES TUNGATE (Loyola University) thought the opportunities were limited:

I don't think the world's most fantastic studio is needed to be innovative, but we have only two cameras. And a very small studio facility. We'll have to be using all our facilities to produce commercials during just those times when we might be innovative. To say nothing of the practical problem of the low cost of syndication compared with local origination.

But WES WALLACE thought the problem was even much deeper:

I'm not sure there is any such thing as innovation or experimentation in broadcasting. As a student of the history of broadcasting, I don't think there's been anything new in broadcasting since 1922. Except maybe for the strip shows and the soap operas. That's literally it, kids. The only thing innovative we're going to be able to do in our regular programming is in some little way doing the news better than they do it next door. Given the demands on people's time and their energies and the money we will have, you can't be creative on a daily basis. It will be once a month or once every six weeks that we can do something that we can be very proud of. And then only because we've put everything we had into that one particular project.

JOSEPH WETHERBY (Duke): We've spent a lot of time talking about making money—which is nice if we are going to stay on the air—but shouldn't we at least ask ourselves what is needed in our programming?

ROBERT STEVENS (Northern Arizona University): Like Bill Parsons, I'm the chairman of an umbrella department. And I too am a bit disappointed that we didn't start with the absolute need of the community but rather with what will compete with the other station, what will sell time, whether to schedule *Mickey Mouse* or *Gilligan's Island*. Am I right to be surprised?

RICK LEVY: If we want to have money to pay for that creative, innovative different kind of program, that money has to come from *Gilligan's Island*.

JOHN GOLDHAMMER: Is it in the interest, convenience and necessity of the viewing audience if no one is watching your station? Let's not confuse the creative process involved in producing a show with the creative process of setting up a program schedule. If we had more time we could follow through the creative process of producing. Our job as programmers is to lay out the skeleton, the framework which allows that creativity to take place. Our creativity is in not laying out a schedule that we can't deliver on, in not laying out local programming that we can't do. Rather, it is in laying out a schedule that will get our station watched, that will turn the sets from off to on, that will draw the audience away from the competitor where it's been for 20 years, Then and only then the creative process of putting together a show can begin.

The SIGMA group had been somewhat more pragmatic. They saw the same problem primarily in terms of the institutional needs of the station they were attempting to set up. Convinced, in the main, of the rightness of their efforts, they were, nonetheless concerned with how the image of the new station might be improved so that the community would recognize the station's value and seek it out. CLAUDE SUMERLIN, however, presented a minority view and a specific recommendation:

We've made all our choices on the basis of whether or not they would make a profit or whether they might satisfy FCC regulations. We haven't chosen anything on the basis of whether it's best for the community. And perhaps stations just don't do it that way. Maybe what we need—maybe what everyone needs—is a code of ethics. A code which starts with a concern for the community.

IOTA also talked of developing a standard, but a standard of quite a different sort.

BUNGE: We're comparing our profitability only with other television stations. A profit margin of 14.6% is pretty healthy by most other business standards. If we talk about a return on investment which compares to other businesses we may have more flexibility in our planning. We could offer a rate of return which would not be so low as to discourage investors. Unless, of course, our assumptions about the market are all wrong. It may well be that the erosion in viewing we've seen this Fall means that the market is beginning to fragment.

JOHN KESHISHOGLOU (Ithaca College): I don't think we can lose sight of the long range implications of cable. Even though only 18 percent of this market, Desolake, has cable now, ultimately its impact on commercial television may be very great.

BARNES: I think we have to realize that this is a realistic, real-life situation in which we have to assume that during a period of time of gearing up and of gaining an audience we're not going to have any income. It's all going to be outgoing. After that, and only after that, we can talk about what is a decent and what is an indecent profit. The problem we have is that as in any profit-making venture our investors expect a return. They expect a high rate of return. That's the whole backbone of the free enterprise system. A man who us willing to take the risk with his capital and to take the responsibility for establishing and running a business is entitled to a return on his investment. Given those realities, profit is not a dirty word.

In TAU, GENE DYBVIG talked of planning for the time when the station would be in the black:

Once we start making a profit I hope we'll try to distinguish ourselves in some way. I would say that as a general rule, the stations around the country that make the most money provide the most service.

GEORGE MITCHELL offered an even broader suggestion to the group:

One of our basic problems is that we deal quantitatively so often in our business. We are a tremendously expensive medium. We're expensive to build and to develop. Even more important, we're expensive to use—expensive for the advertiser to use. So we measure our effect. And we measure quantity. That means we go for the largest audience at any given moment. We don't know whether that audience likes the program. All we know is that they are there. It may be that they are there only because it is the least of three evils. But we have no measure for their attitude. We don't really know how much of a penchant we may have for antagonizing that audience, deep down. When we learn how to measure those things, when we measure the quality of the audience's attention, the quality of their enjoyment, and thus the quality of our service, then, and only then can we really begin to deal with what made you uneasy here today.

Despite the problems they had encountered in devoting so much of their energies to the purchase and scheduling of syndicated programming, each of the four groups was able to find opportunities during the broadcast week to schedule more non-entertainment programming than called for in the CP promises to the FCC. CLAUDE SUMERLIN'S comment to the RHO group prompted BOB STEVENS to suggest, and the group to adopt the notion of following *AM America* with *Am Desolake,* 9:00 to 9:30 Monday through Friday. SIGMA made a similar choice. ROD CLEFTON called attention to the softness of the two network entries on the competition at from 10:00–10:30. *Desolake Today,* a magazine show which he insisted should not be confined to public affairs but should embrace many interests and take advantage of visiting authors, was proposed. LORIN ROBINSON suggested it should tie directly to ascertained problems with one day a week dealing with employment. And the SIGMA concern with image was somewhat allayed by ROBERT JOHN KEIBER (Shaw University) who pointed out that similar shows were doing well in his home market where they were also building prestige for their stations. MARY JEAN THOMAS' concern for encouraging local talent as well as station image found an outlet in a weekly feature delaying *Wide World of Entertainment* and hosted by a new local personality which the station would develop. TAU adopted a weekly public affairs call-in series, 7:00–8:00 P.M. Saturdays. ROY COLLE and CAROL REUSS had urged that the series be run at 10:30 Friday but the group rejected that time period when a comparison of HUT levels showed that with an estimated 10% of available audience in either time period, the broadcast would have 40% more viewers each week in the Saturday period.[11] IOTA also adopted a Saturday Prime Time Access public affairs broadcast and found a weekly spot for *Town Meeting* on Sunday.

CONCLUSION

The growth of the mass media, in fact their very existence, has depended on their ability to develop mechanisms for the syndication of material. No motion picture theater operator would or could dream of making all of his own films. It is estimated that one third of the average American newspaper consists of syndicated features, thereby permitting the publisher to fill 35%, half his news hole for only 10% of his budget.[12] The Radio Corporation of America, in announcing the establishment of the National Broadcasting Company in 1926, indicated that it was seeking "to provide machinery which will insure a national distribution of programs of the highest quality" and expressed the hope "that arrangements may be made so that every event of national importance may be broadcast widely throughout the United States." The ad went on, magnanimously but somewhat unnecessarily, to reassure its readers that "If others will engage in this business the Radio Corporation of America will welcome their action, whether it be co-operative or competitive."[13]

National distribution, of course, came about and was made possible by chain broadcasting, as it was soon called, and competitive networks, as many as the traffic would bear, followed inevitably to the benefit of broadcast audiences throughout the country. For many years, network broadcasts provided the only syndicated service necessary. With the improvement of phonograph recording the increase in musician and other talent costs, and the syphoning off of major advertiser interest to television, syndication came to dominate radio in the form of phonograph records. For the same cost considerations, local television stations have increasingly looked to the syndicator for the bulk of the entertainment programming in the non-network hours. What has given particular urgency to this problem from the business standpoint of the broadcaster, has been the limitation of network time imposed by that circumscription unique to broadcasting among the mass media in this country, the presumption of localism which underlies the licensing process and which has been institutionalized in broadcasting law and regulation. That presumption, and the fear of monopoly control which has historically exerted such a strong influence over government's view of the regulated radio and television systems, have placed limits upon the amount of syndicated material which the broadcaster may obtain from the network. Increasingly, stations have been heard to complain about network incursion into traditionally locally scheduled time periods.

These complaints, of course, do not represent broadcasters' resentment against non-locally produced material, but rather against the terms under which they may receive the network product as opposed to the syndicated product which the broadcaster might obtain from other sources. The institution of the Prime Time Access Rule, having reduced the maximum amount of off-network product which will come into the market by 21 half hours a week, will serve to reduce the number of choices from such other sources which the broadcaster will have available in the future. Some reduction of alternatives will come about as a result of changing social standards which have already inhibited the syndication of some series as too violent for early fringe or family time. An even more important factor in reducing choice will be the fact that network series now have fewer original broadcasts rather than the 39 of years past; it will require as much as five years to build up inventory sufficient to support an off-network re-run. Recently, Wes Harris, Vice-President for Programs of the NBC owned stations, citing these and other factors such as the inclusion of longer forms, made-for-television movies, for example, and higher casualty rates among new series, as compelling reasons, called for local stations to step up efforts to produce their own programming.[14]

A more likely response to the problem is that represented by *Mary Hartman, Mary Hartman*. Confronted by the need to fill an entire schedule with audience attracting programs at less than prohibitive costs, the local broadcaster will continue to look to syndicated material as the key to successful operation.

There is another perspective from which the broadcaster' selection of syndicated programming over locally produced entertainment can be viewed. Scale economies and market power enable networks to offer the program producer such advaantages over what stations might provide, that the networks can and do attract the best stars, the most imaginative writers and the most adept production staffs. Networks can not only outbid single stations, they can and do also outbid the *ad hoc* syndicates which come into being as stations purchase programs produced to meet Access Time requirements in the top 50 markets. Because they have become habituated to receiving programming of network quality, audiences invariably select entertainment programming on the basis of production values. In a Brookings Institution study, the economists Roger G. Noll, Merton J. Peck and John J. McGowan calculate that network entertainment can be delivered at a cost of less than one cent per viewing home.[15] Applying that standard to the Desolake audience, it is apparent that local programming, to be economically competitive, would have to be delivered at a cost of $584.80 per half hour. The study points out that such low budget and consequent low production quality programming obviously generates less revenue by virtue of its reduced audience acceptance. This, in turn, makes for even lower budgets. Economically, they conclude, localism has been a dismal failure.

The premise of localism is that more local programming serves the public interest. But this is not as obvious as its adherents imply. The viewers, by their program choices, have clearly voted for national programming. It typically outdraws its local competitors by many orders of magnitude. Rather than stirring worry, such a record should excite applause—for giving customers what they want. Why, then, the concern on the part of the commission and other observers?

Some argue that television is fundamentally different from most products or services and that consumer sovereignty should not apply. Local programming is different from other products because it does more than fulfill consumer wants; it serves an allegedly important public function.[16]

During the 1960s, then Commissioners Kenneth A. Cox and Nicholas Johnson, the loudest voices for localism which the FCC had heard, produced several studies including an analysis of the 1969 License Renewal Applications of stations in New York State which showed that 13 stations of the 32 presented local programming on less than 10% of the broadcast day. Only two stations exceeded 20%.[17] The two Commissioners also examined television stations in Oklahoma where they found locally produced programming occupying less than 20% of prime and less than 10 percent of daytime. Most of this local programming was news, weather and sports.[18] Noll, Peck and McGowan refer to the Commissioners' comments on local programming in their Oklahoma study:

Commissioners Cox and Johnson are eloquent on this subject: "The greatest challenge before the American people today is the challenge of restoring and reinvigorating local democracy. That challenge cannot be met without a working system of local broadcast media activity serving the needs of each community for information about its affairs, serving the interests of all members of the community, and allowing all to confront the listening public with their problems and their proposals."

The minimal local programming now available hardly serves this purpose. To make stations broadcast more local programming even in prime time would not alleviate the problem, since most viewers would turn to competitive channels that offered network programming. The effective way to assure that the local program is seen by a large fraction of all the population would be to set aside certain prime-time hours in which *all* channels must carry local programming. The FCC's 1970 decision . . . to limit the amount of prime-time programming by networks is a step in this direction, although it was also designed to improve the market for non-network national syndication.

We have considerable doubts about obligatory local programming and about making viewing, in effect, semi-compulsory by withdrawing the alternatives. Yet anything less seems unlikely to further the grand objective that local programming is supposed to serve. The harsh reality is that most viewers do not want to sacrifice even a small fraction of national entertainment to their obligation as local citizens.[19]

This is the background against which the deliberations of the Tarrytown group must be judged. Attempting to work out the often conflicting demands of the station owners, the program producers—with which many of the participants identified—and the public, produced much of the tension as did coming to grips with the suspicion that the public's wishes might not be what they were hoped to be. Much of the frustration resulted from the recognition of the difficulty of achieving the goal of increased diversity in television programs; some frustration no doubt proceeded from the effort which restraining their evangelism always engenders in the cultivated as they confront the more strident products of a popular culture.

When is it wise to subscribe to conventional wisdom? When is it wise and when is it merely conventional? Like the members of the IRTS Faculty Industry Seminar, students who use these materials will have to confront these questions for themselves. Innovation, quality, diversity are goals which broadcasters and students alike must serve. They stand as worthy ends in themselves and their pursuit further help us realize the full potential of our medium. Moreover, vigorous pursuit of these goals assist us in finding ways to unlock our own creativity and that of others.

NOTES

1. *39th Annual Report/Fiscal 1973,* Washington, D.C., Federal Communications Commission, p. 228.
2. *Ibid.,* p. 240.
3. This figure was suggested by Harvey Seslowsky of Film Service Corp. during the SIGMA group discussions.
4. A helpful and readable introduction to the subject of ratings and particularly to their accuracy may be found in Chapter 2 of Martin Mayer, *About Television,* New York, 1972, Harper and Row.
5. Julius Barnathan, Vice-President in charge of Operations and Engineering of ABC and formerly in broadcast research both at Kenyon and Eckhardt and at ABC, has provided an ex-

cellent short guide to the meaning and use of rating information in "The Business of Research" a chapter in *Television Station Management: The Business of Broadcasting,* Yale Roe, New York, 1964, Hastings House.

6. *Ibid.,* pp. 174–6

7. Hours of work vary with type of business and with region. Typically, blue collar workers begin and end their day earlier than do white collar workers. In programming for any station it is important to know the work patterns in the community. For example, the following represents shift times at the principal places of employment in a market in many ways similar to Desolake, Springfield-Decatur-Champaign, Illinois:

SPRINGFIELD

Fiat Allis Construction
8am–4pm
4pm–12m
12m–8am

Sangamo Electric
7am–3;30pm
3:30pm–11pm
11pm–7am

CHAMPAIGN

Kraft Foods
7am–3pm
3pm–11:30pm
10:30pm–7am(part-timers)

Collegiate Cap and Gown
7am–3:30pm (Summer hours–daylight
saving time)
8am–4pm (regular hours)

DECATUR

Catepillar Tractor Co.
7:15am–3:18pm
3:18–11:18pm
11:18pm–7:18am

A.E. Staley Manufacturing Co.

7am–3pm

8. A discussion of the importance of this input is to be found in Albert John Gillen, "Sales Management for the Network Affiliate" and companion chapter, Charles Young "Sales Management for the Independent" in Roe, *loc. cit.*

9. Most of the participants, as students of the mass media in American life, would have had no difficulty in expounding on the extent and the inevitability of such systemic imperatives. George Gerbner, in a particularly insightful essay "Mass Media and Human Communication Theory," in *Human Communication Theory: Original Essays,* Frank E. X. Dance, ed., New York, 1967, Holt, Rinehart and Winston, wrote on this point:

> The media of mass communication—print, film, radio, television—present institutional perspectives, i.e., their own ways of selecting, composing, recording, and sharing symbols and images. They are products of technology, corporate (or other collective) organization, mass production, and mass markets. They are the cultural arms of the industrial order from which they spring.

10. Tandem Productions, Norman Lear and Bud Yorkin, was the production company responsible for *All in the Family.* Tandem or Norman Lear has also gone on to produce *Good Times, Sanford and Son, The Jeffersons, Maude, Hot L Baltimore,* and *Mary Hartman, Mary Hartman* among other series.

11. *Sixty Minutes* increased its total audience when it moved from 10:00 P.M. Tuesdays to 6:00 P.M. Sundays.

12. Peter M. Sandman, David M. Rubin and David B. Sachsman, *Media: An Introductory Analy-*

sis of American Mass Communications, Englewood Cliffs, N.J., 1972, Prentice-Hall, Inc., p. 243. See also *Sydney W. Head, Broadcasting in America: A Survey of Television and Radio,* Boston, 1956, Houghton Mifflin Company, p. 63.

13. Erik Barnouw, *A Tower of Babel,* Volume I in a History of Broadcasting in the United States, New York, 1966, Oxford University Press, p. 188 and plates following.
14. ———— "Into the Breach", *Broadcasting,* February, 16, 1976, p. 68.
15. Roger C. Noll, Merton J. Peck and John J. McGowan, *Economic Aspects of Television Regulation,* Washington D.C., 1973, The Brookings Institution, p. 110.
16. *Ibid.,* p. 111.
17. *Ibid.,* p. 110.
18. *Ibid.,* p. 109.
19. *Ibid.,* p. 111–112.

FOR THE STUDENT

1. Compare local programming at various stations in the 70th to 80th market range.
2. Determine the patterns of network clearance of stations in markets, similar to Desolake.
3. Prepare alternative program plans using the format of Question 4 in Section 4-B of Form 301.
4. Develop alternative plans for various levels of profitability.
5. Analyze the local programming on stations in your own market with respect to its capacity for responding to ascertained needs.
6. Determine, through *TV Guide* or through listings, what local programming, live and recorded, typifies stations in the 75th to 80th markets.

6

News

Submit in Exhibit No. —— the following information concerning the applicant's proposed news program:

A. The staff, news gathering facilities, news services and other sources to be utilized; and

B. An estimate of the percentage of news programs time to be devoted to local and regional news during a typical week.

—Question 5., Part III, Section IV-A, Page 2, FCC Form 301

THE IMPORTANCE OF news to broadcasting and of broadcasting to the news has been apparent at least since the time when the young Marconi was commandeered by an anxious Queen Victoria to keep her posted on the recovery of the Prince of Wales suffering from a knee injury aboard the Royal yacht, lying off the Isle of Wight.[1] In 1963, then Chairman William C. Henry testifying before a House subcommittee described the FCC's interest in news in a statement which Frank Wolf properly describes as "typical of the positions that the FCC has taken in this respect":

> One of the most important services is to contribute to the development of an informed public opinion through the public dissemination of news and ideas concerning the vital public issues of the day. Because of this, the Commission, under the public interest standard, has long recognized the necessity for licensees to devote a reasonable percentage of their broadcast time to the presentation of news and programs devoted to the consideration and discussion of public issues of interest in the community served by the particular station.[2]

Only an apostle of the obvious would trouble to describe how completely the connection between broadcasting and news has come to be accepted. The question is never whether or not to do news broadcasting on a given station as, by way of contrast, one may ask whether or not to seek a network affiliation, but rather, how much news, at what times and under what circumstances. Thus, the problem posed is the development of a format and schedule, and the preliminary questions deal primarily with matters of resource allocation, style, and personnel.

It is, of course, impossible to consider any one element of a station's operation totally in isolation. The program schedule for KIRT has been designed with news in mind. Further, much of the effort in designing that schedule went into establishing a program flow which would deliver significant audiences to the news broadcasts. The point has already been made that news is the keystone of a station's schedule and a prime source of the station's image in the community it serves. This has not always been the case. When television first burst on the scene, news, most frequently taken unedited directly from the wire services, was given to a station announcer to deliver. Even in major markets, the same announcer might be recognized at other times of day wearing a bunny costume on a children's show, interviewing contestants at the wheel of fortune and describing the superiority of a sponsoring supermarket's beefsteak at the kitchen range of the homemaker's program. The major news broadcast of the day consisted of five minutes of news, five minutes of weather, and five minutes of sports, each with its own opening and closing themes and sponsor identification.

In addition to the rip-and-read, the news presented visual information in the form of low resolution stills airmailed in from the wire services and rubber cemented onto shirt cardboard. Characteristically these flip cards would be held on easels stationed to left and right of the news set. Often, pictures would have to be tilted to cut down on the glare. Sometimes they shook. A major pictorial feature would involve two cameras swung around to focus on the easels and intercut on cue. In more elaborate productions, some stills were rephotographed and printed on acetate or glass to be used as rear screen projections. Gradually, 16 millimeter cameras became more reliable, film stocks became more responsive in low light levels, processing equipment became faster and cheaper. News film came to dominate more and more of the news broadcast. Magnetic striping developed enough reliability to be routinely used for interviews. Reporters joined camera crews at the scene. Coincident with these developments, audiences turned more and more to television as their primary news sources. In 1959, the Television Information Office of the National Association of Broadcasters commissioned the Roper Organization to study attitudes toward television and other mass media. The study has been repeated nine times since then, at roughly two year intervals. In answer to the question, "Where do you get most of your news about what's going on in the world?", 57% of a nationwide sample of adults cited the newspapers in 1959. By 1974, the most recent study, fully 65% declared that their primary source was television. Moreover, the percentage of those who, confronted with conflicting stories in different media would place more credibility in television news than in that received via newspapers, magazines or radio, rose from less than 30% to more than 51%, a figure two and a half times as great as television's closest competition.[3]

During the time when the public's acceptance of television news increased so dramatically the public's access to news on its screens was also increasing. In 1953, the critics hailed the first 30-minute news broadcast, which appeared on WCBS-TV in New York, as truly revolutionary. More nearly a weekly magazine than a daily news broadcast—it did, after all, appear only once a week, on Saturday evenings—the broadcast was hardly a news broadcast as we would understand the term today. There was only five minutes of "hard news," delivered by Ned Calmer, followed by five minutes of sports with Jim McKay and five minutes of weather presented by Carol Reed. Another woman, Robin Chandler, delivered five minutes of material of interest to women; Ted Malone, the star of *Between The Bookends,* did a round-up of things to do in New York; and Bill Leonard, now CBS Vice-President for Washington, did yet another New York feature. Finally, a correspondent flew up from Washington each Saturday to do a special piece on the state of the world. That correspondent was Walter Cronkite.

It was not until September 1962 that the first half-hour news appeared from 11:00 to 11:30, again over WCBS-TV, on a daily basis. The following year, 1963, the CBS network early news expanded from 15 minutes to half an hour. In 1965, WNBC-TV, New York, presented the first hour-long local news broadcast.[4] By the early 1970's, two-hour early local news broadcasts, in addition to the network half hours, were to be seen in New York and Los Angeles.

Local news broadcasts could no longer be the throwaways they had clearly been in the days of five minute rip-and-read. Nor, for that matter, were they the loss leaders they were to become. For such exponential growth to occur, news must have been perceived as important to the local station's very survival. And inevitably, a growth industry developed around this fact.

The news consultant appeared—Frank Magid Associates, of Marion, Iowa; ERA of San Francisco; McHugh and Hoffman Inc. Communications Consultants. Since its founding in 1962, McHugh and Hoffman has included among its clients ABC, CBS and NBC, most of the key group-owned stations and many independents.

"We've been in and out of 75 markets over the last 13 to 14 years, and Pete Hoffman and I recently took a look at all of them. Of all the stations that were in number one position in those markets when we started, only five are still in first place in their markets. So you have some idea of the complexity of becoming and staying the number one station in news," Philip McHugh told the Fifth Annual IRTS Faculty-Industry Seminar in Tarrytown. His remarks provided a prelude to the News deliberations of the four groups and would provide a point of departure for us. They appear in their entirety in Appendix 13.

IRTS SEMINAR–Thought-Starter Questions

NEWS

Problem B: Develop a News format and schedule, as well as a Public Affairs schedule for *your* station.

1. Whom are we to serve with our newscasts? (What geographic area, in relation to our technical coverage?)
2. What, if any, syndication or news service should we subscribe to?
3. What can we do to determine what the area's viewers expect of a newscast? (What research can be done to provide us with this information; what specific "special needs" exist in this station's area?)
4. How do you plan to develop news sources within the community—not only the government and other institutions, but in the non-establishment parts, as well? Will you employ stringers, and if so, how will *they* be recruited? What techniques are available to you to develop reliable, inside sources within the community's power structure?
5. Will the station editorialize on-the-air? If so, will News and Editorial operations be separate and independent? How? Who will determine the editorial policies of the station, and who will deliver the on-the-air statements?
6. Whom will the station select as on-the-air newsmen? How do you go about finding skilled journalists who can also be on-camera performers? What training "mechanism" will your station have to develop writers, producer-directors, etc., for News? Is there a role for the local college(s)/universities to play as a source for people?
7. How can the News operation be insulated from internal and external influence? To what extent should it be?
8. Since you have a limited staff, and since the news watch never stops, what can be done to protect yourself during the hours when the newsroom isn't manned?
9. What will be needed in people . . . equipment . . . transportation . . . to adequately cover the news in the area we are to serve?

10. How much of the regularly-scheduled and special (OTO) News and Public Affairs schedule of the network will your station carry?
11. What is a reasonable estimate of the annual total cost of the station's News and Public Affairs operation?
12. Should the station's News operation be self-supporting, or is it to be considered a loss leader?

* * * * *

In light of these questions, and others generated in the Workshop and the Group's discussion/decision on them—*what is the station's News and Public Affairs philosophy, "look" and schedule?*

FACULTY-INDUSTRY SEMINAR DISCUSSIONS

The problem in programming was clear cut. A schedule had to be prepared, each hour of the day had to be accounted for, and the various choices made from among available alternatives entered. Whether or not it might work competitively against the schedules of the other two stations in the market would remain conjectural but there was a final product, the written schedule, for all to see. The task with respect to news did not offer comparably defined parameters. The schedule had already been largely determined, both by the FCC commitment filed in behalf of the group and presented as a given, and by the group's efforts of the day before. Format, staffing, facilities and policy seemed, at least at the outset, more elusive questions. Nonetheless, each of the groups arrived at a roughly similar protocol for solving the problems presented and for considering the thought starter questions. BOB HOYT, Director of News Services, Katz Television, advised the SIGMA group:

One: make a complete study of the competition.
Two: a complete study of the audience. Then, *Three,* put together a news staff and, *Four,* a format which should be drastically different and eventually a lot better than the other two stations.

Study the competition, they did. A cassette had been prepared from the news broadcasts of a station in one market to simulate the news on the dominant station in Desolake. Another cassette, prepared from the news broadcasts in a different market, simulated the other station's early news. Perceptions varied as to the degree of difference between the two simulated newscasts. Many, however, saw the anchor persons on the newscast representing the dominant station to be more authoritative. They also perceived that newscast as being better paced and as being the product of a more clearly defined team. The simulated KGBA broadcast, on the other hand, was seen to have essentially the same format but to be confusing, lacking in depth and devoid of interesting features. It was also scored for its lack of investigative reporting, its failure to provide daylight follow-up on a story which had broken the night before, and for settling for a courthouse steps standup by its reporter when the story in question cried out for interviews with participants. One faculty critic branded the broadcast "film-clip journalism"—allowing the inclusion of a great number of short film pieces to mask the fact that the stories they told were without substance.

Whether or not the simulations presented clearly defined alternatives and even though only a single exposure to a single broadcast on what purported to be the two established competing stations could hardly provide enough data from which to draw meaningful conclusions, the tapes did serve to focus the attention of the group on the kind of choices they would have to make and how the decision-making process would take place in a real life situation. GEORGE SKINNER, Associate Director of News Services, Katz Television, a resource person in the RHO group, described the procedure currently underway in two markets where his firm is advising new applicants, in a lengthy and expensive study of the audience designed to "find the hole—find out what is missing. What are people unhappy with on the other stations and how can we build around it?" KIRT's news would have to be, he counseled, "strong in the areas where the competition is not—investigative reporting, strong features, five-part mini-docs, community service documentaries or whatever. Build a series of elements on that news that will be available only on this station." Noting that KNAC had "flair and promotability," SKINNER warned the group to set aside sufficient funds to promote the new news in the market.

Promotability was a theme discussed in each of the groups. WILLIAM ABER, (News Director, WBZ, Boston) put it this way to the IOTA Group:

> You have to figure out moves in the short haul that will gain you *sampling,* because if the people never feel compelled to turn that tuning knob and take a look at you, then you can be doing the greatest news in the world, you can be doing everything right and spending $4 million, and it won't matter. Over the long haul, you can firm it up, put it in line and shape it. But if you don't get those people at least sampling your broadcast in those initial days, if they don't come over and at least take a look so they can form an opinion, you will never get them.

ED GLICK summed up the IOTA initial strategy:

> The first question has to be: How do we communicate our purpose, first to ourselves and then to the community?

ABER, agreeing, added a strong caveat:

> The fatal mistake many stations have made is looking at publicity as an item separate from that first question. If you are going to promote something in the news then you had damned well better provide it.

Even better, over-provide it. People assume that if you are a newsperson you will be responsible and accurate. If you want to destroy your
credibility, just tell them that you are going to have the greatest report
in the world exposing used car rip-offs and then, for some reason, not
be able to pull it off.

As they considered staffing the news department of the new station, all
four groups agreed that the News Director should be hired at the outset and that
the two other key positions, the individual running the assignment desk at the
beginning of the news gathering process and the person in charge of the production itself at the other end, should be filled by the News Director.

Not surprisingly, since the participants had just heard one of the nation's
foremost consultants address the seminar in plenary session and since two of
the four groups had consultants from a leading station rep firm as resource persons, most advocated bringing in consultants at the outset. One of the arguments which influenced the groups' decisions was the access to information on
people available which the consultants possessed. In addition to their role as
headhunters, consultants seemed appealing since, as one practicing news director told the group he was advising, "If I were going into this market-place and
I were going to spend the millions it will cost and be in the red for a couple of
years under the best of conditions, I would want every scrap of research I could
get and it would not stop at consultants."

Faculty and industry participants alike had troubles reconciling what they
thought needed to be done with the resources described in the sample Construction Permit Application provided. (Exhibit 5, Appendix 4) Five full-time and
three part-time employees were described as too few to hope to compete with
the two established stations. Although two of the groups attempted to work
within the number specified, the other two groups arrived at 15–17 as a far
more realistic number. Similarly, resource persons in three of the groups set
$300–400,000 as probable News Department operating budgets in the first
year, with the higher figure thought to be the more likely.

Particularly in view of the injunction seemingly imposed to hold down
costs, but also because of the many precedents in markets similar in size to
Desolake with which participants were familiar, much attention was given to
examining the pros and cons of various permutations of combined functions.
As an ideal, the resource persons recommended freeing the news director of as
many other duties as possible to concentrate on long range planning, to function as a news executive, and to exercise a supervisory role. The idea of a news
director also functioning as an anchorman was rejected out of hand. In addition
to the demands on the news director's time which the anchor role would involve, such an arrangement would deprive the station of the news director's experience in monitoring that broadcast on a day-to-day basis. In a competitive
situation in which the right anchorman might be the deciding factor, the ability
of the news director to render an objective judgment might be crucial. Simi-

larly, it was felt that the assignment editor role was too demanding on a moment to moment basis to permit the news director the detachment his primary duties require. The news director functioning as producer of the early news, however, was thought to be an acceptable compromise. An alternative scheme had the assignment editor producing the early, and the news director, the late broadcast. A reporter functioning as weekend anchor was also deemed an efficient combination.

On the contrary, the assignment of one reporter to weekend anchor duties and to three days as ombudsman, consumer reporter, action or investigative reporter was rejected on the grounds that an anchorperson must work for the broadest possible audience acceptance while an investigator must often be perceived as relatively abrasive. One group discussed assigning one full time reporter to City Hall, the sheriff's office, the police department and the highway patrol, and another to the county seat. Another group opted for a specialist reporter whose function would be to produce investigative, specialized pieces, mini-documentaries and other features thought to be essential in distinguishing the new KIRT broadcasts.

Some attention was devoted to the comparative desirability of full-time weather reporters in a mid-Western agricultural community with a large lake and attendant recreational activities. The possibility of finding a qualified meteorologist on one of the local colleges was also considered. While the resource persons cautioned that the person who was doing weather was often, as is Elliot in Detroit, one of the most important elements on the broadcast, faculty participants described situations in various markets where the weather was handled by a part time employee or by a person who doubles elsewhere on the station. ACE KELLNER described the situation at WSAZ Huntington, where a broadcasting student does the weekend weather while the Monday through Friday chores are done by a performer who is also Mr. Cartoon earlier in the day. In the same vein, a local radio station was suggested as a source for a weekend sports reporter.

The possibility of finding executives or other reporters at local media was also discussed. Professionals warned that the difference between the demands of newspaper and of television reporting were such as to make the papers a poor source. As for the two existing stations, it became clear to the discussants that there could be few attainable incentives to induce someone to leave an established station whose broadcast already had achieved an audience for an untried station just coming on the air in the same market. On the other hand, the challenge and the opportunity might easily attract qualified professionals from smaller markets or from lower level jobs in comparable markets. Since cities of equivalent size tend to be similar, a journalist could easily make the transition to Desolake.

The TAU group specifically elected to stay within the eight to nine person limitation imposed by the filed CP application and to bring the news operation in for approximately $130,000 a year. Accordingly, TAU spent more time considering the hardware questions, wire services, equipment, etc. As GEORGE MITCHELL pointed out, "When you are short in numbers your only strength is in communications." KNOX HAGOOD suggested the use of scanners, devices which monitor various local police, fire and other emergency frequencies. To maximize the efficiency of such a small staff, the group felt that 2 or 3 cars should be fully radio equipped with scanners as well as intercommunications equipment. In response to the group's concern, MITCHELL described a hot line from the Dayton police department to WKEF-TV's control room, and a severe weather watch service, particularly desirable in areas subject to tornadoes. In the event of a severe weather watch alert or warning, this service sets off a siren in the sheriff's office which is connected directly to the public address system at the station, and thus particularly helpful on weekends when a skeleton staff might miss a wire service bulletin. RAY MOFIELD suggested that KIRT take the free national weather service wire, especially since the only cost involved was in the phone lines. MITCHELL, however, cautioned that in his area they had not found the national weather service to be reliable enough: "We had a tornado watch down south of us about 25 to 30 miles away and we asked the National Weather Service why they hadn't let us know it was coming. They said they had been too busy. A weather service too busy to warn the public of impending disaster! We did an editorial on it." MITCHELL did recommend, however, the National Weather Service Aviation A wire as an excellent and valuable service for a station with someone able to read it. Others in the group questioned whether its cost could be justified.[5]

Cost was one of several questions raised in considering which wire services to subscribe to. CAROLE KAUCIC (Spalding College) proposed determining which service the other two stations carried. If both were taking AP, she suggested, KIRT should take UPI. JAMES TREBLE (Ithaca College) cautioned that his experience revealed a considerable difference in quality between the two services. Others agreed, adding that the direction of that difference varied from state to state. MOFIELD, citing his border location as giving him a valuable vantage point, observed that in his judgment UPI was superior in Illinois while AP was clearly the better service in Kentucky. JOSEPH JOHNSON argued for taking both services for an initial test period, an arrangement confirmed by others as having been acceptable in other markets. Such a test period, he argued, would reveal which better served the new station's needs. At the same time, the station could sample the slide service provided by the two organizations against the graphics package, a basic slide and graphics library augmented as news developments warrant, provided by the ABC newsfilm syndication service, DEF. Since ABC News, like the other network news services, requires a subscription to its news film syndication service, available at a percentage of network rate, as a precondition for taping excerpts from the early *ABC News With Harry Reasoner* for inclusion in the station's late night news broadcast, there was ready agreement to subscribe. Nor, given the clear need for KIRT to identify strongly with ABC, was there any question about taking any other syndication service.

In much the same way that communications and syndicated resources were seen to be critical to the success of a station with a small staff, so, too, equipment occupied considerable attention. Super 8, for obvious reasons, was examined in the light of the experience of those in the group who had made use of it or studied its use on the air. While super 8 capacity was seen to be a helpful adjunct in the event members of the public brought forward unique amateur footage—one example given was of a station which obtained purported UFO sighting film from a viewer—most were somewhat less than sanguine about the use of this format. Although they cited the advances Kodak had recently made toward upgrading its quality and usefulness, particularly in increasing the number of frames per second, several in the group spoke of the discernibly poorer quality of the image when juxtaposed with live cameras or with slides. All who had used it agreed that the sound was unsatisfactory. Another caution raised was in the time required to convert a processor, even an allegedly convertible processor, from 16mm to super-8mm operation.

Electronic News Gathering, ENG, quite to the contrary, was strongly advocated. JOHNSON argued that going into ENG at the very outset "would be money well spent in having something unique in this area to promote in order to convince people that we were really going on the air in a big way." BILL LAWLOR (News Director, WTNH-TV, New Haven, Connecticut), the resource specialist in news for the TAU group, advanced an economic argument in favor of ENG. The station would spend $100,000 a year for film and processing. If the shooting ratio were 4:1—4 feet of film shot to every foot used on the air—a low ratio for most stations, 80% of that $100,000, he reasoned, would literally be thrown away. The amount of money represented by that use of non-recoverable materials could go a long way, over an eight-year amortization, toward paying for ENG. In addition, JOHNSON reminded the group, the storage costs of the retained 20% of material would be considerably less than for the images stored on film. ROYAL COLLE brought up the equipment list filed with the CP Application, calling attention to the remote unit with four color cameras specified. This was described as unnecessary for a station of the size of the proposed KIRT and inconsistent with current and presumably with future industry practice. LAWLOR advised the group that reliable ENG equipment, including associated videotape elements, could be purchased at approximately $75,000 and the desirability of modifying the Form 301, substituting ENG for the remote equipment, was urged. GENE DYBVIG spoke for several of his colleagues:

> ENG is not only for late-breaking stories on this station: we want to make our ENG capability as visible as possible; we want to make heavy use of it. With ENG we can generate public affairs material far more efficiently than we can in the studio. We can get out there where the people are. We can see what they are doing and they can see us doing it.

SIGMA was one of the groups which rejected out of hand the notion of a staff limited to the eight or nine persons listed in Exhibit 5 to Form 301. Although they, like the TAU group, did decide to trade in the remote truck and some of the six studio cameras—PAUL McLENDON (Oral Roberts University) had suggested that whoever devised the equipment list was simply in love with RCA—they devoted most of their time and energy to considering the merits of various formats and their relationship to other questions. LORIN ROBINSON, for example, began the discussion with his suggestion, the format pioneered by the non-commercial San Francisco station, KQED:

> If we accept the need to do something radically different, we might consider the idea of having reporters come in and discuss their stories in a round table format.

> CLEFTON: The difficulty with that open format is implicit in where and when it happened. It began during a newspaper strike and they were able to provide the people of the area with superior, articulate print reporters. I don't know that we will have the same kind of talent to draw on in Desolake.

> ROBINSON: The format has been copied very successfully in Dallas, it was tried in Washington and Pittsburgh, in Chicago, and with some success, in other markets. The same basic format has been adapted to a mix of two kinds of professionals with more broadcast than print journalists.

> MARY JEAN THOMAS: Last Spring, as an awards judge, I sat in judgment on the San Francisco entries and, frankly, I found the KQED newsroom boring. There was a lot of rambling talk on various items, and much repetition rather than good discussion or analysis of the news.

> ROBINSON: Admittedly, there are limitations. That format depends for success on good people interacting.

> KEIBER: We ran into a problem when I was in Washington and we were using that format. The problem was, basically, opposing the show business of the other stations with nothing but the journalistic ability of the people on WETA. The format has potential if you don't ignore the fact that you are on television.

> ANDY POTOS: You have to define what type of people you want to hit. I think you will find a breakdown of any urban American area runs this way: about two percent of the population can be defined as Upper Class. 11 to 13% can be defined as Upper Middle Class, 30 to 34% as Lower Middle Class. Upper Lower Class is between 37 and 40% and

Lower Lower Class is 14 to 16%. I think the objective is to reach the highest number of viewers possible. I think you must find a format that is going to shoot for that demographic area where you have the most people.

CLEFTON: We are talking about a pretty well to do market. I call your attention to the consumer spendable income by household table, which shows that 70% of Desolake households have more than $8,000. 33.4% are over $15,000.

CHARLES PHILLIPS: The early news is on at a time when the audience is building rapidly. Another question we must ask is who is coming home and who will *be* at home to watch at that time. Shift change times, plant closing, other things going on in the town affect the income level of the audience available at that time.

One suggestion was that the five o'clock news be a first person account by the reporters, a tease for the ten o'clock news when the film would be shown. WILLIAM HAWES warned:

It is an erroneous assumption that people who watch your station at five o'clock will watch it at 10. A high percentage of older viewers are available for the early news and they sit around all day wondering what has happened. They want to see pictures. The format suggested has people just sitting on set talking and that works pretty well if you do a wraparound, half an hour before the network news and then a half hour, with the film afterwards. But we have only a half hour. A large portion of the audience won't be watching at ten so they will go over to the competition where the pictures are.

Another proposal for a radically different look was advanced by POTOS:

Start with the set. The newsroom look or the newly adapted modular set. That has a dramatic exciting look with all kinds of shot variety. You can change it around every night. It will let you combine the eyewitness news approach—eyewitnesses coming in to be questioned by the anchorman, with the best of the action format fast pacing, highly visual, many graphics, a lot of film. You can use the best of both.[6]

BOB HOYT advocated a magazine format with a variety of hard and soft features:

Market research tells us that consumer reports, action line features have more response from the audience than anything except for hunting, fishing and leisure time reports in areas like Oklahoma, where half the state buys hunting licenses. It varies with the area, of course. In Detroit, crime features are very popular. I would do a different feature every night. We did the Changing Church in Oklahoma every

Thursday. It was so popular that we had to move it to Monday because all the clergy plugged it from the pulpit on Sunday. Another feature might be the Call for Action. The organization in Washington helps you form a group in your community. 40 or 50 men and women who will devote time to helping people with problems. It's a great story and feature source, it provides a real service to the community and it runs about $1500 a year.

Other features considered included a Market Basket on Thursday calling attention to weekend shopping specials, and the Consumers Reports being syndicated by Consumer's Union. BERT BARER suggested a health feature, THOMAS called for a weekly roundup from the State Capitol, which she described as the source of the least well reported news on television. PHILLIPS cited services such as Boston's Beacon News which provided stringer reports from the Massachusetts capitol as a practical and inexpensive means to cover state government. Finally, the SIGMA Group discussed the relative merits of a double anchor team, with its greatest flexibility in the event of one member's absence, and its attendant increase in pacing, against the increased costs in both salary and development. Similarly, the impact of format on staff and costs, particularly in considering options such as the Eyewitness characteristic inclusion of several reporters on the set was considered.

RHO also opted for an expanded news ataff, reasoning that the CP Application has stated that the news department would "include" eight named staff members. The RHO group devoted most of their attention to setting a tone for their broadcast and arriving at a news philosophy, which they and the resource persons both agreed must underlie any successful operation. "New York, San Francisco, Chicago, Los Angeles are different from the rural Midwest," one participant from a potato-growing area in the East suggested. "In the rural Midwest you don't have to shout so much because there is less background noise. I think the tone of the news can be more subdued." ANDREW BRIGHAM, News Director for WHEN-TV, New Haven, Connecticut, was not so sure:

> Kent State was not in a Metro area. Omaha had riots. Omaha had the sniper incident. Out in the Midwest somewhere they have been shooting calves and you ought to hear the reaction in our urban area to that. You tell me it's nice, quiet and peaceful but I've seen the farmers out there raising holy hell with those animals.

GEORGE SKINNER, the other resource person, spoke from his experience:

> One of our clients at Katz is in Omaha, a town not unlike Desolake. An ABC affiliate also, they were number three in the market and had had a 15 share of the audience for the last ten years. BOB HOYT and I worked five weeks with them, installed a new anchorman, new sports man, new weatherman, and a new set. We put them onto a legitimate, responsible new format. On their opening show they came up with a

45 share and their four week coincidental averages a 40 ever since then. The Midwest is not so different from other parts of the country. They get the same network that New York and Chicago sees and the network sets the style for news.

After considerable discussion, the group set out their individual statements on what the news philosophy of the station should be.

WILLIAM PARSONS: Develop an image independent of the network. Hard hitting—if a person has done something wrong, say so. Totally fair. If someone has done something right, and it is appropriate, say so.

R. JOHN DE SANTO (St. Cloud University): I saw an ABC station come into the Duluth market, and that sounded like the way they managed to do it. They emphasized community problems, the news team was young and hard hitting. I think we should look at the community problems here and do the same thing.

BOB STEVENS: Aggressive investigation. A watchdog of society. But its tone of presentation should be friendly, relaxed.

ACE KELLNER: . . . appeal to the younger adult audience, 18 to 49. Let the news team reflect that.

WES WALLACE: I'd like our station to be the public access station. Get more people on the air talking about their concerns.

ROBERT SCHLATER (Michigan State University): My philosophy would call for good research prior to starting, and for letting people know we are continuing our research into news, into what they want and how we can serve them. Get across the point that we are the station that studies the audience before we make some arbitrary decision. Let them know that and it will be their station.

JOE WETHERBY: Find where the newspapers have dropped the ball. 479,000 people have a news readership of 665,000. Many people are reading more than one paper. Find a way to augment the print media.

JIM TUNGATE: Investigative reporting with a strong emphasis on relating the content to the people in the audience. In view of the heavy reliance on newspapers, be first. Use the ENG for live cut ins.

ALBERT LEWIS (Central Washington State College): A willingness and an ability to be a constructive adversary; advocacy based on thorough investigation; mobility.

MYLES BREEN (Northern Illinois University): Hire a consultant, give him the parameters, and the money available, and stick by what he says. Balance the operating costs and salaries so that it operates on a no loss basis.

HAYES ANDERSON: I agree. But I'd like to know more about our competitors. Be more on the local people's side, follow up on local stories, develop local stories every day.

CARL WINDSOR: Be competitive; as hard hitting as possible.

KEN GREENWOOD: Look at the opportunities in the market; research why it is newsy. This is an area for a people-oriented presentation; beat the competitor with an image of liveliness on the set.

ROBERT LA CONTO (Northern Illinois University): My philosophy is that we are journalists and our responsibility to the people in the community is to show them that they have to learn to vote and run this democratic society. A lot of the discussion so far has not been based on that philosophy but on a crass commercial philosophy that we're going to see what we can do to screw the other guy and beat the other station.

JEFFREY LOWENHAR: Find what the perceptions of the consumers we serve are as to their problems (and the perceptions may or may not match the reality): inflation, economics, schools, community, local taxes. Find those perceptions of need and set about to serve them.

CONCLUSION

As was stated at the outset, the areas to be examined in this section were not as clear-cut as those of programming. News judgments are not fixed and immutable but must always be situational. Basic journalistic values and the fundamental integrity of the individual journalist may be—and it is fervently hoped, are—unshakable but they are ever and again called into play in new and unfamiliar contexts. So, too, the questions posed in this section are judgmental. Their deliberation is no guarantee that they will culminate in precise decisions. Clearly, the problems posed are too complex for complete consideration, let alone solution, in a matter of hours. If there was a note of frustration in the comments of the Tarrytown participants it can be ascribed to that. Twelve questions had been posed; the first question alone could, and does, engage major news organizations in an unending dialogue. No group could contend with more than half the list. What they did succeed in discussing highlighted a fundamental dilemma touched on many times and in many different terms: How can television's journalistic obligation, its accepted mandate to provide news and information accessible to a mass audience, be reconciled with the medium's proclivity to select for the visual, the dramatic, the entertaining? How can this reconciliation take place without significant compromise in the supercharged competitive atmosphere in which a local news organization must survive?

NOTES

1. Erik Barnouw, *A Tower in Babel,* Volume I in *A History of Broadcasting in the United States,* New York, 1966, Oxford University Press, p. 13.
2. Frank Wolf, *Television Programming for News and Public Affairs: A Quantitative Analysis of Networks and Stations,* New York, 1972, Praeger Publishers, p. 60.
3. Burns W. Roper, *Trends in Public Attitudes Toward Television and Other Mass Media: 1959–1974,* New York, 1975, Television Information Office, pp. 3–5.
4. Robert L. Hosking, Vice-President and General Manager, WCBS-TV, address to New York Chapter, National Academy of Television Arts and Sciences, August 30, 1973.
5. Jerry Trapp of AP has provided the following estimate for a mythical 75th market in the Midwest similar to Desolake: 1. Basic News Wire: International, National, Sports, Markets, Business, Weather. 2. State News Wire. 3. Automatic Photo Service (black and white). 4. Color Slide Service, by mail. Cost per week: $525.
6. George Mitchell described to the TAU group a luncheon meeting at which he discussed the Eyewitness format with Al Primo, Executive Producer of *The Reasoner Report* who had previously been News Director at the ABC owned WXYZ-TV in Detroit and was credited with having pioneered the Eyewitness News concept there and later at WABC-TV in New York. Mitchell reported Primo's having enumerated the following elements to the format:

    1. Reporters perceived as people telling the viewers about the stories they had covered in a way that the viewers could identify with the story and empathize with the people involved, by writing the story so that details were what the man-in-the-street could recognize.
    2. Varying the order of the news broadcast so that a sports or weather story might lead it off if that were what people would be most interested in that night.
    3. Deliberate use of sound "presence"—room noise, wild sound, to emphasize the reality of the coverage.
    4. Invariably including a shot of the reporter at the event, even to the extent of shooting the sportscaster in the stands.
    5. Repeated and frequent use of supers, even for long-term anchormen, "so the guy at the end of the bar, who can't hear, can identify the newscaster."
    6. Heavy use of B-roll rather than talking heads. (This refers to the practice, in an interview, of cutting away from the shot of the speaker and continuing his statements as voice-over footage of what he is describing. In practice, the edited actuality film is run on a second or B projector, the sound continues to originate from the track on the A projector and a dissolve or cut to the B roll is made by the control room switcher at time of broadcast.)
    7. The same story is shot twice, with different camera angles and different treatment so that viewers of the late news will get a different presentation and not a mere rebroadcast or cut down version of what had appeared on the early news.
    8. Heavy use of ENG for "credibility."
    9. Developed rapport among members of the team so that their interaction not be perceived as contrived.

FOR THE STUDENT

1. Set up an exchange of tapes for local news broadcasts with a university located in a market similar to Desolake.
2. Prepare a sample news broadcast following plans formulated in the simulation.
3. Visit and prepare analytic descriptions of operations in markets of varying sizes.
4. Develop alternate plans for news operations based on ENG and film modalities.

7

Sales

#20. What is the maximum amount of commercial matter in any 60-minute segment which the applicant proposes normally to allow?

—Section IV-B, PART V
Proposed Commercial Practices

IN 1972, $3,675,000,000 was spent by American advertisers to buy time on television. Of that total, $1,177,400,000 was spent by national and regional advertisers in non-network advertising on local stations, and $810,100,000 was spent by local advertisers.

Each such dollar spent was as a result of a conscious sale. Nothing in television will so affect the future of the student of broadcasting as the nature and volume of television sales, yet no aspect of the industry receives less attention from students or teachers of broadcasting.

Television sales policies directly affect such matters of audience interest as the kind of programs offered, the times at which they are aired and the frequency with which they are run. Television sales costs and policies also directly affect the distribution of information about political candidates and ballot issues. Sales policies may affect the availability of information about such matters as religion, energy, health, nutrition and other vital questions. Yet, even the business community has little understanding of these practices.

Television sales has traditionally been the training ground for top management in the industry. Nevertheless, although every other area of television must turn away applicants in great numbers, there are always opportunities for the ambitious and talented. Still, to all but a few persons in the industry, television sales is both arcane and esoteric.

There is of course, a considerable body of material which deals with advertising on television from the standpoint of the advertiser, the agency, the marketing specialist or media buyer.[1] Textbooks, workbooks, trade publications and siminars have explored and re-explored the relative merits of *reach*—the percentage of a population exposed to a message—and *frequency*—the number of times such an exposure takes place.[2] The relative advantages and disadvantages of television compared to other advertising media, how to mount a multimedia campaign, how to determine the media mix, are topics readily found in the literature.

What is called for in this problem, developing of a rate card, establishing policies, planning a staff and dealing with other such specific task-oriented questions, have not been dealt with, to any great extent, in the descriptions of television sales currently available. In part, this is because the best of the general texts on broadcast management have had to cover so many aspects of sales as to be compelled to provide only a broad description of the typical sales organization and its relationships to other areas of the station. Other texts, however, have been so narrow in their scope that they have tended to become limited to the time and circumstance they described.[3]

It should be obvious to anyone that advertising and other businesses in this economy have a symbiotic relationship with each other. That fact accounts for some of the differences between the sale of advertising time and the sale of the products and services of the businesses and industries which become television's clients. If we examine those difference, we may come to see aspects of the television sales problem which must be understood before this simulation can be successfully carried out.

The most obvious difference between the television salesman and the car dealer to whom he is trying to sell time is that the television salesman has a physically limited inventory which must be disposed of within a specified period of time. The automobile dealer can hold out for a better price until the end of the model year or until the underbody rusts away—whichever is sooner. Even then, all is not lost. The car can be discounted, sold at a loss or, in the extreme, carted away to be sold as scrap. Even the best of con men, however— let alone the best of salesmen—cannot sell last night's news. At some point the television salesman will have had to settle for a price or let the opportunity for obtaining anything go by forever and all time. Under that kind of pressure, there is always a danger as Todd Wheeler, General Sales Manager, WPVI-TV, Philadelphia, Pa., told the TAU Group:

> Everyone I have ever worked for has always suggested to me that whenever you are sold out in any area of your schedule, you have priced that area too low, and you are sold out too soon. Controlling inventory is the most important job of the sales department.

The base unit in television is the 30-second announcement. 10-second announcements are sold at half the price, the rare 60-second announcement at two times the 30-second rate. The number of announcements which can be inserted in any given hour of programming is limited by the station's answer to Question 20 of Section IV-B of the CP Application.[4] It may also be limited by membership or adherence to the NAB Television Code, which includes the voluntary industry self-regulation with respect to standards of commercialization.[5]

To avoid selling out those limited announcements at too low a price or before a new advertiser with an urgent need to enter the market might have a chance to offer more per unit, sales practices and a lexicon unique to broadcasting have been developed. Chief among these is the concept of *fixed* and *pre-emptible* rates. An announcement sold to an advertiser at a pre-emptible rate may be moved to some other time in the schedule if another advertiser comes along who is willing to pay a premium for the initial period. Paying such a premium entitles one to a *fixed,* or *non-pre-emptible* spot.

A station's compensation from the network has already been discussed. This represents, for the typical station, 13.3% of total revenues.[6] Of the remainder, the typical local station will obtain 45.8% from National Sales, which represents the sale of announcements in local time sold to national advertisers. For example, a major oil company may wish to increase its sales in a particular market and augments its purchase of advertising on the networks with advertising placed on the stations in the market in question.

Advertisers buy these announcements through their advertising agencies who maintain offices in major centers, New York, Chicago, Detroit, Los Angeles, San Francisco, Atlanta or several other cities. Since a station in a market of the size of Desolake can hardly afford to have full-time salesmen in each of these cities, it is represented by a firm which, for a fee, serves it and other stations elsewhere in the country. The decision as to which *Rep* firm to choose becomes a critical one for the new station. To assist time buyers operating in the major industry centers, Standard Rate and Data Service (SRDS) publishes a summary of the facilities available at stations throughout the country. This summary, and others such as the *Television Digest Factbook,* include the station's latest *Rate Card,* or price list.

This may be a fixed rate card, which lists only one non-preemptible rate, or a card similar to that for KGBA (Appendix 16) which lists a fixed and a preemptible rate for each time period. Other rate cards may be of the *Grid, Range, Sliding,* or *Pressure Rate* type as exemplified by the card for KNAC. This particular card is typical of those recommended by John Blair and Company, a major rep firm, to its clients. On this card there is a grid of five rates in certain time periods. Sections III, IV and V have three levels of *IP* or *immediate pre-emptible* rates. Which of these might apply at any particular time will be discussed later in this chapter. Section II gives a rate for announcements which are pre-emptible with a two week or two broadcast notice. Announcements sold at Section I rates are fixed.

Stations can adjust their pricing in several other ways. Selling *rotation* allows a station to group certain less desirable time periods together with more sought-after times. Advertisers who buy *rotators* expect to have their spots move through the day part, if the rotation is *vertical* (one day at noon, for example, on the next at 1:00 P.M. and the third at 2:00 P.M.) or through days of the week if it is *horizontal rotation* (the announcement might appear at the same time—in prime time access, for example—but on a Tuesday one week and a Wednesday the next).

Frequently, discounts will be offered for long-term buys—schedules running as long as 52 weeks—although the length of the average *flight,* or schedule purchased for a client, has dropped markedly in recent years.

Another form of discounting is the creation of packages. Packages, which put together combinations of announcements in various day parts, for a special price, allow the station several options. The station's more desirable time periods can be spread out among a number of advertisers as inducements to buy groupings of less popular announcements. Also, some unsought time periods can be tossed in as *CPM Reducers. CPM* refers to *cost per thousand,* a way many agencies may wish to look at the number of viewers who will be reached in a particular buy and the relative cost efficiency of reaching them. CPM Reducers provide additional viewers, generally in programs which are not being easily sold, if at all, and therefore cut the average cost per viewer for the entire buy. Advertisers may also be offered *bonus* spots, generally from the same time periods as CPM reducers are drawn, as an inducement to buy. Sometimes, particularly when the station wishes to sell prestige programs, an advertiser will be rewarded for the purchase by a *bank* of bonus spots in a specified day part which will be scheduled on a pre-emptible basis when available.

Because so much of television's business is conducted on a CPM basis it might be well to examine how to arrive at that figure. If in March, 1975, an advertiser had wished to buy the 8:00 P.M. break on a Tuesday night on WCBS-TV, New York, on a CPM basis using the Nielsen book, he would first have had to convert ratings into homes, since CPM refers to the number of households delivered (and therefore presumably watching) in a given quarter hour.[7] The NSI would give two figures, one for 7:30–8:00 P.M., and another for 8:00–8:30 P.M. The two are averaged to obtain the figure for the 8:00 P.M. break. Thus:

	Rating	Total Households Delivered in Station Area	
7:30–8:00 PM	14.0	909,000	
8:00–8:30 PM	27.0	1,758,000	
8:00 PM Break	20.5	1,333,500	(7)
(Average of 7:30–8:30)			

To obtain the CPM, the rate charged for the spot must be divided by the number of homes. This could be plotted as follows:

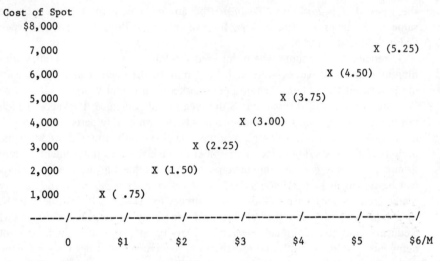

```
Cost of Spot
  $8,000

   7,000                                                          X (5.25)

   6,000                                                X (4.50)

   5,000                                     X (3.75)

   4,000                            X (3.00)

   3,000                  X (2.25)

   2,000         X (1.50)

   1,000    X ( .75)

   ------/---------/---------/---------/---------/---------/---------/
        0       $1       $2       $3       $4       $5      $6/M
```

Thus if $6,000 were charged for the announcement, the 1,333,500 homes would be delivered at a cost per thousand of $4.50. At $3,000 the CPM would be $2.25.

Obviously, if the spot purchased were part of a plan or of a package, the various times in the package would have to be averaged to arrive at the CPM for the buy.

Now let us apply the same concept to the Tuesday night break in Desolake. Again, we will use half hours since the Desolake NSI is not broken out by quarter hour periods.

KNAC's ratings converted into homes, would be as follows:

		Total Households
	Ratings	(DMA-Designated Market Area)
7:30–8:00 PM	29	74,820*
8:00–8:30 PM	31	79,980
8:00 PM Break	30	77,400

With such numbers, a charge of $6,000 would represent a CPM of $77.50. $3,000 for the announcement would mean a CPM of $38.75. Clearly, the abscissa of the chart must change.

A price of $100 for the announcement would represent a CPM of $1.29, slightly under the national average for 1975 of $1.39. Batten, Barton, Durstine & Osborn, Inc., N. W. Ayer and other agencies prepare lists of CPM which they are prepared to meet in particular sized markets.[8]

(* A rating of one is equal to one per cent of 258,000, the total number of television households in the Desolake DMA.)

Cost of Spot

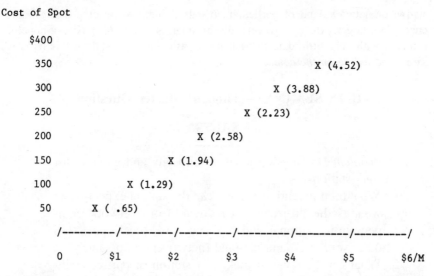

```
$400

 350                                             X (4.52)

 300                                   X (3.88)

 250                              X (2.23)

 200                    X (2.58)

 150             X (1.94)

 100        X (1.29)

  50    X ( .65)

   /---------/---------/---------/---------/---------/---------/

   0      $1        $2        $3        $4        $5        $6/M
```

Each salesman for the station or for the rep firm is given a *list*. His list names the agencies and accounts on which he and he alone may call so that salesmen in the same organization do not compete endlessly with each other for the same prospective sale and can cover the marketplace in a systematized fashion. Obviously, the quality of the list is a mark of the relative productivity of the salesman and in turn can determine his earnings. The local salesman, in a market of the size of Desolake, will spend more time with actual retail merchants and less, if any, with agencies. One of his tasks will be to assist the retail advertiser to make use of co-op advertising. A local appliance dealer, for example, may be able to obtain a portion of the cost of advertising from the appliance manufacturer. In other instances, the manufacturer may make commercials available for the local dealer's tag at the conclusion of the announcement, a mention of the local dealer's store as the place where the product may be obtained.

A salesman for an established station will be able to use the rating history of the time period or of the package to persuade the prospective customer of the efficiency of the purchase. In the largest markets, New York and Los Angeles, ratings are available in the form of "overnights," the results of *coincidentals,* surveys taken by telephone during the broadcast itself and on the desk of rating service customers the next morning. In large markets, rating services provide weekly estimates, all year long. In some of the larger markets there are monthly reports eight months of the year. In all NSI markets, there are so-called *sweep* periods, in November, February and May when ratings are measured. Before these books appear with the results of the sweeps, the station must, as in the case of a brand new station, sell on the basis of estimates. To some extent, these can be derived from what the program in question has done in other, presumably similar markets, from an evaluation of the competition, of special promotional plans, of the effect of other, highly visible programs on the station or network, and of particular appeals thought to be of possible influence. To a larger extent, however, the salesman is selling *blue sky*—a hopeful estimate with very little data to back it up. Attempting to sell on this basis is said to be *selling on the come.*

IRTS SEMINAR—Thought Starter Questions

—SALES

Problem D: Develop a sales philosphy and strategy for *your* stations.

1. What total potential revenue can the station expect—and what is the projected breakdown, from network compensation, national and regional spot, local spot, "all other sources," and national (network) co-op sales?
2. What can be done to make our station of particular interest to local advertisers? Should we have a "charter year" rate? Should we try to sell on-the-come, at discounted prices until we have established a saleable audience level, or should we go flat-out against the competition at directly competitive prices?
3. What rate card innovations—without declaring a price war—can we hope to develop to attract national and regional spot dollars?
4. Is it good business for the station to establish a differential rate structure for local as opposed to national/regional advertisers?
5. What part of our inventory shall we make available on a pre-emptible basis?
6. What criteria shall we establish for selection of a national station representative? (In addition, do we need a national sales effort, other than that of our rep firm?)
7. What will be the structure and size of our local sales operation?
8. Will we subscribe to the NAB, and thereby adhere to its Code guidelines on the amount of advertising as well as product restrictions? (As a new station, will this be an inhibition to sales and to our getting off the ground?)
9. Will we accept religious advertising—in the form of programs supplied by a religious group, for which we only sell the *time?* What about religious spot advertising?

10. What will our policy be on political advertising? Will we have special rates? (In this connection, what will our posture be on Section 315—equal time?)

11. Should we accept advertising for guns and ammunition? What about over-the-counter proprietaries or other products that are on the "questionable" list (i.e. products which the FDA or any other agency has not banned as yet, but which may fall into questionable categories, such as analgesics, artificial sweeteners, aerosol-dispenser products, etc.?) To what extent, and by what mechanism should we exercise control over the acceptability of commercials in terms of taste, substantiation of claims, etc?

12. What syndicated rating service should we subscribe to? How do we handle advertiser/agency requests for submitting plans based on research of the other major syndicated service? (We can't afford both.)

13. What incentives can we offer local advertisers (other than price)—i.e., copy-writing . . . no-fee commercial announcers . . . point of sale merchandising . . . production services, etc.—to attract them to our station?

* * * * *

In light of these questions, and others generated in the Workshop and the Group's discussion/decision on them—*what is the overall sales plan and policy of the station?*

FACULTY-INDUSTRY SEMINAR DISCUSSIONS

Participants in each of the four groups seemed to approach the problems in the same fashion. In part because they seemed to feel less secure in making judgements in sales than in either programming or news, in part because they recognized that they would have access to the knowledgeable specialists in the field over a very short period of time, each group independently sought more counsel from the resource persons than had been the case with the other topics. The sessions were characterized by give and take from the group as a whole, less discussion and more direct questioning. Leaving specific details to subcommittee meetings or their later deliberation, they concentrated on four or five broad areas.

Considerable time was given over to considering whether such a thing as a sales philosophy could be articulated for the proposed station, and what, if any, function that might serve. To some extent, what was being talked about involved specific policies the station would adopt with respect to how its sales force carried out their duties. To a larger, and more important extent, the subject dealt with the kinds of relationships the station would set up with agencies, advertisers, its competitors and the community in which it was preparing to do business. Stripped of all platitudes of good neighborliness and responsibility, there is the essential recognition of the fact that a new station must get past the business community's inevitable first impression of its management as a planeload of carpet-baggers. Unlike the retailer who can choose to remain in a hospitable location or to move to the next town, a broadcaster is inevitably forced to succeed in the community he is licensed to serve. Like a telephone company or an electric power supplier, he has no option but to remain where his most important investment, in this case the license, dictates. Since his business will thus depend on the long term financial consequences of his policies, he must be careful to avoid short term gains which would have a deleterious effect on the climate in which the station must continue to operate over time. In practical terms, the weight the management puts on this question may well determine both the particular kind of rep firm sought and the kind of local sales force hired. A station which decides that its best interests lie in maximizing profits initially by selling at significantly reduced rates in such a manner as to attract considerable business away from the competition will hire a sales force geared to that kind of activity, and a rep who will carry out that basic sales philosophy on the national scene.

Strategically, such a procedure might succeed in shaking up a market considerably. MANN REED, Regional Sales Manager for WTEV, Providence, Rhode Island, reported, for example, that before WTEV came on the air in 1963 as the third station in the market, the other two stations each had a single salesman. Now, each of the three stations has five or six on the street. Obviously, the market had become stagnant, the salesmen were functioning as order takers, growth was at a minimum and the comparatively more aggressive philosophy of the new-comer opened up an enormous amount of new business for each of the stations.

The downside contingency of such a course of action might be the setting off of a price war. Not only would this work to the advantage of the older stations, in the short run, since they would still be selling on the basis of a history of success, but it would also seriously affect the stability of the market. This would act to every station's disadvantage in several related ways. To accommodate a new station, there must be growth in the total sales in the market. In part, this can come about by the growth of a market or its surrounding region, in terms of population as well as in terms of business activity. Desolake, for example, had gone through a period of enormous growth during the previous decade. One of the impulses toward investing in the proposed new station must be the belief that not all of this growth has been proportionately reflected in television advertising sales by the two existing stations.

The only other possibility for growth in any market, and what the new station must ultimately have to depend on after the initial readjustment of the market to the presently unrepresented population growth, lies in the allocation of more national sales dollars to the market and in the attraction of industries and advertisers not hitherto seen advertising on television. If the market has passed through a period of great price instability and a general depression in pricing has set in, much of the gains in increasing business to reflect population growth will have been offset by the lower return per unit of inventory. Even more important, the national rates will have been depressed and the national interest in the market as growing, important and stable will have been eroded. The increase in national sales allocation must depend, not only on the realization of the growing importance of the market, but also on the faith the media-buying community can place in the responsibility of the broadcasters to operate responsibly. National sales has always suffered from a fear that purchases on a station thousands of miles away carry no guarantee that a schedule will run as ordered and that therefore the results can not be evaluated with assurance. An unstable market, however attractive its lowered prices might seem locally, will be perceived as unreliable and will be approached warily by national buyers. There is little likelihood that the allocations to the market would rise. Rather, fewer dollars would be coming into the market next year since a national advertiser who had been able to buy 100 rating points (i.e., the sum total of rating points his schedule would represent) for 10 percent less than he had budgeted, would not only most likely shift 10 percent of his dollars next year into another market, he might also tend to think of the first market as declining in importance. If the market should, for some marketing reason, become more appealing, print and radio and other media would gain at the expense of television.

In each of the groups there developed this curious balance between, on the one hand, the intense spirit of competition which is essential to any successful sales effort, and, on the other hand, a realization that the individual station, and particularly a new station, had a responsibility to the market itself. One way in which this responsibility is continually called into question is the way which a station deals with an excess of inventory. Inventory and its control attracted considerable attention from the resource persons in the group discussions. A station's inventory is, at any given moment, the total of unsold announcements scheduled. The inventory which will become available for any given day is calculated by adding the number of commercial positions available in each daypart. Thus, for prime time, the station generally has 60 seconds between hour long programs, and 30 seconds at the internal half hour break.

Adherence to the NAB Code, the industry's voluntary standard for commercial practices, or the station's own standards, which, as in the case of the Westinghouse or some other group owned stations, may be more stringent, will determine how much commercial time may be available in local time. Currently, for example, the NAB Code will permit 16 minutes per hour in local, non-prime time programming.[9] There may be no more than four interruptions in a prime-time hour program and no more than four non-program elements in any one of these interruptions. Children's programming may contain only nine minutes 30 seconds; news programs may have additional interruptions due to the fact that news is recognized to be different in nature from dramatic programming, for example, where longer periods of continuity may be assumed to be desirable so that the audience can intelligently follow the plot of the show.

The number of availabilities, subject to the restraints noted, are figured for each hour in each daypart and the salesmen and traffic department, the unit which keeps track of which announcements have been scheduled in which available position, can calculate what the station's inventory will be for any given day and for whatever longer period of time the station wishes to examine.

Occasionally, developments in programming will greatly affect the inventory available. The preemption of a network program on an OTO—one time only—basis will increase the inventory available for a particular day. If a network series is to be preempted, the station's inventory may be increased significantly for an entire quarter. If a network affiliate elects to carry the home games of the local big league baseball team, the effect could be considerable, not only on the station's own inventory, but also on the entire market. Every daytime hour during which baseball is played might add as many as 29 additional 30-second announcements to be sold. That increase in volume of units to be sold can be tremendously disruptive, since the natural tendency is to depress the price to the point where a sizable proportion of the availabilities are sold. The example was cited in one group of such a situation in one station, an NBC affiliate, with not only local baseball to sell, but also a regionally networked daytime talk show, their own *Phil Donahue Show* and an hour variety show at noon to say nothing of *Tonight* and 90-minutes of news. Succumbing to the temptation to move a large part of their inventory, they began to sell at rates which approached those charged by the UHF station in their intermix market. Obviously, that put the UHF station at a tremendous disadvantage since the same amount was more efficient in terms of CPM on the over-inventoried VHF station.

A related problem is that of overselling. Although overselling is less likely to directly result in depressing the entire market, this practice can adversely dispose local merchants towards television advertising altogether. A station habitually engaging in a deliberate practice of selling every announcement several times, particularly when it is compounded, as sometimes happens, by a failure to advise in advance those whose commercial will not run, can establish a climate of distrust which affects others in the market. One such example described involved a CBS affiliate which delayed the start of *The Waltons*. Thus the break before was expanded by 60 seconds. This doubled the amount of time adjacent to the program. The station offered the adjacencies for very little on the grounds that there was such a large inventory on that night, thereby attracting many advertisers who bought this appealing spot as part of a package. The station had deliberately sold more inventory than was available and proceeded to swing clients into less desirable time periods or less desireable months of the year. Swinging, as it is called, is described as a fairly common device stations use to obtain sales for nonexistent or scarce inventory when advertisers are anxious to buy and then rescheduling the announcements into the traditionally slow months of the year. Advertisers who have coordinated multi-media purchase plans or have special merchandising commitments to fill are understandably irritated by the practice.

To some extent, what the new station will do in establishing its own practices will be determined by what the competition has already conditioned the market to consider the norm. If the two established stations have managed to maintain an integrity in their rate structure, if their rate cards are adhered to and therefore reflect essentially what the selling rates in the market are, advertisers will demand that the newcomer behave in the same way. There are many areas, however, where the practice in the market cannot serve as a guide to the station.

Religious broadcasting can bring in several thousand dollars a week in addition to counting against promised religious broadcasting in the License Application. Whether or not to accept paid religious broadcasting depends more on an assessment of the religious preferences of the community, the identity of the groups seeking time and on the station's own policies than on the practices in the market. In many cities, one station will see nothing wrong with accepting such programs while other stations in the same market will refuse them on the grounds that religious or other non-entertainment programming should not be preempted by those with the funds to put across their ideas but should be allocated by the station to groups or persons holding a number of different opinions. Similarly, every station must decide for itself what the threshold of taste in advertising is to be. The first station in the market carrying advertisements for hard-sell home improvement, second mortgages, loans and other complex consumer credit businesses, mail order novelties of questionable value, guns and ammunition, personal advice, land sales, computer dating services, contraceptives, or other sensitive products or service categories will suffer some loss of prestige. A station refusing to carry a particular category of advertising may attract no notice whatsoever beyond the walls of the advertising agency seeking to place the business. Yet such a station must predetermine the policy it will adhere to in accepting advertising. What will it do when the lean days are at hand? Business will be good in the fourth quarter, to be sure, particularly in a year like 1976, as the sales resource persons pointed out, But how much will the station compromise its rate cards when the four-wall movie house deals appear in January?[10] Perhaps the most succinct guidelines in answer to this and related questions were those implicit in GENE DYBVIG's observation in the TAU discussions:

There is a pragmatic reason for us to be very ethical in all our dealings in Desolake. In our home country, we are only 100,000 people. In

such a community, the advertisers are a very close-knit group; they all
belong to the same organizations. If someone buys a spot in your news
for X dollars and someone else gets it for less. . . .

BRIAN COBB, Sales Manager, WNGE, Nashville, saw the station's sales
philosophy as a key to determining which rep firm would be the most desirable.
As he told the IOTA Group, the sales philosophy of the national must match
that of the local sales force, and different rep firms' sales staffs have differing
approaches. Clearly, the selection of the best possible rep firm is one of the
most important decisions a station must make in the area of sales. National
sales will bring in somewhere between 30 and 60% of the station's revenue and
all of that will be placed as a result of the sales efforts of the rep.

A number of factors enter into the decision. *Broadcasting Yearbook 1975*
lists 233 station representative firms.[11] Station representatives fall into two
major categories, "short list" and "long list" firms. Short list firms represent a
limited number of stations, selecting them carefully, generally in much larger
markets than Desolake, and concentrating all their energies on those few. Long
list firms, one of which would be the likely choice for the 75th market, represent many more stations in markets of varying sizes. Frequently, they group
their sales teams by market size so that one team might service, for example,
markets in the 50–75 market range on the supposition that their problems would
be most similar. Some reps have a number of UHF stations, others may
specialize in representing independent stations. Some reps seem to specialize in
representing stations affiliated with a particular network. Others provide basic
services to a station including research, rate card development, syndication,
barter and movie title selection, sales training, programming or news consultancy. Success with stations of the same size or of the same network affiliation
or success with a station facing problems such as KIRT will face in entering a
long established market would be criteria which might weigh heavily in making a decision. Support services available would also be a factor. Yet another
consideration would be the strength of the rep firm offices in particular sales
centers. Blair Television, one of the larger firms, maintains offices in nine
cities in addition to New York. The importance of representation in Atlanta, St.
Louis or San Francisco, however, will vary from market to market. If a station
is located in the West, it may expect considerable business from San Francisco
and Los Angeles agencies. To such a station a rep firm with a strong office in
each of those cities might be more important than it would be to a small market
station in the East. In any event, the decision as to which rep firm to use will
not, for a late third entry in the nation's 75th market, be entirely up to the
station. Reps, not too surprisingly, beat a path to the door of stations in the
larger markets; in a market of size we are studying, the station might well have
to solicit representation. As an inducement, the station will have to offer more
than other stations might. Some stations pay as little as 8% to a rep firm; KIRT
Desolake may expect to pay as much as 15%, at least in the beginning.

If the choice of a rep can be seen to be important because 40 per cent of the station's business may be done through the rep firm's offices, then the staffing of the station's own sales department can be seen to be even more important. That group will not only bring in more than half of the station's total revenue, it will also to a large extent embody the image of the station to the business community and to much of the nonbusiness leadership in the region. Further, once the station has become established and is competing with the two older stations for a reasonable market share, it will be primarily through the efforts of this sales force in attracting customers new to television advertising that the station will have any hope of growth. Not surprisingly, the sales management resource persons urged a carefully selected, highly motivated force working within the discipline of clear sales goals. One resource person even went so far as to suggest a specified number of calls per week, on the grounds that a sufficient number of new business presentations would have to return a certain percentage on time invested.

The size of the sales force, as well as its makeup, must be determined by weighing a number of factors, JACK CONDIOTO, General Sales Manager for WTEV, New Bedford, Mass., urged the RHO Group to consider the size and makeup of the competition's sales force as the most important criterion. Much of the task of the sales force, at least initially, will be to sell against the other stations. The level of individual service they can provide their customers would have to condition the staffing of the new station, he argued. All the resource persons agreed that management in the sales department involved too much detail work for a single sales manager. In some smaller markets, the general manager himself serves as the liaison with the station's rep. Whatever the merits of that arrangement, it would be impossible, in a start up operation, as there would be too many demands on the general manager's time for the day by day contacts required. The question becomes, therefore, whether to make the general sales manager the department head, the person who maintains contact with the rep and thus might be away from the station fairly regularly, or to give the general sales manager immediate supervision and control over local sales, with a second sales executive functioning as national sales manager and maintaining contact with the rep. A third alternative would be to have two sales managers, reporting to the general sales manager, one for national, one for local and regional, the local sales manager serving as back up and presumably in training for the top spot. One advantage to having the local sales manager serve as assistant to the general sales manager, whether the general sales manager were himself handling national sales or whether there were a third sales management executive designated as national sales manager, is that there is then less competition for *avails*—unsold spots—and the problems the rep faces are more easily understood. All agreed that the local sales manager should not carry a list. Having control of inventory, he would be able to function at a tremendous advantage over his other salesmen and would thus destroy their incentive.

The participants had been given a description of a typical sales department in the 90th to 100th markets. The structure of this typical station consisted of a general sales manager, a national sales manager who not only maintained liaison with the station's representative but also handled regional business. There were five salesmen and a local sales manager who carried a list of prestige accounts such as department stores and bottlers in addition to his managerial duties. Besides questioning the effectiveness of this practice there was considerable discussion on the number of salesmen the station should have. One view held that three would be the maximum in the beginning since selling purely on speculation, before the first rating results were obtained, would require a highly disciplined, skilled force of experienced salesmen sharing detailed research and experienced enough to be thoroughly prepared. A Kansas City station, in the 23rd market, was cited as having only three while a Boston station, in the nation's 5th market, was described as having five. REYNARD CORLEY, General Sales Manager at WMAR-TV Baltimore, described for the SIGMA Group a station in the 106th market with which he was familiar as having four and looking for a fifth sales person. The problem, he indicated, was that the accounts in a small market involved such small dollar amounts that the station had to have far more clients than in a larger market. Salesmen in that market, he reported, averaged some 30 calls a day.

Ultimately, the decision as to the size of the sales staff will depend on how many can be supported on the business available in the market. Some argued that even this factor can be adjusted by intermixing experienced salesmen with trainees. The need for experienced salesmen was acknowledged in view of the difficulty of selling an untried schedule; the need for trainees was argued on the grounds that the station would eventually be forced to develop its own sales and sales management talent to replace those sales persons who would inevitably leave for greater opportunities in larger markets. Promoting sales management from within would encourage those men and women with developing management skills to share successful presentations or creative sales plans. Trainees could obviously be attracted from the local universities, perhaps even beginning their careers before graduation.

Some discussants advocated hiring the experienced sales force away from the other stations. This would give the station's sales team, it was argued, a feel for the market. It might also provide the station with significant intelligence on the competition's plans and practices. Counter arguments included the likelihood of embittering the competitive climate, of stimulating price warring and of blurring an opportunity to take advantage of the station's novelty. Attracting at least one salesman from a local radio station and another from a local newspaper were cited as ways to increase the credibility of the pre-rating book sales presentations while also helping to develop a knowledge of the market. Surveying local advertisers and agencies on a regular basis, perhaps every three months, was described in the TAU Group as a fairly standard practice in the industry to determine which salesmen in the market were giving the best service, calling on clients most regularly, appearing to do the best job. Ideally, the station would learn that it was its own salesmen. If a competitor's salesman turned out to be the most effective in the market, the station might attempt to woo him to cross the street. Failing that, it was suggested, the station might even help him get a fabulous new job in another market.

To attract the kind of sales force needed for a new station in an established market, strong incentives are required. In general, salesmen are compensated in one of three ways. The NAB reports that 8% of the profit-making stations in Desolake's market range pay salesmen salaries, 39% pay a smaller salary with commission on top, and 52% pay straight commission with a guaranteed minimum. (Appendix 14) The description of a typical station in the 90th–100th market furnished to the participants reported the practice in that range market was a $150 per week draw against future commissions with commission averaging 10% on new and 8 % on repeat business. Salesmen were said to average, on this basis, $14,000–$30,000 per year in the market range. A typical salary for a general sales manager was given as $30,000 plus a $5,000–$7,000 bonus to stimulate increased sales. National sales managers' compensation was given at $25,000. Local sales managers were described as making $15,000 in salary, $10,000 in commissions and an additional $3,000–$5,000 as an incentive to top last year's sales.

Some felt these figures to be too low. While noting that, in any event, some kind of guarantee would have to be worked out for the first year of operation, ARNOLD ROUTSON, General Sales Manager of WBNS-TV, Columbus, Ohio, told the RHO Group: "I don't think you can find a good salesman anywhere in broadcasting today who will work for a salary." One participant in another group described a station which had converted to a liberal salary figure to counteract a series of raids on its sales personnel. Sales went dramatically down over the next year but rose as soon as a commission plan was reinstated. Some way must be found, each group agreed, to provide compensation for the fact that during the first year salesmen will have to be selling in the face of established stations as well as having to persuade prospective clients to take a chance on the unknown. One suggestion advanced was that commissions go as high as 15 per cent. Other proposals included liberalized draws not subject to review for an entire year, split compensation—part salary, part commission—and a declining split. This latter suggestion would start with a high proportion of salary and work toward an increasing proportion of commission, a plan described by proponents as being both protective and motivating. FRANK DI PROSA, Vice-President and Sales Manager of WOKR, Rochester, New York, suggested his station's method of compensating new salesmen as the method KIRT should adopt. This calls for straight salary for the first three months, followed by a three-month period of working on a draw against commissions. After six months, the salesmen are placed on straight commission with the explicit understanding that if, at the end of that first six months, they are unable to exceed their draw, there either is insufficient business in the market to support them or they simply do not have the makings of good salesmen or women. DI PROSA stated that the system has been used effectively for more than 10 years.

Whatever the specifics, any compensation should both depend on and serve to stimulate sales. Thus, a commission rate figured on the basis of expected annual local sales and what percentage would be required to insure an adequate living to each of the salesmen, assuming they averaged the same gross, could be increased for an individual salesman should his sales exceed a certain expected quota. If the increase applied across the board, that is to say, on total sales and not just on the amount above an established goal, the incentive would be even greater. One suggestion advanced was that the new station grant double commissions on any sales made prior to the station going on the air.

Traditionally, sales management has been rewarded by granting an override, a commission on the sales of the entire unit reporting to the particular manager. Since his task is essentially to maximize the efficiency of his sales force, such an incentive serves further to stimulate increased sales. Most frequently, this override is on gross sales, rather than on net profit, the argument in favor of gross being the additional incentive to the manager who may distrust or disagree with the station's computation of net figures. The arguments on the other side are twofold. First, net computations provide for closer cost controls. Second, high gross dollar figures may actually hide net losses. A hypothetical example of this was posed by TODD WHEELER. An ambitious and unscrupulous sales manager, merely passing through a market en route to greater earnings in the next higher market, might sell a client on carrying a Saturday night beauty pageant, available as a package, which would pre-empt network programming. The price to the client might be considerable thereby resulting in a considerable personal profit to the sales manager on the gross sale. The net on such a transaction might be far less attractive to station management, however. To the cost of acquiring the program would have to be added the loss of network compensation and of national spot sales pre-empted by the event. Although the gross would appear to be high, the entire venture might represent a loss to the station or, at the best, a gain insufficiently great to justify the disruption to established sales patterns which it would represent. Nonetheless, the station will have to devise attractive override, bonus and other incentives if it is to attract and retain good sales management during the critical early years. A number of alternatives were considered by the four groups including percentages of the company, stock options, and profit sharing plans based on self-imposed goals. Retaining a good manager for a three-year period was described as a desireable and reasonable goal.

One incentive plan which involved salesmen as well as sales management and had evolved to prevent raiding of the staff by the competing stations in the Dayton market was outlined by GEORGE MITCHELL. He told of having arranged a trade deal to provide new cars every year for each of his salesmen. The cars are not only for them to use in making sales calls but also for their personal use. "The trade deal means the station hasn't laid out cash and the salesmen know that," MITCHELL said, "and it doesn't sound like much at all. But it inspires a tremendous amount of loyalty to my station when a salesman realizes that to take that offer from the station across the street he's got to out and buy a brand new car first thing tomorrow morning."

Trade deals are similar to barter. In barter, the station receives a program in exchange for a certain number of spots; trade deals involve the exchange of program announcements, generally through a company specializing in setting up such deals, for almost any kind of merchandise or service. Stations must sometimes trade as high as two for one—spot positions worth twice the list price of the merchandise received. Sometimes, trades can be arranged directly with suppliers on a one to one basis. Like barter, trading has its adherents and its detractors. MARK CONRAD, General Sales Manager of WEBC-TV, Greenville, South Carolina, for example, while acknowledging the efficacy of the incentive, advocated buying the automobile for cash, one from each of the dealers in town or on a rotating basis, but avoiding trade deals at all cost: "Too often, when a general manager wants a new car, he makes a trade deal with the Lincoln dealer and simply ruins a good customer. First of all, he has to make exceptions. He can't let the dealer have his most valuable positions, the Olympics or NCAA, for example. Second, the salesman who calls on the Lincoln dealer is getting no commission on the deal so he stops dropping in every week. He doesn't do the pre-planning necessary to get the trade worked off in a year as the station was supposed to. The result? The Lincoln dealer feels cheated; he doesn't think much of the professionalism of your sales team; you have kept him off the air a full year when you could have been getting hard dollars; he loses confidence in television because he hasn't gotten any of the good selling positions. You have lost a client. Also you have antagonized a good salesman."

Determining a station's rates must by now be seen as far more complex than merely setting a price which it is hoped an advertiser might be induced to pay. The rate card is an important device in maximizing income. It can also be an important tool in increasing inventory. C. RICHARD BURNTON, General Sales Manager, WBAY-TV, Green Bay, Wisconsin, ascribes the fact that his station can be 70 percent sold out at all times, and nearly 100 percent sold out in peak periods, fall and spring, largely due to the rate card they have devised. FRANK DI PROSA traced through one of the ways a rate card can assist in maximizing available inventory for the TAU Group. An NBC affiliate, he points out, would have to consider the spots adjacent to *Sanford And Son* and to *Chico And The Man* as among the most desirable on the station. Priced at $1,000 in a particular market, they might be easily sold for a 13-week period. If, however, they were priced at $2,000 it is unlikely that anyone would come along offering to buy them either for an extended period or even on a one time only basis. Should this happen, the station would stand to make considerable money. Should it not, the spots would then be available to sweeten prospective sales. Throwing in one of those adjacencies might, for example, succeed in landing an order for 80% of the business a major advertiser would be placing in the market during a particular period. The unreasonably high price has served to keep the inventory open and thus given the station a chance to increase its market share and its revenues.

Such a procedure presupposes a sliding rate card with established preemptibility levels. It probably also presupposes, to take advantage of national sales opportunities, a rate card which was not differential. One argument for differential rate cards, which specify a higher rate for national sales, is that a local advertiser may not need to reach the entire coverage area audience as a national advertiser does. Thus, a lower local rate was seen by its proponents as making it easy for local businesses new to television. Others argued that the two stations already in the market will have developed a habit of television advertising which would make such a rate unnecessary unless the other stations were offering it and KIRT could not meet that price. Another difficulty with the differential rate has arisen in some markets where national advertisers have chosen to place business through their local bottler, or distributor. Conversely, some local merchants have chosen to make use of out-of-town agencies. Much local business, however, is not placed through any agency and therefore does not involve a 15% commission. One argument for a differential rate holds that some of that savings could be passed on to the advertiser. Recently, however, local agencies have been purchasing generic commercials from production houses, adding a tag for the local advertiser, and demanding a full commission whether or not they have been involved in the original purchase of the advertising time.

A different question arises with respect to whether the station will opt for a fixed rate card, a two-section card, or one similar to the Blair, five-section grid card already in use by one station in the market. RICK LEVY presented the two most likely alternatives to the RHO Group as a *fixed* card, at least for the first three to six months of operation, which would assure the advertiser of running, thereby building confidence and good will toward the newcomer station, and a *sliding* card which "allows the market to tell us what the rates will be. The late news on KNAC sells for between $75 and $150. Depending on the time of year and the amount of business, the market will tell us how much they can get for it. If it fills up at $75, they start selling it at $90, pre-empting advertisers to do so. If it fills up at $90, they can sell it at $110." Other proponents of pressure rate cards point to their usefulness in national sales. Different agencies may assign a particular rate to the market, planning to buy it at $75, $90, or $110, for example. A sliding card easily accommodates them. Similarly, if a station has strong demographics, a good women 18–49 showing in a particular day part, and an agency expresses interest in that particular demographic profile, a salesman can know immediately what would be a good price to ask for. On the other hand, if the agency wanted to make the same buy on a CPM basis, he would be able to go toward the low end of the card. As TODD WHEELER put it, "You just don't know what the value of your spots will be. In Philadelphia, we started selling our early news at $900. Now it is selling at $1600 a spot. Advertisers simply wanted to get on the air in that time period. It has nothing to do with cost efficiency. They simply wanted to get on the air. It was just supply and demand. But if we didn't have a way to accommodate that pressure, we would have missed out on as much as $500 a spot!''

Other variables may come into play in determining which of the rates on a grid becomes the selling rate. PHILIP JONES, General Sales Manager for WTAE, Philadelphia, cited, in addition to time of year and demographics such considerations as the length of the flight, the size of the purchase, and the other accounts the agency making the buy might control.

Rates must be determined for each day part. After the station has been on the air for several weeks, special coincidentals can be ordered for the most important day parts. Before that time, however, rates must be set on the basis of estimates which will neither touch off a price war depressing the level to a point from which no station in the market can recover in the predictable future, nor price the new station out of the running. RHO had determined to counterprogram the other station's early news with entertainment at six o'clock. RICK LEVY and the sales resource team talked the group through the process they would follow in pricing *Bewitched* at that hour.

The HUT level at six is 47 with KNAC dominating the time period with a 30 rating. The new station coming on the air can be expected to increase the HUT level to some extent; *Bewitched* has a strong family appeal and has historically done well with children and teens. Since there had been 30,000 children and 20,000 teens watching *I Dream of Jeanie* on KNAC at 4:30 but the number of children had dropped to 1,000 and the number of teens to 4,000, it is reasonable to assume that *Bewitched* will bring back some of that lost audience. LEVY and the others assumed that the HUT level could thus be brought up to 55, an estimate they agreed was conservative.

The next question to be answered is how much of that 55 HUT level could be attracted to KIRT. Since the decision had been made that the new station would present its news at 5:30 and thus be the first news in the market, and since some of the viewers currently watching the dominant KNAC news may wish to see *Bewitched,* it might be estimated that 10% of KNAC'S audience could be persuaded to change. An even greater percentage of the number two station, KBGA, perhaps as much as 30 percent, might be wooed away. This would now give KNAC a 25 rating and KBGA a 12. KIRT, having also picked up all the tune in audience, would have an 18 and would be second in the market at that hour.

The rate cards for the two older stations show a range of $90–$110 for the early news. Because of the dominance of the KNAC broadcast, it can be assumed that they are selling at the $110 level while KBGA is selling at $90. Since it is a safe assumption that the number two news will not outdraw entertainment, a reasonable price for KIRT would be $90.

What has been determined is a selling rate for the particular time period, even as the $90 price being paid for KBGA's news represents the selling price. When the card is made up to reflect that price, the top of the card will have to be high enough so that the station will not feel disadvantaged at a time when demand is high. The lower rates must have enough of a spread to accommodate a variety of situations. Many of the resource persons agreed that the card would show rates within $5–$10, on the average, of the other cards.

A specific illustration of the difference between rate card and selling rate might be seen in a further example stemming from the same analysis of the potential of *Bewitched* in the six o'clock time period. An advertiser seeking to buy at $3.00/rating point would be willing to spend, therefore, 3 X 18 or $54 per announcement in *Bewitched*. The station's willingness to sell at that price when the stated rate was $90 would be perceived by the advertiser as indicating that the station had severe doubts about the accuracy of its prediction of audience levels. Yet syndicated entertainment counter-programmed against news is primarily of interest to the national spot buyer rather than to the local account. A way out of the quandary might be found by offering the advertiser the announcement at $90 but with a 20% charter discount. Thus, the station might maintain its $90 rate and its rate card integrity while still placing the spot, now discounted to a selling rate of $72, within range of the buyer's initial asking price.

Charter discounts, favorable rates for initial advertisers on a new station, are traditional and serve to facilitate advertisers' buying the unknown and unrated new channel. Since the first day on the air means an automatic 30% increase in inventory in virtually every day part of the Desolake market, devices such as a special discount would serve to cushion the flooding of the market and reduce the rush of long term price depression. Groups discussing whether to offer a discount and if so, under what terms, were cautioned that offering a charter discount—or a discount at any time for long term buys—would have the effect of stimulating the competition to offer a similar price reduction. In any such confrontation, the new station would be bound to suffer by comparison with an established program on an established channel. On the other hand, limiting discounts by requiring a particular amount of purchase before the discount would take effect and strictly limiting the time during which a charter discount would apply were seen as ways to prevent the station from losing money in the event of early success. A time limit would mean that the station would not suffer from a sell out of choice inventory at untenable rates if the first rating book would justify selling those announcements for much more money. Another alternative discussed was providing no discount, but rather bonus spots on a 3 for 2, 2 for 1, 5 for 3 or some basis. This would mean that a purchase within a specified time, perhaps before the station actually went on the air, would entitle the buyer to 3 announcements for every 2 purchased, etc. The advantage of such an arrangement was held to be psychological since a repeat buy would not be at a higher rate, as would be the case when a discount went off. Nonetheless, some pointed out, bonus spots might also create inventory problems when rating data comes in to justify higher rates.

Other topics which engaged the groups in their discussions included the relative merits of the two rating services, NSI and ARB, and which should be selected if the station determined it could afford only one. Some felt that the station might be required, by competitive pressures, to purchase both services. Practice in the market was an important factor to be considered, since the station could be put at a critical disadvantage if local advertisers were expecting ARB data, as many of the experts reported they very well might, and the station subscribed only to Nielsen. On the other hand, the New York and Chicago agencies do their purchasing on the basis of NSI, although for San Francisco agencies ARB was the dominant index. Pricing for the services was estimated at $11,000 for Neilsen, $15,000 for ARB in a market of Desolake's size. In either case, there would be 3 books a year, those for the November, March and May sweeps.

Similarly, there was discussion in some groups about subscribing to other services such as the Television Bureau of Advertising. TVB, among other things, prepares sales presentations tailored to particular industries to use in attracting clients who have never advertised on television. Another service discussed was BAR, the Broadcast Advertiser's Reports, a service which provides stations and their representative firms with a record of what commercials the competition broadcast. One suggestion, since BAR has a 3 to 4 week delay, was hiring students to monitor the opposition on a day by day basis during the most critical hours, noting what commercials ran at what times.

BAR came into being and continues because advertisers had reason to question how many of the commercials placed actually ran as ordered. There are those few stations which have from time to time engaged in fraudulent practices such as double-billing or failing to notify an advertiser that he was entitled to a make-good for a spot which did not air or which was broadcast with such technical problems as to render the audio or video incomprehensible. Every station, however, has the very real problem of getting all the announcements sold onto the air in the time period specified and under whatever conditions were specified in the order. These might include a live announcer reading voice over copy, a dealer tag slide, or a combination of the two. Keeping track of the inventory of announcements available, those sold, and at what prices, is the mission of the station's Traffic Department. In some stations, this department also handles the process of getting the individual commercial into the hands of the telecine or videotape technician who must physically put it on the air. In other stations, this operation function may be spun off into another department.

Participants in the seminar were informed that the typical station in the market range backed up its sales department with a traffic manager and three other employees. Two commercial producer/copy writers were also described as typical. These persons actually produce commercials for local advertisers who do not have or choose to have agencies available to them. Some discussion centered around the location and use of these critical units. Some advocated having the traffic manager report to the general sales manager, where that individual handles local sales, or to the local sales manager in instances where he is the sales executive who supervises inventory. Others recommended following the practice in some stations of having traffic report to the business manager to facilitate the billing which traffic's records would have to generate.

The desirability of leasing a computer service such as BIAS was also considered. Other topics discussed included the question of collections, most station sales executives telling the groups that their stations followed a practice of charging back commissions to salesmen after an account remained unpaid for 90 days. Some described a policy of requiring salesmen to handle collections. Others recommended the establishment of a local credit association, if one is not already in existence in the market, to advise KIRT and other stations of problems with questionable clients. In a market where only 10 percent of the business will come through advertising agencies, collection might occupy more of a station's attention than in larger markets. Mention was also made of those stations which choose to accept doubtful clients on the grounds that if the time remained unsold, they would certainly receive no revenue from it whereas even a doubtful client might eventually pay.

The use of the station's production facilities for commercial production requires careful consideration. It was pointed out that it has become traditional for a new station to offer production services in part as an incentive to advertisers to come onto that station. Some resource persons warned, however, that stations had found themselves wishing to give out a bone and winding up giving away the whole carcass. Stations had offered free production amounting to $4,000 to $5,000 worth of services in order to land a few-hundred dollar order. Often, also, the station would see the production showing up on a competitive station which might even have been given a bigger schedule. Some stations, usually one to a market, had developed into production houses and actually found a significant source of revenue. Many stations, not functioning as production houses, charge out of pockets costs and provide other services free so long as the commercial is to be used on that station. Copies of the commercial for other stations would be supplied at a designated fee. Still other stations maintained two production rate cards, one for commercials for use on their own air, a much higher one for use elsewhere.

Whenever combination of sales policies the prospective station adopts, one thing should be clear from the discussions of the IRTS seminar. A sales department must be organized with far more critical goals than merely bringing in sales. Not only must the sales department compete for a share of the market as great as if not greater than its share of audience would warrant, it must also view itself, as the station's only significant profit center, as charged with managing inventory so that revenue can be maximized at all times. It is a far more complex, demanding and creative process than those who have not examined it ever imagine. Moreover, there is the reward of realizing, as GEORGE MITCHELL pointed out:

> We perform a service in making a local advertiser's goods and services known to the community. We are helping the advertiser become a successful businessman. If we help enough of them become successful businessmen, we will become successful businessmen. There can be enormous pleasure in watching a client grow over time. There is a man in our town who used us exclusively over the years and he has become the number one Frigidaire dealer in the world. It is nice to see that happen.

NOTES

1. A good annotated bibliography—one of many, it must be emphasized—is to be found in Leo Bogart, *Strategy in Advertising,* New York, 1967, Harcourt, Brace and World.
2. *Ibid.,* p. 143–161.
3. An example of the former might be the chapter on Broadcast Sales in Ward L. Quaal and James A. Brown, *Broadcast Management: Radio-Television,* New York, 1976, Hastings House. The latter is exemplified by the chapters by Gillen, Young, Sias, and Zeigler in *Television Station Management; The Business of Broadcasting,* Yale Roe, ed., New York, 1964, Hastings House.
4. The question is open ended. However, Question 18, addressed to Renewal Applicants, and asking about Past Practices, requests information as to the number of hours in the station's schedule during the composite week during which there were a) up to and including eight minutes, b) over eight and up to 12 minutes, c) over 12 and up to and including 16 minutes, and d) over 16 minutes. The question further asks for the amount of commercial time and the day and time of each broadcast in category D. It should be apparent to licensees that 16 minutes is the preferred cut-off point.
5. NAB Television Code limitation are nine minutes in prime-time for affiliates, twelve minutes for independents; 16 minutes in non-prime time and nine minutes 30 seconds on Saturday or Sunday mornings, 12 minutes Monday to Friday in children's time, defined as "those hours other than prime time in which programs initially designed for children under 12 years of age are scheduled."
6. _____ *NAB Television Financial Report 1976,* Washington 1976, National Association of Broadcasters, p. 2.
7. This example is taken from an excellent primer on how agencies use CPM as a guide in buying time prepared by Mary L. McKenna, Vice-President for Market Research, Metromedia, Inc. Mrs. McKenna's "step-by-step consideration of broadcasting business fundamentals" was filed on January 19, 1976 as a Supplement to Comments of Metromedia, Inc. *In the Matter of Petition for Inquiry into the Need for Adequate Television Service for the State of New Jersey,* Docket No. 20350.
8. *Ibid.,* p. 6. McKenna also cites a J. Walter Thompson study in connection with a 1975 study of media cost trends (_____, "New Look at Media Cost Trends: 1965–1980." *Media Decisions,* Vol. 10, No. 2, February 1975) in which, based on a 9.5 rating in all television markets, 1975 fringe time average CPM was computed to be $1.39, up one cent since the year before, but down three cents since the $1.42 1973 figure, the highest of the previous decade.
9. _____, *The Television Code,* Nineteenth Edition, New York, June, 1976, National Association of Broadcasters. The full text of the Seventeenth Edition, April 1973, appears as Appen-

dix B in Charles S. Steinberg, ed., *Broadcasting: The Critical Challenges,* New York, 1974, Hastings House.

10. Some motion picture producers or distributors rent movie houses, bring in the film and place their own advertising. The movie theater, instead of itself presenting and promoting a film, has thus been rented out in the same way a store or apartment is rented out, on a so-called, four-walls basis. Since the rentors are coming in to town with the express purpose of getting whatever profit they can and then moving onto the next town, their media buys are apt to be opportunistic.

11. _____, *Broadcasting Yearbook, 1975,* Washington, Broadcasting Publications Inc., pp. D-8 - D-14. Advertisers may also consult the individual station listing in the *Yearbook,* or in SRDS, to discover which rep firm it retains. The value of the representative to the advertiser, often over looked in thinking about the problem, is made clear by Roger Barton: "It would be an almost impossible task for an advertising agency to keep in touch with 577 television stations or even with 50. The agency time buyer can, through the representative, learn immediately almost anything he needs to know about programs or rates of the stations they represent." *Media in Advertising,* New York, N.Y., 1964, McGraw-Hill, p. 215. A helpful discussion of the role of and the value of the rep to the station is to be found in Quaal and Brown, *op. cit.,* pp. 269–272.

FOR THE STUDENT

1. From SRDS or other sources obtain rate cards for various stations in your own market. What may be learned from their comparison?

2. Determine what rep firms are engaged by stations in the 70th to 100th markets. What inferences if any may be drawn concerning the experience of particular firms with respect to market size, independent stations, network affiliation or other factors?

3. What ancillary services do stations in your market obtain from their representatives?

4. Using lowest unit rate obtained from political broadcasting reports, calculate probably maximum income for various day parts for stations in your market.

5. Determine compensation policies, and their rationale, for your market.

6. Analize the organizational structure of stations in your market with respect to local and national sales and such sales support functions as traffic, commercial production, operations, market research and sales promotion.

8

Promotion

FROM NINE TO TEN P.M., on Tuesday, October 28, 1975, the program on Channel 13 in New York captured its time period with a phenomenal 36 share. Similarly, it drew 36% of the total viewing audience in Pittsburgh, 30% in Boston, 28% in Washington and 20% in Houston. What made its success phenomenal was that Channel 13 in New York and the stations in the other cities mentioned are all Public Broadcasting stations. *The Incredible Machine,* a *National Geographic* series broadcast about the human body, broke all records for PBS audience levels.[1] In New York, where it played opposite a Perry Como special on CBS, *The Rookies* on ABC, the last half of a David Brinkley Bicentennial special and the first half of *Police Story,* on NBC, it more than doubled the previous house record 17 share which the first of the *Monty Python Flying Circus* series had registered.[2] PBS's audience research chief, Alan Cooper, estimated that a total of 20 million Americans watched the broadcast or its repeats during the week on the 250 PBS stations on which it played.[3]

What accounted for the broadcast's success? Surely, the competition was not weak. In New York, in addition to the three commercial network offerings, there were *The Merv Griffin Show,* a movie and a syndicated mystery on three independent VHF stations as well as at least four UHF stations available. In three immediately subsequent sweep periods, WNET, Channel 13, averaged between a three and a four share from 9 to 10 P.M. on Tuesdays.[4]

131

Admittedly, the *National Geographic* series was well known. It had been on commercial networks for nine previous years. Furthermore, the words "National Geographic" had become a household term decades before, thanks to the society's magazine. Yet such recognition might even carry with it some negative feelings. Some viewers might think the series or its usual subject matter, wild life, old hat. The series had never in all its nine years garnered any thing like the audience attracted to *The Incredible Machine*.

The subject matter, films actually taken inside parts of the human body, was fascinating.[5] Health and biology teachers assigned the broadcast as required viewing. But school children doing their homework, even with their parents looking on, could not account for a 36% share of the audience. What did, of course, was the most massive promotional campaign in Public Broadcasting's history.

Gulf Oil Corporation, in what was the largest single corporate grant ever made to PBS, underwrote 12 *National Geographic* specials to be broadcast over a three-year period. Gulf's first entry into Public Broadcasting, the grant of $3,720,000 for the David Wolper productions was through Gulf's hometown Pittsburgh station, WQED. In addition to the program grant, Gulf also pledged at least $1 million a year to promote the specials.[6] Gil Goetz, a spokesman for Gulf, was quoted as saying that "around $900,000" was spent on promoting *The Incredible Machine*, the first program in the series.[7] The production of the broadcast came to only $250,000.[8] Sources at WNET describe the campaign as consisting of seven elements:

— 30 second *TV spots* on NBC and CBS.
— *Newspaper ads* placed in all PBS markets.
— Saturation *radio campaign* in top 25 markets.
— Broad *magazine campaign* in both mass and selected publications.
— *Bill stuffers* went to 3.5 million Gulf credit card holders.
— *Posters* were sent to 19,000 Gulf service centers.
— *Internal promotion* to Gulf employees.[9]

The magazine campaign included mentions in corporate ads as well as ads for the broadcast alone.[10]

Dr. Thomas Skinner, Vice President of WQED and the station's executive producer for the series, said of the premiere broadcast's success: "We proved that when public TV mounts a complete advertising and promotion campaign for a program of real quality, we can be competitive with commercial networks."[11]

It is seldom that one can, with assurance, assign effect to cause and particularly to any single cause. In fairness it must be said that there are many who are unwilling to do so in this case. They cite the promise of first-time-ever camera techniques, and especially, the appeal of the subject matter. To be sure, it is hard to imagine a sizeable audience attracted to a scholarly discourse on the iconography in 12th Century Bukovinian handcraft, no matter how extensive

Magazine ads for *The Incredible Machine*

Magazine	Corporate Ad*	'Incredible Machine' Ad**
Atlantic		1
Audubon		1
Black Enterprise	1	
Harpers		1
National Observer		1
Newsweek		1
New Yorker		1
N.Y. Times Magazine		1
People		1
Saturday Review/World	1	
Scientific American		1
Smithsonian	1	
Sports Illustrated		1
Time		1
U.S. News and World Report		1
Washingtonian	2	
Young Professional Groups:		
AMA Magazine	1	
Juris		1
Medical Dimensions	1	
New Engineer	1	

*Emphasis on Gulf but including mention of the series.
** Emphasis on the program."

the advance publicity. Surely 20 million people would not have stayed with the broadcast were the subject matter not compelling and the production not of the highest standard. But 20 million people would never have known that *The Incredible Machine* was worth sampling, let alone staying with, without the promotional campaign which called it to their attention.

A television program is most successful in attracting an audience when it is perceived, before the fact, as a significant event. A presidential debate will surely be the subject of tomorrow's conversation, the Superbowl is a once in a year event not to be missed by anyone with an interest in sports or spectacles, the Olympics bring into quadrennial focus nationalism, youth, excellence, and competition. Most special events become the subjects of so much advance media attention that they seem to promote themselves. It would be difficult not to know that a Bicentennial was being celebrated or that a President was about to be elected. But television's anomaly is that it not only carries, and to an extent, creates legitimately anticipated events; each station also presents between 126 and 168 hours of all kinds of programming a week. Against the presumption of the routine, that which is noteworthy, different, or for any other reason particularly appealing, may often be overlooked. Anyone who has been associated with a television station is accustomed to hearing the rueful plaint, "Oh, if only I had known a program like that was going to be on . . ." All too often, this comes after the person identified as Associated-With-A-Television-Station has patiently and courteously provided a recent example of the kind of program that his or her questioner had just demanded in an accusation which begins with "Why doesn't television ever do . . ."

The task of audience promotion can thus be seen to consist of informing the potential audience of the genuinely unusual, the impending event. With respect to the commonplace, it is finding and announcing whatever is different enough to cause a viewer's break in his routine, a change in habit, a turning away from the competition. As the Thought-Starter Questions indicate, the promotion problem for the new station in Desolake has both a short and a long term component. In the short term, the advent of a third station must be built into a significant event of which the entire community is completely aware, the curiosity of every member of the potential audience must be aroused, they must be persuaded to thoroughly sample the new station's product, and, by no means to be overlooked, they must be given reasons to bolster their feelings that the programs they see on the new station are worth breaking habits for. The tools a new station has to accomplish these ends, like the tools available to a station for its on-going promotion, include advertising, publicity, and exploitation.

While advertising entails adequate budgeting, informed media selection and creative message development, effective publicity demands a sensitivity to the needs and desires of the various publications which report news of television's activities. Exploitation is the enlisting of community forces, institutions and energies to provide promotion of the station through their own or joint activities. Planning to use these tools with maximum effectiveness in promoting the station to its audience and the related development of a plan to promote the station to the time-buying community through sales promotion is the task at hand. A station's public consists of many segments. Good promotion tries to reach them all—viewers as well as advertisers.

IRTS SEMINAR—Thought-Starter Questions

AUDIENCE PROMOTION

PROBLEM E: Develop an audience promotion and a sales promotion campaign for *your* station.
1. What should my initial "premiere week" ads and on-air and radio spots say to the viewer?
2. In which media do I want to place most of my advertising dollars for the initial campaign?
3. Which programs on my schedule lend themselves best to featuring in our station's audience promotion efforts?

(Do we have an up-front show . . . or image . . or quality . . . that will serve as the "consumer benefit" we focus on in audience promotion?)

4. What will I say about my local news to distinguish it from the competition's and to influence viewers to change their long-term viewing habits?

5. What do I want to say in my advertising about my station, overall, which will offer a convincing alternative to the other commercial stations, other than just providing different network programs?

6. What do I really know about the attitudes of viewers to the other two competing stations? What are their image-weaknesses and how can we show our new station as filling this void?

7. What is the best medium for a continuing, on-going audience-promotion campaign to increase awareness of my station and its programs? What other media should be used? How often? How?

8. Do I need an advertising agency? If so, how will I choose one for my station? What criteria do I set? Why these criteria?

9. Are we getting maximum benefit from the allocations of our promotion budget to the various media?

SALES PROMOTION

1. How do I most effectively communicate to the national and local advertising community the importance of Desolake's third network affiliated station?

2. Since Desolake is not a top-25 (or even a top-50) market, how do I convince agencies/clients that they need my station? What "story" do I have to tell advertisers/agencies about our station or Desolake that will draw their attention (and advertising dollars) to us?

3. What do I know about the image of my competitors with the agency/client fraternity: How do I determine the weaknesses of the competition, be it in servicing clients, poor internal scheduling and billing procedures, or whatever, so that I may avoid them and use that as a selling point?

4. Should I have an on-going advertising and/or direct mail program for agencies and clients? If so, what form should it take, what sales points should it make, and how frequent should it be?

5. What is the agency/client fraternity expecting from my new station? Do I know what their needs are in Desolake? Their problems? The advantages they already enjoy?

6. What are the things I want our station representative to most strongly focus upon and develop during initial encounters with agency and client representatives?

7. Do I want to invest in a useable premium item (like an ash tray, etc.) to distribute to all Desolake buyers and prospects? Or is something like this essentially meaningless?

FACULTY-INDUSTRY SEMINAR DISCUSSIONS

Promotional plans, at least at the outset, are not as easy to quantify or to objectify as certain other aspects of a new station's operations. Nonetheless, the RHO Group began its deliberations by attempting to do precisely that. KEN GREENWOOD set forth both a list of goals and a statement of principle against which to assess strategic alternatives:

> I would suggest that a goal for the end of the first year, would be being second in the market in audience level among 18 to 49's. I think this is reasonable. In the second year, our goal ought to be second in the market overall. In the third year, we ought to be first in the target demographic group, 18 to 49's. These are reasonable goals for audience levels. As to community awareness, by the end of the second year we should be as well known as any other medium in the community; at the end of the third year, we should be the best known medium in the community.

To achieve these ends, GREENWOOD suggested the following objectives for community awareness, to create consciousness in the following order of:

1. Dial Position
2. The Local Stations Personalities
3. Network Programs
4. Specials: Olympics, etc.

In each group, participants agreed that call letters were of far less importance to the audience than were dial numbers. Audiences turn to channels, not to call letters.

Similarly, in the TAU Group, WILLIAM MOCKBEE, Director of Research, WCVB-TV, Boston, spoke of the problem of the new station in the market:

You may be owned by local business, operated by local business, employ local business people. You are still a carpet-bagger because you disturb the status quo; you disturb what has been traditional in the marketplace for 20 years.

Drawing on his own experience in establishing the new station in Boston after the demise of WHDH, MOCKBEE saw the problem for any new station as twofold: first, the identity problem—whatever the station wished to project to counteract the carpet-bagger image; and second, the recognition problem—what the station is and hopes to become. Clearly, with so many programs which might be promoted some ordering of priorities is necessary. The easiest would involve assigning priorities according to the potential audience and thus the potential revenue, of every program on the entire station schedule. Such a protocol, most of the resource persons seemed to agree, might mask some other considerations. We have already seen the extent to which local news dominance, although news may represent a smaller audience than prime time access, for example, can determine the extent of a station's total sales and audience success. Promotional planning must have such considerations firmly in mind.

A central question in planning station promotion is the extent to which it shall be done "in house" (by your own staff) and the extent to which an outside agency shall be consulted. Here the four groups developed cogent arguments which supported antithetical views on the desirability of having any outside advertising agency involvement. MOCKBEE, for example, owner of a Boston agency before joining WCVB-TV, strongly urged the TAU Group not to make use of an agency at all. MOCKBEE contended, as did some of the promotion resource persons working with other groups, that the two roles the agency would have to play—representative of the station in its own advertising campaigns and prospective customer of the station on behalf of the agency's other clients—were mutually exclusive. He declared that WCVB-TV was better served, after it had discontinued a previous relationship with an agency. JIM COPPERSMITH, citing his experience with one of MOCKBEE's Boston competitors, advised IOTA against using an agency for quite a different reason: ". . . you have a constant battle between your own creative process and your own creative people and the advertising agency. Each group spends all its time and energy criticising the other group's work; nothing constructive is accomplished." PAUL BISSONETTE, Creative Services Director for KYW-TV, Philadelphia, advising the RHO Group, took quite the opposite position:

You can never be hurt by having another creative head to work with you. You simply cannot possibly think of all the ideas yourself, mobilize all the resources yourself, tap all the trade deals yourself. These are services that an agency can perform for you and it does not have to cost you a nickel.

BISSONETTE felt the agency could "divorce its two selves" sufficiently; on the contrary, he suggested, being a client would get the station a foot in the agency's door. FRANK TUOTI, WPIX-TV, New York Vice President for Marketing, advised the SIGMA Group that a local agency, familiar with the market, would not only cost nothing since it would work on commissions in all but the nation's largest markets, but would actually save the station money since the agency would be familiar with the most cost-effective ways of mounting a campaign in that particular market. TUOTI and JUDY JURISICH, Promotion Manager, WSKB-TV, Boston, agreed that a good working relationship would be set up to offset the problems some feared to be inevitable. Others cautioned that selection of one agency involved rejection and possible consequent alienation of all others in the market. JAMES CHIRUMBULO, Program Manager, WTNH-TV, New Haven, Connecticut, advocated using an agency on a short term or consultancy basis to mount a campaign prior to the station's premiere, thus taking advantage of the agency's market expertise at a time when the work load of the station would be at peak level. In short, both resource persons and station management disagreed among themselves on the desirability of using an agency, offering strong arguments on each side of the question.

Whichever decision the station makes with respect to hiring an agency, the task before it remains the same. The agency would be merely one means toward the desired ends. Another resource which might be available to the new station, depending on whether or not the station chooses to affiliate with ABC, is the body of promotional materials developed by the network to promote its programs and personalities. This often involves, as the groups discussed, cooperative projects with locally placed print ads partially paid for out of network funds. Surprisingly, at least to some of the participants, these co-op arrangements were not perceived as unmixed blessings by station promotion departments. The products of centralized planning which so sought to standardize the network's efforts from market to market, the ads were produced at the network headquarters, often featured only network programming and sometimes included several call letters where newspaper distribution reached into more than one station's coverage area. In the event that a station wished to produce its own newspaper or other print ads, the network reserved the right to prior approval, if co-op funds were to be made available. Promotion resource people describing their network's promotional campaigns or their staffs were often reminiscent of what COPPERSMITH had described as station or agency representatives talking of each other's work.

Obviously, this is an area fraught with tension. At a minimum, what was described involved the reconciling of the ideas of two groups of creative persons with respect to content, style, scheduling and selection of media. One person told of seeing car cards on every New York City bus advertising a network's flagship station on the very day he was told by a network promotion liaison that car cards were too inefficient for co-op advertising in his and other markets. Offsetting these irritants, of course, is the considerable sum which may come into the market on a 50 per cent matching fund basis with materials tied, thematically and stylistically, to the high visibility on-air network promotion for the new program season. In Dayton, Ohio, the nation's 41st market, the seasonal premiere fund was reported as $2,600, half being paid by the network and half by the station. In New Haven, part of the nation's 21st market, Hartford, the sum was reportedly $20,000. Further, special funds were said to be available to promote new affiliates. In Dayton, when the station went on the air in 1964, this amounted to $10,000. One additional caution was mentioned by station representatives: network co-op funds are generally specified to be cash only. Stations may not "trade out" for their portion of the advertising.

Trading forms an important component of a station's advertising budget. Although many stations, as has been noted in Chapter 6, make it a matter of policy to discourage trade deals, most stations permit trade with other media for the purposes of advertising. Most of the resource persons advocated setting up promotion budgets which carefully distinguished trade expenditures from other items, salaries and cash expenditures for other media.

The relative effectiveness of various media, essential to determine before planning and budgeting could be carried out, occupied much of the time and attention of the discussants. Industry representatives agreed that broadcasting was the most effective means for promoting broadcasting. Specifically, on-air promotion was seen to be a television station's best medium for attracting an audience to a particular broadcast. Moreover, this can and should be used from the first moment the new station goes on the air, every random sampling being perceived as an opportunity to bring yet another prospective program to the attention of the sampler. Further, as ANDREW POTOS pointed out to the SIGMA Group, unless plans to use station time for promotion purposes are put into effect at the very outset, the station faces another problem:

> Normally a station in a big market—the first to the 25th, for example—will run anywhere from 6,000 to 7,000 commercial units per month. There is no way in the world that KIRT will be running that many units. In a market of Desolake's size, the maximum will probably be between 3,500 and 4,000 units in a given month. That means 2,000 or more units may go unsold. They are available for public service announcements and for whatever other use the station wishes to make of them. They are also an important and valuable promotional resource.

On-air announcements, obviously, will not be possible before the station is in operation. Prior to that time, the consensus held, radio provided the second best alternative. Radio listeners, it has been established, also watch television. This is especially true of daytime and drive time listeners. Further, radio provides a natural means for promoting television personalities. Many network news and sports figures do features on their network radio; their familiarity to affiliated radio stations' listeners can be exploited. Stars of the network entertainment broadcasts, particularly those about whom the audience may have read or whom they may have frequently seen on talk shows, can be enlisted to do radio spots promoting their shows on the new station. Radio spots can also be easily adapted from existing network fall premiere week materials.

In using radio, BILL MOCKBEE cautioned the TAU Group, attention should be given to the class as well as to the format of the stations available. Drive time would probably not be available for trade, nor, for that matter, would the dominant station in the market. Also, the price structure of the dominant station may reflect the buyer's market frequently encountered at leading stations in many radio markets today. Whether the intention is to purchase with cash or with time, however, it is important to select stations with an eye to the extent of the market they cover. Some AM frequencies, for example, are designated as local. Two of the seven Desolake AM stations are on local frequencies. Stations operating on those frequencies must use low power transmitters and their signals may not be able to reach the entire coverage area of the television station.[12] Also, since radio stations' formats are so specialized, they may present particular advantages by targeting advertising to specific segments of the audience. For example, MOCKBEE pointed out, ABC's network product appeals primarily to an 18–49 audience. Some programs however, appeal to older audiences. Accordingly, in promoting his ABC affiliate, he selects both contemporary and MOR—middle of the road—formats, the former appealing to the younger and the latter to the older-viewing segments of his audience. MOCKBEE also described a very successful promotion of a documentary on the place of the Boston Symphony Orchestra in the life of the community. In that instance WCVB-TV deliberately avoided the classical music stations, on the reasonable grounds that their audiences would be aware of the program through other media and would make a point of watching. Instead, the station concentrated its radio promotion on a rock station and on one with an MOR format. Partially, at least, because of the radio campaign, the documentary broadcast was first in its time period.

It is doubtful that anyone could produce a similar story in support of outdoor advertising. Billboards, by themselves, would hardly be credited with having developed a sufficient audience to win a time period for any particular program. Yet, billboards properly used, were seen to perform an important role in conjunction with other media. Billboards are especially effective in establishing a presence, a sense of expectation, or, as RAY STEELE argued before his colleagues in the RHO Group, an identity. STEELE advocated, as did members of the other groups, a billboard campaign to establish the channel number before going on air. PAUL BISSONETTE reminded the group that billboards can be relatively expensive, especially in terms of the three-way trades—billboards traded for a car which is, in turn, traded for air time on the station—made necessary by the fact that billboard companies, unlike newspapers and magazines, have no need to sell their products to members of the public. JIM CHIRUMBULO advised the IOTA Group to confine billboard activity to high traffic density routes and to points where traffic slowdowns habitually occur. Bill-boards, by the estimates of the outdoor advertising industry, must make their impact in eight to ten seconds, a fact which supports their effectiveness in establishing a new channel number. Billboard purchases can be made, it was pointed out in another group, to assure 25, 50, or 100% showing in combinations of locations which can be scientifically demonstrated to be seen by 25, 50 or 100% of the city's vehicular traffic within a given period.

KIRT, it has been shown, can expect to have as many as 2,000 or more unsold positions per month in its first year of operation. Three way trades for that time, as would be required for outdoor advertising, would seem, at first glance, to pose no problems. The trouble with three-way trades, however, is that they inevitably involve an additional inducement to the parties. Trades of this nature are almost never on a one-to-one basis, but almost always require the station to provide time equivalent to two or three times the value of what they get in return. The advertiser, whoever it might ultimately prove to be, will get two or three times the amount of air time for his contribution that he would have obtained by paying cash. Viewed another way, a potential advertiser on the station has been given the time at a 50 or even a 66% discount; he will be unwilling to purchase time at a later date at rate card or selling price, having once enjoyed such a discount. No such problem exists with respect to the newspaper or magazine with whom the station trades. In these cases, the trades are at one-to-one rates—a dollar's worth of air time for a dollar's worth of *TV Guide* space, for example. In addition, the station's advertising will reach an already pre-selected audience. Many studies show the television page to be the second or third most frequently seen page in newspapers; *TV Guide*'s readers are invariably interested in what is playing on television that day. Placement on the television page in the important newspaper or newspapers in a community, space adjacent to a day's listing in *TV Guide* or similar newspaper-distributed publications, can thus be seen to be very valuable, indeed. Further, ABC, like the other networks, merits a 52-week discount from *TV Guide,* a savings which can be passed on to affiliated stations. If the local papers will trade—some simply will not—such arrangements are probably, in the opinion of the participants in all four groups, to be sought.

JUDY JURISICH further reminded the SIGMA Group of the need to provide *TV Guide* and the local newspapers with accurate, up-to-date information on schedules, a massive chore requiring several days clerical work, but essential. She also recommended the servicing of suburban and outlying newspapers known to print many of the handouts supplied them, and also recognized as more read, more thoroughly, than the metropolitan papers. It was pointed out that prudence and fairness would suggest setting aside a certain proportion of the station's promotion budget to reward these papers with some paid advertising since their small individual circulations would probably not warrant the station's offering them trade deals even were they inclined to welcome such arrangements.

The importance of a separate and substantial trade budget has already been established. Each of the four groups also argued that the cash budget for a new station should also be substantial. The average selling expenses, including promotion and salesman's commissions—exclusive of agency and rep commissions—is 14.8% for profit-making affiliated stations.[13] JURISICH estimated ongoing promotion budgets as averaging two to four per cent per year. Four per cent is $40,000 per million dollars of revenue, or an average of $97,000 for the average profit-making affiliate in Market range 7, the 76th to 100th markets.[14] The inadequacy of this amount for publicizing a new station can be easily seen in one set of figures, as laid out by KEN HARWOOD and his colleagues in IOTA. A radio campaign before the station's premiere would almost undoubtedly have to be paid for in cash since the station could not yet trade out air time. Assuming that the objective was to make it impossible for any man, woman or child to overlook the exact day and hour of the station's first broadcast, a reasonable promotion plan would include a saturation campaign on local radio. Twenty-four announcements on each of 12 stations at an average cost of $17 would run to $4,800 a day or $35,000 in the week before air. REY BARNES suggested 10% of anticipated first year's gross as not unusual for a new station going on the air; COPPERSMITH, specifying a 60 share for the opening day, advocated at least $100,000 be set aside just for advertising the station's premiere.

Ultimately, the promotion problem for KIRT will come down to an ongoing series of campaigns designed to manufacture a sense of the event often enough, consistently enough, to insure the maximum possible awareness of its products. Since the methods to make the potential audience aware will have been designed with the additional criterion of making the programs, news and entertainment, local and national alike, absolutely irresistible, the campaigns will bring about sufficient audience sampling so that the programs can have the chance to develop their maximum potential.

The station will make use of a range of media, numerous devices—slogans, sounders, musical tags, generic on-air campaigns, contests, community activities—to keep itself before the public. Never again, though, will the station have the opportunity which the premiere presents. First of all, the advent of a new television station in a community the size of Desolake has to be the biggest predictable news event of the year. The opportunities for legitimate free publicity are manifest. Secondly, one of the two characteristics of a significant event, that it be demonstrably worth the public's anticipation, is clearly present. They have heard of the stars and many of the shows they will be seeing. Personalities can even be brought into town to further whet the audience's appetites. The ascertainment process will have made at least temporary publicity agents of scores of importantly connected residents, the building of facilities will have taken place over time. The facilities themselves, the tower, the studios are structures which call attention to themselves. It was reported, for example, that when Kaiser's station signed on in San Francisco they held open house on two consecutive Sundays: "The police had to come—the lines never stopped. We marched 8,000 people through that station." That natural curiosity which people seem to have about television and how it works can be further exploited; crowds waiting in line can be shown as teasers for upcoming shows; news and program personalities can actually greet the visitors, and the potential audience members can be taken one further step toward loyalty by having their views solicited on community issues or programming features they would welcome. As FRANK TUOTI, commenting on the benefits of planned year-round exploitation put it: "The untapped free participatory resources of the community are beyond our imaginings." At no time will that statement be more accurate than when KIRT-TV first goes on the air.

To insure that no opportunity is overlooked in optimizing the promotional possibilities inherent in the opening of the station, the question of when and how to go on the air becomes crucial. Since, presumably, the potential audience has been whipped up to fever pitch, they will all want something to merit their tuning in. Fall brings the premieres of the new shows, a traditional time for transit viewing; late summer, however, would make the full network fall campaign available, promising even more delights. Not only does Desolake have a full schedule of shows new to the market, soon there will be even better ones. January might permit opening with the Superbowl. In more than one group, the notion grew of opening with a telethon, either the *Jerry Lewis Muscular Dystrophy Telethon* on Labor Day weekend with its ready-made roster of big stars and feature acts, or a specially mounted local telethon. In either case, the telethon format would permit ample opportunities for local participation, both by dignitaries and by personalities, and for insertion of promos for upcoming shows. Stars of ABC shows, it was argued, might be persuaded to tape special localized inserts which would plug their shows. The telethon proponents asserted that the format provided maximum opportunity to attract an audience to watch the station's own on-air promotion, its most effective means for developing sampling audiences. Other proposals, called for opening with a special hour-long promotional show leading into a broadcast with high intrinsic appeal.

SUMMARY

Programming provides a product, by production or acquisition; news results in a daily overview of the affairs of the community and of the world; sales brings in the dollars that make possible everything a station undertakes. Promotion may bring in an audience. Without effective promotion there is no audience; with promotion, however, although there is an audience it is impossible to ascribe its presence absolutely to the efforts of the promoter. Promotion is thus viewed as a support function. But unlike many other support functions, promotion specifically requires creative people. In some stations, it is now labeled Creative Services, or Communications, or something else which acknowledges this characteristic. Creativity and the background status usually accorded staff functions are often incompatible. For that reason alone, most promotion people describe themselves as undervalued, misunderstood and seldom given the co-operation they need to perform their tasks as well as they might.[15]

As was pointed out in the beginning of this chapter, no television program can attract the audience who might wish to watch it unless they are made aware that it is on. At the very least, every program must be announced. Many programs, even most, require more assistance in reaching their potential. They must not only be announced, they must, in some way be explained, touted, exploited, glorified, puffed. Any possible reason for a viewer to wish to set aside all other alternatives for his or her life at that particular moment must be found and driven home. This is what the promotion department is really there for. If they do their work well, the program will get its largest possible audience, the news will lead the market, there will be plenty of material to develop into sales promotion and the sales figures will climb.[16] The plan for audience and for sales promotion is an essential step toward those ends.

NOTES

1. Les Brown, "Record Public-TV Rating for 'Incredible Machine'," *The New York Times,* October 30, 1975.

2. John J. O'Connor, "TV: Machine Sets Networks Reeling". *The New York Times,* October 31, 1975.

3. Arthur Unger, "Ratings Boom for 'Quality' Public TV," *The Christian Science Monitor,* November 10, 1975.

4. NSI, New York, N.Y. DMA Household Shares, time period basis, November '75, July '75, March/April '75. Nielsen lists the following UHF stations in the market: WBTB, Channel 68; WEDW, Channel 49; WLIW, Channel 21; WNJB, Channel 58; WNJM, Channel 50; WNJU, Channel 47; WNYC, Channel 31; WNYE, Channel 25; WXTV, Channel 41. All are not seen throughout the market area. Channel 68 is located in Newark, New Jersey, as is Channel 47, a Spanish-language station. Channel 41, also a Spanish-language station, is located in Paterson, New Jersey. Channels 50 and 58, located in Montclair and New Brunswick respectively, are New Jersey Public Broadcasting Authority stations actually functioning as repeaters of Channel 52, Trenton. Channel 21 is located in Garden City, New York, about 20 miles from Manhattan on Long Island. Channel 31 is a New York City owned station; Channel 25 is operated by the New York City Board of Education. Channel 49 is a public station operating in Bridgeport, Connecticut.

5. Subsequent to its first broadcast, *The Incredible Machine* was discovered to have included sequences filmed inside the bodies of rabbits and monkeys, contrary to the assertions made on the broadcast and in its advance publicity, thus touching off considerable controversy as to whether the public had been deceived. Dennis B. Kane, chief of the television division of the National Geographic Society, in accepting the blame for not including a disclaimer on the broadcast, estimated the amount of such footage as being less than five per cent of the broadcast. Repeat showings following the disclosures carried a clarification. Les Brown, "Geographic Special on Body Used Some Animals," *The New York Times,* November 15, 1975; Tom Shales, "A Flaw in the Machine?", *The Washington Post,* November 14, 1975.

6. Tom Shales, " 'Incredible Machine': A Winner for PBS," *The Washington Post,* November 1, 1975.

7. Unger, *op. cit.*

8. Shales, November 1, *op. cit.*

9. From a presentation used by the WNET development department. (Although NBC and CBS

accepted advertising for the broadcast, ABC, reportedly, refused to accept any commercials for what it correctly perceived to be a competitive broadcast. Brown; Unger; O'Connor; Shales, November 1; *op. cit.*)

10. *Ibid.*
11. Shales, November 1, *op. cit.*
12. A listing of AM frequencies by Class may be found in Exhibit 3.2 in Sydney W. Head, *Broadcasting in America: A Survey of Television and Radio,* 3rd Edition, Boston, 1976, Houghton Mifflin Company, p. 41.
13. Appendix 17, taken from Table 27, *NAB Television Financial Report,* 1976, Washington, the National Association of Broadcasters.
14. *Ibid.*
15. *vide* Howard W. Coleman, "Advertising, Promotion and Publicity", in *Television Station Management:* The Business of Broadcasting, edited by Yale Roe, New York, 1964, Hastings House, *passim.*
16. Sales promotion materials will include press releases, copies of biographical materials on station personalities, details on awards, copies of special citations and anything else which will assist the sales force in describing the station and its product to perspective buyers. Frequently, stations will develop standard presentation binders, themselves sales tools, into which those materials or suggested campaign presentations for clients can be slipped. Most stations will also supply their salesmen and reps with a body of standard materials. Typical is the kit used by radio station KBBQ-KFOX, Los Angeles, which contains:

   1. Audience composition: an analysis by occupation, income, education, automobile ownership.
   2. The radio market; call letters, dial positions, power, format.
   3. Market data and comparative rank: Population, number of households, spendable income; spendable income per household; spendable income per capita; retail sales; retail sales per household; sales of representative goods, food, drug, general merchandise, etc.
   4. A description of the typical country music station listener, particularly his leisure/consumption habits.
   5. The demographics of the country music audience.

The materials may be seen in Jay Hoffer, *Managing Today's Radio Station,* Blue Ridge Summit, Pa., 1968, Tab Books, pp. 241–254.

FOR THE STUDENT

1. Determine the attitudes of local broadcasters toward the use of agencies.
2. Prepare summaries of local rates in various media. On the basis of those rates, estimate levels of expenditure for the various stations.
3. Can promotional strategies be inferred from on-air, print or other advertising of local stations? Compare your perceptions with the stations' description of their campaigns.
4. Compare advertising strategies of an independent and of network affiliates in the same or comparable markets.
5. Obtain copies of previous year's network pre-season promotional packages.

9

Financial Planning

ONE IMPORTANT QUESTION remains to be discussed. The initial charge was to devise and describe an economically viable commercial television station: the station's plans must insure a profit. It is imperative that, at some clearly specified point, the new station's income exceed its expenditures. In Tarrytown, because time was limited, there was no specific session set aside for consideration of income versus expenditure. Each of the groups, however, detailed individuals or committees to develop projections. Thus, in their final report, IOTA presented an estimate of $800,000 in sales for the first year and planned programming and news budgets to stay within that figure. SIGMA estimated Desolake as a $6 million television market and KIRT-TV's share during its first year at 14 to 18%. Accordingly, they planned to keep the expense budget below $1 million. The other groups made comparable decisions. No realistic simulation, no matter how pressed for time, could overlook such fundamental considerations.

Presumably, costs have been or can be arrived at for all the plans laid thus far, using program cost figures, representative salaries and other figures supplied in the Appendices. Some of these costs are inescapable and not subject to change; it is simply impossible to operate a station without certain personnel, for example. The exact number and allocation of the personnel, however, is subject to a number of variables, many of them within the discretion of the management. Signing on or off at a different time might easily reduce the number of technicians required; electing to do an additional news broadcast would increase personnel in many categories—cameramen, reporters, director, among others—and would also involve expending more on news film and in processing costs.

The planning which has thus far taken place has exemplified the essence of the process: the selection, within specified constraints, of what appear to be the best possible choices in programming, news, sales, community relations and promotion for meeting the station's stated goals. These decisions involve the judgment of the planners, as individuals or corporately, with respect to what the station's product, its programming and news, will look like and what it will represent. Decisions have been made on the basis of professional projections of viewer preferences, personal taste, and good faith judgments with respect to the public interest. Program selection has taken into account such additional factors as the history of a particular program in other markets, the probability of new audiences being attracted to the use of television in a given time period, the likelihood of a specific program drawing away audience from dissimilar programs on the two other stations, the ability of a program to meet unmet needs when it is forced to compete with programs of the same type, the effect of programs on either side of the time period and the effect of the program itself on them and their ability to attract audiences.

Similarly, the News Department has been designed and staffed to provide the best possible service within the constraints as understood. Just as it would have been counter-productive to establish arbitrary cost constraints before even examining the context in which the station was to operate, the nature of the market and of the competition, so too it would be irresponsible to make capricious changes after the fact solely on the basis of cost considerations. Yet a point is always reached when any management would insist—and quite properly—that costs be examined in terms of probable revenues.

Central to such a comparison is accurate accounting. Historically, stations have combined that function with other related business management tasks in a unit known variously as Business Affairs, Administration or the Controller's Office. Some of these functions, in addition to accounting, are billing and collecting; credit management; banking; insurance; payroll and taxes; personnel and the related industrial relations and contract negotiation functions; purchasing; facilities maintainance and office management; budgets and controls; forecasting and planning.[1] Increasingly, the business unit, whatever its designation, has come to use sophisticated computer models to make its role less of an historical recording of what has happened than a predictive determination of probable developments and the elaboration of alternative strategies to deal with them. Similarly, the personnel in the unit has become more professional with an increasing reliance on MBA's with skills in forecasting, particularly with respect to revenues.

Estimating future revenues involves using one of two methods. The first is estimating the probable revenue for each program, day by day, day part by day part, hour by hour. This means estimating the audience for a particular broadcast[2] and computing what the audience would be worth were the time period sold out at the CPM rates prevailing for that time period in that market, figures which may be arrived at by examining what the competition is able to charge. Since it is highly unlikely that a new station will sell out, even in a time of year of peak demand, the projected revenue for the time period will be a percentage of computed maximum potential. When all time periods are thus analyzed, their cumulative revenue provides a projection of the station's income.

This protocol involves a detailed estimate making allowances for readjustments due to variables—network lead-in or the availability of a particular syndicated series, for example. It also involves a two step estimate: the estimated audience share is the basis for determining the maximum rate to be charged; a further estimate of the percentage of inventory which might be sold yields the forecast revenue for each time period. In some cases, such a micro-analytic process may generate far more accurate predictions than would be available using any other method. For example, in counterprogramming a family appeal syndicated series opposite a news program, the station can draw upon detailed historical data on the series' performance in attracting various demographic groups as well as the rating services computations of the number of persons in particular groups not hitherto being attracted to television during the time period or, with even greater significance, turned away at the conclusion of earlier programming. In the absence of such data, however, it would be difficult to develop meaningful estimates. On the contrary, there is a very great possibility of elaborating a fiction too attenuated to rely upon.

A second method of forecasting revenue might be more helpful. That method involves the estimating of market share on an annual basis. For markets where there are three or more commercial stations, the FCC publishes revenue and expense data summaries.[3] For other markets, data may be extrapolated from NAB figures for typical stations in the market range.[4] Thus, NAB figures for Market Size 7 (ARB Markets 76 to 100) detailing profit margin, time sales, total revenue, total and selected expense items, would provide a background for estimating the total market in Desolake.

These data are, of course, historical. What is needed is a means by which to predict future developments in the market. Economists and planners use data other than past performance. They will examine various economic indicators such as retail sales volume, fluctuations in disposable income, shifts in local or regional economies, industrial production, housing starts, and other descriptors of the economy of the nation or of the market to develop models for predicting future market size. Economists differ in their judgment of the comparative utility of particular factors in this process. Despite these differences, a number of highly sophisticated and uncannily accurate models for estimating future television markets have been devised. JANE LOKSHIN, Director of Economic Research and Senior Economist for RCA outlined some of her thinking at the Tarrytown Seminar. Concerned with macro-analysis, and looking at the entire American economy in order to assess the future of broadcasting on a national scale, she uses such indicators as industrial production, retail sales adjusted to exclude the effects of inflation, trends in payroll employment, real consumer income, gross private domestic investment, especially change in business inventories and producers' durable equipment, to predict the economic climate and its effect on television: "There is usually a four or five quarter lag between an upturn in profits and a subsequent upturn in advertising."

AARON COHEN, then Vice President for Research of the NBC Television Network, estimated that Ms. LOKSHIN and her colleagues have been accurate with respect to forecasting network business for NBC, to within one percent on an annual and three to four percent on a quarterly basis. Major market station forecasters also report accuracy within a very small percentage. In New York and some other major markets, the accuracy of forecasting share of market can be judged on a monthly basis. In those major markets, stations submit their total revenues for the month, in confidence, to one of the large and prestigious accounting firms. In New York, Arthur Young and Company serves this function. They, in turn, inform the station what percentage of the total market that figure represented for the month in question. Although the figures for individual competing stations are not revealed, the market is broken down in terms of total share by independent and by affiliate stations. Thus the accuracy of the stations' forecasting of share of market can be determined on a month by month basis and need not wait, as is the case in most markets, for the annual FCC total market summary.

In estimating share of market, it is important to recognize that the total revenue in the market will vary each year. One of the largest variations will occur during the first year of operation of the new station. During that year, the total inventory of television time available in the market will increase by fifty percent. Where before there were 18 minutes for sale in any given prime-time hour, for example, now there will be 27. This will bring about a reduction in price since, at the beginning, no new advertising dollars will be coming in to the market. Rather, the national advertisers will probably spend the same amount as last year but divide their purchases among three stations where before they were divided between two. Similarly, until the new station is established, local advertising will come from the same sources as before, again divided by three rather than by two. What will develop is a classic economic situation in which a limited number of dollars will be sought by a greatly expanded and competitive television market. In such a situation, a buyer's market develops and price inevitably falls. In the very near future, however, the decline in price should result in the attraction of advertising dollars now being spent elsewhere in the market. A Brookings Institution study of television economics explains:

The factors governing supply and demand in television advertising are in several ways unique. From the standpoint of the individual advertiser, television is a substitute for other media, so that his demand for television advertising, all other things being equal, is highly elastic—that is, a small percentage change in price leads to a large percentage change in demand—at a price per household comparable with prices in other media (corrected for differences among the media in the productivity per household of advertising). In this range, advertisers switch rapidly from other media to television as the (relative) price of television advertising per viewer-minute falls.[5]

The result of this fall in price will be a shift in advertising dollars from radio and, probably to an even greater extent, from newspapers. Thus, if at the inception of a new station the total advertising revenue for the market were divided as follows:

Television	Radio	Newspapers	Other
30%	20%	45%	5%

one might expect a shift to television of as much as 10% in the first year after the introduction of the third station and of an additional five percent in the second year. This shift will generally not continue thereafter, since the effects of the price reduction in a market in which television has been offered for twenty years will be rapid and will not involve any secondary price reduction due to increased audience. As Noll, Peck and McGowan have found, "evidence . . . suggests that once two stations are available, the total audience is insensitive to a change in the number of stations."[6]

How can we determine the advertising revenues for any particular market? Since broadcasters are required to report their revenues to the FCC and since these revenues are, in most cases, published, as has been pointed out earlier, it is easy to estimate the size of the Desolake market. The typical station in the ARB 76th to 100th markets had a total revenue in 1975 of $2,298,500.[7] Using that figure as a guide, one could assume that the equivalent of the 75th market, with two commercial stations, would have television advertising revenues in excess of $4.6 million. An even more accurate estimate might be arrived at by looking at the total market figures in a range of markets of approximately the same size as derived from figures reported to the FCC.[8] The average revenue in the five television markets was $5,814,565. Although radio markets are not exactly coterminous with television markets, revenue figures may also be obtained for radio from the FCC summary. In the five markets under consideration, there are 47 AM and AM/FM stations reporting an average market revenue of $2,547,565.[9] FM-only figures in the 73rd through 77th markets averaged an additional $223,752.[10] Thus:

Market Size	Market	Total
73	Fresno	$6,964,963
74	Springfield–Decatur–Champaign (Ill.)	$7,621,667
75	Portland–Poland Springs (Me.)	$5,065,702
76	Chattanooga	$4,800,783
77	Spokane	$4,619,710

Newspaper revenues are not as easily obtained. Newspapers are not federally regulated, as are radio and television stations, and do not accordingly have to make their earnings as licensees a matter of public record. Furthermore, most newspapers are still held by family trusts; they do not even have to make their annual reports to stockholders widely available as publicly traded corporations must. Ways to estimate newspaper advertising revenue are, however, available. Annually, *Editor and Publisher,* a trade magazine for publishers and advertisers, publishes a compilation of retail, general, automotive, financial, classified and total advertising linage. For 1975, the data detailed advertising carried by 1,319 newspapers in 735 cities. Total linage for the five markets we have been considering was as follows:

City	Number	When Published	Linage	
Fresno	1	Evening/Sunday	35,224,761	
Springfield	1	Morning/evening/Sunday	26,348,854	
Portland	3	Morning/Evening/Sunday	35,037,285	
Chattanooga	1	Evening/Sunday	18,110,188	
Spokane	2	Morning/Sunday Evening	41,985,283	(11)

Average linage for the five cities was 31,341,000.

Standard Rate and Data Service publishes *Newspaper Rates and Data,* a listing similar to that published for radio or television stations which gives the advertising rates for newspapers in various markets.[12] From such data, approximation of revenues can be derived. Rates are usually quoted in terms of lines, 14 agate lines being equal to one column inch. A *flat rate* means that the rate does not vary no matter how much space is used or how often the advertising is placed. An *open rate,* or *sliding scale rate* denotes that bulk and frequency discounts are applied.[13] In the Appendices to this volume, open rates are given for the two Desolake newspapers.

In the event a newspaper quotes only a flat rate, that figure might be multiplied by the total linage to arrive at the advertising revenue for a given year. Where the newspaper quotes an open rate, an estimate must be made as to the probable actual percentage of full rate obtained.

If one were to assume that all advertising sold in the two daily papers and one Sunday newspaper in Desolake were sold at the equivalent of the lowest open rate given, the total volume, assuming total linage in Desolake to be equal to the average linage of the same five markets we have been considering, would be $18,804,600. This is more than three times the probable total of the television market and something between five and six times the size of the total local sales registered by the two Desolake stations, assuming local to represent 60% of total revenue. This figure is remarkably consistent with estimates derived in other studies. One such study conducted by CBS found that newspaper revenues equalled 7.5 to 10 times the local portion of television revenue in the 25 markets studied. Further, the study found that a most significant factor in determining what that multiple would be is the number of newspapers in the market. If one newspaper dominates the market, the total advertising revenue is relatively small. The presence of a second newspaper of consequence made for a much larger total revenue. In general this would seem to be because retailers are far less cognizant of cost per thousand figures than of the amount of advertising they believe necessary to cover the market.

Atlanta and Houston are the nation's 16th and 14th largest markets. Atlanta has 818,500 ADI television households; Houston has only 38,000 more. Yet Houston has two major competing newspapers, the *Post,* a morning paper with a Sunday edition, and the *Chronicle,* which appears in the evening and also publishes on Sunday. Annual linage for the daily papers is close to 98,000,000. Total linage in Houston is 140,442,000. In Atlanta, with the commonly published *Constitution,* a morning paper, and *Journal,* which publishes in the evening, and a single combined Sunday paper, total linage was 96,967,000. Linage in the dailies was 76,719,000. Thus, although Houston has only 5% more households, advertising linage in Houston was almost 45% greater than in Atlanta.[14] In smaller markets, where retail competition is less acute, the ratio of newspaper advertising revenues to local television is probably in the range of five to seven to one.[15]

Once the expected growth of the market as a result of attracted dollars from other media is calculated, two other factors must be entered. Inflation will cause a rise in price and consequent rise in revenues on top of the expected enlarged market. Even after the market stabilizes and the effect of adding a third station is no longer felt, inflation at a probable rate of 5% per year will still have to be considered. So too will the effect of population growth; revenues will rise proportionately. Since television stations are selling access to audiences on a cost-per-thousand basis, a growth in population will make television advertising inevitably more efficient; more households can be delivered for the same cost, thereby reducing the CPM for the given time period.

This fact has significant long-term implications since newspapers and other print media always encounter a rise in costs in order to accommodate an increase in readership. Although a television station can deliver its programs with no consequent change in production or delivery costs as population increases within its coverage area, every increase in a newspaper's circulation demands the printing of more newspapers and the incurring of higher delivery costs. Thus the relative efficiency will favor television over newspapers so long as television's basic production costs do not rise so much more rapidly than newspapers' as to render television non-competitive. Population growth will vary from market to market. Figures for any given city are available from the Chamber of Commerce or from the United States Census Bureau. The rate of population growth for Desolake can be extrapolated from the growth rate for the previous decade, available in Appendix 2.

Over time, there is no reason to believe that the new station's revenue will not reach 33% of a three-station market. Initially, however, there are several factors which will impede the station in reaching anywhere near its potential. The market will be undergoing profound changes with the introduction of the third station. At the very beginning, these changes will inevitably favor the more stable, older stations. The new station, on the other hand, will be experiencing some start up problems. At the very least, a new team will be unable to assure advertisers that their commercials will be given service at the same level of efficiency customary at the older stations. Also, there will be a lengthy period before the new station has developed its agency relationships. Much of the station's business, as has been pointed out, must be conducted on faith, at least until the first and probably the second and third rating books appear. Persuading agencies to do business on that basis involves developing a trust that the schedule will run as ordered, that the pre-emption policy is applied as agreed upon and that billings are accurate. Developing billing procedures which are not only accurate but thorough and timely, and developing credit and collection mechanisms will take time.

How the budget will correspond to the expected revenue based on estimated share of market will vary with such factors as the extent of capitalization of the station, the expectations of the financial principals and the policies of the management. One successful general manager, looking at the Desolake problem, cautioned that if the market were estimated at six million, the total budget of the station should not exceed one million dollars if the station wished to break even during the first year. This figure he arrived at by considering that total revenues would be at most $1.75 million in the first year. However, since cash flow will be far slower than usual in the first year and since there will have to be heavy expenditures for features and other syndicated products which will be amortized very heavily for their first and second plays, the operating budget would have to be set at considerably below the anticipated revenue. Other observers, thinking in terms of being able to carry the station for several years before showing a profit, would be willing to sanction a larger budget.

The table entitled "Affiliated Revenue and Expense Yardsticks Market Size 7 (ARB 76–100)" found in Appendix 7 presents a form for assembling financial data so that budgeted expense items may be compared with estimated revenue. The items shown in this NAB summary are those which are reported to the FCC. Another and perhaps a more helpful form, in that it more nearly represents the structure of the typical station's operation today, is that devised by the Institute of Broadcasting Financial Management (IBFM) and published in their *Accounting Manual for Broadcasters* [16]. This breaks cost and expenses down into Operating, Selling and General Expenses. Operating expenses are grouped under the following headlines: Program and Production; Transmitter; Studio; News and Public Affairs. Selling expenses are divided into Sales Department and Advertising.

Historically, television program production expenses, like motion pictures before them, have been broken down into *Above-the-Line* and *Below-the-Line* costs. Although the heavy black line across the page is widely thought to divide the creative from the craft elements, a more useful distinction as far as films are concerned is between those elements and persons whose services are individually negotiated and those—below-the-line—whose services are not. Above-the-line elements include: Story; Producer; Director; Cast; and expenses directly associated with them. Below-the-line expenses include technical; scenic; wardrobe; make-up and hairdressing; location expenses; transportation; film processing; film or tape stock; music; and other show costs. [17] For purposes of planning, such a matrix helps discipline thinking about local production and particularly about the production of major station efforts.

A far more troublesome concept in arriving at a station's budget is the need to establish a film amortization schedule. Unlike syndicated programming which is purchased on a per-episode price basis, film is purchased in packages and at a rate which covers a number of "plays" over a specified long term. For purposes of this exercise, all film purchases are assumed to be for five plays per title over five years. At first glance, it would appear that each run of each film would cost the station $200. Indeed, some authorities have suggested that the station write off the showings at that rate, or even that the five allowable runs be charged off evenly throughout the contract term, a suggestion which has been hotly disputed by most financial planners:

> . . . on the grounds that (1) it fails to give accounting recognition to the fact that films included in a package are rarely of the same quality, (2) it fails to recognize that the necessity of maintaining attractive programming often causes station management to forego reruns to which they are technically entitled, and (3) it ignores the prevailing belief among broadcasters that programs normally earn a smaller amount of revenue from each successive re-showing. For these reasons, this method is generally considered unsatisfactory.[18]

Let us examine these objections in some detail. There may be any number of reasons why a station might not wish to show every film in a purchased package its full number of allowable plays. One particular film may do unusually well in a particular market; another film may do unusually poorly. A station buying Premium Package 2 from Metromedia might find it impossible to run *Class of '63* in a market where the high school football team met with a tragic accident in that year. Many stations found themselves with films in which Ronald Reagan appeared which could not be played during his bid for the Republican Presidential nomination. A particular market may have been so saturated with one genre of film, the Western perhaps, that no such film, no matter how well made or how well received elsewhere, can be played anywhere but in children's time. It should be obvious that films cannot be considered equally valuable.

Less obvious, but perhaps more important, is the fact that two showings of the same film cannot be equated. When a film package is purchased, it represents an asset to the station, an asset which will never again be worth as much. When the new station goes on the air, for example, most of its films will never have been seen in the market. Their exploitational value is at its highest. Once a given film has been seen, it will lose some of that value. After its second showing, it will lose still more. If films are written off at the same rate for each showing, the declining value of the station's film library may be masked and management might well be deprived, in the name of cost control, from acting in time to maintain the commercial viability of its film programming. Moreover, the true value of the station's assets may not be reflected in its P & L statements.

To avoid these problems, most stations amortize their film packages according to a formula which is front-loaded to account for the declining value of a library as its films have been shown. Many such formulas have been devised. One of the simpler, and one frequently used by stations, is one which requires periodic review to assure that permitted runs are converted into expected runs to avoid excessive writing off of unused plays at the expiration of a particular contract:

Percentage charged to each showing	Number of showings permitted or expected			
	2	3	4	5
First......................	65	50	40	35
Second....................	35	35	30	25
Third......................	--	15	20	20
Fourth....................	--	--	10	15
Fifth.....................	--	--	--	5
Total Percentage	100	100	100	100 (19)

Other formulas involve the conversion of day parts into prime time or into early fringe, in much the same manner as network affiliation agreements convert time, based on difference in earning power. A percentage of the film package contract price is then charged off each year based on the station's forecast of the use to which the package will be put.[20]

Let us assume, to take a much simplified example, that the station has purchased a package of 12 films which it plans to run in four regular 90-minute time periods, its weekly early fringe film series, a weekly late fringe period, a Saturday afternoon and a Sunday morning series. The contract period is three years. Five plays are permitted. The station plans to run one film a month in its early fringe series during the first year and give each film its second run, during the same year, in the late fringe series. During the second year, each film will get its third play in the late fringe series and its fourth in the Saturday afternoon time period. During the third year, each title will get a fifth play on Sunday morning. Again, for the purposes of simplifying the example, let us assume that late fringe is worth 60% of early fringe, the Saturday afternoon period is worth 40%, and the Sunday morning worth 20%. Since the film is calculated to run 90 minutes, we can convert the schedule into the equivalent of early fringe hours as follows:

First Year

12 X 1.5 X 100% = 18.0
12 X 1.5 X 60% = 10.8

                  28.8

Second Year

12 X 1.5 X 60% = 10.8
12 X 1.5 X 40% = 7.2

                  18.0

Third Year

12 X 1.5 X 20% = 7.2

Since this totals 54 fringe hour equivalents, the package can be charged off proportionately as follows:

```
First year  (28.8 hrs).....    53.4%

Second year (18 hrs).......    33.3%

Third year  (7.2 hrs)......    13.3%
```

Another variant would account for the difference in accuracy of forecasting and the likelihood that changes in the station's scheduling would be more apt to happen at the end of the contract period. Under this method, each year is given a discounted value. Thus the annual equivalent broadcast hours in the preceding example would be discounted as follows:

	Equivalent Hours	Discounted Value	Amount
First year	28.8	100%	28.8
Second year	18.0	80%	14.4
Third year	7.2	60%	4.3
			47.5

Under this formula, the write-off would be as follows:

	Discounted Hours	Percentage of 47.5
First year	28.8	61%
Second year	14.4	30%
Third year	4.3	9 %
		100%

Obviously, such discounting permits the station to write off even more of the total package costs in the first years of a long term contract thus avoiding the necessity of writing off heavy amounts of unplayed product at the end of a contract term and also providing a more realistic framework for examining the asset value of film library packages. Further, since the last two methods amortize packages rather than individual films they take into account the differences among titles within a package.

Whichever accounting methods are adopted, it should be clear that accurate forecasting is the key to budgeting and that budgeting is essential to the operation of a profitable commercial station. As Joseph K. Mikita, Vice-president, Finance, Westinghouse Broadcasting Company, put it in an often quoted statement:

Forecasting has become a necessity in television broadcasting because of the high cost of operation and because the profit margin is highly susceptible to unfavorable variations in an increasing sales pattern. There is a reasonably fixed level of operating costs which bears little or no relation to the amount of commercial business the station enjoys. Beyond this level of fixed costs, or break-even volume, the television station can convert a substantial part of sales improvements into operating profit. Conversely, a drop-off in business is generally reflected in reduction in operating profit. It is essential, therefore, that for a healthy growth in profitability, the gross business improvement inherent in a young and dynamic industry contain within itself a satisfactory margin of profit. The measure of profitability must therefore be applied to new ventures in programming, promotion, facilities improvement and, in fact, to any other area designed to increase the gross revenue of a station.[21]

Mikita was writing of a station already in operation; his statements are equally, if not more, relevant to a new station.

NOTES

1. Joseph K. Mikita, "The Controller's Role in Management," in Yale Roe, ed., *Television Station Management: The Business of Broadcasting,* New York, 1964, Hastings House, provides a more detailed examination of many of these functions as long performed. Another interesting analysis of their relation to total station operation as seen in an NAB survey of broadcasting organizational structure can be found in Sydney W. Head, *Broadcasting in America: A Survey of Radio and Television,* Third Edition, Boston, 1976, Houghton Mifflin Company, pp. 218–220.
2. *vide,* discussion on projected audience share in Programming, *supra.*
3. ————. *39th Annual Report/Fiscal Year 1973,* Federal Communications Commission, pp. 223–243.
4. ————, *NAB Television Financial Report 1976,* Washington, D.C., National Association of Broadcasters. Table 8, Table 27 and Table 60 are reproduced in Appendix 7.
5. Roger G. Noll, Morton J. Peck and John J. McGowan, *Economic Aspects of Television Regulation,* Washington, D.C., 1973, The Brookings Institution, p. 34.
6. *Ibid.,* p. 36.
7. *loc. cit.,* Table 8.
8. 39th Annual Report, op. cit., pp. 239–241.
9. *Ibid.,* pp. 260–266.
10. *Ibid.,* pp. 255–257.
11. ————. "Report of Newspaper Advertiser Linage for 1975", *Editor and Publisher,* May 29, 1976, pp. 1L–11L.
12. *Newspaper Rates and Data,* published monthly by Standard Rate and Data Service, includes market data, information about newspapers in general and listings for individual papers. A typical listing includes information under the following categories: Personnel; Representative; Commission and Cash Discounts; Advertising Rates; General; Line Rate; Color; Classifications (special rates for sections such as Amusements or Financial); Inserts and Preprints; Position Charges; Classified; Supplements; Contract and Copy Regulations; Closing Time; Mechanical Measurements; and Circulation.

13. Roger Barton, *Media in Advertising,* New York, 1964, McGraw-Hill, pp. 79–83.
14. "Report of Newspaper Advertiser Linage for 1975", *op. cit.*
15. Care must be exercised in attempting to develop income from linage figures. Such factors as daily versus Sunday differentials, differences in cost for various classifications of advertising: local, national, amusements, classified, etc., may prove misleading.
16. Ward L. Quaal and James A. Brown, *Broadcast Management: Radio and Television,* 2nd Edition, New York, 1976, Hastings House, p. 284., *et seq.* contains a copy of the form and a valuable discussion of the topic.
17. Warde B. Ogden, *The Television Business: Accounting Problems of a Growth Industry,* New York, 1961, The Ronald Press Company, pp. 36–38.
18. *Ibid.* p. 132.
19. *Ibid.*
20. *Ibid.* pp. 133–137 contain a discussion of various amortization formulas upon which the following section draws heavily.
21. *loc. cit.* pp. 94–95.

FOR THE STUDENT

1. Based on what is available public knowledge about a station in your market, its rate card, its program schedule, data on employment in its public files, FCC reports, and what can be surmised from data on comparable stations, develop an estimated annual budget.

10

Conclusion:
Faculty and Industry
Proposals

LIKE THOSE WHO are using this book to work out their own solutions to the simulation problem, the four groups of participants at the IRTS Fifth Annual Faculty–Industry Seminar meeting in Tarrytown devised program schedules, news departments, ascertainment plans, rate cards, and promotional campaigns for the new commercially viable VHF in Desolake. As a final step before committing their plans to paper, each group met with the General Manager of a successful station who was charged, in this instance, with taking the role of the major financial backer of the proposed station. IOTA Group met with Lawrence P. Fraiberg, Vice-President and General Manager of WNEW-TV, New York. RHO Group met with Alan J. Bell, Vice-President and General Manager of KYW-TV, Philadelphia, Pa. TAU Group met with Bob J. Wormington, President and General Manager of KMBA-TV, Kansas City, and SIGMA Group met with Arthur A. Watson, Executive Vice-President and General Manager of WNBC-TV, New York. Some of the General Managers projected themselves fully into the role of wary stockholders; all served to bring to bear their own experienced judgment on the groups' plans.

If there was an expected similarity in certain aspects of the four solutions to the problem, there was, nonetheless, great diversity in emphasis. There was also variety in their style of presentation, as can be seen in what follows.

IOTA PRESENTATION

Rapporteurs: F. Dennis Lynch (Cleveland State University)
John Keshishoglou (Ithaca College)

LYNCH:

	We're going to tell you about the
Take 5	new boy in town...
	KIRT-TV, Channel 5
	the vital voice of Desolake, Kansouri.
	KIRT-TV plans to serve the community
Service	better than the existing media by . . .
	presenting quality programs of
	entertainment, news and community
Service	service.
Quality	
	By these means and by the way IOTA
	Group has programmed the station,
	it will deliver . . .
Profit	
Service	a profit.
Quality	

Young Active Stylish	Channel 5 will have a young, active and stylish look. By that we don't mean it will be stylish in the sense of Cher,

but crisp, distinct, professional...

from the graphics down to the way each

cameraman shoots--professional.

Young Active Stylish All-family FIVE	The station will be programmed as an all-family station and it will be targeted primarily to the 18 to 49 age group and to women. We will be going after that demographic group specifically.

We programmed the station for immediate impact through counter programming. We rejected the alternative—which we considered to the extent of drawing up a program schedule—of making a slower impact on the community and on the market through parallel programs. It is our hope to come close to breaking even during the first year of operation.

The first major programming decision we made was to affiliate, a decision made for a number of reasons:

One: Affiliates can charge more for time.
Two: Programming costs will be less.
Three: First run programming will be available to us.
Four: Network news sources and resources will be available to us.
Five: Network sports programs will be available.
Finally: Affiliation does not preclude selective pre-empting for local
            programming.

With that decision to affiliate with ABC in mind, let us look at the group's specific decisions of the program schedule and the now familiar opposition schedules so that you can see the contrast. We are offering what we hope will prove to be an attractive alternative:

KNAC	KGBA		KIRT	COMMENTS
Rural		6	AG SHOW	
"		:30	NEW ZOO REVIEW	Some children's shows in the morning.
News	News	7	MICKEY MOUSE	
Today	"	:30	BEVERLY HILLBILLIES	
"	Capt. Kang.	8	ROMPER ROOM	
"	"	:30	"	
Celeb Sweep	Spinoff	9	DINAH!	followed by DINAH!
Wheel Fortune	Gambit	:30	"	A woman's group until we join the network at
High Rollers	Rattle Tale	10	GILLIGAN'S ISLAND	
Hlwood Squares	Love of Life	:30	ABC NETWORK HAPPY DAYS	10:30 and stay with network through the soap opera period.
Magic Marble	Young and Restless	11	SHOWOFF	
Jackpot	Search for Tomorrow	:30	ALL MY CHILDREN	We decided against running a noon news program.
News	Weather Woman's World	12	RYAN'S HOPE	
Days of Our Lives	As The World Turns	:30	MAKE A DEAL	
"	Guiding Light	1	$10,000 PYRAMID	
Doctors	Edge of Night	:30	RHYME AND REASON	
Another World	Price Is Right	2	GENERAL HOSPITAL	
"	Match Game	:30	ONE LIFE TO LIVE	

Now look at the early fringe period:

KNAC	KGBA		KIRT	COMMENTS
Somerset	Musical Chairs	3	LAND OF GIANTS	Again we are offering alternatives.
Be My Guest	Mike Douglas	:30	"	
Jeannie	"	4	VOYAGE TO THE BOTTOM OF THE SEA	We picked old ABC shows because they will be first run in the Desolake Area.
Huck and Yogi	"	:30	"	

Let me side track from the program schedule for just a moment here to tell you something of the promotion schedule now that you have seen some of the programs.

We are going to be using in our promotion a Channel 5 country slogan:

Channel	"Desolake is Channel 5
5 Country	Country!"

Kid—	We will promote the several kinds of
Dinah!—	programs we have as "Adventure Country,"
Adventure—	"Mystery Country," and so on. We will
Movie—	use this in radio spots and in our own
	on air promotion.
Country	

Kid—	
Dinah!—	
Adventure—	The high point of this will be:
Movie—	"Channel 5 is going to be your
	country."
Country	
Your Country	

Now let's return to early fringe time and to the lead in to prime time access.

KNAC	KGBA		KIRT	COMMENTS
Truth or Consequences	Dialing for Dollars	5	BOWLING FOR DOLLARS	Here, in early fringe and the lead in to prime time access we offer new adventure and bowling for a strong lead to what we consider the key program EYEWITNESS NEWS.
NBC News	CBS News	:30	EYEWITNESS NEWS	
Local News	Local News	6	ABC NEWS	
Various	Various	:30	ADAM 12	We initially had decided not to try to go up against the NBC affiliate's news programs because one look at the ratings shows they are very solid. So we were going to program only late news. Then we decided it would be good programming to move into the early period with proper promotion and proper lead in. So we are going against their network with our local news, then network news and ADAM 12 as a strong lead in to network programming.
NBC Network	CBS Network	7	ABC NETWORK	

Now let me talk for a moment about our news department and about our news broadcasts. The key point is that we believe news to be vitally important to the station—both for the station's image and for its income. And the key to our success will be the time of our broadcasts:

	We are not going to be like the competition—insensitive to viewers. We are not going to deal with the
Responsible Responsive Reporting	institutions or with the power structure in the community. We are going to deal with the individuals. We are going to be responsive to all--particularly to the Blacks in our audience.

We will have a style, a professional look which tells our audience we have made a major commitment to news.

Our procedure will be to hire a news director and a news consultant. They will determine the format and hire the rest of the staff.

Responsible	The staff will include a city reporter
Responsive	and a suburban reporter, a third reporter—
Reporting	anchor person and full time
(And Reporters!)	sports and weather people.

We will have three cameramen and we will commit to ENG at the first opportunity.

The format will be based on the news consultant's market research and designed to identify voids and fill them, aiming the program towards the 18 to 49 market and to women.

The news director will be charged specifically by management to relate all news items to the individual—to use all available technology to say that . . .

	we care about the community and about
We Care	the people. We are professionals—
We Know	we know what is important, we know
Issues	how to select what is important,
Technology	we can provide the background and
Professional	the content. We are involved with
	issues as well as events.

We use all available technology not to present an image but to tell the story as clearly as possible. To develop and project a feeling of professionalism.

We have a team, confident and with a sense of humor, but not frivolous. We take news seriously.

As a matter of policy, the news director will be insulated from pressures from within or from without. He will be given complete responsibility for the news consistent with the license responsibilities of management.

The station will editorialize when needed and will do documentaries, minidocs and features in response to community needs developed in the ascertainment process. These, too, will be aimed at the 18 to 49 audience.

Now let us return to the program schedule for late fringe, the period after network prime time programming:

KNAC	KGBA		KIRT	COMMENTS
News	News	10	PERRY MASON	Once again, KNAC is
Tonight	CBS Movie	:30	" "	very stong in its
"	"	11	LOCAL NEWS	late news so we are
"	"	:30	MOVIE	counterprogramming.
Tomorrow	Off	12	"	Eventually, when our
"		:30	"	quality begins to tell,
Off		1	OFF	we hope to move our news

up to 10 and compete

directly.

Saturday morning is the children's hour—"Kid Country" followed by "Adventure Country"—we stay with network until we bring in our VOYAGE TO THE BOTTOM OF THE SEA and ADAM 12:

KNAC	KGBA		KIRT	COMMENTS
Network		7	ABC NETWORK	
local movies				
local sports				
		5:30	VOYAGE TO THE	After ADAM 12, we go to
NBC News	CBS News		BOTTOM OF THE SEA	the network.
Lawrence	HeeHaw	6	"	Late fringe is the same
Welk		:30	ADAM 12	as Monday–Friday:
"	"			PERRY MASON followed

by News at 11.

On Sunday, we have religion and ABC until 11:00:

KNAC	KGBA		KIRT	COMMENTS
local and		7	RELIGION	
religion				
"		9:30	ABC	
"		11	TOWN MEETING	This program incorporates

the various commitments

for public service prog-

ramming that we made to

the FCC in the applicat-

ion.

The TOWN MEETING program will focus on minority groups, the elderly, and others that we promised special programs for. We felt the TOWN MEETING format would not only be cheaper to produce but would also be more flexible than the programs that were laid out in the application.

Ascertainment will be a continuing responsibility for management; all management level staff are charged in written policy to conduct ascertainment interviews whenever they talk to anyone in the community. For the general public survey we will hire an ABD from Piedmont University who will, with his students and his research class, provide us with a continuing ongoing ascertainment and with other research to meet the needs of a new station in the market. The phone log, the letters we receive, what we learn from community activities, what the news department learns—all will form a part of the ascertainment. As a matter of policy, our staff meetings will cover the results of these surveys so that they are translated into programming, and not just filed away. There will be documentaries and mini-docs in the news dealing with the community problems, and six times a year we will move our TOWN MEETING into prime time for a major forum with a live studio audience and with phone-in facilities.

After the weekly TOWN MEETING on Sundays, more action and adventure:

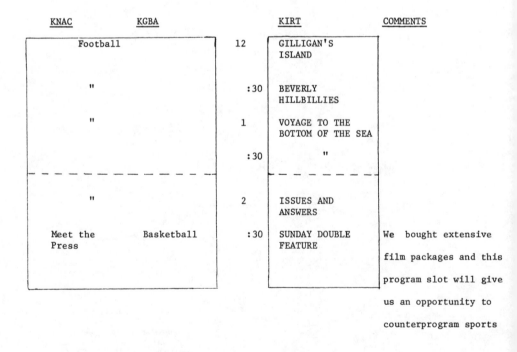

KNAC	KGBA		KIRT	COMMENTS
Football		12	GILLIGAN'S ISLAND	
"		:30	BEVERLY HILLBILLIES	
"		1	VOYAGE TO THE BOTTOM OF THE SEA	
		:30	"	
"		2	ISSUES AND ANSWERS	
Meet the Press	Basketball	:30	SUNDAY DOUBLE FEATURE	We bought extensive film packages and this program slot will give us an opportunity to counterprogram sports

KNAC	KGBA		KIRT	COMMENTS
Network		6	ABC NETWORK	on the other networks
				We can also cut back to
News	News	10	ABC NEWS/LOCAL	one or no feature to
Movie	Movie	:30	MOVIE	accommodate ABC Sports.
Sign-off	Sign-off		SIGN-OFF	

We have talked of spending money—$237,000 for programming, approximately $250,000 for news. We turn now to the side of the station that is going to make big money. We plan a very aggressive sales posture. We will assert that Channel 5 can do it better than any other medium in Desolake.

We will hire a general sales manager who will be a local person, possibly hired from the competition, but certainly one who knows the local market. He will be responsible for local sales and he will have a local sales staff of three. We felt that that was a little small but it would permit us to give very good incentives to the salesmen. We would expect each of them to sell about $5,000 a week, which would give them a fairly good income, on 10% commission. We expect our first year's local sales to be about $800,000.

KIRT's salesmen will be required, again as a matter of policy, to make calls on clients that are not yet advertising on television. To help them, we will prepare a distinctive, high quality sales presentation, again featuring the young demographics that we hope to track. We will vigorously attract advertisers from all media and not just seek to take advertising away from the other two stations in the market.

There will be a national sales manager responsible to the general sales manager. We plan to select a national rep with a very good record of selling difficult properties like ABC affiliates and independents. The Petry Organization would be our first choice. Tele-Rep, RTV are among others we would consider. We will pay up to 15% commission to the rep.

We will subscribe to the NAB code and we'll take both ARB and Nielsen. If we have to cut back to only one it would be ARB.

We will have a single rate card and it will be quite similar to those of the other two stations. We do not plan to attract our advertising by making price cuts because we do not want to destabilize the market. Instead, we will offer other incentives, good service, production services to our accounts at a break-even cost, for example. We hope eventually to have production as a profit center, but in the beginning if the advertiser is going to place the commercial with us exclusively, we will produce it for him on a break-even basis. We will do a limited amount of trade offs—except to the other media where we will trade off very generously.

Now for our promotion plans. We have a promotion manager hired from the competition or at least from elsewhere in the market, a long time resident of Desolake who understands advertising, production, and publicity. Our first year promotion budget will be $100,000, which is a little high compared to the figures we have, but we feel that it would be very quickly returned to the station.

We will have a three part campaign. First, prior to the opening of the station, it is our goal that every man, woman and child in Desolake will know that Channel 5 is coming to town. We will be number one on opening night with at least a 60 share. The keynote of the campaign will be that a vital new force is coming to Desolake, and that people who view Channel 5, KIRT-TV will be highly entertained. For the opening campaign, and, just for that, we will hire an advertising agency, and they will design for us the graphic look of the station, everything from the letterhead to the logo on the news vehicles. The campaign will begin three weeks before opening and will peak during the last week. We will use supermarket throw-aways, the local paper—particularly Sunday TV supplements—and we will use billboards. Our primary effort will be in radio, particularly during the last week. The radio spots will feature the various "countries" of Channel 5 and will use ABC star talent on the spot. For example, we might have Robert Young—who plays Marcus Welby—say: "Marcus Welby is coming to 5—5 is coming to Desolake—Desolake is coming to 5." We will also promote our news personalities, we will encourage them to take part in the laying of corner stones and the christening of babies and so on all over town, so they begin to get known.

The second part of the promotion will be the opening night, the presentation. We plan to open on Monday the week before Labor Day, at six o'clock with a short dedication program followed by the ABC promotional reel film followed by excerpts from some of our station programs. This will lead into the evening network programming. We will have an open house and a barbeque for local advertisers and community leaders, and at that time we will give away free soy sauce.

The third part of the promotional campaign will be the on-going promotion for the station, once we are on the air, and our primary vehicle here will be the station itself. We will also use the local newspaper in preference to *TV Guide*. We will also expect that the manager of the station will promote us by speaking at various service clubs. For sales and other promotional uses we'll prepare a slick folder which can cover up some rather unslick, more up-to-date promotional material inside—maps, reasons to buy, and so on. And we will prepare cassettes for use by our salesman—for the salesmen to take to the reps to show them the kinds of things that we're doing in Desolake.

I hope I managed to convince you that we're going to have a very exciting station.

KESHISHOGLOU: I want to clear up one point. I don't think we really decided we were going to give away any soy sauce; I believe the decision was we were going to use the soy sauce to baste a roast pig.

LYNCH: Let the record show that.

RHO PRESENTATION

Rapporteurs: Robert Schlater (Michigan State University)
Ray L. Steele (University of Pittsburgh)

KIRT-TV Community Affairs/Ascertainment

KIRT-TV, through its community affairs director, with the advice of station management who accepted a commitment to community development and enhancement as a condition of employment, will, on a continuing basis, ascertain the problems and concerns of the general community and community leaders via multiple inputs. Ours will be an open door. KIRT-TV will center its news and public affairs programming on reporting, investigating, discussing, and providing forums on those subjects which, in the judgment of station management, appear worthwhile and where the need or interest of the community is apparent. Presentation of community problems and concerns shall be done on a regular basis throughout the broadcast week, and special in-depth programs of significant problems will be programmed at appropriate times throughout the broadcast day.

KIRT-TV's management team will develop a Community Advisory Council with whom to meet and discuss ascertainment needs and means of answering community needs.

Promotion

I. Station Goals
   A. Audience Level
      1. First year, second in market in 18–49 year age group.
      2. Second year, second in total viewers.
      3. Third year, first in target area 18–49 year olds.
   B. Community Level
      1. First year, Channel 5 equally well recognized in market as other
         two TV stations.
      2. Second year, Channel 5 best known TV channel in total market.
      3. Third year, Channel 5 retains position as best known TV channel.
      II. Pre-air date Promotion
   A. Slogan: "Five is Alive".
   B. Tradeout with radio station, newspapers, TV Guide, also ABC network promotion.
   III. On Air-First
   A. Premiere broadcast, telethon for local charity, which will help to promote it. Features ABC-TV personalities, local community leaders appearing and answering phones. Station management and personalities serve as hosts.

IV. A. Major initial emphasis is promotion of network entertainment, i.e., "A new entertainment opportunity".

B. Hire local ad agency.

C. Invest in experienced promotion person.

V. First year special promotional budget—$50,000.

KIRT-TV Programming (RHO)

DAY TIME M-F	KIRT-TV	KNAC-TV	KBGA-TV
6:30AM		Rural Report	
7:00	AM America	Today	Morning News
8:00	AM America	Today	Captain Kangaroo
9:00	AM DESOLAKE	Celeb. Swpstakes	Spin-off
9:30	ROMPER ROOM	Wheel of Fortune	Gambit
10:00	ROMPER ROOM	High Rollers	Tattletales
10:30	Happy Days	Hollyood Squares	Love-Life; News
11:00	Showoffs	Mag. Marb. Mach.	Young & Restless
11:30	All My Children	Jackpot	Search for Tomorrow
12:00PM	Ryan's Hope	Noon Report	News
12:30	Let's Make Deal	Days of Our Lives	As the World Turns
1:00	$10,000 Pyramid	Days of Our Lives	As the World Turns
1:30	Rhyme and Reason	Doctors	Edge of Night
2:00	General Hospital	Another World	Price Is Right
2:30	One Life To Live	Another World	Match Game '75
3:00	DINAH	Somerset	Musical Chairs
3:30	DINAH	Be Our Guest	Mike Douglas
4:00	DINAH	Huck & Yogi	Mike Douglas
4:30	HOGAN'S HEROS	Drum of Jeanie	Mike Douglas
5:00	ABC News	Truth Or Consequences	Dialing for Dollars
5:30	KIRT NEWS	NBC News	CBS News
6:00	BEWITCHED	KNAC Evening Report	KBGA Newsroom

EVENING	MONDAY	TUESDAY	WEDNESDAY	THURSDAY	FRIDAY
6:30	LCL MOVIE	THAT GIRL	THAT GIRL	THAT GIRL	THAT GIRL
7:00	LCL MOVIE	Happy Days	When Things	Barney Milr	Mobile 1
7:30	LCL MOVIE	Welcome Bk	That's Mama	On the Rocks	Mobile 1
8:00	ABC Movie	Rookies	Baretta	Streets SF	ABC Fri Movie
8:30	ABC Movie	Rookies	Baretta	Streets SF	ABC Fri Movie
9:00	ABC Movie	Medical Ctr	Strsky Htch	Harry O	ABC Fri Movie
9:30	ABC Movie	Medical Ctr	Strsky Htch	Harry O	ABC Fri Movie

EVENING

M-F	KIRT-TV	KNAC-TV	KBGA-TV
10:00	KIRT-TV NEWS	Nite Report	News
10:30	FBI	Tonight Show	CBS Late Movie
11:30	ABC WW Ent.	Tonight Show	CBS Late Movie
12:00	ABC WW Ent.	Tomorrow	CBS Late Movie
12:30	ABC WW Ent.	Tomorrow	
1:00 AM	SIGN OFF		

- Public Affairs pre-empts 6:30–7 PM programming on night or nights each month when reports of local public affairs are released as per licensee promise in Exhibit 3 of FCC application.
- AM DESOLAKE will tape daily (for next day's) broadcast with local people discussing the subject on the day's *AM America* or other subjects. Public service opportunity as well as follow up to the network program.
- Tape facilities available 10:30–3:00 daily for AM DESOLAKE and also for weekend and other delayed material.
- 3 PM Woman's time—we appeal strongly to 18–49's.
- 5 PM *ABC News* will be the first in the market.
- 6 PM BEWITCHED the strongest possible alternate programming and a money maker.
- 6:30 Mondays. The local movie as a lead in to football. There are few local movies in the market and movies are profitable. On other nights, THAT GIRL will appeal to the 18–49 age group.
- 10 PM The toughest competition of the day and where we will put most of our budget, most of our promotion, most of our time.

KIRT-TV Weekend Programming

SAT'DAY	KIRT TV	KNAC TV	KGBA TV
7:00	Hong Kong Phooey	Emerg. 4	Pebbles & Bam Bam
7:30	New Tom & Jerry	Sigmund	Bugs Bunny
8:00	Great Grape Ape	Secret Life of Wkty	Bugs Bunny
8:30	Odd Ball Couple	Pink Panther	Scooby-Do
9:00	New Adv. of Glgn	Land of Lost	Shazams/Iris Hour
9:30	Uncle Croc's 1k	Run, Joe Run	Shazams/Iris Hour
10:00	Uncle Croc's Blk	Bynd Pln of Apes	Far Out Space Nuts
10:30	The Lost Saucer	West Wind	Ghost Busters
11:00	Speed Buggy	Josie & Psy Cts	Harlem Globetrotters
11:30	American Bandstnd	Go U.S.A.	Fat Albert
12:00PM	American Bandstnd	Local	Children's Film Fest
12:30	TALKING TO YOUTH	Indian Country	Children's Film Fest
1:00	College Football	Bible Story	Death Valley Days
1:30	College Football	Gilligan's Island	H.S. Football
2:00	College Football	Local Movie	H.S. Football
3:30	College Football	Various	Various
4:00	ABC WW Sports	Yogi Gang	Various
4:30	ABC WW Sports	Good News	Various
5:00	ABC WW Sports	Knight Hour	Various
5:30	ABC Evening News	NBC Sat'day News	CBS Sat'day News
6:00	Barbary Coast	Lawrence Welk	Hee Haw
6:30	Barbary Coast	Lawrence Welk	Hee Haw
7:00	ABC Sat Nite Movie	Emergency	Jeffersons
7:30	ABC Sat Nite Movie	Emergency	Doc
8:00	ABC Sat Nite Movie	KNAC Sat Movie	Mary Tyler Moore
8:30	ABC Sat Nite Movie	KNAC Sat Movie	Bob Newhart
9:00	ABC Sat Nite Movie	KNAC Sat Movie	Carol Burnett
10:00	KIRT NEWS	KNAC Night Report	KBGA News
10:30	KIRT MOVIE	Various	Star Wrestling

SAT'DAY	KIRT TV	KNAC TV	KGBA TV
11:00	KIRT MOVIE	Weekend Tonight	Star Wrestling
11:30	KIRT MOVIE	Weekend Tonight	Hank Thompson
12:00AM	KIRT MOVIE		
12:30	BEWITCHING CINEMETTE		
2:00	SIGN-OFF		

- 12:30 TALKING TO YOUTH pre-taped public affairs.
- 6:00 Barbary Coast is a network show delayed from Monday night.
- 12:30 BEWITCHING CINAMETTE is a low budget horror film designed to capture whatever late night audience is available and to fill out the promised 126 hours per week of programming.

SUNDAY	KIRT TV	KNAC TV	KBGA TV
7:30AM	RELIGIOUS	Local	Meet a Friend
8:00	RELIGIOUS	Local	Valley of Dinosaurs
8:30	CAPTAIN NOAH	Oral Roberts	Cath. of Tomorrow
9:00	CAPTAIN NOAH	Truth:Word	Lamp Unto Feet
9:30	Devlin	Day-Discovery	Old Time Gospel
10:00	These Are Days	Rex Humbard	Old Time Gospel
10:30	Make A Wish	Rex Humbard	Face The Nation
11:00	VARIOUS	Faith For Today	Calvary Temple
11:30	VARIOUS	Herald-Truth	Calvary Temple
12:00PM	NOTRE DAME FTBL	NFL Football	NFL Today
12:30	NOTRE DAME FTBL	NFL Football	NFL Football
1:00	DOUBLE FEATURE	NFL Football	NFL Football
3:00	DOUBLE FEATURE	Meet the Press	NFL Football
3:30	DOUBLE FEATURE	Meet the Press	NBA Basketball
4:00	LOCAL FB REVUE	Various	NBA Basketball
4:30	LOCAL FB REVUE	Judy	NBA Basketball
5:00	Issues/Answers	Judy	NBA Football
5:30	ABC News	NBC News	NBA Basketball
6:00	Swiss Family Rob.	Disney	Three for the Road
7:00	$6 Million Man	Family Holvak	Cher

SUNDAY	KIRT TV	KNAC TV	KBGA TV
8:00	ABC Sunday Movie	NBC Myst. Movie	Kojak
9:00	ABC Sunday Movie	NBC Myst. Movie	Bronk
10:00	KIRT TV NEWS	KNAC Nite Report	KBGA News/Weather
10:30	LOCAL MOVIE	Sunday Nite Movie	Movie
11:30	LOCAL MOVIE	Sunday Nite Movie	Bobby Goldsborough
12:30	SIGN OFF		

- 7:30 AM Taped and/or syndicated religion.
- 8:30 CAPTAIN NOAH is a cartoon show.
- 11:00 on alternate Sundays, PROBLEMS OF THE ELDERLY, RECREATION TODAY; 11:30 CORE SOUL DEN and THE NEIGHBORHOOD, local public affairs broadcasts described in the license application and pretaped during the week.
- 12:00 PM NOTRE DAME FOOTBALL is syndicated.
- 4:00 LOCAL FOOTBALL REVUE is live and tape.

News Department

NEWS POLICY: KIRT-TV will be a constructive adversary with investigative, people-oriented reporting. Specifically:

1. KIRT TV news will feature heavy, local, in-depth investigative reporting.

2. KIRT TV will editorialize on local issues.

3. The station will provide thorough coverage of outlying areas (one news team assigned to this "beat.") As an option, stringers might be utilized to supplement the team coverage.

4. The station's mobile unit will be used as much as possible to provide local live coverage on "big" events.

5. The station will seek out community opinion for newscasts through "man on the street"/guest interviews etc.

NEWS STAFF: Seventeen full timers—total salaries $238,500 per year as follows:

1 News Director	$25,000
1 Assgn/Editor	20,000
1 Producer/Director	15,000

1 Anchorman	20,000	
1 Sports Director	17,000	
1 Meteorologist	17,000	
1 Reporter/Weekend Anchor	20,000	
4 General Reporters	48,000	($12,000 each)
3 Camerapersons	28,500	($9,500 each)
2 Reporter/Camerapersons	21,000	($10,500 each)
1 Secretary	7,000	
	$238,500	

SUPPLEMENTAL: AP Broadcast Wire, ESSA WX Wire, Desolake Police Wire, all local papers, news slide service.

NEWS SCHEDULE: Weekdays: Two 4-minute cut-ins between 7 and 9 AM, plus 5-minute insert into AM DESOLAKE: KIRT TV NEWS 5:30–6:00 PM.

Daily: KIRT TV NEWS 10–10:30 PM Monday–Sunday.

Sales

PHILOSOPHY: In the first year KIRT will concentrate on building a strong *local market* as the major revenue source with emphasis on developing new broadcast advertisers and a strong sales service reputation to include skill in copy-writing, production, and point of sale merchandising.

For 90 days, the foresight of charter advertisers will be rewarded by receiving a 10% discount on the rate card.

We will subscribe to the NAB Code.

In rate development we will allow room for flexible development by our management team with the general expectation that rates will not differ greatly from the other stations and will not be less than the current second station in the market at this time. A single rate card for national and regional sales will be used and a long list national representative, like Katz, will be sought with Peters, Griffin and Woodward and H-R Television as alternatives.

RESEARCH: We will subscribe to one television audience market report selected by the management. Arbitron telephone concentrates will be used for the first year.

Organization

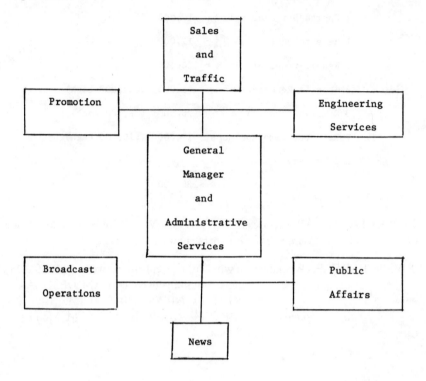

KIRT-TV Revenue

	First Year	Second Year	Third Year
Network	$200,000	$225,000	$250,000
National	300,000	535,000	1,020,000
Local	900,000	1,190,000	1,530,000
	$1.400,000	$1,950,000	$2,800,000
Less Discount	210,000	292,500	420,000
Net Revenue	$1,190,000	$1,657,500	$2,380,000

First Year Expenses

By NAB Classifications

		Salary	Total
Technical	Chief	$20,000	
	Staff	64,000	
		$84,000	$143,000
Sales	Sales Manager	$25,000	
	Local Sales Manager	22,000	
	Staff	53,000	
		$100,000	$177,000
General & Administration			
	General Manager	$30,000	
	Business Manager	15,000	
	Staff	35,500	
		$80,500	$430,000
Programming			
	Programm Director	$18,000	
	News Director	25,000	
	Public Affairs Director	12,000	
	Staff	148,000	
		$203,000	$390,000
			$1,140,000
Additional Promotion (First Year)			50,000
			$1,190,000

TAU PRESENTATION

Rapporteurs: Carol Reuss (Loyola University)
                Donald Agostino (Indiana University)

Programming

In regard to programming, this is an interim report, which will attempt, generally, to describe plans for the new station in Desolake. More complete programming will be developed when the program staff is hired.

The program schedule summarized below is predicated on three assumptions:

1. KIRT-TV must be viable, competitive, potentially profitable.
2. Care must be taken to guard against overburdening facilities and the staff, especially at the beginning of operations.
3. It is advisable to use a strategy of counter-programming against the established stations in Desolake and to program in the action-entertainment personality of ABC-TV because KIRT-TV will be an ABC affiliate.

For accounting purposes, two program plans are proposed at this time for management approval. One is based on the proposition that our news staff, at day one, will be capable of developing meaningful new programs appropriate to metro-Desolake; the other, that we should concentrate news gathering and production efforts into one superb local newscast at 10:00 PM Monday through Friday, thus not spreading ourselves too thin, competitively.

Thus, KIRT-TV programming will follow one of these two tracks:

Track One

7:00 – 9:00 AM	Network (Good Morning America)
9:00 – 10:30	DINAH
10:30 – 3:30	Network
3:30 – 4:00	GAME (DEALER'S CHOICE, DIAMOND HEAD)
4:00 – 5:30	LIGHT SITUATION (Three)
5:00 – 6:30	BONANZA
6:30 – 7:00	BOWLING FOR DOLLARS
7:00 – 10:00	Network
10:00 – 10:30	LOCAL NEWS

10:30 – 1:00	Network (Wide World Of Entertainment)
1:00	NEWS HEADLINES/SIGN OFF

Track Two

7:00 – 9:00 AM	Network (Good Morning America)
9:00 – 10:30	DINAH
10:30 – 3:30	Network
3:30 – 4:00	GAME (DEALER'S CHOICE, DIAMOND HEAD)
4:00 – 5:30	MOVIE
5:30 – 6:00	Network Nes
6:00 – 6:30	LOCAL NEWS
6:30 – 7:00	BOWLING FOR DOLLARS
7:00 – 10:00	Network
10:00 – 10:30	LOCAL NEWS
10:30 – 1:00	Network (Wide World of Entertainment)
1:00	NEWS HEADLINES/SIGN OFF

Weekend programming will rely heavily on the network. The Saturday program schedule, as now planned, will be:

7:00 – 12:00 noon	Network
12:00 – 2:30	MOVIE
2:30 – 6:00	Network, including Network News (5:30)
6:00 – 7:00	COMMUNITY AFFAIRS (Locally generated)
7:00 – 10:15	Network
10:15	MOVIE

The Sunday program schedule, as now planned, will be:

7:00 – 1:00	Network, PAID RELIGIOUS, COMMUNITY AFFAIRS
1:00 – 5:00	Network (Sports)
5:00 – 6:00	COMMUNITY AFFAIRS (Locally generated)
6:00 – 10:15	Network
10:15	MOVIE

The programs above call for scheduling syndicated strips, to engender continuity, and films and appropriate news team efforts of real service to the community.

News

The on-air news look for KIRT-TV should be fast but intelligible, visuals with every story, a believable and easily identifiable anchor, use of effects, but not to excess, clear separation between news and commentary, good sports coverage and weather with radar.

In line with the programming noted in another section of this interim report, KIRT-TV will have to choose one of two news options. Option One calls for two half-hour news programs on weekdays (6 and 10 P.M.) and use of network news on weekends. Two locally produced news programs will tax the new station's staff considerably. Option Two calls for one newscast per day, at 10 P.M., with network news on weekends. The KIRT-TV news staff will also produce the community affairs programs, scheduled now for an hour on Saturday and an hour on Sunday.

The news philosophy will be to provide viewers with current and complete information in news stories which have impact on the citizens of Desolake; to provide this news with visuals, for high attention impact and visibility. The 10 P.M. news should include evening news events as well as reports of events which occur throughout the day. Special attention will be given to investigative/feature reporting of locally significant news. The station's news team will strive for impact and image as well as accuracy and fairness.

The news department staff will consist of nine persons: a news director, newsperson as anchor, reporters who write and report on-air, cinematographers, and others. Stringers will be hired from the metro-county area, all of whom will be considered independent contractors for stories. Eventually, interns from the area colleges can be worked into the program.

News equipment and sources, other than the reporters noted above, will include: one major wire service, (to begin, both AP and UPI will be contracted for on a trial run), one weather bureau wire; scanner radio; one ENG color camera and accessories; the ABC DEF news service; one single system 16 mm camera and accessories, with processing to be arranged with other media on a contract basis; other standard news room equipment and supplies.

The news service areas will be principally the metro-county area, with outlying coverage by stringers, as noted above.

Staffing for the KIRT TV news department will begin as soon as possible, with every effort made to hire from the area because it is deemed wise to have as many members of the staff skilled in local history, politics, etc., as possible. Area radio stations and newspapers should be sources of some news personnel.

Transportation for the news department will include two station wagons, equipped with two-way radios, and one motorcycle.

Details for the news operation will be spelled out more precisely when a news director is hired. He or she should develop such detailed plans.

The station's editorial policy, however, should include care for using the airwaves for good, solid editorials. Station editorials will be aired at least twice a week and rebuttal time will be encouraged on non-editorial days. Editorials will be researched and outlined by the news director, who will call upon his staff as necessary. The general manager will deliver the editorials on air.

The first year's budget for KIRT-TV news will be approximately $130,000. Specific budgetary details will be devised by the news director.

Sales

One of the assumptions of this planning is that the station, at the beginning, where we have no performance data, holds to an annual operating budget no larger than $1,000,000.

Based on a total market potential of $6,000,000 and an estimate that KIRT TV can reasonably expect to attract 14% to 18% of the television dollars in the market area, our top estimate of our potential for the first year will be approximately $1-million gross sales.

We realize that this will be a loss for this year, when capitalization is considered, but management is prepared to stand this deficit at the beginning.

The sales organization will include: General sales manager, who will also handle national sales. Local sales manager, who will also carry list. Three salespersons. At the beginning they will be on salary and draw; ultimately they will be on straight commission. The plan is to hire as many of these as possible from the other Desolake area media because KIRT TV needs the acceptance, credibility, and experience of persons known and respected locally.

Since we are a locally originated new station, we will stress service to local businesses in order to give them the best advertising buys for their dollars. We will not offer special rates to any advertisers under the guise of "charter" or discounted prices at the beginning of operations because it is too difficult to terminate such offers or the discount aura they might engender. Our space rates will be held slightly under the competition until we prove we have an audience that allows for higher rates.

We will have one rate card. Since we are beginning operations, we feel we don't have choices on setting a portion of our inventory that will be available on a pre-emptible basis.

We will solicit presentations from a variety of national sales representatives who are presently handling small stations and markets adequately. Our consultants, Mitchell and Mockbee, suggest that we definitely contact Avery-Knodel about national accounts because of the representative's record with other smaller operations. Whichever national representative is chosen, we should work closely with the rep to get assistance with programming, research, and production problems.

Because of the cost, we will not subscribe to the NAB but we will indicate adherence to its Code guidelines on the amount of advertising aired and on product restrictions. In all cases, the general manager and program manager will make final decisions on possible objectionable advertisements and programs. The general manager will devise a schedule for times of broadcast of products and services that might be inappropriate during certain viewing times. The staff will be made aware of these policies.

We will accept religious advertising, programs supplied by religious groups, and religious spot advertising and the general manager shall be apprised of these so as to avoid any that might be inappropriate to our market.

We will accept political advertising, and notify such advertisers that we will adhere to FCC guidelines regarding same.

We will subscribe to the same rating service as our competitors for two reasons: we cannot afford two services and we want to be able to be compared across the board with our competition.

Incentives to local advertisers will include copy-writing, no-fee commercial announcers, production services, and (in the first months of operation) counter cards and photos of staff for display, as well as advertiser product/service promotion.

Our sales policies, like our programming and public service policies, are based on KIRT TV having a professional staff throughout. We will show our market that professionalism develops as integrity and service—integrity and service that is important to every person in our area. We recognize that while we will be the "new kids on the block," so to speak, newness can mean freshness, vigor, enthusiastic service when professionals join talents. We will tap our energies and our creative professionalism and the energies and professionalism of our advertising representative for the benefit of our advertisers and our viewers.

Community Affairs/Ascertainment

From a philosophical and policy standpoint, ascertainment and community affairs are two complementary elements of public service. In the view of KIRT TV, they are also a two-step process because a conscientious ascertainment effort will assist in developing valuable community affairs functions.

The station's ascertainment mechanism will follow the guidelines established by the FCC. In other words, ascertainment will be conducted on two levels: 1. A survey of community leaders, conducted in group interviews. 2. A survey of the general community.

The group interviews, in cooperation with the other local stations, will be efficient and economical and will tend to lead to a closer relation with the other stations and might possibly blunt some of the initial antagonism that a new station might encounter. The general community ascertainment will be handled by

KIRT TV staff, assisted by selected local university students. Professional research organizations will not be used initially because of costs and the desire to have our personnel involved in the area.

There will be continuous ascertainment activities during the year, including luncheons and meetings with community leaders, solicitation of comments from citizens, and possibly some mail questionnaires.

Community affairs programming will evidence the station's public service philosophy. At KIRT-TV there will be two primary categories of community affairs programming at the beginning: 1. Programs of non-controversial/human interest variety, both syndicated and locally originated. 2. Programs indicating local needs.

One hour will be scheduled on Saturday and on Sunday for local interest programming, some of which will be controversial and will involve call-in's. We will look for a reputable telethon as a valuable charity and also to promote Channel 5.

The second type of community programming will result directly from the station's ascertainment program. We will plan programs that deal directly with the needs and issues of the community, as reflected in the contact that the station has with community leaders and other citizens.

In dealing with the problems of our market, KIRT-TV's philosophy is that a problem of one group in society affects the entire community. Therefore, varied needs and problems will be integrated into the station's regularly scheduled programming, particularly the hour-long periods on Saturdays and Sundays.

In an effort to build community awareness as well as participation, KIRT-TV will report community affairs in the regular newscast and will editorialize and allow for replies. The news director and community affairs director will maintain records of the issues covered and the amount of time devoted to each.

Documentaries will not be used as vehicles for community affairs programs until the station becomes more solvent financially and the staff becomes more experienced.

Community affairs inevitably involves the establishment of policies dealing with relations with community persons and groups. It will be the policy of KIRT-TV to establish and maintain a dialog with these persons. However, from a programming standpoint, it will be impossible to meet demands of all groups. This is further justification for relating individual group problems to the community as a whole. With proper planning and communication with the groups within the community, we feel that this is possible.

Promotion

We are entering a market with two well established stations and must overcome the image of intruders. We feel the existing stations have not been forced to work very hard to keep an audience or advertisers. In fact, they have probably been indifferent. We want to come in as friends, neighbors, folksy good guys with something new and positive to offer.

Our opening promotion will be built around the theme of "A new family on the block." We will build on family entertainment of the variety found on ABC. Prior to going on-air we will use heavy newspaper advertising to get use of ABC cooperative dollars. Since we will start broadcasting in January, we will give away printed Christmas shopping bags all over the area to try to build audience awareness.

Our program promotional emphasis will be on the local news, public affairs, BOWLING FOR DOLLARS, sports (especially the coming Olympics) and the strong network shows. All will close with "You all come to Channel 5." We will do a heavy promotion of ENG, which should be very visible everytime there is a big crowd—such as at sports events, and the extra service of radar weather. This could be themed: "Looking Out for You." We know that NBC has a strong dominance over CBS in this market; the NBC station has a slick news format and a strong news dominance, so we must show our local concern.

We will use radio with a mix of the ABC radio affiliates promoting shared personalities on the network and KLTD, the strong middle-of-the-road station. KLTD was chosen because this is probably the station most listened to by the opinion leaders.

Channel 5 is between Channels 3 and 8 on the dial so we should benefit by some stopovers at channel switching times. We should therefore use heavy on-air promotion at normal switching times.

For promotion to the advertising communities, we will prepare a station promotional piece to be used locally and by the representatives. We should also buy an advertisement in *Broadcasting* to build visibility nationally. Nationally, we must build the uniqueness of the market: Soybean capital, three large sports stadiums, a strong mix of urban and rural, an isolated market that makes an ideal test market. We should then go out for test market advertising.

We must convince the advertising community that we are serious business people who will serve the interests of the area. We will promote the fact that we have hired local people with a knowledge of the area and with experience in the area. We must show that we pledge ourselves to an ethical business practice with computer billing and logging. We care! (The other stations have not found this necessary.)

We will run a contest for national time buyers on estimates of our performance in the first February/March rating books. The prize can be modest (a smoked turkey, for example). Hopefully, we can do better than expected.

Overall, our promotion will emphasize that we are professionals. We will make the effort to serve our community, our viewers, and advertisers alike.

Admittedly, our plans for KIRT-TV are commercial. They are less creative than we would wish them to be. They are more prosaic than we would wish them to be. We realize, however, the tremendous financial outlay that the establishment (yes, creation) of a new TV station represents and we propose annual assessments to determine when we can branch out and do more exciting programming for our mid-west audience and, equally, for our commercial interests.

SIGMA PRESENTATION

Rapporteurs: William Hawes (University of Houston)
Brian R. Naughton (Marquette University)

The abiding philosophy of the management of KIRT-TV, Desolake, is to remember always that it is serving a metropolitan, a suburban and a rural population—a large number of human beings.

We want to make money, it is true, but the community comes first. In order to do this, we have attempted to make trade-outs in our program schedule. Some features we wish to point out:

1. FARM REPORT: We begin the 18-hour day in this rural area with what we plan will be more than the usual pap—our farmers are sophisticated and we plan to give them what they need to be informed.

2. ROMPER ROOM: A local personality working with young children. Desolake has a lot of kids.

3. DESOLAKE TODAY: An opportunity for ongoing input from the community—community leaders, visiting dignitaries, the people who are in town.

4. GILLIGAN'S ISLAND and STAR TREK: Kidult programming to lead into a hardhitting five o'clock news.

5. On Saturdays, a local sports program with taped and perhaps some live portions—local sports is very important in this market.

6. Sunday mornings we devote a good deal of time to religion—our market is in Bible Belt America. Various religious groups can purchase time at 8 AM and there is a shared local religious program at 9 AM featuring all kinds of religious activity, musical groups as well as the preachers, in a flexible format. The children's religious program, DAVEY AND GOLIATH follows.

7. The Sunday morning movie is in a time period which we can pre-empt for cultural activities, the orchestra, the light opera, for example.

8. The PUBLIC AFFAIRS programs can be live or taped depending on staff availabilities.

KIRT-TV, Desolake, Kansouri, Program Schedule (Monday–Friday)

6:00AM	(L)	FARM REPORT
6:30	(L)	NOT FOR WOMEN ONLY
7:00	(N)	Good Morning America
9:00	(L)	ROMPER ROOM
10:00	(L)	DESOLAKE TODAY
10:30	(N)	Happy Days
11:00	(N)	Show Offs
11:30	(N)	All My Children
12:00PM	(N)	Ryan's Hope
12:30	(N)	Let's Make A Deal
1:00	(N)	$10,000 Pyramid
1:30	(N)	Rhyme & Reason
2:00	(N)	General Hospital
2:30	(N)	One Life To Live
3:00	(N)	You Don't Say
3:30	(L)	GILLIGAN'S ISLAND
4:00	(L)	STAR TREK
4:30	(L)	" "
5:00	(L)	LOCAL NEWS
5:30	(N)	ABC News
6:00	(L)	HOGAN'S HEROS
6:30	(L)	ADAM 12
7:00	(N)	NETWORK
10:00	(L)	LOCAL NEWS
10:30	(N)	ABC Wide World of Entertainment (Except Friday--Local Movie DB WWE Sun 10:30)

KIRT-TV Program Schedule Saturday

7:00AM	(N)	Hong Kong Phooey
7:30	(N)	Tom & Jerry
8:00	(N)	Great Grape Ape
8:30	(N)	The Odd Couple
9:00	(N)	New Adventures of Gilligan
9:30	(N)	Uncle Crock
10:00	(N)	" "
10:30	(N)	Lost Saucer
11:00	(N)	Speed Buggy
11:30	(N)	American Bandstand
12:00PM	(N)	" "
12:30	(L)	LOCAL SPORTS (VT)
1:00	(N)	NCAA Football
4:00	(N)	Wide World of Sports
5:30	(L)	SCIENCE FICTION MOVIE (Light Horror)
7:00	(N)	Network
10:00	(N)	ABC News
10:15	(L)	LOCAL NEWS
10:30	(L)	BLOCKBUSTER MOVIE (With Host)
12:30	(L)	LATE MOVIE
2:30	(L)	LATE LATE MOVIE

KIRT-TV Program Schedule Sunday

7:00AM	(L)	PAID RELIGIOUS PROGRAM
7:30	(L)	" " "
8:00	(L)	LOCAL RELIGIOUS (Council of Churches)
8:30	(L)	" "
9:00	(L)	DAVEY & GOLIATH

KIRT-TV Program Schedule Sunday (cont.)

9:30	(N)	Devlin
10:00	(N)	These Are The Days
10:30	(N)	Make A Wish
11:00	(L)	SUNDAY MOVIE (Possible Pre-empt Slot)
1:00PM	(L)	PUBLIC AFFAIRS PROGRAM
1:30	(N)	Issues and Answers
2:00	(L)	PUBLIC AFFAIRS
2:30	(N)	Directions
3:00	(L)	LAST OF THE WILD
3:30	(L)	BIG MOVIE
6:00	(N)	Network
10:00	(N)	ABC News
10:15	(L)	LOCAL NEWS
10:30	(N)	ABC Wide World of Entertainment (DB From Friday)

News Format and Schedule

Format

--------	Billboard NEWS in last minutes of STAR TREK
5:00:00	Visual tease open
5:01:00	Commercials
5:03:00	Lead story or film open or both
5:03:30	News, flexible at 3-4 minutes; 10 o'clock includes national news
5:07:30	Commercials
5:08:30	News, flexible at 3-4 minutes
5:12:30	Commercials
	Possible feature and roll to weather
	Weather, flexible at 2-1/2 to 3 minutes

```
Possible world weather 0:30 minutes

Commercials

Possible consumer report, stock market,

    farm report, state capitol report

Sportscast

Commercials

Editorial, when needed

Promo for local news

Promo for network
```

Setting: Modular with flexibility

Graphics: Should be strong: same for slide package

Staff: Duo anchor at 5 and 10 P.M.
Weather person, (possibly from university meteorology department) Sportscaster. Others: 5 reporters; 2 camera operators; 1 film editor; 1 assignment editor; 1 news director. Total news staff, 14. Internship program to be encouraged.

Format: Include best of existing news formats

Editorials: To be read by general manager, based on committee decision of community problems. Committee to consist of general manager, news director, perhaps someone from the community. Editorials aired as needed. All editorials will be in accordance with the fairness doctrine and other regulations such as Section 315. Political editorializing will be determined later depending in part on what other stations in the market are doing. The general manager has the final decision on editorials.

Rationale: Problem One (Programming)

1. KIRT-TV will seek ABC network affiliation: 1. Strong basic programming from network. 2. Strong promotion from network. 3. Independent too expensive to program and make profit.

2. KIRT-TV's FCC license application program promises were met as follows:

1. NEWS: 7 hours 30 minutes, consisting of news at 5 and 10 P.M. (5 hours) plus half hour total weekend local news plus network (3 hours). (The minimum will be exceeded by 1 hour per week)

2. PUBLIC AFFAIRS: 2 hours, consisting of two half hour local programs

on weekend: DESOLAKE TODAY (2½ hours); plus a half hour per month in prime time.

3. LOCAL LIVE: Newscasts at 5 and 10 PM; ROMPER ROOM; possibly DESOLAKE TODAY.

3. KIRT-TV's fringe time is for kid-ults; GILLIGAN'S ISLAND, STAR TREK, HOGAN'S HEROS. Prime access is for kid-ults with ADAM 12.

4. KIRT-TV's image is something for everyone (evenly divided between 18–49 and over 49 plus kids); yes, including news and public affairs for adults plus kids ROMPER ROOM and GILLIGAN'S ISLAND, STAR TREK in addition to network on Saturday mornings; DAVY & GOLIATH on Sunday.

5. Above selections for schedule based on availabilities. Representative costs: GILLIGAN'S ISLAND, $40.00 per telecast, LAST OF THE WILD, barter; NOT FOR WOMEN ONLY, $15.00.

6. KIRT-TV's small studio will be in heavy production weekdays, but can accomplish production schedule. Videotape used in preference to much film because of limited processing facilities in community.

7. Production of both local program production and commercial is expected to extent studio schedule will allow.

8. KIRT-TV will clear all network programming from ABC. Delayed broadcast for *Wide World of Entertainment* from Friday night to Sunday night.

9. KIRT-TV will seek some local sports programming in addition to network.

10. KIRT-TV will invest in local news staff doubling as talent—possible promotion director to host movie, possible public affairs director to host public affairs programs. All on air personnel within $150 to $250 per week range.

11. KIRT-TV will take network except for Friday when it will have local movie package.

News Format and Schedule: Public Affairs

Format

FARM REPORT is produced locally but includes some pre-taped features. Local weather and news will be included as well as information concerning agriculture. While the farm show is not classified as public affairs, this program includes more than news of agriculture.

ROMPER ROOM is a daily program for pre-schoolers. It is hosted by local talent and follows the familiar format.

DESOLAKE TODAY is a local origination public affairs program appearing daily. It is hoted by the public affairs director. Certain local issues will be discussed, celebrities interviewed and features concerning local community life will be included.

Public Affairs on the Weekend. Two programs on public affairs will be included at 1 and 2 P.M. Saturday. These programs will probably be taped earlier in the week. They will include discussions with leaders in business, education and those areas of the community wherein ascertainment research indicates a need for the airing of matters of community importance.

Public Affairs in Prime Time. Once a month a public affairs program will be produced to quality standards. Community input will be solicited to encourage citizens' participation, so that citizens will have "access" to the airwaves.

Schedule

Daily: 6:00 A.M. FARM REPORT
                9:00 ROMPER ROOM
                10:00 DESOLAKE TODAY
Weekends: (Sunday)
                1:00 P.M. Public Affairs
                2:00 Public Affairs
Prime Time: One hour monthly Public Affairs program (Monday–Sunday, 6–11 P.M.)

Policy

KIRT-TV enters the market with a strong local news and public affairs commitment. News and public affairs will be the most featured programming in all advertising and promotion and constitutes all of the locally produced programming of the station. The news staff makes up one third of the station personnel and will account for its major programming expenses. Public affairs is designed to provide maximum participation of citizens in discussions and demonstrations of problems and solutions.

One hour per month the station will pre-empt prime time programming to present documentaries and special programs of interest and importance to the community at large.

The early news is scheduled at 5 P.M. to get a lead on the competition. Regular extended features will offer information and service to the community in matters which are timely and important, but not breaking news items. Editorials, when vital to the interests of the community, will be featured at the end of the program.

Community Affairs/Ascertainment

Ascertainment is to be made through research, consisting of a survey of community leaders and other citizens. This survey is to be completed by station personnel and college students involved in internship programs. Age groups, racial and religious considerations will be included in the study. The study will be made as required. The news staff and the general manager will be out in the community continually gathering community feedback on an informal basis, especially by telephone. TV station does not intend *to solve* problems; however, "Access" is interpreted by the management as being an opportunity for citizens to express their point of view. Citizens will be given a chance to do this in accordance with FCC regulations of fairness and reasonable consideration of community problems. It is management's responsibility to make clear to its public the role the station can and wants to play in the total community problem solving process.

The Public Affairs Director or the News Director may anchor the public affairs programming listed above. The station intends to encourage an on-going dialogue with community members and its staff through these programs.

Periodic surveys will attempt to determine whether the Desolake community likes the programs and whether they are aiding community solutions to problems by airing them for public attention.

At present no pool ascertainment surveys are contemplated, nor does the management intend to make specific agreements with minorities. Instead, it intends to research the needs of everyone and program accordingly in good faith.

The General Manager and Program Director and host of DESOLAKE TO-DAY will be chief representatives of the station in on-going ascertainment of community response to station programming. The General Manager is expected to spend 50% of his time in community relations work.

Philosophy

The station intends to have as aggressive a sales posture as possible, but its service to the community through its programming has the edge on decisions. This is to say that the Program Director is hired second to the General Manager, and that the Sales Manager does not make programming decisions, although cooperation and counsel is encouraged from all concerned. Major management decisions are based on the collective thinking of the department heads, and any position developed is then reflected in sales philosophy. KIRT-TV is a NAB Code station.

Strategy

Desolake in the 75th market believed to yield $2.8 million to $3.2 million the first year. Local sales have the greatest potential. The stations revenue will be 60% local sales; 32% national sales; 5% network; 3% other. Approximately $8 million market.

To tap this potential, salesmen are expected to sell "on the come," that is by painting a picture of potential for programming and station service without having an established track record.

Thus, a flexible rate card is desirable, using a 5-level grid with Level One at a fixed rate and the other four levels pre-emptable by the General Manager of the station. The rate card will stay within $5.00 to $10.00 of the rate card of

KNAC. Rates for production services will be related to whether spots are aired on KIRT-TV.

The sales staff will consist of a General and Local Sales Manager, a National Sales Manager, four local sales people. At least one sales person should come from a station in the market or a local newspaper, or radio. The rest should be young, bright, aggressive, personable.

KIRT-TV will hire a regional sales representative (but not an advertising agency). One that is not too big so that the account is unimportant, but one that has an established record.

KIRT-TV will subscribe only to the Nielsen Rating Service. Further research may be conducted by college interns paid to do the job.

It is understood that salesmen will often write their own copy, and that on air personnel, especially news personnel, will not appear on competing stations in the market. News personnel cannot sell products or services on the air. Salesmen are also responsible for collecting their money from clients. Salesmen will have a drawing account otherwise work on commission.

The Traffic Department will consist of two or three people, including a traffic manager, one person for inventory of availabilities.

Audience Promotion

Although the station does not intend to hire any advertising agency, it intends to use ABC network promotion at maximum, especially when it goes on tthe air during "premiere" week. A strong, crisp visual promotion campaign will be designed by station personnel including the Promotion Director and station artist. Local participation by citizens, from youngsters drawing pictures for station IDs to college students, will be solicited.

Dominant image is, "The folks on five—your kind of people."

Promotion material is to be placed on local radio stations, metro and suburban newspapers, *TV Guide,* and on billboards in heavy traffic areas. Emphasis on all copy and promotion is "Channel 5." "5" becomes central image for visuals such as billboards which might show five-person news team, including duo anchor, weathercaster, sportscaster and ABC anchorman (Reasoner).

Promotional campaign is to have a preliminary campaign to the effect that a new station is coming into the market. Once on the air, on-air promotion will follow using Jerry Smith promotion package plus music option, music plus "donut" jingles and/or several packaged possibilities in addition to station staff's inventions.

Promotion Schedule

One year before opening of station: General Manager, Promotion Manager, Program Manager begin community contests and publicity releases.

Six months before opening: Creative services contracted for billboards, radio promos, logos, etc. Agreements with network for their season promotions.

Three months before opening: Begin to step up releases.

Six weeks before open: Billboard teasers, radio teasers.

One month before opening: Full promotion in all media. Barter and trade off with radio and weeklies. Hypo season and *CHANNEL 5*. Begin "Folks on Five" promos.

One day before the opening of season for ABC fall schedule and opening of station, stage gala event in 38,000-seat arena with ABC stars, politicians, entertainers and local dignitaries. Self coverage and hopefully coverage by other stations and press. Barter with stadium management for mentions of attractions.

On-going promotions once on the air: 1. Sunday visitation at station; 2. On-air local and network; 3. Radio and newspapers; 4. Use local radio personalities as movie host; 5. Kid art contests; college student contests; 6. Slogan contests. Much of foregoing is to be paid for by barter-trade arrangements, on 50-50 basis with flexibility. Fifty percent bottom line trade-out.

Sales Promotion Campaign Schedule

One year before opening; General Manager, Program Manager, Sales Manager hired. Internal decisions made during first six months.

Six months before: Begin tease opening of the station, limited publicity.

Four months before: Hire sales staff.

Sales promotion and audience promotion campaigns run in concert, reinforce each other.

After station is on the air: Set objectives of first quarter of station on the air based on the fourth quarter financial return. Projection by management for entire year made thereafter and reviewed regularly.

KIRT-TV Station Staff

1 General Manager	1 Secretary
1 Chief Engineer	12 Engineers
1 Program Director	2 Promotion & Scheduling
1 Production Manager	7 Production Staff
	4 Producer/Directors
	1 Public Affairs Talent/Producer
	1 *Romper Room* Talent/Producer
1 News Director	13 News Staff
1 Traffic Manager	2 Staff
2 Sales Managers	4 Staff
1 Business Manager	1 Clerical
Total Staff 51 persons.	

Epilogue

ONE KNOWLEDGEABLE CRITIC, upon reading the manuscript, suggested that this chapter be entitled something like "How the Experts Put It All Together." This would have been accurate—the four panels were composed of knowledgeable professionals—but it would also have been misleading. It would have suggested that the conclusions they came to proceeded solely from their expertise, from a professionalism denied to less experienced students. To be sure, any simulation reflects the sum of the experience of the participants. But of even more importance in determining its outcome are the built-in systematic imperatives. Perhaps the only point on which journalists and lawyers always agree is that the nature of the question predetermines the nature of the answer. So, too, in a simulation, the questions posed direct the answers.

In this simulation, the charge was to develop a commercially viable station for a mythical market in the American mid-west where two VHF stations had been in existence for the previous 20 years. Academics are circumscribed by such a charge; professionals readily acknowledge that they are defined by it, and, as in all four groups, solutions flow from its demands. Thus, the ascertainment process is determined not only by the regulations but more especially by the prospect of competitive challenge; programming concentrates on the syndicated rather than the original; news planning does not begin with the tantalizing prospect of a two-hour broadcast but rather from the pragmatic evaluation of what is being done in the market; promotion recognizes that no broadcast can succeed unless its existence is known; budgets are determined with the objective of assuring a return on investment.

The new station will require not only risk capital but long term investment. This involves banks and, ultimately, the whole range of investors—mutual funds, pensions, insurance companies and private investors. In turn, the station within a framework of Federal regulations, will engage in journalism and present entertainment, a sort of newspaper publisher and movie theatre operator combined, deriving revenue not from the sale of tickets but from that most intangible quantity, advertising time. The wonder is not that the decisions of such a medium foster caution; the wonder is that it can work at all. A successful KIRT-TV is no more a miracle than any American broadcasting station.

Appendix 1

FCC FORM 301: *APPLICATION FOR AUTHORITY TO CONSTRUCT A NEW BROADCAST STATION*

FCC Form 301
January 1971

Section I

Form Approved
Budget Bureau No. 52-R0014

UNITED STATES OF AMERICA
FEDERAL COMMUNICATIONS COMMISSION

Application for Authority to Construct a New Broadcast Station or Make Changes In an Existing Broadcast Station

INSTRUCTIONS

A. This form is to be used in applying for authority to construct a new standard, commercial FM, or television broadcast station, or to make changes in existing broadcast stations. This form consists of this part, Section I, and the following sections:

Section II, Legal Qualifications of Broadcast Applicant
Section III, Financial Qualifications of Broadcast Applicant
Section IV-A, Statement of Program Service of Broadcast Applicant (AM-FM)
Section IV-B, Statement of Program Service of Broadcast Applicant (TV)
Section V-A, Standard Broadcast Engineering Data
Section V-B, FM Broadcast Engineering Data
Section V-C, Television Broadcast Engineering Data
Section V-G, Antenna and Site Information
Section VI, Equal Employment Opportunity Program

B. Prepare three copies of this form and all exhibits. Sign one copy of Sections I, IV-A, and IV-B. Prepare one additional copy (a total of four) of Section V-G and associated exhibits, and one additional copy (a total of four) of Section V-C and associated exhibits. File all the above with Federal Communications Commission, Washington, D. C. 20554. A SEPARATE AND COMPLETE APPLICATION (IN TRIPLICATE) MUST BE FILED FOR EACH AM STATION, EACH FM STATION, AND EACH TV STATION.

C. Number exhibits serially in the space provided in the body of the form and list each exhibit in the space provided on page 2 of this Section. Show date of preparation of each exhibit, antenna pattern, and map, and show date when each photograph was taken.

D. The name of the applicant stated in Section I hereof shall be the exact corporate name, if a corporation; if a partnership, the names of all partners and the name under which the partnership does business; of an unincorporated association, the name of an executive officer, his office, and the name of the association. In other Sections of the form the name alone will be sufficient for identification of the applicant.

E. Information called for by this application which is already on file with the Commission *(except that called for in Section III which is more than 90 days old and in Section V-G)* need not be refiled in this application provided (1) the information is now on file in another application or FCC Form filed by or on behalf of this applicant; (2) the information is identified FULLY by reference to the file number (if any) the FCC form number, and the filing date of the application or other form containing the information and the page or paragraph referred to, and (3) after making the reference, the applicant states: "No change since date of filing." Any such reference will be considered to incorporate into this application all information, confidential or otherwise, contained in the application or other form referred to. The incorporated application or other form will thereafter, in its entirety, be open to the public. (See Section 1.526 of the Commission's Rules and Regulations, "Records to be maintained locally for public inspection by applicants, permittees, and licensees."

F. This application shall be personally signed by the applicant, if the applicant is an individual; by one of the partners, if the applicant is a partnership; by an officer, if the applicant is a corporation; by a member who is an officer, if the applicant is an unincorporated association; by such duly elected or appointed officials as may be competent to do so under the laws of the applicable jurisdiction, the applicant is an eligible government entity; or by the applicant's attorney in case of the applicant's physical disability or of his absence from the United States. The attorney shall, in the event he signs for the applicant, separately set forth the reason why the application is not signed by the applicant. In addition, if any matter is stated on the basis of the attorney's belief only (rather than his knowledge), he shall separately set forth his reasons for believing that such statements are true.

G. Before filling out this application, the applicant should familiarize himself with the Communications Act of 1934, as amended, Parts 1, 2, 73 and 17 of the Commission's Rules and Regulations and the Standards of Good Engineering Practice.

H. BE SURE ALL NECESSARY INFORMATION IS FURNISHED AND ALL PARAGRAPHS ARE FULLY ANSWERED. IF ANY PORTIONS OF THE APPLICATION ARE NOT APPLICABLE, SPECIFICALLY SO STATE. DEFECTIVE OR INCOMPLETE APPLICATIONS MAY BE RETURNED WITHOUT CONSIDERATION.

File No.

1. Name of applicant (See Instruction D)

Street Address

City	State	ZIP Code

2. Name and address of person to whom communications should be sent, if different from item 1

Name

Street Address

City	State	ZIP Code

3(a). Purpose of application (check one)

☐ New Station   ☐ Change existing station facilities

(b). If this application is for a change in existing facilities, complete Section I plus any other Sections necessary to show all substantial changes in information previously filed with the Commission, and indicate below the Sections completed and filed with this application.

Section II	Section V-A
Section III	Section V-B
Section IV-A	Section V-C
Section IV-B	Section V-G
	Section VI

4. Requested facilities

Type of station (as Standard, FM, Television)

Frequency	Call	Channel No.	Power in kilowatts		Minimum hours operation daily
			Night	Day	

Hours of operation

Unlimited	Sharing with (Specify Stations)	Other (Specify)
Daytime only		
Limited		

Station location

City	State

5. In the space below refer to information already on file with the Commission which, in accordance with Instruction E, may be incorporated in this application by proper reference.

File or Form No. and Date	Section No.	Paragraph No.

FOR COMMISSION USE ONLY

THE APPLICANT hereby waives any claim to the use of any particular frequency or of the ether as against the regulatory power of the United States because of the previous use of the same, whether by license or otherwise, and requests an authorization in accordance with this application. (See Section 304 of the Communications Act of 1934).

THE APPLICANT represents that this application is not filed for the purpose of impeding, obstructing, or delaying determination on any other application with which it may be in conflict.

THE APPLICANT acknowledges that all the statements made in this application and attached exhibits are considered material representations, and that all the exhibits are a material part hereof and are incorporated herein as if set out in full in the application.

CERTIFICATION

I certify that the statements in this application are true, complete, and correct to the best of my knowledge and belief, and are made in good faith.

Signed and dated this .... day of ...., 19 ....

(This Section should not be signed and dated until all the following Sections and Exhibits have been prepared and attached.

INCLUDE FILING FEE WITH THIS APPLICATION. SEE PART 1 OF FCC RULES FOR AMOUNT OF FEE.

....
(NAME OF APPLICANT)

By ....
(SIGNATURE)

WILLFUL FALSE STATEMENTS MADE ON THIS FORM ARE PUNISHABLE BY FINE AND IMPRISONMENT U. S. CODE, TITLE 18, SECTION 1001.

Title ....

If applicant is represented by legal or engineering counsel, state name and post office address:

EXHIBITS furnished as required by this form:

Exhibit No.	Section and Para. No. of Form	Name of officer or employee (1) by whom or (2) under whose direction exhibit was prepared (show which)	Official title

F.C.C. Form 301	FEDERAL COMMUNICATIONS COMMISSION	Section II
LEGAL QUALIFICATIONS OF BROADCAST APPLICANT	Name of Applicant	

INSTRUCTIONS

As used in paragraphs 6 to 10 and 19 to 21, both inclusive, of Section II of this form, the words "party to this application" have the following meanings, respectively: In case of *an individual applicant*, the applicant. In case of a *partnership applicant*, all partners, including limited and silent partners. In case of a *corporate applicant*, all officers, directors, stockholders of record, persons owning the beneficial interest in any stock, subscribers to any stock, and persons who voted any of the voting stock at the last stockholders meeting. In case of *any other applicant*, all executive officers, members of the governing board, and owners or subscribers to any membership or ownership interest in the applicant. (Note: If the applicant considers that to furnish a complete answer to the paragraphs referred to would be an unreasonable burden, it may request the Commission for a waiver of the strict terms of this requirement.)

1. Applicant is (Check one): An individual ☐ , a general partnership ☐ , a limited partnership ☐ , a corporation ☐ , an unincorporated association ☐

2. If applicant is not an individual, give the State, District, Territory or Possession under the laws of which it is organized.

3. Submit as Exhibit No.   three copies (ONE COPY CERTIFIED) each of the Articles and By Laws, if applicant is a corporation or incorporated association, or three copies (ONE COPY SIGNED) of the partnership agreement, if applicant is a partnership. (ARTICLES MUST BE CERTIFIED BY SECRETARY OF STATE OR OTHER PROPERLY DESIGNATED STATE OFFICIAL AND BY LAWS MUST BE CERTIFIED BY APPROPRIATE OFFICIAL OF THE COMPANY)

4. If applicant is a corporation or an unincorporated association, indicate specifically by reference to page and paragraph of the articles of incorporation or of association, the charter powers relied upon by the applicant to show that it is legally empowered to construct and operate the proposed station. If the articles of incorporation do not specifically authorize kind of business sought to be entered into, attach a statement from Secretary of State or other officer interpreting the language relied upon.

5. Complete Tables I and II on pages 3 and 4.

CITIZENSHIP AND OTHER STATUTORY REQUIREMENTS (See instructions above)

6. If applicant is an individual, is the applicant a citizen of the United States; or, if applicant is not an individual, are all parties to this application citizens of the United States?   Yes ☐   No ☐

If the answer is "No", state the name and citizenship of each person who is not a citizen of the United States.

7. Is United States citizenship of any party to this application claimed by reason of naturalization?   Yes ☐   No ☐

If so, state the name of such party, the date and place of issuance of final certificate of naturalization, certificate number, and name and location of court authorizing issuance of same.

8. Is United States citizenship of any party to this application claimed by reason of naturalization of a parent?   Yes ☐   No ☐

If so, state the name of such party, the name of the parent to whom the final certificate was issued, the age of the party to this application at the time the certificate was issued, and any additional facts relied on to establish citizenship, in addition to the information required by Paragraph 7 hereof.

9. (a) Is applicant or any party to this application a representative of an alien or of a foreign government?   Yes ☐   No ☐

(b) If applicant is a corporation, is more than 20 percent of the capital stock owned of record or may it be voted by aliens or their representatives, or by a foreign government or a representative thereof, or by any corporation organized under the laws of a foreign country?   Yes ☐   No ☐

(c) If applicant is a corporation and is controlled by another corporation or corporations, is more than 25 percent of the capital stock of such controlling corporation or corporations owned of record or may it be voted by aliens, their representatives, or by any corporation organized under the laws of a foreign country?   Yes ☐   No ☐

(d) If the answer to any of the foregoing parts of this paragraph is "Yes", submit as Exhibit No.   a full disclosure concerning the persons and matters involved.

10. (a) Has applicant or any party to this application had a station license revoked by order or decree of any Federal court?   Yes ☐   No ☐

(b) Has the applicant or any party to this application been found guilty by a Federal court of the violation of the laws of the United States relating to unlawful restraints and monopolies and to combinations, contracts, or agreements in restraint of trade?   Yes ☐   No ☐

(c) Has the applicant or any party to this application been finally adjudged guilty by a Federal court of unlawfully monopolizing or attempting unlawfully to monopolize radio communications, directly or indirectly, through the control of the manufacture or sale of radio apparatus, through exclusive traffic arrangements, or by any other means, or to have been using unfair methods of competition? (See Section 313 of the Communications Act of 1934)   Yes ☐   No ☐

(d) Has the applicant or any party to this application been found guilty by any court of (1) any felony, (2) any crime, not a felony, involving moral turpitude, (3) the violation of any State, territorial or local law relating to unlawful lotteries, restraints and monopolies and combinations, contracts or agreements in restraint of trade, or (4) using unfair methods of competition?   Yes ☐   No ☐

FCC Form 301	LEGAL QUALIFICATIONS	Section II, Page 2

10. (Continued)

e. Is there now pending in any court or administrative body against the applicant or any party to this application any action involving any of the matters referred to in Paragraphs 10a, b, c, and d above?　　Yes ☐ No ☐

f. Have voluntary proceedings in bankruptcy been instituted by, or have involuntary proceedings in bankruptcy ever been brought against applicant or any party to this application?　　Yes ☐ No ☐

g. Are there outstanding any unsatisfied judgments or decrees against applicant or any party to this application?　　Yes ☐ No ☐

h. If the answer to any of the foregoing parts of this paragraph is "Yes", submit as Exhibit No.　　a full disclosure concerning the persons and matters involved, identifying the court and the proceeding (by dates and file numbers), stating the facts upon which the proceeding was based or the nature of the offense committed, and the disposition of the matter.

CORPORATE APPLICANT

INSTRUCTION: If applicant is a corporation, answer paragraphs 11 to 16, inclusive.

11. Stock of corporation

(a) Class of stock	(b) Par value	(c) Vote per share	(d) No. shares authorized	(e) No. shares issued	(f) No. shares subscribed	(g) Total number stockholders

12. At the last meeting of stockholders were any shares of stock voted by proxy?　　Yes ☐ No ☐

If so, state

Class of stock	No. of shares	Meeting date	No. voted by stockholders in person	No. voted by proxy	Name of each proxy voting 1 percent or more of each class

13. In connection with the stockholders and stock subscribers named in Table I to this form, is the beneficial owner of the stock a person other than the owner of record or subscriber?　　Yes ☐ No ☐

If so, submit as Exhibit No.　　a statement of (a) the name of the owner of record, or subscriber, (b) the name of the beneficial owner, (c) the conditions under which the owner or subscriber holds any votes or has subscribed for such stock, and (d) a copy of any contract or other instrument relating to such conditions.

14. Has applicant any other obligations or securities authorized or outstanding which bear voting rights either absolutely or upon any contingency?　　Yes ☐ No ☐

If so, submit as Exhibit No.　　a statement of (a) the nature of such securities, (b) the face value or par value, (c) the number of units authorized, (d) the number of units issued and outstanding, (e) the number of units, if any, proposed to be issued, (f) the conditions or contingency upon which such securities may be voted, and (g) facts showing whether or not such securities have been voted or entitled to be voted in the past 5 years and at the present time.

15a. Is applicant corporation, directly or indirectly, controlled by another corporation or legal entity?　　Yes ☐ No ☐

b. Is 10 percent or more of the stock of applicant corporation owned by another corporation or legal entity?　　Yes ☐ No ☐

c. If the answer to any of the foregoing parts of this paragraph is "Yes", state below the name of such other corporation or legal entity, and submit as Exhibit No.　　(a) a statement of how such control, if any, exists and the extent thereof, and (b) with respect to such other corporation or legal entity, a statement answering paragraphs 11 to 15, inclusive and the information requested in Tables I and II of this section.

16. Is the corporation or legal entity named in paragraph 15 in turn a subsidiary?　　Yes ☐ No ☐

If so, state below the name of such other parent corporation or legal entity, and submit as Exhibit No.　　a statement for each such corporation or legal entity answering paragraphs 11 to 16, and the information requested in Tables I and II of this section, to and including the organization having final control.

UNINCORPORATED ASSOCIATION (OR OTHER LEGAL ENTITY)

INSTRUCTION: If applicant is an unincorporated association or a legal entity other than an individual, partnership or corporation, answer paragraphs 17 and 18.

17. State the nature of the applicant, cite the laws under which organized, and submit as Exhibit No.　　a copy of such laws.

18. State the total number of members or persons holding any ownership interest in the applicant.

LEGAL QUALIFICATIONS

Table I

INSTRUCTIONS: *If applicant is an individual*, fill out columns (a) and (b) stating (a) applicant's name and residence (home) address or addresses, and (b) applicant's date and place of birth. *If applicant is a partnership*, fill out columns (a), (b), (c) and (g), stating as to each general or limited partner (including silent partners): (a) name and residence (home) address or addresses, (b) date and place of birth, (c) nature of partnership interest (i.e. general or limited), and (g) percent of ownership interest. *If applicant is a corporation or an unincorporated association*, fill out all columns, giving the information requested as to all officers, directors and members of the governing board. In addition, give the information as to all stockholders, stock subscribers, holders of membership certificates of other ownership interests, unless the applicant has more than 20 stockholders, stock subscribers or holders of membership certificates or other ownership interests, in which case furnish the information as to all persons owning 3 percent or more of the capital stock, membership or ownership interest, and all persons who voted 3 percent or more of such stock or interest at the last meeting of stockholders, members or owners. *If applicant is a corporation or unincorporated association*, state in columns (g) the percent of voting stock or voting interest held, (d) whether or not the individual is a director or member of the governing board (Yes or No), (e) the number of shares of stock of all classes or membership interests held, and (f) the number of shares of stock of all classes or membership interests subscribed for.

NAME AND RESIDENCE (home) ADDRESS(es)	DATE AND PLACE OF BIRTH	NATURE OF PARTNERSHIP INTEREST OR OFFICE HELD	DIRECTOR OR MEMBER OF GOVERNING BOARD (Yes or No)	NO. SHARES OF EACH CLASS OF STOCK OR NO. OWNERSHIP INTERESTS		PERCENT OF OWNER-SHIP OF PARTNERSHIP OR PERCENT OF VOTING STOCK OR MEMBERSHIP
				Now held	Subscribed	
(a)	(b)	(c)	(d)	(e)	(f)	(g)

204

Table II

BUSINESS AND FINANCIAL INTERESTS

INSTRUCTIONS: The purpose of Table II is to obtain information concerning the occupation, business, and financial interests, at the present time and during the past 5 years, of the applicant and of each party to this application named in Table I. In column (a) list the names of all individuals or organizations listed in column (a) of Table I. In column (b) state the principal occupations and businesses in which each party named is engaged at the present time or has been engaged at any time during the past 5 years and, in addition, state any other business or financial enterprise in which such party has now or within the past 5 years has had either a 25% or greater interest or any official relationship. In each case, state in column (b) the firm name, the principal place of business, and the nature of the business engaged in. In case the party has been associated in business with any other person or persons, state the name of each such other person. In column (c) state the extent and nature of the interest, official relationship, employment, or association, giving approximate dates.

(a) Name of party	(b) Firm name, principal place of business, and nature of business	(c) Extent and nature of interest, etc. (giving dates)

FCC Form 301	LEGAL QUALIFICATIONS	Section II, Page 5

OTHER BROADCAST INTERESTS (See instructions on page 1)

19. Does applicant or any party to this application have now, or has applicant or any such party had, any interest in, or connection with, the following:

(a) Any standard, FM, or television broadcast station? Yes ☐ No ☐

(b) Any application pending before the Commission? Yes ☐ No ☐

(c) Any application which has been denied by the Federal Communications Commission? Yes ☐ No ☐

(d) Any broadcast station the license of which has been revoked? Yes ☐ No ☐

If the answer to any of the foregoing parts of this paragraph is "Yes", show particulars in the table below:

(1) Name of party having such interest	(2) Nature of interest or connection (giving dates)	(3) Call letters of station or file number of application	(4) Location

20. Is the applicant or any party to this application controlled, directly or indirectly, by any person who has any interest in or connection with any broadcast station or application of the type referred to in Paragraphs 19(a) to (d)? If so, submit as Exhibit No.   giving full particulars.   Yes ☐ No ☐

21. (a) Are any of the parties to this application related to each other (as husband, wife, father, mother, brother, sister, son or daughter)?   Yes ☐ No ☐

(b) Does any member of the immediate family (i.e., husband, wife, father, mother, brother, sister, son or daughter) of any party to this application have any interest in or connection with any other broadcast station or pending application?   Yes ☐ No ☐

(c) If answer is "Yes" to either (a) or (b) above, state (a) names of the persons, (b) relationship, (c) nature and extent of such interest or connection, (d) name of applicant or call letters of station, (e) file number of application, and (f) location of station or proposed station involved.

OWNERSHIP AND CONTROL OF STATION

22. The Commission is seeking in this paragraph information as to contracts and arrangements now in existence, as well as any arrangements or negotiations, written or oral, which relate to the present or future ownership, control or operation of the station; the questions must be answered in the light of this instruction.

(a) Applicant's control over the station is to be by reason of: (Indicate by check mark)

Ownership ☐   Lease ☐   Other authority ☐

(b) Name and address of the owner of the station (if other than the applicant)

(c) Will the applicant have and maintain absolute control of the station, its equipment, and operation, including complete supervision of the programs to be broadcast? If "No", explain   Yes ☐ No ☐

(d) Are there any documents, instruments, contracts or understandings relating to ownership, management, use or control of the station or facilities, or any right or interest therein?   Yes ☐ No ☐

If so, attach as Exhibit No.   copies of all such documents, instruments or contracts and state the substance of oral contracts or understandings.

FCC Form 301	FEDERAL COMMUNICATIONS COMMISSION	Section III

**FINANCIAL QUALIFICATIONS
OF BROADCAST APPLICANT**

NAME OF APPLICANT

The Commission is seeking in the questions that follow information as to contracts and arrangements now in existence, as well as any arrangements or negotiations, written or oral, which relate to the present or future financing of the station; the questions must be answered in the light of this instruction.

IF CONTEMPLATED EXPENDITURES ARE LESS THAN $5,000 COMPLETE PARAGRAPH 1 OF SECTION III ONLY.

1. a. Give estimated initial costs of making installation for which application is made. If performed under a contract for the completed work, the facts as to such contract must be stated in lieu of estimates as to the several items. In any event, the cost shown must be the costs in place and ready for service, including the amounts for labor, supervision, materials, supplies and freight. Cost items such as professional fees, mobile and STL equipment, non-technical studio furnishings, etc., should be included under "Other Items" below, and itemized.

	COLUMN I (USE ONLY WHEN ITEMIZING)	COLUMN II (TOTAL)
Antenna System: (Including antenna, antenna tower, transmission line, phasing equipment, ground system, coupling equipment and tower lighting.)	$	$
RF Generating Equipment: (Including transmitter, tubes, filters, diplexer, remote control equipment, and automatic logger.)		
Monitoring and Test Equipment: (Including frequency monitor, phase monitor, modulation monitor, oscilloscope, dummy load, vectorscope, video monitors.)		
Program Origination Equipment: (Including control consoles, film chains, cameras, audio tape equipment, video tape equipment, program and distribution amplifiers, limiters, and transcription equipment.)		
Acquiring Land:		
Acquiring, Remodeling or Constructing Buildings:		
Other Items: (Itemize Below)		
Legal Costs:		
Engineering Costs:		
Installation Costs:		
Other Miscellaneous:		
Total Other Items:		
Total Construction Costs:		
Add Estimated Cost of Operation for First Year:		
Total First Year Costs To Be Met By Applicant:		
Estimated Revenues For First Year:		

| FCC Form 301 | FINANCIAL QUALIFICATIONS | Section III, Page 2 |

Item 1 (continued)

b. State the basis of the estimates in (a), Page 1, Section III, including (in the case of an application for a new broadcast station) complete itemization of cost of operation for the first year, including cost of proposed programming, as Exhibit No. ____ to this application.

c. The proposed construction is to be financed and paid for in the following manner. The financial plan should provide for sufficient funds to construct the station and operate it for a period of one year. If the applicant plans to rely on revenues from operation of the proposed station for any portion of operating expenses, supply as Exhibit No.____ data in support of revenue estimate.

	COLUMN I (USE ONLY FOR LOANS AND DEFERRED CREDIT)	COLUMN II (NET TOTAL)
Existing Capital:	$	$ _____
New Capital:		_____
Loans from Banks or Others:	_____	
(Less repayments of principal and interest @ ____% due during first year):	_____	
Net Total Available from Loans:		_____
Profits from Existing Operations:		_____
Donations:		_____
Other Sources: *(Specify)*		_____
Deferred Credit from Equipment Supplier:	_____	
(Note: If 1st payment is due upon shipment, include 14 monthly payments. If due in 30 days, 13 monthly payments. If due in 60 days, 12 monthly payments, etc.)		
(a) Less: Down Payment ____%	_____	
(b) Less: 1st Year Payment to Principal	_____	
(c) Less: 1st Year Interest @ ____%	_____	
Net Deferred Credit Available:		_____
Net Total Available:		

2. a. Attach as Exhibit No.____ a detailed balance sheet of applicant as at the close of a month within 90 days of the date of the application showing applicant's financial position. If the status and composition of any assets and liabilities on the balance sheet are not clearly defined by their respective titles, attach as Exhibit No.____ schedules which give a complete analysis of such items.

b. Attach as Exhibit No.____ a statement showing the yearly net income, after Federal income tax, for each of the past 2 year received by applicant from any source.

3. Furnish the following information with respect to the applicant only. If the answer is "None" to any or all items, specificall so state:

a. Amount of funds on deposit in bank or other depository: $	b. Name and address of the bank in which deposited (Include ZIP Code)

c. Name and address of the party in whose name the money is deposited (Include ZIp Code)

d. Conditions of deposit (in trust, savings, subject to check, on time deposit, who may draw on account and for what purpose, or other condition).

e. Are the funds deposited for the specific purpose of constructing and operating the station? ☐ Yes ☐ No
If "No," explain.

FUNDS, PROPERTY, ETC., TO BE FURNISHED BY
PARTIES CONNECTED WITH APPLICANT OR BY OTHERS

4. Submit as Exhibit No. ____ a statement setting forth the full name and address of each person (whether or not connected with applicant, but including partners, shareholders, or subscribers to capital stock of the applicant) who has furnished or will furnish funds, property, service, credit, loans, donations, assurances, or other things of value, or will assist in any other manner in financing station. For each person (other than financial institutions or equipment manufacturers) who has furnished or will furnish one percent or more of the total of things of value, excluding loans from financial institutions and equipment credit, supply the additional information requested in a. to d. below. For financial institutions or equipment manufacturers, supply the additional information requested in e.below. ("Furnish" or "furnished" as herein used includes payments for capital stock or other securities, loans and other credits, gifts and any other contributions.)

a. For each person who has agreed to furnish funds, purchase stock, extend credit, or guarantee loans, submit a copy of the agreement by which each person is so obligated, showing the amount, rate of interest, terms of repayment, and security, if any. If no security is required, so state.

b. For each person (except financial institutions) who has agreed to furnish funds or purchase stock, but who has not already done so, submit a balance sheet or, in lieu thereof, a financial statement showing all liabilities and containing current and liquid assets sufficient in amount to meet current liabilities (including amounts payable during the next year on long term liabilities) and, in addition, to indicate financial ability to comply with the terms of the agreement. The balance sheets submitted should segregate receivables and payables to show the amounts due within one year and those due after one year. The term and liquid assets refers to items such as cash, or loan value of insurance, government bonds and publicly traded securities (provided, however, that such securities must be identified by the market or exchange on which traded, at their current market value), or other assets which may be readily used or converted to provide funds to meet the proposed commitments. Current assets such as accounts receivable which result from normal operation of a business, inventory, etc., are not considered as a readily available source of funds without a specific showing that such assets can be relied upon to provide funds to meet proposed commitments. However, if accounts receivable have been "aged" and certified collectible within 90 days by a Certified Public Accountant, three-fourths (3/4) of such accounts receivable will be treated as "liquid." If a balance sheet or a financial statement does not clearly indicate liquid and current assets sufficient in amount to meet current liabilities and in addition, sufficient liquid assets to meet the proposed commitments, it should be supplemented by a statement showing the manner in which non-liquid assets will provide such funds. When the applicant relies upon "non-liquid assets," a statement must be submitted showing the extent to which such assets have liens or prior obligations against them. All balance sheets, or financial statements submitted in accordance with this section must be dated. In any event, a mere statement of total assets and total liabilities, or a statement of net worth, is not acceptable under the terms of this section.

c. Net income after Federal income tax, received for the past two years by each person who will furnish funds, property, service, credit, loans, donations, assurances, or other things of value. (A statement that income tax for the required periods was in excess of a certain specified amount will be sufficient.)

d. If applicant or any person named in the exhibit has pledged, hypothecated or otherwise encumbered any stocks or other securities for the purpose of providing applicant with funds for construction of the station herein requested, submit a statement explaining each such transaction.

e. For financial institutions or equipment manufacturers who have agreed to make a loan or extend credit, submit a copy of the document by which the institution or manufacturer has indicated its willingness to provide such loan or credit, showing the amount of loan or credit, terms of payment or repayment of loan, collateral or security required, and rate of interest to be charged. If there are any special requirements such as a moratorium on principal or interest, or a waiver of collateral, etc., it must be shown on the document of credit. In the event such document requires special endorsements or guarantees, a statement from the party or parties required to provide such endorsement or guarantee must be submitted with the document as supporting evidence of their willingness to so provide.

FCC Form 301	FEDERAL COMMUNICATIONS COMMISSION	Section IV-A
STATEMENT OF AM OR FM PROGRAM SERVICE (See instructions, Sec. IV-A, pages 7 and 8.)	Name of Applicant	
Call letters of station	City and state which station is licensed to serve	

PART I

Ascertainment of Community Needs

1. A. State in Exhibit No._____ the methods used by the applicant to ascertain the needs and interests of the public served by the station. Such information shall include (1) identification of representative groups, interests and organizations which were consulted and (2) the major communities or areas which applicant principally undertakes to serve.

   B. Describe in Exhibit No._____ the significant needs and interests of the public which the applicant believes his station will serve during the coming license period, including those with respect to national and international matters.

   C. List in Exhibit No._____ typical and illustrative programs or program series (excluding Entertainment and News) that applicant plans to broadcast during the coming license period to meet those needs and interests.

NOTE: Sufficient records shall be kept on file at the station, open for inspection by the Commission, for a period of 3 years from the date of filing of this statement (unless requested to be kept longer by the Commission) to support the representations required in answer to Question 1. These records should *not* be submitted with this application and need not be available for public inspection.

PART II

Past Programming

2. A. State the total hours of operation during the composite week: _____

   B. Attach as Exhibit No. _____ one exact copy of the program logs for the composite week used as a basis for responding to questions herein. Applicants utilizing automatic program logging devices must comply with the provisions of Sections 73.112(c) and 73.282(c). Automatic recordings will be returned to the applicant. Exact copies will not be returned.

   If applicant has not operated during all of the days of the composite week which would be applicable to the use of this form, applicant should so notify the Commission and request the designation of substitute day or days as required.

3. A. State the amount of time (rounded to the nearest minute) the applicant devoted in the composite week to the program types (see Definitions) listed below. Commercial matter within a program segment shall be excluded in computing time devoted to that particular program segment (e.g., a 15-minute news program containing 3 minutes' commercial matter shall be counted as a 12-minute news program).

	Hours	Minutes	% of Total Time on Air
(1) News	....	....	.... %
(2) Public Affairs	....	....	.... %
(3) All other programs, exclusive of Entertainment and Sports	....	....	.... %

   B. If in the applicant's judgment the composite week does not adequately represent the station's past programming, applicant may in addition provide in Exhibit No._____ the same information as required in 3-A above (using the same format) for a calendar month or longer during the year preceding the filing of this application. Applicant shall identify the time period used. Applicant need not file the program logs used in responding to this question unless requested by the Commission.

4. List in Exhibit No._____ typical and illustrative programs or program series (excluding Entertainment and News) broadcast during the year preceding the filing of this application which have served public needs and interests in applicant's judgment. Denote, by underlining the Title, those programs, if any, designed to inform the public on local, national or international problems of greatest public importance in the community served by the applicant. Use the format below.

Title	Source*	Type*	Brief Description	Time Broadcast & Duration	How Often Broadcast

5. Submit in Exhibit No._____ the following information concerning the applicant's news programs:

   A. The staff, news gathering facilities, news services and other sources utilized; and

   B. An estimate of the percentage of news program time devoted to local and regional news during the composite week.

6. In connection with the applicant's public affairs programming, describe its policy during the past renewal period with respect to making time available for the discussion of public issues and the method of selecting subjects and participants.

*See Definitions Section IV-A, Page 7

7. Describe briefly the applicant's program format(s) during the past 12 months (e.g., country and western music, talk, folk music, classical music, foreign language, jazz, standard pops, etc.) and the approximate percentage of time per week devoted to such format(s).

8. State how and to what extent (if any) applicant's station contributed during the past license period to the over-all diversity of program services available in the area or communities served.

9. Was the applicant affiliated with one or more national, regional or special radio networks during the past license period? Yes_____ No_____. If "yes," give name(s) of network(s): _____

0. State the number of public service announcements broadcast by the applicant during the composite week: _____

1. A. If this application is for an FM station, did the programming duplicate that of any AM station?

   Yes_____ No_____.("Duplicate" means simultaneous broadcasting of a particular program over both the AM and FM stations or the broadcast of a particular FM program within 24 hours before or after the identical program is broadcast over the AM station—Section 73.242(a) of the Rules and Regulations.)

   B. If the answer is "yes," identify the AM station by call letters; describe its relation to the FM station; and state the number of hours each day in the composite week that were duplicated.

2. A. In applicant's judgment, does the information supplied in this Part II adequately reflect its past programming? Yes _____ No _____.

   B. If "no," applicant may attach as Exhibit No._____ such additional information as may be necessary to describe accurately and present fairly its program service.

   C. If applicant's programming practices for the period covered by this statement varied substantially from the programming representations made in applicant's last renewal application, the applicant shall submit as Exhibit No. _____a statement explaining the variations and the reasons therefor.

PART III

Proposed Programming

3. State the proposed total hours of operation during a typical week:_____

4. State the minimum amount of time the applicant proposes to devote normally each week to the program types (see Definitions) listed below. Commercial matter within a program segment shall be excluded in computing time devoted to that particular program segment (e.g., a fifteen-minute news program containing 3 minutes' commercial matter shall be computed as a 12-minute news program.)

	Hours	Minutes	% of Total Time on Air
(1) News....................................	....	....	.... %
(2) Public Affairs	....	....	.... %
(3) All other programs, exclusive of Entertainment and Sports.............	....	....	.... %

Submit in Exhibit No._____ the following information concerning the applicant's proposed news programs:

A. The staff, news gathering facilities, news services and other sources to be utilized; and

B. An estimate of the percentage of news program time to be devoted to local and regional news during a typical week.

16. In connection with the applicant's proposed public affairs programming describe its policy with respect to making time
available for the discussion of public issues and the method of selecting subjects and participants.

17. Describe the applicant's proposed programming format(s), e.g., country and western music, talk, folk music, classical
music, foreign language, jazz, standard pops, etc., and the approximate percentage of time per week to be devoted to such
format(s).

18. State how and to what extent (if any) applicant proposes to contribute to the over-all diversity of program services availabl
in the area or communities to be served.

19. State the minimum number of public service announcements applicant proposes to present during a typical week: _____

20. Will the applicant be affiliated with one or more national, regional, or special radio networks? Yes_____ No_____.
If "yes," give name(s) of networks(s): _____

21. A. If this application is for an FM station will the programming duplicate that of any AM station? Yes_____ No_____.
("Duplicate" means simultaneous broadcasting of a particular program over both AM and FM stations or the broadcast of
a particular FM program within 24 hours before or after the identical program is broadcast over the AM station—Section
73.242(a) of the Rules and Regulations.)

B. If the answer is "yes," identify the AM station by call letters; describe its relation to the FM station; and state the
number of hours each day proposed to be duplicated.

PART IV

Past Commercial Practices

22. Give the following information with respect to the composite week:

	All Hours	6 A.M. - 6 P.M.
A. Total broadcast time	....	....
B. Time devoted to commercial matter:		
(1) Amount in hours and minutes	....	....
(2) Percentage	.... %	.... %

FCC Form 301   STATEMENT OF AM OR FM PROGRAM SERVICE   Section IV-A, Page 4

23. State the number of 60-minute segments of the composite week (beginning with the first full clock hour and ending with the last clock hour of each broadcast day) containing the following amounts of commercial matter:

    A. Up to and including 10 minutes ....

    B. Over 10 and up to and including 14 minutes ....

    C. Over 14 and up to and including 18 minutes ....

    D. Over 18 minutes ....

List each segment in category (D) above, specifying the amount of commercial time in the segment, and the day and time broadcast.

24. A. In the applicant's judgment, does the information supplied in this Part IV for the composite week adequately reflect its commercial practices?   Yes_____ No_____ .

    B. If "no," applicant may attach as Exhibit No._____such additional material as may be necessary to describe adequately and present fairly its commercial practices.

    C. If applicant's commercial practices for the period covered by this statement varied substantially from the commercial representations made in applicant's last renewal application, the applicant shall submit as Exhibit No._____ a statement explaining the variations and the reasons therefor.

PART V
Proposed Commercial Practices

25. State the maximum percentage of commercial matter which the applicant proposes normally to allow during the following segments of a typical week:

        6 a.m. - 6 p.m. .... _____%

        All hours .... _____%

If applicant proposes to permit this level to be exceeded at times, state under what circumstances and how often this is expected to occur, and the limits that would then apply.

26. What is the maximum amount of commercial matter in any 60-minute segment which the applicant proposes normally to allow?

If applicant proposes to permit this amount to be exceeded at times, state under what circumstances and how often this is expected to occur, and the limits that would then apply.

PART VI
General Station Policies and Procedures

27. State the name(s) and position of the person(s) who determines the/day-to-day programming, makes decisions, and directs the operation of the station covered by this application and whether he is employed full-time in the operation of the station.

28. A. Does the applicant have established policies with respect to programming and advertising standards (whether developed by the station or contained in a code of broadcasting standards and practices) to guide the operation of the station?

Yes_____ No_____.

    B. If "yes," attach as Exhibit No._____ a brief summary of such policies. (If the station relies exclusively upon the published code of any national organization or trade association, a statement to that effect will suffice)

29. State the methods by which applicant undertakes to keep informed of the requirements of the Communications Act and the Commission's Rules and Regulations, and a description of the procedures established to acquaint applicant's employees and agents with such requirements and to ensure their compliance.

30. If, as an integral part of its station identification announcements, applicant makes or proposes to make reference to any business, profession or activity other than broadcasting in which applicant or any affiliate or stockholder is engaged or financially interested, directly or indirectly, set forth typical examples and approximate frequency of their use.

31. State the number of station employees: _____ . If the station has or proposes to have ten or more employees, state in Exhibit No._____ the number of full-time and part-time employees in the programming, sales, technical, and general and administrative departments. Do not list the same employee in more than one category. However, if an employee performs multiple services, this may be so shown by identifying him with his various duties e.g., if two employees are combination announcers and salesmen, the list would include an entry of "two programming-sales".

PART VII
Other Matters and Certification

2. Applicant may submit as Exhibit No._____ any additional information which, in its judgment, is necessary adequately to describe or to present fairly its services and operations in relation to the public interest.

3. The undersigned has familiarized himself with paragraph 7 of the Instructions on page 7 of Section IV-A concerning signature requirements and in light of its provisions does hereby:

   A. Acknowledge that all the statements made in this Section IV-A and the attached exhibits are considered material representations and that all the exhibits are a material part hereof and are incorporated herein as if set out in full in the application form; and

   B. Certify that the statements herein are true, complete, and correct to the best of his knowledge and belief and are made in good faith.

SIGNED AND DATED this .... day of .... , 19 ....

....
(NAME OF APPLICANT)

By: ....
(SIGNATURE)

....
(PLEASE PRINT NAME OF PERSON SIGNING)

....
(TITLE)

WILLFUL FALSE STATEMENTS MADE IN THIS FORM ARE PUNISHABLE BY FINE AND IMPRISONMENT. U. S. CODE, TITLE 18, SECTION 1001.

Instructions, General Information and Definitions
for AM-FM Broadcast Application

1. *Applicants for new AM or FM stations, and major changes when required* (see paragraph 2) shall file this Section IV-A with respect to Ascertainment of Community Needs (Part I), Proposed Programming (Part III), Proposed Commercial Practices (Part V), General Station Policies and Practices (Part VI) and Other Matters and Certification (Part VII).

2. *Applicants for major changes in facilities* (as defined in Sections 1.571(a)(1) and 1.573(a)(1) of the Commission's Rules) need not file this Section IV-A unless there is proposed a substantial change in programming, increased facilities serving a substantial amount of new area or population, or unless the information is requested by the Commission.

3. A. The replies to the following questions constitute representations on which the Commission will rely in considering this application. Thus time and care should be devoted to the replies so that they will reflect accurately applicant's responsib consideration of the questions asked. It is not, however, expected that the licensee will or can adhere inflexibly in day-to day operation to the representations made herein.

   B. Replies relating to future operation constitute representations against which the subsequent operation of the station will be measured. Accordingly, if during the license period the station substantially alters its programming format or commercia practices, the licensee should notify the Commission of such changes; otherwise it is presumed the station is being operat substantially as last proposed.

4. The applicant's attention is called to the Commission's "Report and Statement of Policy re: Commission En Banc Program ming Inquiry," (FCC 60-970; 25 Federal Register 7291; 20 Pike and Fischer Radio Regulation 1902), copies of which are available upon request to the Commission; and also to the material contained in Attachment A and Attachment B to this Section.

5. A legible copy of this Section IV-A and the exhibits submitted therewith shall be kept on file available for public inspectio at any time during regular business hours. It shall be maintained at the main studio of the station or any other accessible place (such as a public registry for documents or an attorney's office) in the community to which the station is or is propos to be licensed.

6. *Network Programs.* Where information for the composite week is called for herein with respect to commercial matter or pro gram type classification in connection with national network programs, the applicant may rely on information furnished by the network.

7. *Signature.*
   This Section IV-A shall be signed in the space provided at the end hereof. It shall be personally signed by the applicant, if the applicant is an individual; by one of the partners, if the applicant is a partnership; by an officer of applicant, if a corporation or association. *SIGNING OF THIS SECTION IS A REPRESENTATION THAT THE PERSON WHO SIGNS IS FAMILIAR WITH THE CONTENTS OF THIS SECTION AND ASSOCIATED EXHIBITS, AND SUPPORTS AND APPROVES THE REPRESENTATIONS THEREIN ON BEHALF OF THE APPLICANT.*

Definitions

The definitions set out below are to be followed in furnishing the information called for by the questions of this Section IV-A The inclusion of various types and sources of programs in the paragraphs which follow is not intended to establish a formula for station operation, but is a method for analyzing and reporting station operation.

8. *Sources* of programs are defined as follows:

   (a) A *local program* (L) is any program originated or produced by the station, or for the production of which the station is primarily responsible, and employing live talent more than 50% of the time. Such a program, taped or recorded for later broadcast, shall be classified as local. A local program fed to a network shall be classified by the originating station as local. All non-network news programs may be classified as local. Programs primarily featuring records or transcrip tions shall be classified as recorded even though a station announcer appears in connection with such material. How ever, identifiable units of such programs which are live and separately logged as such may be classified as local (e.g. if during the course of a program featuring records or transcriptions a non-network 2-minute news report is given and logged as a news program, the report may be classified as local).

   (b) A *network program* (NET) is any program furnished to the station by a network (national, regional or special). Delayed broadcasts of programs originated by networks are classified as network.

   (c) A *recorded program* (REC) is any program not defined above, including, without limitation, those using recordings, transcriptions, or tapes.

9. *Types* of programs are defined as follows:

   If a program contains two or more identifiable units of program material which constitute different program types as herein defined, each such unit may be separately logged and classified.

   The definitions of the first eight types of programs, (a) through (h) are not intended to overlap each other, and these types will normally include all the programs broadcast. The programs classified under (i) through (k) will have been classified under the first eight and there may be further duplication among types (i) through (k).

   (a) *Agricultural programs* (A) include market reports, farming or other information specifically addressed, or primarily of interest, to the agricultural population.

FCC Form 301   Section IV-A, Page 8

Definitions - Cont.

(b) *Entertainment programs* (E) include all programs intended primarily as entertainment, such as music, drama, variety, comedy, quiz, etc.

(c) *News programs* (N) include reports dealing with current local, national, and international events, including weather and stock market reports; and when an integral part of a news program, commentary, analysis and sports news.

(d) *Public Affairs programs* (PA) include talks, commentaries, discussions, speeches, editorials, political programs, documentaries, forums, panels, round tables, and similar programs primarily concerning local, national, and international public affairs.

(e) *Religious programs* (R) include sermons or devotionals; religious news; and music, drama, and other types of programs designed primarily for religious purposes.

(f) *Instructional programs* (I) include programs, other than those classified under Agricultural, News, Public Affairs, Religious or Sports, involving the discussion of, or primarily designed to further an appreciation or understanding of, literature, music, fine arts, history, geography, and the natural and social sciences; and programs devoted to occupational and vocational instruction, instruction with respect to hobbies, and similar programs intended primarily to instruct.

(g) *Sports programs* (S) include play-by-play and pre- or post-game related activities and separate programs of sports instruction, news, or information (e.g., fishing opportunities, golfing instruction, etc.).

(h) *Other programs* (O) include all programs not falling within definitions (a) through (g).

         *   *   *   *   *   *   *   *

(i) *Editorials* (EDIT) include programs presented for the purpose of stating opinions of the licensee.

(j) *Political programs* (POL) include those which present candidates for public office or which give expression (other than in station editorials) to views on such candidates or on issues subject to public ballot.

(k) *Educational Institution programs* (ED) include any program prepared by, in behalf of, or in cooperation with, educational institutions, educational organizations, libraries, museums, PTA's or similar organizations. Sports programs shall not be included.

). *Commercial matter* (CM) includes commercial continuity (network and non-network) and commercial announcements (network and non-network) as follows:

(a) *Commercial continuity* (CC) is the advertising message of a program sponsor.

(b) *A commercial announcement* (CA) is any other advertising message for which a charge is made, or other consideration is received.

    (1) Included are (i) "bonus" spots, (ii) trade-out spots, and (iii) promotional announcements of a future program where consideration is received for such an announcement or where such announcement identifies the sponsor of the future program beyond mention of the sponsor's name as an integral part of the title of the program (e.g., where the agreement for the sale of time provides that the sponsor will receive promotional announcements, or when the promotional announcement contains a statement such as "LISTEN TOMORROW FOR THE [NAME OF PROGRAM] BROUGHT TO YOU BY [SPONSOR'S NAME]").

    (2) Other announcements including but not limited to the following are *not* commercial announcements:

        (i) Promotional announcements, except as defined above;

        (ii) Station identification announcements for which no charge is made;

        (iii)Mechanical reproduction announcements;

        (iv)Public service announcements;

        (v) Announcements made pursuant to Sections 73.119(d) or 73.289(d) of the Rules that materials or services have been furnished as an inducement to broadcast a political program or a program involving the discussion of controversial public issues;

        (vi) Announcements made pursuant to the local notice requirements of Sections 1.580 (pre-grant) and 1.594 (designation for hearing) of the Rules.

A public service announcement (PSA) is any announcement (including network) for which no charge is made and which promotes programs, activities, or services of federal, state or local governments (e.g., recruiting, sales of bonds, etc.) or the programs, activities or services of non-profit organizations (e.g., UGF, Red Cross blood donations, etc.), and other announcements regarded as serving community interests, excluding time signals, routine weather announcements and promotional announcements.

A program is an identifiable unit of program material, logged as such, which is not an announcement as defined above (e.g., if, within a 30-minute entertainment program, a station broadcasts a one-minute news and weather report, this news and weather report may be separately logged and classified as a one-minute news program and the entertainment portion as a 29-minute program).

Composite Week - Seven days designated annually by the Commission in a Public Notice and consisting of seven different days of the week.

Typical Week - A week which an applicant projects as typical of his proposed weekly operation.

ATTACHMENT A

Attention is invited to the Commission's "Report and Statement of Policy Re: Commission En Banc Programming Inquiry" released July 29, 1960 - FCC 60-970 (25 Federal Register 7291; 20 Pike and Fischer Radio Regulation 1902).

Pursuant to the Communications Act of 1934, as amended, the Commission cannot grant, renew or modify a broadcast authorization unless it makes an affirmative finding that the operation of the station, as proposed, will serve the public interest, convenience and necessity. Programming is of the essence of broadcasting.

A broadcast station's use of a channel for the period authorized is premised on its serving the public. Thus, the public has a legitimate and continuing interest in the program service offered by the station, and it is the duty of all broadcast permittees and licensees to serve as trustees for the public in the operation of their stations. Broadcast permittees and licensees must make positive, diligent and continuing efforts to provide a program schedule designed to serve the needs and interests of the public in the areas to which they transmit an acceptable signal.

In its above-referenced "Policy Statement," the Commission has indicated the general nature of the inquiry which should be made in the planning and devising of a program schedule:

"Thus we do not intend to guide the licensee along the path of programming; on the contrary, the licensee must find his own path with the guidance of those whom his signal is to serve. We will thus steer clear of the bans of censorship without disregarding the public's vital interest. What we propose will not be served by pre-planned program format submissions accompanied by complimentary references from local citizens. What we propose is documented program submissions prepared as the result of assiduous planning and consultation covering two main areas: first, a canvass of the listening public who will receive the signal and who constitute a definite public interest figure; second, consultation with leaders in community life -- public officials, educators, religious (groups), the entertainment media - agriculture, business, labor, professional and eleemosynary organizations, and others who bespeak the interests which make up the community."

Over the years, experience has shown both broadcasters and the Commission that certain recognized elements of broadcast service have frequently been found necessary or desirable to serve the broadcast needs and interests of many communities. In the Policy Statement, referred to above, the Commission set out fourteen such elements. The Commission stated:

"The major elements usually necessary to meet the public interest, needs and desires of the community in which the station is located as developed by the industry, and recognized by the Commission, have included: (1) Opportunity for Local Self-Expression, (2) The Development and Use of Local Talent (3) Programs for Children, (4) Religious Programs, (5) Educational Programs, (6) Public Affairs Programs, (7) Editorialization by licensees, (8) Political Broadcasts, (9) Agricultural Programs, (10) News Programs, (11) Weather and Market Reports, (12) Sports Programs, (13) Service to Minority Groups, (14) Entertainment Programming."

It is emphasized that broadcasters, mindful of the public interest, must assume and discharge responsibility for planning, selecting and supervising all matter broadcast by their stations, whether such matter is produced by them or provided by networks or others. This duty was made clear in the Commission's Policy Statement, page 14, paragraph 3:

" Broadcasting licensees must assume responsibility for all material which is broadcast through their facilities. This includes all programs and advertising material which they present to the public. With respect to advertising material the licensee has the additional responsibility to take all reasonable measures to eliminate any false, misleading, or deceptive matter and to avoid abuses with respect to the total amount of time devoted to advertising continuity as well as the frequency with which regular programs are interrupted for advertising messages. This duty is personal to the licensee and may not be delegated. He is obligated to bring his positive responsibility affirmatively to bear upon all who have a hand in providing broadcast matter for transmission through his facilities so as to assure the discharge of his duty to provide (an) acceptable program schedule consonant with operating in the public interest in his community. The broadcaster is obligated to make a positive, diligent and continuing effort, in good faith, to determine the tastes, needs and desires of the public in his community and to provide programming to meet those needs and interests. This, again, is a duty personal to the licensee and may not be avoided by delegation of the responsibility to others."

ATTACHMENT B

Attention is invited to the Commission's Public Notice entitled "Ascertainment of Community Needs By Broadcast Applicants," released August 22, 1968 - FCC 68-847, (33 Federal Register 12113).

The Commission issues this Public Notice to provide broadcast applicants with a better understanding of the showing called for in response to Part 1, Sections IV-A and IV-B, the programming sections of application forms. Deficient showings delay definitive action on applications and impose a costly workload burden on the Commission.

In a recent case, Minshall Broadcasting Company, Inc. (petition to enlarge issues) 11 FCC 2d 796 (1968), the Commission reiterated the four elements of the showing to be made in response to Part 1:

    (a) Full information on the steps the applicant has taken to become informed of the real community needs and interests of the area to be served.

    (b) Suggestions which the applicant has received as to how the station could help meet the area's needs.

    (c) The applicant's evaluation of those suggestions.

    (d) The programming service which the applicant proposes in order to meet those needs as they have been evaluated

In another recent case, Andy Valley Broadcasting System, Inc. (petition to deny) FCC 68-290 (1968), the Commission held that a survey of community needs is mandatory and that "applicants, despite long residence in the area, may no longer be considered, ipso facto, familiar with the programming needs and interests of the community."

Before detailing the information needed in the four elements set forth above, it is appropriate to state our belief that if the processes of Part 1 are carried out in good faith, the programming service will be rooted in the people whom the station is obligated to serve and who will be in a much better position to see that the obligation to them is fulfilled, thus lessening the enforcement burden of the Commission.

Part 1, Question 1.A., requires consultation with leaders in community life—public officials, educators, religious, the entertainment media, agriculture, business, labor, professional and eleemosynary organizations, and others who bespeak the interests which make up the community. Report and Statement of Policy Re: Commission En Banc Program Inquiry, 20 RR 1902.

Consultations with community leaders: Such consultations are to help determine the needs of the community from the standpoint of the group represented by the leader being consulted; should include a representative range of groups and leaders to give the applicant a better basis for determining the total needs of the community; and should identify them by name, position and organization. The purpose of such consultations should be to elicit constructive information concerning community needs, and not mere approval of existing or pre-planned programming.

Suggestions received: The second of the above four elements is largely self-explanatory, but, importantly, the listing should include the significant suggestions as to community needs received through the consultations with community leaders, whether or not the applicant proposes to treat them through its programming service.

Applicant's evaluation: What is expected of the applicant is that he will evaluate the relative importance of those suggestions and consider them in formulating the station's over-all program service.

Programming service proposed to meet the needs as evaluated: The fourth element set out in Minshall should be set out in response to Question 1.C., and calls for relating the program service to the needs of the community as evaluated, i.e., what programming service is proposed to meet what needs.

The foregoing information is also expected of all applicants for increased facilities serving a substantial amount of new area population. KTBS, Inc., 1 RR 2d 1054 (1964).

Section 1.526 of the Commission Rules requires licensees of broadcast stations to keep on file locally for public inspection a copy of its applications (which include Sections IV-A and IV-B) as well as exhibits, letters, other documents, and correspondence with the Commission pertaining to the application.

FCC Form 301	FEDERAL COMMUNICATIONS COMMISSION	Section IV-B
STATEMENT OF TELEVISION PROGRAM SERVICE	Name of Applicant	
Call letters of station	City and state which station is licensed to serve	

(See Instructions, Sec. IV-B, page 7)

PART I

Ascertainment of Community Needs

1. **A.** State in Exhibit No.____the methods used by the applicant to ascertain the needs and interests of the public served by the station. Such information shall include (1) the major communities or areas which applicant principally undertakes to serve and (2) identification of representative groups, interests and organizations which were consulted.

   B. Describe in Exhibit No.____the significant needs and interests of the public which the applicant believes his station will serve during the coming license period, including those with respect to national and international matters.

   C. List in Exhibit No.____typical and illustrative programs or program series (excluding Entertainment and News) that applicant plans to broadcast during the coming license period to meet those needs and interests.

   D. Describe in Exhibit No.____the procedures applicant has or proposes to have for the consideration and disposition of complaints or suggestions coming from the public.

NOTE: Sufficient records shall be kept on file at the station, open for inspection by the Commission, for a period of 3 years from the date of filing of this statement (unless requested to be kept longer by the Commission) to support the representations required in answer to Question 1. A, B, and C. These records should *not* be submitted with this application and need not be available for public inspection.

PART II
Past Programming

2. **A.** State the total hours of operation during the composite week: _____

   B. Attach as Exhibit No._____one exact copy of the program logs for the composite week used as a basis for responding to questions herein. Applicants utilizing automatic program logging devices must comply with the provisions of Section 73.670(c). Automatic recordings will be returned to the applicant. Exact copies of program logs will not be returned.

   If applicant has not operated during all of the days of the composite week which would be applicable to the use of this form, applicant should so notify the Commission and request the designation of substitute day or days as required.

3. **A.** State the amount of time (rounded to the nearest minute) the applicant devoted in the composite week to the program types (see Definitions) listed below. Commercial matter within a program segment shall be excluded in computing time devoted to that particular program segment (e.g., a 15-minute news program containing 3 minutes' commercial matter shall be counted as a 12-minute news program).

	Hours	Minutes	% of Total Time on Air
(1) News	....	....	.... %
*(2) Public Affairs	....	....	.... %
*(3) All other programs, exclusive of Entertainment and Sports	....	....	.... %

   * Attach as Exhibit No._____ a brief description of each program included in these categories.

   B. If in the applicant's judgment the composite week does not adequately represent the station's past programming, applicant may in addition provide in Exhibit No._____the same information as required in 3-A above (using the same format) for a representative period during the year preceding the filing of this application. Applicant shall identify the time period used. Applicant need not file the program logs used in responding to this question unless requested by the Commission.

4. List in Exhibit No._____ typical and illustrative programs or program series (excluding Entertainment and News) broadcast during the year preceding the filing of this application which have served public needs and interests in applicant's judgment. Denote, by underlining the Title, those programs, if any, designed to inform the public on local, national or international problems of greatest public importance in the community served by the applicant. Use the format below. (*NOTE:* If applicant's response includes any program described in Question 3, give title of program and refer to that Question without further details.)

   A. Title: E. Time broadcast & duration:

   B. Source*:   F. Number of times broadcast:

   C. Type*:   G. Extent, if any, to which community
   D. Brief description: leaders or groups involved:

5. State below the amount of time (in hours and minutes) by source* for programs in the composite week. (The response shall be in terms of total program time, including commercial matter.)

	Local	Network	Recorded
8 a.m. - 6 p.m.	....	....	....
6 p.m. - 11 p.m.	....	....	....
All other hours	....	....	....

*See Definitions—Sec. IV-B, page 7.

. Submit in Exhibit No. _____ the following information concerning the applicant's news programs:

A. The staff, news gathering facilities, news services and other sources utilized; and

B. An estimate of the percentage of news program time devoted to local and regional news during the composite week.

. In connection with the applicant's public affairs programming, describe its policy during the past renewal period with respect to making time available for the discussion of public issues and the method of selecting subjects and participants.

, Was the applicant affiliated with one or more national television networks during the past license period?
Yes _____ No _____

If so, give name(s) of Network(s): ....

If applicant had more than one such affiliation, which network was the principal source of network programs?

....

State the number of public service announcements broadcast by the applicant during the composite week: ....

A. In applicant's judgment, does the information supplied in this Part II adequately reflect its past programming?
Yes _____ No _____ .

B. If "no," applicant may attach as Exhibit No._____ such additional information as may be necessary to describe accurately and present fairly its program service.

C. If applicant's programming practices for the period covered by this statement varied substantially from the programming representations made in applicant's last renewal application, the applicant shall submit as Exhibit No. _____ a statement explaining the variations and the reasons therefor.

PART III

Proposed Programming

State the proposed total hours of operation during a typical week:_____

State the minimum amount of time the applicant proposes to devote normally each week to the program types (see Definitions) listed below. Commercial matter within a program segment shall be excluded in computing time devoted to that particular program segment (e.g., a fifteen-minute news program containing 3 minutes' commercial matter shall be computed as a 12-minute news program.)

	Hours	Minutes	% of Total Time on Air
(A) News..	....	....	.... %
(B) Public Affairs	....	....	.... %
(C) All other programs, exclusive of Entertainment and Sports.............	....	....	.... % .... %

State below the amount of time (in hours and minutes) proposed to be devoted to programs in a typical week by <u>source*</u>. (The response shall be in terms of total program time, including commercial matter.)

	Local	Network	Recorded
8 a.m. - 6 p.m.	....	....	....
6 p.m. - 11 p.m.	....	....	....
All other hours	....	....	....

Submit in Exhibit No._____ the following information concerning the applicant's proposed news programs:

A. The staff, news gathering facilities, news services and other sources to be utilized; and

B. An estimate of the percentage of news program time to be devoted to local and regional news during a typical week.

See Definitions—Sec. IV-B, page 7.

.5. .In connection with the applicant's proposed public affairs programming, describe its policy with respect to making time available for the discussion of public issues and the method of selecting subjects and participants.

16. State the minimum number of public service announcements applicant proposes to present during a typical week: _____

17. Will the applicant be affiliated with one or more national television networks during the coming license period? Yes _____ No _____ . If so, give name(s) of network(s): _____
_____

If more than one such affiliation is expected, which, if any, does applicant now expect to be the principal source of network programs? _____

PART IV

Past Commercial Practices

18. State the number of 60-minute segments of the composite week (beginning with the first full clock hour and ending with th last full clock hour of each broadcast day) containing the following amounts of commercial matter:

A. Up to and including 8 minutes .... _____ .
B. Over 8 and up to and including 12 minutes .... _____
C. Over 12 and up to and including 16 minutes .... _____
D. Over 16 minutes .... _____

List each segment in category (D) above, specifying the amount of commercial time in the segment, and the day and time broadcast:

9. A. In the applicant's judgment, does the information supplied in this Part IV for the composite week adequately reflect its commercial practices? Yes_____ No_____ .

B. If "no," applicant may attach as Exhibit No._____ such additional material as may be necessary to describe adequately and present fairly its commercial practices.

C. If applicant's commercial practices for the period covered by this statement varied substantially from the commercial representations made in applicant's last renewal application, the applicant shall explain the variations and the reasons therefor:

PART V

Proposed Commercial Practices

What is the maximum amount of commercial matter in any 60-minute segment which the applicant proposes normally to allow? _____

If applicant proposes to permit this amount to be exceeded at times, state under what circumstances and how often this is expected to occur, and the limits that would then apply.

PART VI

General Station Policies and Procedures

21. State the name(s) and position of the person(s) who determines the day-to-day programming, makes decisions, and directs the operation of the station covered by this application and whether he is employed full-time in the operation of the station.

22. **A.** Does the applicant have established policies with respect to programming and advertising standards (whether developed by the station or contained in a code of broadcasting standards and practices) to guide the operation of the station?

    Yes_____ No_____.

    B. If "yes," attach as Exhibit No._____ a brief summary of such policies. (If the station relies exclusively upon the published code of any national organization or trade association, a statement to that effect will suffice)

23. State the methods by which applicant undertakes to keep informed of the requirements of the Communications Act and the Commission's Rules and Regulations, and a description of the procedures established to acquaint applicant's employees and agents with such requirements and to ensure their compliance.

24. If, as an integral part of its station identification announcements, applicant makes or proposes to make reference to any business, profession or activity other than broadcasting in which applicant or any affiliate or stockholder is engaged or financially interested, directly or indirectly, set forth typical examples and approximate frequency of their use.

25. **A.** State the total number of station employees:_____ .

    B. Describe in Exhibit No._____ the applicant's plans for staffing the station including the number of employees in the programming, sales, technical, and general administrative departments. Do not list the same employee in more than one category. However, if an employee performs multiple services, this may be so shown by identifying him with his various duties (e.g., if two employees are combination announcers and salesmen, the list would include an entry of "two programming-sales".

FCC Form 301   **STATEMENT OF TV PROGRAM SERVICE**   Section IV-B, Page 6

26. State whether the applicant:

A. Has a policy of broadcasting programs to meet public needs whether or not commercial sponsorship is available or appropriate. Yes_____ No_____

If "yes", in Exhibit No._____ give examples to illustrate application of station's policy during the 12 months preceding the filing of this application.

B. Has a policy of preempting time to present special programs. Yes_____ No_____

If "yes", in Exhibit No._____ give examples to illustrate application of station's policy during the 12 months preceding the filing of this application.

PART VII
Other Matters and Certification

27. Applicant may submit as Exhibit No._____ any additional information which, in its judgment, is necessary adequately to describe or to present fairly its services and operations in relation to the public interest.

28. The undersigned has familiarized himself with paragraph 7 of the Instructions on page 7 of Section IV-B concerning signature requirements and in light of its provisions does hereby:

A. Acknowledge that all the statements made in this Section IV-B and the attached exhibits are considered material representations and that all the exhibits are a material part hereof and are incorporated herein as if set out in full in the application form; and

B. Certify that the statements herein are true, complete, and correct to the best of his knowledge and belief and are made in good faith.

SIGNED AND DATED this .... day of .... , 19 ....

....
(NAME OF LICENSEE)

By: ....
(SIGNATURE)

....
(PLEASE PRINT NAME OF PERSON SIGNING)

....
(TITLE)

WILLFUL FALSE STATEMENTS MADE IN THIS FORM ARE PUNISHABLE BY FINE AND IMPRISONMENT. U. S. CODE, TITLE 18, SECTION 1001.

Instructions, General Information and Definitions
for TV Broadcast Application

1. **Applicants for new televisions stations, and major changes when required** (see paragraph 2) shall file this Section IV-B with respect to Ascertainment of Community Needs (Part I), Proposed Programming (Part III), Proposed Commercial Practices (Part V), General Station Policies and Practices (Part VI) and other Matters and Certification (Part VII).

2. **Applicants for major changes in facilities** (as defined in Sections 1.571(a)(1) and 1.573(a)(1) of the Commission's Rules) need not file this Section IV-B unless there is proposed a substantial change in programming, increased facilities serving a substantial amount of new area or population, or unless the information is requested by the Commission.

3. **A.** The replies to the following questions constitute representations on which the Commission will rely in considering this application. Thus time and care should be devoted to the replies so that they will reflect accurately applicant's responsible consideration of the questions asked. It is not, however, expected that the licensee will or can adhere inflexibly in day-to-day operation to the representations made herein.

   B. Replies relating to future operation constitute representations against which the subsequent operation of the station will be measured. Accordingly, if during the license period the station substantially alters its programming format or commercial practices, the licensee should notify the Commission of such changes; otherwise it is presumed the station is being operated substantially as last proposed.

4. The applicant's attention is called to the Commission's "Report and Statement of Policy re: Commission En Banc Programming Inquiry." (25 Federal Register 7291; 20 Pike and Fischer Radio Regulations 1902; FCC 60-970), copies of which are available upon request to the Commission; and also to the material contained in Attachment A and Attachment B to this Section.

5. A legible copy of this Section IV-B and the exhibits submitted therewith shall be kept on file available for public inspection at any time during regular business hours. It shall be maintained at the main studio of the station or any other accessible place (such as a public registry for documents or an attorney's office) in the community to which the station is or is propose to be licensed.

6. **Network Programs.** Where information for the composite week is called for herein with respect to commercial matter or program type classifications in connection with network programs the applicant may rely on information furnished by the network.

7. **Signature.**

   This Section IV-B shall be signed in the space provided at the end hereof. It shall be personally signed by the applicant, if the applicant is an individual; by one of the partners, if the applicant is a partnership; by an officer of applicant, if a corporation or association. *SIGNING OF THIS SECTION IS A REPRESENTATION THAT THE PERSON IS FAMILIAR WITH THE CONTENTS OF THIS SECTION AND ASSOCIATED EXHIBITS, AND SUPPORTS AND APPROVES THE REPRESENTATIONS THEREIN ON BEHALF OF THE APPLICANT.*

Definitions

The definitions set out below are to be followed in furnishing the information called for by the questions of this Section IV-B. The inclusion of various types and sources of programs in the paragraphs which follow is not intended to establish a formula for station operation, but is a method for analyzing and reporting station operation.

8. **Sources** of programs are defined as follows:

   (a) **A local program** (L) is any program originated or produced by the station, or for the production of which the station is substantially responsible, and employing live talent more than 50% of the time. Such a program, taped, recorded, or filmed for later broadcast shall be classified by the station as local. A local program fed to a network shall be classified by the originating station as local. All non-network news programs may be classified as local. Programs primarily featuring syndicated or feature films, or other non-locally recorded programs shall be classified as "Recorded" (REC) even though a station personality appears in connection with such material. However, identifiable units of such programs which are live and separately logged as such may be classified as local (e.g., if during the course of a featu film program a non-network 2-minute news report is given and logged as a news program, the report may be classified a local).

   (b) **A network program** (NET) is any program furnished to the station by a network (national, regional or special). Delayed broadcasts of programs originated by networks are classified as network.

   (c) **A recorded program** (REC) is any program not defined in (a) and (b) above, including without limitation, syndicated programs, taped or transcribed programs, and feature films.

9. **Types** of programs are defined as follows:

   If a program contains two or more identifiable units of program material which constitute different program types as herein defined, each such unit may be separately logged and classified.

   The definitions of the first eight types of programs, (a) through (h) are not intended to overlap each other, and these types will normally include all the programs broadcast. The programs classified under (i) through (k) will have been classified under the first eight and there may be further duplication among types (i) through (k).

   (a) **Agricultural programs** (A) include market reports, farming or other information specifically addressed, or primarily of interest, to the agricultural population.

Definitions - Cont.

(b) *Entertainment programs* (E) include all programs intended primarily as entertainment, such as music, drama, variety, comedy, quiz, etc.

(c) *News programs* (N) include reports dealing with current local, national, and international events, including weather and stock market reports; and when an integral part of a news program, commentary, analysis and sports news.

(d) *Public Affairs programs* (PA) include talks, commentaries, discussions, speeches, editorials, political programs, documentaries, forums, panels, round tables, and similar programs primarily concerning local, national, and international public affairs.

(e) *Religious programs* (R) include sermons or devotionals; religious news; and music, drama, and other types of programs designed primarily for religious purposes.

(f) *Instructional programs* (I) include programs, other than those classified under Agricultural , News, Public Affairs, Religious or Sports, involving the discussion of, or primarily designed to further an appreciation or understanding of, literature, music, fine arts, history, geography, and the natural and social sciences; and programs devoted to occupational and vocational instruction, instruction with respect to hobbies, and similar programs intended primarily to instruct.

(g) *Sports programs* (S) include play-by-play and pre- or post-game related activities and separate programs of sports instruction, news, or information (e.g., fishing opportunities, golfing instruction, etc.).

(h) *Other programs* (O) include all programs not falling within definitions (a) through (g).

*   *   *   *   *   *   *

(i) *Editorials* (EDIT) include programs presented for the purpose of stating opinions of the licensee.

(j) *Political programs* (POL) include programs which present candidates for public office or which give expression (other than in station editorials) to views on such candidates or on issues subject to public ballot.

(k) *Educational Institution programs* (ED) include any program prepared by, in behalf of, or in cooperation with, educational institutions, educational organizations, libraries, museums, PTA's or similar organizations. Sports programs shall not be included.

. *Commercial matter* (CM) includes commercial continuity (network and non-network) and commercial announcements (network and non-network) as follows:

(a) *Commercial continuity*   is the advertising message of a program sponsor.

(b) *A commercial announcement*   is any other advertising message for which a charge is made, or other consideration is received.

  (1) Included are (i) "bonus" spots, (ii) trade-out spots, and (iii) promotional announcement of a future program where consideration is received for such an announcement or where such announcement identifies the sponsor of the future program beyond mention of the sponsor's name as an integral part of the title of the program (e.g., where the agreement for the sale of time provides that the sponsor will receive promotional announcements, or when the promotional announcement contains a statement such as "TOMORROW SEE - -⌊NAME OF PROGRAM⌋ - - BROUGHT TO YOU BY - -⌊SPONSOR'S NAME ⌋").

  (2) Other announcements including but not limited to the following are *not* commercial announcements:

   (i) Promotional announcements, except as defined above;

   (ii) Station identification announcements for which no charge is made;

   (iii)Mechanical reproduction announcements;

   (iv)Public service announcements;

   (v) Announcements made pursuant to Section 73.654(d) of the Rules that materials or services have been furnished as an inducement to broadcast a political program or a program involving the discussion of controversial public issues;

   (vi)Announcements made pursuant to the local notice requirements of Sections 1.580 (pre-grant) and 1.594 (designation for hearing) of the Rules.

A public service announcement (PSA) is any announcement (including network) for which no charge is made and which promotes programs, activities, or services of federal, state, or local governments (e.g., recruiting, sales of bonds, etc.) or the programs, activities or services of non-profit organizations (e.g., UGF, Red Cross blood donations, etc.), and other announcements regarded as serving community interests, excluding time signals, routine weather announcements and promotional announcements.

A program is an identifiable unit of program material, logged as such, which is not an announcement as defined above (e.g., if, within a 30-minute Entertainment program, a station broadcasts a one-minute news and weather report, this news and weather report may be separately logged and classified as a one-minute news program and the entertainment portion as a 29-minute program).

Composite Week - Seven days designated annually by the Commission in a Public Notice and consisting of seven different days of the week.

Typical Week - A week which an applicant projects as typical of his proposed weekly operation.

ATTACHMENT A

Attention is invited to the Commission's "Report and Statement of Policy Re: Commission En Banc Programming Inquiry" released July 29, 1960 - FCC 60-970 (25 Federal Register 7291; 20 Pike and Fischer Radio Regulation 1902).

Pursuant to the Communications Act of 1934, as amended, the Commission cannot grant, renew or modify a broadcast authorization unless it makes an affirmative finding that the operation of the station, as proposed, will serve the public interest, convenience and necessity. Programming is of the essence of broadcasting.

A broadcast station's use of a channel for the period authorized is premised on its serving the public. Thus, the public has a legitimate and continuing interest in the program service offered by the station, and it is the duty of all broadcast permittees and licensees to serve as trustees for the public in the operation of their stations. Broadcast permittees and licensees must make positive, diligent and continuing efforts to provide a program schedule designed to serve the needs and interests of the public in the areas to which they transmit an acceptable signal.

In its above-referenced "Policy Statement," the Commission has indicated the general nature of the inquiry which should be made in the planning and devising of a program schedule:

"Thus we do not intend to guide the licensee along the path of programming; on the contrary, the licensee must find his own path with the guidance of those whom his signal is to serve. We will thus steer clear of the bans of censorship without disregarding the public's vital interest. What we propose will not be served by pre-planned program format submissions accompanied by complimentary references from local citizens. What we propose is documented program submissions prepared as the result of assiduous planning and consultation covering two main areas: first, a canvass of the listening public who will receive the signal and who constitute a definite public interest figure; second, consultation with leaders in community life -- public officials, educators, religious (groups), the entertainment media - agriculture, business, labor, professional and eleemosynary organizations, and others who bespeak the interests which make up the community."

Over the years, experience has shown both broadcasters and the Commission that certain recognized elements of broadcast service have frequently been found necessary or desirable to serve the broadcast needs and interests of many communities. In the Policy Statement, referred to above, the Commission set out fourteen such elements. The Commission stated:

"The major elements usually necessary to meet the public interest, needs and desires of the community in which the station is located as developed by the industry, and recognized by the Commission, have included: (1) Opportunity for Local Self-Expression, (2) The Development and Use of Local Talent (3) Programs for Children, (4) Religious Programs, (5) Educational Programs, (6) Public Affairs Programs, (7) Editorialization by licensees, (8) Political Broadcasts, (9) Agricultural Programs, (10) News Programs, (11) Weather and Market Reports, (12) Sports Programs, (13) Service to Minority Groups, (14) Entertainment Programming."

It is emphasized that broadcasters, mindful of the public interest, must assume and discharge responsibility for planning, selecting and supervising all matter broadcast by their stations, whether such matter is produced by them or provided by networks or others. This duty was made clear in the Commission's Policy Statement, page 14, paragraph 3:

" Broadcasting licensees must assume responsibility for all material which is broadcast through their facilities. This includes all programs and advertising material which they present to the public. With respect to advertising material the licensee has the additional responsibility to take all reasonable measures to eliminate any false, misleading, or deceptive matter and to avoid abuses with respect to the total amount of time devoted to advertising continuity as well as the frequency with which regular programs are interrupted for advertising messages. This duty is personal to the licensee and may not be delegated. He is obligated to bring his positive responsibility affirmatively to bear upon all who have a hand in providing broadcast matter for transmission through his facilities so as to assure the discharge of his duty to provide (an) acceptable program schedule consonant with operating in the public interest in his community. The broadcaster is obligated to make a positive, diligent and continuing effort, in good faith, to determine the tastes, needs and desires of the public in his community and to provide programming to meet those needs and interests. This, again, is a duty personal to the licensee and may not be avoided by delegation of the responsibility to others."

ATTACHMENT B

Attention is invited to the Commission's Public Notice entitled "Ascertainment of Community Needs By Broadcast Applicants," released August 22, 1968 - FCC 68-847, (33 Federal Register 12113).

The Commission issues this Public Notice to provide broadcast applicants with a better understanding of the showing called for in response to Part 1, Sections IV-A and IV-B, the programming sections of application forms. Deficient showings delay definitive action on applications and impose a costly workload burden on the Commission.

In a recent case, Minshall Broadcasting Company, Inc. (petition to enlarge issues) 11 FCC 2d 796 (1968), the Commission reiterated the four elements of the showing to be made in response to Part 1:

(a) Full information on the steps the applicant has taken to become informed of the real community needs and interests of the area to be served.

(b) Suggestions which the applicant has received as to how the station could help meet the area's needs.

(c) The applicant's evaluation of those suggestions.

(d) The programming service which the applicant proposes in order to meet those needs as they have been evaluated.

In another recent case, Andy Valley Broadcasting System, Inc. (petition to deny) FCC 68-290 (1968), the Commission held that a survey of community needs is mandatory and that "applicants, despite long residence in the area, may no longer be considered, ipso facto, familiar with the programming needs and interests of the community."

Before detailing the information needed in the four elements set forth above, it is appropriate to state our belief that if the processes of Part 1 are carried out in good faith, the programming service will be rooted in the people whom the station is obligated to serve and who will be in a much better position to see that the obligation to them is fulfilled, thus lessening the enforcement burden of the Commission.

Part 1, Question 1 A, requires consultation with leaders in community life—public officials, educators, religious, the entertainment media, agriculture, business, labor, professional and eleemosynary organizations, and others who bespeak the interests which make up the community. Report and Statement of Policy Re: Commission En Banc Program Inquiry, 20 RR 1902.

Consultations with community leaders: Such consultations are to help determine the needs of the community from the standpoint of the group represented by the leader being consulted; should include a representative range of groups and leaders to give the applicant a better basis for determining the total needs of the community; and should identify them by name, position and organization. The purpose of such consultations should be to elicit constructive information concerning community needs, and not mere approval of existing or pre-planned programming.

Suggestions received: The second of the above four elements is largely self-explanatory, but, importantly, the listing should include the significant suggestions as to community needs received through the consultations with community leaders, whether or not the applicant proposes to treat them through its programming service.

Applicant's evaluation: What is expected of the applicant is that he will evaluate the relative importance of those suggestions and consider them in formulating the station's over-all program service.

Programming service proposed to meet the needs as evaluated: The fourth element set out in Minshall should be set out in response to Question 1 C., and calls for relating the program service to the needs of the community as evaluated, i.e., what programming service is proposed to meet what needs.

The foregoing information is also expected of all applicants for increased facilities serving a substantial amount of new area or population. KTBS, Inc., 1 RR 2d 1054 (1964).

Section 1.526 of the Commission Rules requires licensees of broadcast stations to keep on file locally for public inspection copy of its applications (which include Sections IV-A and IV-B) as well as exhibits, letters, other documents, and correspondence with the Commission pertaining to the application.

FCC Form 301	FEDERAL COMMUNICATIONS COMMISSION	Section V - A

STANDARD BROADCAST ENGINEERING DATA	Name of applicant	

1. Indicate by check mark the purpose of this application. (The items of this Section that are applicable to, and must be answered for, each category are shown to the right of the category.)

☐ Construct a new station
☐ Change station location to a different
   city or town
☐ Change power
☐ Change transmitter location   } All
☐ Change frequency   items
☐ Change from DA to Non-DA
☐ Change from Non-DA to DA
☐ Change in antenna system
   (including increase in height
   by addition of FM or TV antenna)

☐ Install new Auxiliary Transmitter
☐ Install new Alternate Main   } 2 thru 7,
   Transmitter   and 10
☐ Change transmitter (non type
   accepted)
☐ Change Main Studio Location to
   point outside city limits and not   } 2 thru 7
   at transmitter site
☐ Change Hours of Operation
☐ Other (specify): _____   2 thru 7
       (and appropriate other items)

If this application is not for a new station, summarize briefly the nature of the changes proposed:

---

2. Facilities requested

Frequency	Hours of operation	Power in kilowatts Night Day

3. Station location

State	City or town

4. Transmitter location

State	County

City or town	Street Address (or other identification)

5. Main studio location

State	County

City or town	Street and number, if known

6. Remote control point location

State	City or town

Street Address (or other identification)

7. Transmitter

Make	Type No.	Rated Power

(If the above transmitter has not been accepted for licensing by the F.C.C., attach as Exhibit No.   a complete showing of transmitter details. Showing should include schematic diagram and full details of frequency control. If changes are to be made in licensed transmitter include schematic diagram and give full details of change.)

8. Modulation monitor

Make	Type No.

9. Frequency monitor

Make	Type No.

---

10. Antenna system, including ground or counterpoise

Non-Directional Antenna:

Day ☐   Night ☐

Directional Antenna:

Day only (DA-D) ☐
Night only (DA-N) ☐
Same constants and power day
and night (DA-1) ☐
Different constants or power
day and night (DA-2) ☐

(If a directional antenna is proposed submit complete engineering data. Show clearly whether directional operation is for day or night or both. If day and night patterns are different give full information on each pattern. This information is in addition to the information in Paragraph 10 and is submitted as Exhibit No.   and signed by the engineer who designed the antenna system.)

Type radiator	Height in feet of complete radiator above base insulator, or above base if grounded.
Overall height in feet above ground. (Without obstruction lighting)	Overall height in feet above mean sea level. (Without obstruction lighting)
Overall height in feet above ground. (With obstruction lighting)	Overall height in feet above mean sea level. (With obstruction lighting)

If antenna is either top loaded or sectionalized, describe fully as Exhibit No.

Excitation   Series ☐   Shunt ☐

Geographic coordinates to nearest second.
For direction antenna give coordinates of center of array.
For single vertical radiator give tower location.

North latitude	West longitude
° ' "	° ' "

If not fully described above, give further details and dimensions including any other antennas mounted on tower and associated isolation circuits as Exhibit No.   (Height figures should not include obstruction lighting.)

Submit as Exhibit No.   a plat of the transmitter site showing boundary lines, and roads, railroads, or other obstructions; and also layout of the ground system or counterpoise. Show number and dimensions of ground radials or if a counterpoise is used, show height and dimensions.

11. Attach as Exhibit No.   a sufficient number of aerial photographs taken in clear weather at appropriate altitudes and angles to permit identification of all structures in the vicinity. The photographs must be marked so as to show compass directions, exact boundary lines of the proposed site, and locations of the proposed 1000 mv/s contour for both day and night operation. Photographs taken in eight different directions from an elevated position on the ground will be acceptable in lieu of the aerial photographs if the data referred to can be clearly shown.

12. Allocation Studies:

A. Attach as Exhibit No.   map or maps, having reasonable scales, showing the 1000, 25, 5, 2, normally protected and interference-free contours in mv/m for both day and night operation both existing and as proposed by the application. (NOTE: The 2 mv/m night contour need not be supplied if service is not rendered thereto.)

B. (1) For daytime operation, attach as Exhibit No   an allocation study, utilizing Figure M-3 of the Rules or an accurate full scale reproduction thereof and using pertinent field strength measurement data where available, a full scale exhibit of the entire pertinent area to show the following:

    (a) Normally protected, the interference-free, and the interfering contours for the proposed operation along all azimuths.

    (b) Complete normally protected and interference-free contours of all other proposals and existing stations to which objectionable interference would be caused.

    (c) Interfering contours over pertinent arcs of all other proposals and existing stations from which objectionable interference would be received.

    (d) Normally protected and interfering contours over pertinent arcs of all other proposals and existing stations which require study to show the absence of objectionable interference.

    (e) The 0.1 mv/m groundwave contour of Class I-B stations and appropriate studies to establish compliance with Section 73.187 when operation is proposed on a U. S. Class I-B channel.

    (f) Plot of the transmitter location of each station or proposal requiring investigation, with identifying call letters, file numbers, and operating or proposed facilities.

    (g) Properly labeled longitude and latitude degree lines, shown across entire exhibit.

(2) For daytime operation, when necessary to show more detail, attach as Exhibit No.   an <u>additional</u> allocation study, utilizing World or Sectional Aeronautical charts to clearly show interference or absence thereof.

(3) For daytime operation, attach as Exhibit No   a tabulation of the following:

    (a) Azimuths along which the groundwave contours were calculated for all stations or proposals shown on allocation study exhibits required by Paragraph 12B above.

    (b) Inverse distance field strength used along each azimuth.

    (c) Basis for ground conductivity utilized along azimuths specified in (3) (a). If field strength measurements are used, the measurements must be either submitted or be properly identified as to location in Commission files.

C. For nighttime operation, attach as Exhibit No.   , allocation data to include the following:

(1) Proposed nighttime limitation to other existing or proposed stations with which objectionable interference would result, as well as those other proposals and existing stations which require study to clearly show absence of objectionable interference.

(2) All existing or proposed nighttime limitations which enter into the nighttime R.S.S. limitation of each of the existing or proposed facilities investigated under C (1) above.

(3) All existing and proposed limitations which contribute to the R.S.S. nighttime limitation of the proposed operation, together with those limitations which must be studied before being excluded.

(4) A detailed interference study plotted upon an appropriate scale map if a question exists with respect to nighttime interference to other existing or proposed facilities along bearings other than on a direct line toward the facility considered.

(5) Utilizing an appropriate scale map, clearly show the normally protected and interference-free contours of each of the existing and proposed stations which would receive nighttime interference from the proposed operation.

(6) The detailed basis for each nighttime limitation calculated under C (1) (2) (3) and (4) above, including a copy of each pertinent radiation pattern in the vertical plane and basis therefor.

13. Attach as Exhibit No.   tables of the areas and populations within the contours included in Paragraph 12 (A) above, as well as within the normally protected and interference-free contours of each station or proposed operation to which interference would be caused according to the Commission Rules.

(NOTE: See the Standard Broadcast Technical Standards. All towns and cities having populations in excess of those given in Section 3.182(g) are not to be included in the tabulation of populations within the service contours. The latest Census Minor Civil Division maps are to be used in making population counts, subtracting any towns or cities not receiving adequate service, and where contours cut a minor division assuming a uniform distribution of population within the division, to determine the population included in the contours unless a more accuract count is made.)

14. Attach as Exhibit No.   map or maps having reasonable scales clearly showing the following:

(a) Proposed antenna location

(b) General character of the city or metropolitan district, particularly the retail business, wholesale business, manufacturing, residential, and unpopulated areas (by symbols, cross-hatching, colored crayons, or other means)

(c) Heights of buildings or other structures and terrain elevations in the vicinity of the antenna, indicating the location thereof.

(d) Transmitter location and call letters of all radio stations (except amateur) and the location of established commercial and government receiving stations within 2 miles of the proposed transmitter location. Call letters and locations of broadcast stations, including FM and television, within 5 miles must be shown.

(e) Terrain

15. If this application is for modification of construction permit state briefly as Exhibit No.   the present status of construction and indicate when it is expected that construction will be completed.

I certify that I represent the applicant in the capacity indicated below and that I have examined the foregoing statement of technical information and that it is true to the best of my knowledge and belief.

Date _____   Signature_____
                                                    (check appropriate box below)

                                           ☐ Technical Director   ☐ Chief Operator
                                           ☐ Registered Professional Engineer
                                           ☐ Consulting Engineer

CC Form 301	**FEDERAL COMMUNICATIONS COMMISSION**	Section V-B

FM BROADCAST ENGINEERING DATA	Name of applicant

. Purpose of authorization applied for: (Indicate by check mark)

(If application is for a new station or for any of the changes numbered B through D, complete all paragraphs of this form; if change E is of a character which will change coverage or increase the overall height of the antenna structure more than 20 feet, answer all paragraphs, otherwise complete only paragraphs 2 and 10 and the appropriate other paragraphs; for changes F through H, complete only paragraph 2 and the appropriate other paragraphs; for change I, complete only paragraphs 2 and 5.)

A. ☐ Construct a new station
B. ☐ Change effective radiated power or antenna height above average terrain
C. ☐ Change transmitter location
D. ☐ Change frequency

E. ☐ Change antenna system
F. ☐ Change transmitter
G. ☐ Install auxiliary or alternate main transmitter
H. ☐ Other changes (specify)
I. ☐ Change studio location

If this is not for a new station, summarize briefly the nature of the changes proposed.

---

2. Facilities requested

Frequency   Channel No. . . . .

Mc/s.

Effective Radiated Power	Antenna height above average terrain
Horizontal kw	Horizontal feet
Vertical kw	Vertical feet

3. Station location

State	City or town

4. Transmitter location (principal community)

State	County
City or town	Street Address (or other identification)

5. Main studio location

State	County
City or town	Street address

6. Remote control point location

State	City or town

Street Address (or other identification)

7. Transmitter

Make	Type No.	Rated Power

(If the above transmitter has not been accepted for licensing by the F.C.C., attach as Exhibit No.   a complete showing of transmitter details. Showing should include schematic diagram and full details of frequency control. If changes are to be made in licensed transmitter include schematic diagram and give full details of change.)

8. Modulation monitor

Make	Type No.

---

9. Frequency monitor

Make	Type No.

10. (a) Antenna structure:

Is the proposed construction in the immediate vicinity or does it serve to modify the construction of any standard broadcast station, FM broadcast station, television broadcast station, or other class of radio station? If "Yes", attach as Exhibit No.   complete engineering data thereon.   YES ☐   NO ☐

Submit as Exhibit No.   a vertical plan sketch for the proposed total structure (including supporting building if any) giving heights above ground in feet for all significant features.

Overall height in feet above ground. (Without obstruction lighting)	Overall height in feet above mean sea level. (Without obstruction lighting)
Overall height in feet above ground. (With obstruction lighting)	Overall height in feet above mean sea level. (With obstruction lighting)

Height of antenna radiation center in feet above mean level.
Horizontal
Vertical

Geographical coordinates of antenna (to nearest second)
North latitude   West longitude
    0   '   ''   0   '   ''

(b) Antenna data

Make	Type No. or description
No. of sections	Antenna power gain
Horizontal	Horizontal
Vertical	Vertical

If directional antenna is proposed, give full details including horizontal and vertical plane radiation patterns, as Exhibit No.

Is electrical or mechanical beam tilting proposed?   YES ☐   NO ☐
If so, describe fully in Exhibit No.
including horizontal and pertinent vertical radiation patterns.

Will antenna be altered to provide null fill-in?   YES ☐   NO ☐
If yes, describe fully in Exhibit No.

| FCC Form 301 | FM BROADCAST ENGINEERING DATA | Section V-B, Page 2 |

Transmission line proposed to supply power to the antenna from the transmitter

Make	Type No.	Description

Size (nominal transverse dimension) in inches	Length in feet	Rated efficiency in percent for this length

15. Attach as Exhibit No. _____ map(s) (Sectional Aeronautical Charts where obtainable) of the area proposed to be served and show drawn thereon:

(a) Proposed transmitter location and the radials along which the profile graphs have been prepared;
(b) The 3.16 mv/m and the 1 mv/m contours predicted;
(c) Scale of miles.

Areas and population: (1960 or later census.)

Area (sq. mi.) within 1 mv/m contour	Population within 1 mv/m contour

12. Proposed operation

Transmitter power output in kilowatts	Power dissipation within transmission line in kilowatts

Antenna input power in kilowatts	Effective radiated power in kilowatts (Must be same as shown in Para. 2) Horizontal Vertical

16. (a) Attach as Exhibit No. _____ a map(s) (topographic where obtainable, such as U. S. Geological Survey quadrangles) for the area within 15 miles of the proposed transmitter location and show drawn thereon the following data:

1. Proposed transmitter location--accurately plotted;
2. Transmitter location and call letters of all radio stations (except amateur) and the location of established commercial and government receiving stations within 2 miles of the proposed transmitter location;
3. Proposed location of main studio;
4. Character of the area within 2 miles of proposed transmitter location, suitably designated as to residential, business, industrial, and rural nature;
5. At least eight radials each extending to a distance of ten or more miles from the proposed transmitter location, one or more of which must extend through the principal city or cities to be served.

13. Will the studios, microphones, and other equipment proposed for transmission of programs be designed for compliance with the FM Technical Standards?   YES ☐ NO ☐

If this application is for modification of construction permit state briefly as Exhibit No. _____ the present status of construction and indicate when it is expected that construction will be completed.

(b) Attach as Exhibit No. _____ profile graphs for the radials in (a) (5) above. Each graph shall show the elevation of the antenna radiation center. Identify each graph by its bearing from the proposed transmitter location. Direction true north shall be zero azimuth and angles measured clockwise. Show source of topographical data on each.

17. From the profile graphs in 16(b), for the eight mile distance between two and ten miles from the proposed transmitter location, and in accordance with the procedure prescribed in Section 73.313 of the Commission Rules, supply the following tabulation of data:

Radial bearing (degrees true)	Average elevation of radial (2-10 mi.) in feet above mean sea level	Height in feet of antenna radiation center above average elevation of radial (2-10 mi.)	Predicted distance in miles to the 3.16mv/m contour	Predicted distance in miles to the 1mv/m contour
0 ____0	____feet	____feet	____mi.	____n
45				
90				
135				
180				
225				
270				
315				
(*)				

Average _____

Antenna height above average terrain _____ feet (horizontal) / _____ feet (vertical)
(Average of above listed heights -- must be identical with Paragraph 2)

*Radial over principal community if not included above. Do not include in average.

I certify that I represent the applicant in the capacity indicated below and that I have examined the foregoing statement of technical information and that it is true to the best of my knowledge and belief.

_____ Signature _____
date

(check appropriate box below)

☐ Technical Director   ☐ Chief Operator   ☐ Registered Professional Engineer   ☐ Consulting Engineer

FCC Form 301	FEDERAL COMMUNICATIONS COMMISSION	Section V-C
TELEVISION BROADCAST ENGINEERING DATA	Name of applicant	

1. Purpose of authorization applied for: (Indicate by check mark)

(If application is for a new station or for any of the changes numbered B through D, complete all paragraphs of this form; if change E is of a character which will change coverage or increase the overall height of the antenna structure more than 30 feet, answer all paragraphs, otherwise complete only paragraphs 2 and 7 and the appropriate other paragraphs; for changes F through I, complete only paragraph 2 and the appropriate other paragraphs; for change J, complete only paragraphs 2, 5 and 16(b).

A. ☐ Construct a new station

B. ☐ Change effective radiated power or antenna height above average terrain

C. ☐ Change transmitter location

D. ☐ Change frequency

E. ☐ Change antenna system

F. ☐ Construct or change auxiliary antenna system

G. ☐ Change transmitter

H. ☐ Install auxiliary or alternate main transmitter

I. ☐ Other changes (specify)

J. ☐ Change studio location

2. Facilities requested

Frequency

_____ _____ Mc.

Channel No. ....

Effective Radiated Power (visual)	Effective Radiated Power (aural)	Antenna height above average terrain
In dbk:	In dbk:	
In kw:	In kw:	feet

3. Station location (principal community)

State	City or town

4. Transmitter location

State	County
City or town	Street Address (or other identification)

5. Main studio location

State	County
City or town	Street address

6. Transmitters

Visual

Make	Type No.	Rated power
		In dbk:
		In kw:

Aural

Make	Type No.	Rated Power
		In dbk:
		In kw:

(If the above transmitter has not been accepted for licensing by the F.C.C., attach as Exhibit No.   a complete showing of transmitter details. Showing should include schematic diagram and full details of frequency control. If changes are to be made in licensed transmitter include schematic diagram and give full details of change.)

(a) Describe in Exhibit No.   means which will be used for determining and maintaining power output of the transmitters to the values specified in this application.

(b) Multiplexer: Make _____ Type No. ____

Rated input power _____ dbk

Rated loss: Visual _____ db   Aural _____ db

7. (a) Antenna structure

Is the proposed construction in the immediate vicinity of any other radio station or will the proposed transmitting antenna be supported by the antenna structure of any other radio station? If "Yes", attach as Exhibit No.   complete engineering data showing details and effect upon other station.
Yes ☐   No ☐

Submit as Exhibit No.   a vertical plan sketch for the proposed total structure (including supporting building if any) giving heights above ground in feet for all significant features.

Overall height in feet above ground. (Without obstruction lighting)	Overall height in feet above mean sea level. (Without obstruction lighting)
Overall height in feet above ground. (With obstruction lighting)	Overall height in feet above mean sea level. (With obstruction lighting)

Height of antenna radiation center in feet above mean sea level.   feet

Geographical coordinates of antenna (to nearest second)
North latitude   0   '   "   West longitude   0   '   "

How were coordinates determined?

Indicate by check mark the zone in which structure is located.   1 ☐   2 ☐   3 ☐

(b) Antenna data

Visual

Make	Type No.

Number of sections	Rated input power in dbk	Power gain in db

Aural (if separate)

Make	Type No.

Number of sections	Rated input power in dbk	Power gain in db

If directional antenna is proposed, give full details including horizontal and vertical plane radiation patterns, as Exhibit No.

Is electrical or mechanical beam tilting proposed? If so, describe fully in Exhibit No. including horizontal and pertinent vertical radiation patterns.
Yes ☐   No ☐

Will antenna be altered to provide null fill-in?   Yes ☐   No ☐

If yes, describe fully in Exhibit No.

| FCC Form 301 | TELEVISION BROADCAST ENGINEERING DATA | Section V-C, Page 2 |

8. Transmission line proposed to supply power to the antenna from the transmitter

(a) Visual			(b) Aural (if separate)		
Make	Type No.	Rated input power in dbk	Make	Type No.	Rated input power in dbk
Size (nominal inside transverse dimensions) in inches	Length in feet	Power loss in db for this length	Size (nominal inside transverse dimension) in inches	Length in feet	Power loss in db for this length

9. Proposed operation

(a) Visual			(b) Aural		
Transmitter power output (after vestigial side-band filter, if used) In dbk: In kw:	Multiplexer loss in db:	Input to transmission line in dbk:	Transmitter power output In dbk: In kw:	Multiplexer loss in db:	Input to transmission line in dbk:

Transmission line power loss in db:	Antenna input power in dbk:	Antenna power gain in db:	Effective radiated power In dbk: In kw:	Transmission line power loss in db:	Antenna input power in dbk:	Antenna power gain in db:	Effective radiated power In dbk: In kw:

10. Modulation monitors

(a) Visual monitor or monitoring equipment

Make	Type No.

(b) Aural monitor

Make	Type No.

11. Frequency monitors

(a) Visual monitor

Make	Type No.	Accuracy

(b) Aural monitor

Make	Type No.	Accuracy

12. If the above monitors or monitoring equipment have not been approved by the F.C.C., include as Exhibit No. _____ a brief technical description of each.

13. Will the studios, cameras, microphones, and other equipment proposed for transmission of programs be designed for compliance with the Commission's Rules?   Yes ☐   No ☐

14. (a) Attach as Exhibit No. _____ a map(s) (topographic where obtainable, such as U. S. Geological Survey quadrangles) for the area within 15 miles of the proposed transmitter location and show drawn thereon the following data:

1. Proposed transmitter location—accurately plotted;
2. Transmitter location and call letters of all known radio stations (except amateur) and the location of known commercial and government receiving stations within 2 miles of the proposed transmitter location;
3. Character of the area within 2 miles of proposed transmitter location, suitably designated as to residential, business, industrial, and rural nature;
4. At least eight radials each extending to a distance of ten or more miles from the proposed transmitter location, one or more of which must extend through the principal city to be served.

(b) Attach as Exhibit No. _____ profile graphs with reasonably large scales for the radials in (a) (4) above. Each graph shall show the elevation of the antenna radiation center. Identify each graph by its bearing from the proposed transmitter location. Direction of true north shall be zero azimuth, with angles measured clockwise. Show source of topographical data on each.

15. From the profile graphs in 14(b), for the eight mile distance between two and ten miles from the proposed transmitter location, and in accordance with the procedure prescribed in the Commission's Rules, supply the following tabulation of data:

Radial bearing (degrees true)	Average elevation of radial (2-10 mi.) in feet above mean sea level	Height in feet of antenna radiation center above average elevation of radial (2-10 mi.)	Effective radiated power in radial direction	Predicted distance in miles to the Grade A contour	Predicted distance in miles to the Grade B contour
0	.... feet	.... feet	.... dbk	.... mi.	.... mi.
45					
90					
135					
180					
225					
270					
315					
(*)					
Average	....				

*Radial over principal community if not included above. Do not include in average.

Antenna height above average terrain _____ feet (Must be identical with Paragraph 2)

| FCC Form 301 | TELEVISION BROADCAST ENGINEERING DATA | Section V-C, Page 3 |

16. Attach as Exhibit No.   map(s) (Sectional Aeronautical charts where obtainable, preferably without aeronautical overlay) of the area proposed to be served and shown drawn thereon:

    (a) Proposed transmitter location and the radials along which the profile graphs have been prepared;

    (b) The studio location and boundaries of the principal community;

    (c) The predicted Grade A and Grade B contours from 12 above;

    (d) The required minimum field strength contour;

    (e) Scale of miles.

17. Attach as Exhibit No.   a sufficient number of aerial photographs taken in clear weather at appropriate altitudes and angles to show the nature of the surrounding terrain in the vicinity of the proposed transmitter site. The photographs must be marked so as to show compass directions. Photographs taken in eight different directions from an elevated position on the ground will be acceptable in lieu of the aerial photographs if the area can be clearly shown.

Give date photographs were taken.

18. Will the minimum required value of field strength predicted in accordance with the method prescribed in the Commission's Rules, be provided over the entire principal community proposed to be served?

          Yes ☐   No ☐

19. Will the main studio be located within the limits of the principal community proposed to be served.

          Yes ☐   No ☐

20. (a) Does the proposed transmitter location comply with the minimum separation requirements of the Commission's Rules?

          Yes ☐   No ☐

    (b) If any co-channel separations are proposed that are less than the applicable minimum separation requirement plus 20 miles, or if other channel separations are proposed that are less than the applicable minimum separations plus 10 miles, list such separations below. (Include existing stations, proposed stations and cities which appear in the table of assignments; the location and geographical coordinates of each antenna, proposed antenna or reference point as appropriate; the distance to each from the proposed transmitter location; and the method used in each instance to measure the distance.) If none, so state.

21. If this is an application for modification of construction permit state briefly as Exhibit No.   the present status of construction and indicate when it is expected that construction will be completed.

    I certify that I represent the applicant in the capacity indicated below and that I have examined the foregoing statement of technical information and that it is true to the best of my knowledge and belief.

Date _____   Signature _____

                          (check appropriate box below)

        ☐ Technical Director   ☐ Chief Operator

        ☐ Registered Professional Engineer

        ☐ Consulting Engineer

FCC Form 301   **FEDERAL COMMUNICATIONS COMMISSION**   Section V-G (Antenna

ANTENNA AND SITE INFORMATION (see instruction B, Section 1)	Name of applicant

Legal Counsel

Address

Consulting Engineer

Address

Class of station	Facilities requested

1. Location of antenna

State	County	City or Town

Exact antenna location (street address) (If outside city limits, give distance and direction from, and name of nearest town)

Geographic coordinates (to be determined to nearest second. For directional antenna give coordinates of center of array.) For single vertical radiator give tower location.

North latitude			West longitude		
0	'	"	0	'	"

Purpose of application (Check appropriate box)

a. New antenna construction ☐
b. Alteration of existing antenna structures ☐
c. Change in location ☐

2. Features of surrounding terrain

List any natural formations or existing man-made structures (hills, trees, water tanks, towers, etc.) which, in the opinion of the applicant, would tend to shield the antenna from aircraft and thereby minimize the aeronautical hazard of the antenna.

Submit as Exhibit No. ____ a chart on which is plotted the exact location of the antenna site, and also the relative location of the natural formations and/or the existing man-made structures listed above.

The chart used shall be an Instrument Approach Chart (or the landing chart on reverse side thereof), or a Sectional Aeronautical Chart, choice depending upon proximity of the antenna site to landing areas. 1/ In general, the Sectional Aeronautical Chart should be used only when the antenna site is more than 10 miles from a landing area or when an Instrument Approach Chart is unobtainable. 1/ These charts may be purchased from the U. S. Coast and Geodetic Survey, Washington, D. C. 20852

1/ Exception - Where the proposed antenna site is within the boundary of a landing area for which no Instrument Approach Chart is available, submit a self-made, large scale map showing antenna site, runway(s) and existing man-made structures listed above.

3. Designation, distance, and bearing to center line of nearest established airway within 5 miles:

4. List all landing areas within 10 miles of antenna site. Give distance and direction to the nearest boundary of each landing area from the antenna site.

Landing Area	Distance	Direction
(a)		
(b)		
(c)		

5. Description of antenna system (If directional, give spacing and orientation of towers).

Type

Description of tower(s)

Self-supporting	Guyed			Tubular (Pole)		
Tower (height figures should include obstruction lighting)	#1	#2	#3	#4	#5	#6
Height of radiating elements						
Overall height above ground						
Overall height above mean sea level						

If a combination of Standard, FM, or TV operation is proposed on the same multi-element array (either existing or proposed) submit as Exhibit No. ____ a horizontal plan for the proposed antenna system, giving heights of the elements above ground and showing their _orientation_ and spacing in feet. Clearly indicate if any towers are existing.

Submit as Exhibit No. ____ a vertical plan sketch for the proposed total structure (including supporting building if any) giving heights above ground in feet for all significant features. Clearly indicate existing portions, noting painting and lighting.

Is the proposed antenna system designed so that obstruction lights may be installed and maintained at the uppermost point(s)?   Yes ☐   No ☐

6. Is the proposed site the same or immediately adjoining the transmitter-antenna site of other stations authorized by the Commission or specified in another application pending before the Commission?   ☐ Yes   ☐ No

If the answer is "Yes", give: CALL LETTERS _____ FILE NUMBER _____

I certify that I represent the applicant in the capacity indicated below and that I have examined the foregoing statement of technical information and that it is true to the best of my knowledge and belief.

_____   Signature _____
(date)

(check appropriate box below)

☐ Technical Director   ☐ Chief Operator   ☐ Registered Professional Engineer   ☐ Consulting Engineer

FCC Form 301	FEDERAL COMMUNICATIONS COMMISSION	**Section VI**
EQUAL EMPLOYMENT OPPORTUNITY PROGRAM	Name of Applicant	
:all letters of station	City and state which station is licensed to serve	

Applicants for construction permit for a new facility must file equal employment opportunity programs or amendments to those programs in the following exhibit.

Submit as Exhibit No.   the applicant's equal employment opportunity program for the station, and its network operation if the applicant operates a network, indicating specific practices to be followed in order to assure equal employment opportunity for Negroes, Orientals, American Indians and Spanish Surnamed Americans in each of the following aspects of employment practice: recruitment, selection, training, placement, promotion, pay, working conditions, demotion, layoff, and termination. The program should reasonably address itself to such specific practices as the following, to the extent they are appropriate in terms of station size, location, etc. A program need not be filed if the station has less than five fulltime employees or if it is in an area where the relevant minorities are represented in such insignificant numbers that a program would not be meaningful. In the latter situation, a statement of explanation should be filed.

1. To assure nondiscrimination in recruiting:

    a. Posting notices in station employment offices informing applicants of their equal employment rights and their right to notify the Federal Communications Commission or other appropriate agency if they believe they have been the victim of discrimination.
    b. Placing a notice in bold type on the employment application informing prospective employees that discrimination because of race, color, religion, national origin, or sex, is prohibited and that they may notify the Federal Communications Commission or other appropriate agency if they believe they have been discriminated against.
    c. Placing employment advertisements in media which have significant circulation among minority-group people in the recruiting area.
    d. Recruiting through schools and colleges with significant minority-group enrollments.
    e. Maintaining systematic contacts with minority and human relations organizations, leaders and spokesmen to encourage referral of qualified minority applicants.
    f. Encouraging present employees to refer minority applicants.
    g. Making known to all recruitment sources that qualified minority members are being sought for consideration whenever the station hires.

2. To assure nondiscrimination in selection and hiring:

    a. Instructing personally those of your staff who make hiring decisions that minority applicants for all jobs are to be considered without discrimination.
    b. Where union agreements exist:
        (1) Cooperating with your unions in the development of programs to assure qualified minority persons of equal opportunity for employment;
        (2) Including an effective nondiscrimination clause in new or re-negotiated union agreements.
    c. Avoiding use of selection techniques or tests which have the effect of discriminating against minority groups.

3. To assure nondiscriminatory placement and promotion:

    a. Instructing personally those of the station staff who make decisions on placement and promotion that minority employees are to be considered without discrimination, and that job areas in which there is little or no minority representation should be reviewed to determine whether this results from discrimination.
    b. Giving minority group employees equal opportunity for positions which lead to higher positions. Inquiring as to the interest and skills of all lower paid employees with respect to any of the higher paid positions, followed by assistance, counselling, and effective measures to enable employees with interest and potential to qualify themselves for such positions.
    c. Reviewing seniority practices and seniority clauses in union contracts to insure that such practices or clauses are nondiscriminatory and do not have a discriminatory effect.

4. To assure nondiscrimination in other areas of employment practices:

    a. Examining rates of pay and fringe benefits for present employees with equivalent duties, and adjusting any inequities found.
    b. Advising all qualified employees whenever there is an opportunity to perform overtime work.

U.S. GOVERNMENT PRINTING OFFICE : 1971 O - 415-800

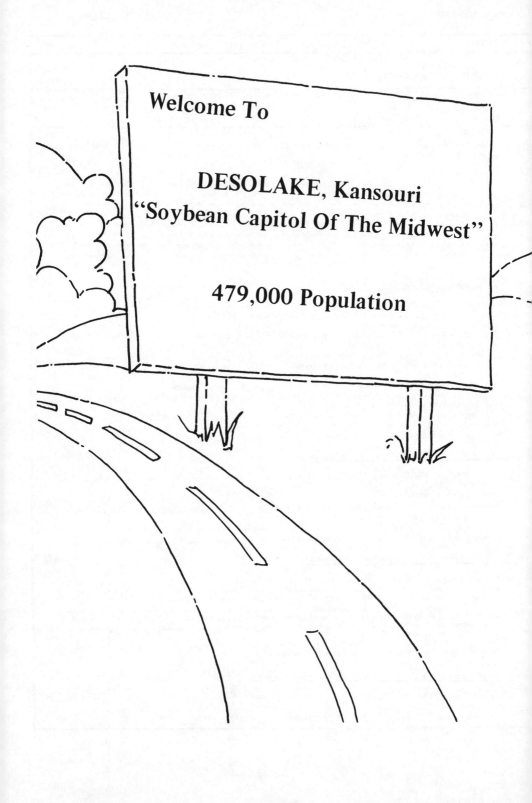

Appendix 2

WELCOME TO DESOLAKE, KANSOURI:
A Brief Description of the City of License

DESOLAKE, Kansouri

DESOLAKE is the equivalent of the 75th market in the nation and has

has an average population growth rate of 30 percent over the past decade.

Wight counties comprise the DMA (ADI) market area, encompassing 673,000

persons, 71 percent of whom are concentrated in the Three Metro Counties

of Lard, Henry and Hataway.

City Government

The city of DESOLAKE has a population of 110,653. Its government

officials are elected every four years in a city-wide election. There

are a Mayor, Vice-Mayor, who also serves as President of the City Council,

and 18 Councilmen. Of these, sic are at-large and the remaining 12 are

elected from the 12 Councilmanic Districts.

The Three Metro Counties

Lard County, of which DESOLAKE CITY is the county seat, covers 476
square miles. Its total population is 259,200 of which 148,547 live
outside the DESOLAKE CITY limits. The county has a Board of Commissioners
made up of a Board Chairman and four Commissioners elected every four years.

Hathaway County is the second most populous county in the DESOLAKE area,
with 132,000 persons spread over an area of 261 square miles.   **Three**
Commissioners, including a Chairman, make up the government. Hathaway
County is the location of the two largest institutions of higher learning
Piedmont University (enrollment 3,800) and Alliance Tech, an engineering
school with an enrollment of 2,200.

Henry County covers an area of 299 square miles and is the site of
DESOLAKE International Airport. It is governed by three Commissioners
and has a population of 100,800.

Non-Metro Counties

The five non-metro counties of Buttington, Caldwell, Morgan, Twonsend
and Luster are essentially farmland with a total population of 132,000.
Principal crops are wheat, soy beans and alfalfa. Small industry also
dots the five non-metro counties but is mostly concentrated in Caldwell
and Buttington Counties.

Metropolitan DESOLAKE's population is 83 percent white, 12.2 percent Black
and 4.8 percent Spanish-speaking and Other.

POPULATION AND POPULATION CHARACTERISTICS

Households

Population 1970	258,000
1960	198,000 (1960-70 Growth Rate: 30%)
1950	145,000

Black Population	12.2%
Spanish "	4.8%
White and Other	83.0%

Age Composition
Under 5	8.5%
18-64	61.5%
65+	7.1%

# Counties	DMA (8)	NSI (10)	METRO (3)
Total TvHH	258,000	272,000	205,000
Total Persons	673,000	701,000	479,000
Total Adults (18+)	482,000	–	–
Women	252,000	–	–
W18-49	110,000	–	–
Men	230,000	–	–
M18-49	141,000	–	–
Teens (12-17)	78,000	–	–
Children (2-11)	113,000	–	–

DMA COUNTIES	TvHH		
		Color HH	69%
		VHF%	92%
Lard (M)	108,000	CATV%	18%
Henry (M)	42,000		
Buttington	13,000		
Caldwell	16,000		
Morgan	8,000		
Townsend	5,000		
Luster	11,000		
Hathaway (M)	55,000		
	258,000		

(M) = Metro Counties

GROWTH AND DEVELOPMENT
_____

DESOLAKE'S 30% growth rate over the past decade has been matched
by corresponding growth in construction.

Within the past five years, DESOLAKE has begun and completed
the construction of 18 new office buildings, 26 warehouses, 11
manufacturing plants, 3 major retail outlets, 9 motels, 3 high-
rise apartment buildings and one high-rise condominium, 3 high
schools and 4 grade schools, three major shoppings centers,
plus a new sports arena/convention center.

The new DESOLAKE City Arena has a capacity of 28,000 with an
adjacent shopping center, and the new DESOLAKE Hotel with a 300
room capacity and the nearby Fairmont Motel, with a   150-room
capacity.

1974 CONSUMER SPENDABLE INCOME (BY HOUSEHOLD)

$ 0 2,999	7.2%
$3,000 - 4,999	6.9%
$5,000 - 7,999	14.1%
$8,000 - 9,999	11.4%
10,000 -14,999	27.0%
$15,000+	33.4%

RETAIL SALES DATA

	DMA	METRO
Total Retail Sales	1,462,000,000 (.02% of U.S.)	1,105,000,000
Food	292,000	222,000
Gen. Merchandise	151,000	130,000
Automobile	289,000	219,000
Drug	41,000	32,000
Furniture/Household	56,000	44,000

EDUCATION
_____

Two schools of higher learning have attracted students from
every state and several foreign countries.

Piedmont University (3,800) is one of the foremost agricultural
schools in the western hemisphere, and also offers an excellent
School of Dentistry and School of Business Administration.

Alliance Tech (2,200) has earned a reputation as an outstanding
school of engineering, offering courses in higher mathematics,
aeronautical engineering, aerospace technology. Alliance Tech

1974 EMPLOYMENT DATA & CHARACTERISTICS

	# Employed	% of Total Employment
Agriculture	9,450	7%
Construction	15,600	12%
Manufacturing	16,300	12%
Transportation	1,050	1%
Communications	1,680	1%
Education	14,700	11%
Public Administration	16,600	12%
Retail Stores	14,800	11%
Financial	2,300	2%
Entertainment/Recreational	1,250	1%
Welfare, Religious	3,110	2%
Misc. Industry	4,920	4%
All Other	33,500	25%
Total Employed	135,260	

is one of the principal university sources of technicians and engineers to the governmental and commercial aeronautical and aerospace programs.

Other degree-granting colleges and schools:

John Hamilton College   Morley Junior College
Christian Baptist College   Morley School of Pharmacy
Claymore Heights College   Gerhardt School of Law
Interdenominational Seminary   Hathaway Junior College

Total enrollment: 7,400

CULTURAL AND RECREATIONAL

DESOLAKE is home for the Piedmont Panthers, boasting one of the nation's top gridiron powers among smaller universities. The Panthers are perennial winners of the Tri-State College Conference and twice during the last five years have been invited to play in the Cherry Bowl post-season classic.

The Alliance Tech Ramblers also provide exciting football
for area residents, is a team which has been improving with each
season, and last year was runner-up in its division.

Professional sports is represented by the ABA Sentinels, an
expansion team which has already established itself as a
playoff contender. The Capitols are a colorful Triple A
baseball team that has spawned more than 15 major league
baseball players.

MAJOR SPORTS ATTRACTIONS

Professional   Basketball   ABA   - Sentinels
                        Baseball   Triple A - The Capitols

College   Football   Alliance Tech
                                      Piedmont

                        Basketball   Alliance Tech
                                      Piedmont

MAJOR SPORTS ARENAS

City Stadium   38,000 Capacity (Basketball, Wrestling,
(Indoor, City owned)   Rodeos, Conventions)

Alliance Tech Stadium   33,000 (Football)

Piedmont Stadium   29,000 (Football)

The Desolake Symphony Orchestra and the Desolake Light Opera
Company are renowned throughout the mid-west for their artistic
achievment.   The Desolake Repertory Company also distin-
guishes itself for its Shakespearean Summer Festival and the
presentation of both contemporary and classical productions.

The Desolake Museum of Primitive American Art, the Piedmont
University Agricultural Museum and the Desolake Science
Pavilion rank as important contributions to the cultural life
of Desolake.

Other Cultural/Sports/Tourist Attractions

State Camping Show
2 Ice Skating Rings
Desolake Sports Car Show
Desolake Horse Show
Desolake Livestock Show

College Tennis, Wrestling
Desolake Hunt and Steeplechase
Piedmont University Baseball, Basketball
Alliance Tech Basketball
Desolake Farmers Market
Luster County Zoo
Peak Point Mountain State Park
14 Public Golf Courses
Morgan County Stock Car Racing
Happy Islands Park

COMMUNICATIONS/MEDIA

DESOLAKE has a wide variety of communication/entertainment media:

> Two commercial network affiliated TV stations
> One educational PBS-affiliated TV station
> Six commercial FM radio stations
> Seven commercial AM radio stations
> One city-owned non-commercial FM radio station
> Three major metropolitan newspapers
> Eleven suburban newspapers
> One city/suburban magazine of current events

There are no common ownerships: Desolake's newspapers, AM, FM and TV stations are independent of each other.

TELEVISION STATIONS

KNAC-TV
Channel 3
NBC Network Affiliation

KBGA-TV
Channel 8
CBS Network Affiliation

KEA-TV   (Educational)
Channel 13
Public Service Broadcasting

RADIO MEDIA

AM STATIONS	KHZ/ MHZ	Affiliation	Format	:60 Rate Open $	End $
KLTD	590	CBS	MOR	26	18
KNHD	710	ABC/C	Contemp.	22	16
KAC	890	–	C-W	20	15
KML	1100	NBC	News	15	10
KPLD	1240	MBS	Talk	16	12
KFXT	1380	–	Rock	14	10
KOP	1450	–	Beautiful Music	14	10

FM STATIONS					
KFHU-FM	93.7	ABC/FM	MOR	18	14
KDID-FM	96.1		C-W	14	10
KAVO-FM	98.3		Rock	20	16
KQSR-FM	101.2	ABC/I	Classical	14	12
KPOT-FM	103.6		Black	12	8
KMLS-FM	106.1		Contemp.	14	10

PRINT MEDIA

NEWSPAPERS

	STAR TELEGRAM	CITY REGISTER	
	M-Sat Morning	M-F Evening	Sunday
Circulation	110,000	78,000	138,000
Readers per Issue	1.4	2.0	2.7
Total Readership	154,000	156,000	372,600
Open Line Rate	$1.06	$0.61	$1.28
Page Size	8 Col x 300 Lines 2400 Lines	8 Col x 300 Lines 2400 Lines	8 Col x 300 Lines 2400 Lines

MAGAZINES

TV Guide	28,000	Circulation
Weekly	$250	Cost per Page

The Gazetter	16,000	Circulation
Monthly	$190	Cost per Page
(area events, dining)		

OUTDOOR BILLBOARDS

Kroner Outdoor Advertising Inc.
450 24-sheet outdoor billboards (175 illuminated)
 12 Painted Billboard Spectaculars, premium locations

50 24-sheet boards	$2,700 per month
100 " "	$5,000 " "

Painted billboard spectaculars $1200 each. year's contract

SUBURBAN NEWSPAPERS

		Circulation
Busingdale Bugle	Weekly	5,800
Caldwell County Sentinel	Daily-E	3,700
Cavington News	Daily-E	1,800
Peak Mountain Courier	Weekly	1,100
The Jefferson Record	Daily-M	4,300
The Townsend Crier	Daily-E	2,700
Desolake Monitor	Weekly	4,800
Southside Sentinel	Weekly	1,900
The Morgan Star	Daily-E	1,600
The Buford Observer	Daily-E	2,200
Rockdale Citizen	Daily-M	3,100
		33,000

Appendix 3

FEDERAL COMMUNICATIONS COMMIS-SION PRIMER on Part I, Section IV-A and IV-B of Application Forms concerning Ascertainment of Community Problems and Broadcast Matter to Deal with Those Problems

A. **General**

1. Question: With what applications does this Primer apply in answering Part I, Section IV (A or B) of the application forms?

    Answer: With applications for:

    a. construction permit for new broadcast stations;

    b. construction permit for a change in authorized facilities when the station's proposed field intensity contour (Grade B for television, 1 mV/m for FM, or 0.5 mV/m for AM) encompasses a new area that is· equal to or greater than 50% of the area within the authorized field intensity contours.

    c. construction permit or modification of license to change station location;

    d. construction permit for satellite television station, including a 100% satellite;

    e. the assignee's or transferee's portion of applications for assignment of broadcast license or transfer of

control, except in <u>pro forma</u> cases where Form 316 is
appropriate.

Educational organizations filing applications for educational non-
commercial stations are exempt from the provisions of this Primer.

2. Question: If Section IV (A or B) has been recently submitted,
    must an applicant conduct a new ascertainment of community
    problems and submit a new Section IV?

    Answer: Needless duplication of effort will not be required.
    Prior filings within the year previous to the tender of the present
    application will generally be acceptable, where they were filed by the
    same applicant, for the same station or for another station in the
    same community and there are no significant coverage differences in-
    volved. Parties relying on previous filings must specifically refer
    to the application relied on and state that in their judgment there
    has been no change since the earlier filing. Proposed assignors and
    transferors of control are not required to file Part I even where they
    must file other parts of Section IV.

3. Question: What is the general purpose of Part I, Section IV-A
    or IV-B?

    Answer: To show what the applicant has done to ascertain
    the problems, needs and interests of the residents of his
    community of license and other areas he undertakes to serve
    (See Question 6, below), and what broadcast matter he proposes
    to meet those problems, needs and interests, as evaluated.
    The word "problems" will be used subsequently in this Primer
    as a short form of the phrase "problems, needs and interests."
    The phrase "to meet community problems" will be used to
    include the obligation to meet, aid in meeting, be responsive
    to, or stimulate the solution for community problems.

4. Question: How should ascertainment of community problems
    be made?

    Answer: By consultations with leaders of the significant
    groups in the community to be served and surrounding areas
    the applicant has undertaken to serve, and by consultations
    with members of the general public. In order to know what
    significant groups are found in a particular community, its
    composition must be determined, see Question and Answer 9.
    The word "group" as used here is broad enough to include
    population segments, such as racial and ethnic groups, and
    informal groups, as well as groups with formal organization.

5. Question: Can an applicant rely upon long-time residency in
    or familiarity with, the area to be served instead of making
    a showing that he has ascertained community problems?

    Answer: No. Such an ascertainment is mandatory.

6. Question: Is an applicant expected to ascertain community
    problems outside the community of license?

Answer: Yes. Of course, an applicant's principal obligation
is to ascertain the problems of his community of license. But
he should also ascertain the problems of the other communities
that he undertakes to serve, as set forth in his response to
Question 1(A) (2) of Section IV-A or IV-B. Applicants for
stations licensed to more than one city, or for channels assigned
to two or more cities; or proposed transferees or assignees of stations
which have obtain waiver of the station identification rules to permit
secondary identification with additional cities, are expected to
ascertain problems in each of the cities. If an applicant chooses
not to serve a major community that falls within his service contours
a showing must be submitted explaining why. However, no major city
more than 75 miles from the transmitter site need be included in the
applicant's ascertainment, even if the station's contours exceed
that distance.

7. Question: Must the ascertainment of community problems
    for the other areas the applicant undertakes to serve be
    as extensive as for the city of license?

    Answer: No. Normally, consultations with community
    leaders who can be expected to have a broad overview
    of community problems would be sufficient to ascertain community
    problems.

8. Question: Should an applicant for a major change in
    facilities (see Answer 1(b), above) make a new ascer-
    tainment of community problems for the entire service
    area or just the additional area to be served?

    Answer: Only the additional area to be served need be
    subjected to a new ascertainment of community problems.
    Only communities or areas covered by Question and Answer
    6 need be ascertained, to the extent indicated in Answer 7.

9. Question: How does an applicant determine the composition
    of his city of license?

    Answer: The applicant may use any method he chooses, but
    guesswork or estimates based upon alleged area familiarity
    are inadequate. Current data from the U.S. Census Bureau,
    Chamber of Commerce and other reliable studies or reports
    are acceptable. The applicant must submit such data as is
    necessary to indicate the minority, racial, or ethnic
    breakdown of the community, its economic activities,
    governmental activities, public service organizations, and
    any other factors or activities that make the particular
    community distinctive.

10. Question: If the applicant shows consultations with leaders
    of groups and organizations that represent various economic,
    social political, cultural and other elements of the community,
    such as government, education, religion, agriculture, business,
    labor, the professions, racial and/or ethnic groups, and
    eleemosynary organizations, is the applicant still required to
    submit a showing in support of its determination of the
    composition of the community?

Answer: Yes. The purpose of requiring a determination of the community is to inform the applicant and the Commission what groups comprise the community. The applicant must use that information to select those who are to be consulted as representatives of those groups. That determination may be challenged on a showing, including supporting data, that a significant group has been omitted. The "significance" of a group may rest on several criteria, including its size, its influence, or its lack of influence in the community.

B. Consultations with Community Leaders and Members of the General Public.

11(a). Question: Who should conduct consultations with community leaders?

Answer: Principals or management-level employees. In the case of newly formed applicants who have not hired a full staff and are applying for new stations, or for transfer or assignment of an authorization, principals, management-level employees, or prospective management-level employees, must be used to consult with community leaders.

11(b). Question: Who should consult with members of the general public?

Answer: Principals or employees. In the case of newly formed applicants who have not hired a full staff and are applying for new stations, or for transfer or assignment of an authorization, principals, employees or prospective employees may conduct consultations. If consultations are conducted by employees who are below the management level, the consultation process must be supervised by principals, management-level employees, or prospective management-level employees. In addition, the applicant may choose to use a professional research or survey service to conduct consultations with members of the general public.

12. Question: To what extent may a professional research or survey service be used in the ascertainment process?

Answer: A professional service would not establish a dialogue between decision-making personnel in the applicant and community leaders. Therefore, such a service may not be used to consult community leaders. However, a professional service, as indicated in Answer 11(b), may be used to conduct consultations with the general public. A professional service may also be used to provide the applicant with background data, including information as to the composition of the city of license. The use of a professional research or survey service is not required to meet Commission standards as to ascertaining community problems. The applicant will be responsible for the reliability of such a service.

13(a). Question: With what community leaders should consultations
be held?

Answer: The applicant has already determined the
composition of the community, and should select for
consultations those community leaders that reflect that
composition. Groups with the greatest problems may be
the least organized and have the fewest recognized spokesmen. Therefore, additional efforts may be necessary to
identify their leaders so as to better establish a dialogue
with such groups and better ascertain their problems.

13(b). Question: With what members of the general public should
consultations be held?

Answer: A random sample of members of the general public
should be consulted. The consultations should be designed
to further ascertain community problems which may not have
been revealed by consultations with community leaders. In
addition to a random sample, if the applicant has reason
to believe that further consultations with a particular
group may reveal further problems or may elicit viewpoints
that will give him further insight into its problems, he
is encouraged to consult with additional members of that group.

14. Question: How many should be consulted?

Answer: No set number or formula has been adopted. Community
leaders from each significant group must be consulted. A
sufficient number of members of the general public to assure
a generally random sample must also be consulted. The
number of consultations will vary, of course, with the size
of the city in question and the number of distinct groups
or organizations. No formula has been adopted as to the
number of consultations in the city of license compared to
other communities falling within the station's coverage
contours. Applicants for stations in relatively small communities that are near larger communities are reminded that
an ascertainment of community problems primarily in the
larger community raises a question as to whether the station
will realistically serve the smaller city, or intends to
abandon its obligation to the smaller city.

15. Question: When should consultations be held?

Answer: In preparing applications for major changes in the facilities of operating stations, a complete new ascertainment must
be made within six (6) months prior to filing the application.
Applicants for a new facility, or the party filing the
assignee or transferee portion of an application for
assignment or transfer, are also required to hold consultations with six (6) months prior to filing an appropriate
application.

16. Question: Is a showing on the ascertainment of community
problems defective if leaders of one of the groups that

comprise the community, as disclosed by the applicant's study, are not consulted?

Answer: The omission of consultations with leaders of a significant group would make the applicant's showing defective, since those consulted would not reflect the composition of the community.

17. Question: In consultations to ascertain community problems, may a preprinted form or questionnaire be used?

Answer: Yes. A questionnaire may serve as a useful guide for consultations with community leaders, but cannot be used in lieu of personal consultations. Members of the general public may be asked to fill out a questionnaire to be collected by the applicant. If the applicant uses a form or questionnaire, a copy should be submitted with the application.

18. Question: In consulting with community leaders to ascertain community problems, should an applicant also elicit their opinion on what programs the applicant should broadcast?

Answer: It is not the purpose of the consultations to elicit program suggestions. (See Question and Answer 3.) Rather, it is to ascertain what the person consulted believes to be the problems of the community from the standpoint of a leader of the particular group or organization. Thus, a leader in the educational field would be a useful source of information on educational matters; a labor leader, on labor matters; and a business leader on business matters. However, it is also recognized that individual leaders may have significant comments outside their respective fields, and the applicant should consider their comments with respect to all community problems. The applicant has the responsibility for determining what broadcast matter should be presented to meet the ascertained community problems as he has evaluated them.

19. Question: If, in consulting with community leaders and members of the general public, an applicant receives little information as to the existence of community problems, can he safely assume that only a few problems actually exist?

Answer: No. The assumption is not safe. The applicant should re-examine his efforts to determine whether his consultations have been designed to elicit sufficient information. Obviously, a brief or chance encounter will not provide adequate results. The person interviewed should be specifically advised of the purpose of the consultation. The applicant should note that many individuals, when consulting with a broadcast applicant, either jump to the conclusion that the applicant is seeking programming preferences, or express community problems in terms of exposure or publicity for the particular group or groups with which they are affiliated. The applicant may properly note these comments, but should ask further questions designed to elicit more extensive responses as to community problems.

20. Question: In responding to Part I of Section IV-A or IV-B how should the applicant identify the community leaders consulted?

Answer: By name, position, and/or organization of each. If further information is required to clearly identify a specific leader, it should be submitted.

21. Question: Should the information elicited from a community leader, from the standpoint of the group he represents, be set forth after his name?

Answer: It is not required, but the applicant may find it desirable. The information can be set forth in a general list of community problems.

C. Information Received.

22. Question: Must all community problems which were revealed by the consultations be included in the applicant's showing?

Answer: All ascertained community problems should be listed, whether or not he proposes to treat them through his broadcast matter. An applicant need not, however, list comments as to community problems that are clearly frivolous.

D. Applicant's Evaluation

23. Question: What is meant by an "applicant's evaluation" of information received as to community problems?

Answer: The applicant's evaluation is the process by which he determines the relative importance of the community problems he has ascertained, the timeliness of the various comments, and the extent to which he can present broadcast matter to meet the problems.

24. Question: Is the applicant's evaluation to be included in his application?

Answer: It is not required. Where the applicant's broadcast matter does not appear to be sufficiently responsive to the community problems disclosed by his consultations, the applicant may be asked for an explanation by letter of inquiry from the Commission. See Questions and Answers 25 and 26.

25. Question: Must an applicant plan broadcast matter to meet all community problems disclosed by his consultations?

Answer: Not necessarily. However, he is expected to determine in good faith which of such problems merit treatment by the station. In determining what kind of broadcast matter should be presented to meet those problems, the applicant may consider his program format and the composition of his audience, but bearing in mind that many problems affect and are pertinent to diverse groups of people.

26. Question: If an applicant lists a number of community problems but in his evaluation determines that he will present broadcast matter to meet only one or two of them, would the proposal be defective?

Answer: A prima facie question would arise as to how the proposal would serve the public interest, and the applicant would have the burden of establishing the validity of his proposal.

27. Question: As a result of the evaluation process, is an applicant expected to propose broadcast matter to meet community problems in proportion to the number of people involved in the problem?

Answer: No. For example, the applicant, in his evaluation (see Question and Answer 23) might determine that a problem concerning a beautification program affecting all the people would not have the relative importance and immediacy of a problem relating to inadequate hospital facilities affecting only a small percentage of the community, but in a life-or-death way.

E. Broadcast Matter to Meet the Problems as Evaluated

28. Question: What is meant by "broadcast matter"?

Answer: Programs and announcements.

29. Question: In the application, must there be a showing as to what broadcast matter the applicant is proposing to what problem?

Answer: Yes. See Public Notice of August 22, 1968, FCC 68-847, 13 RR 2d 1303. The applicant should give the description, and anticipated time segment, duration and frequency of broadcast of the program or program series, and the community problem or problems which are to be treated by it. One appropriate way would be to list the broadcast matter and, after it, the particular problem or problems the broadcast matter is designed to meet. Statements such as "programs will be broadcast from time to time to meet community problems," or "news, talk and discussion programs will be used to meet community problems," are clearly insufficient. Applicants should note that they are expected to make a positive, diligent and continuing effort to meet community problems. Therefore, they are expected to modify their broadcast matter if warranted in light of changed community problems. If announcements are proposed, they should be identified with the community problem or problems they are designed to meet.

30. Question: Can an applicant specify only announcements and no programs to meet community problems?

Answer: A proposal to present announcements only would raise a question as to the adequacy of the proposal.

The applicant would have the burden of establishing that
announcements would be the most effective method for meeting
the community problems he propose to meet. If the burden
is not met by the showing in the application, it will be
subject to further inquiry.

31. Question: What is meant by devoting a "significant proportion"
of a station's programming to meeting community problems?
/City of Camden 18 FCC 2d 412, 421, 16 RR 2d 555, 568 (1969)/

Answer: There is no single answer for all stations. The time
required to deal with community problems can vary from community
to community and from time to time within a community. Initially,
this is a matter that falls within the discretion of the applicant.
However, where the amount of broadcast matter proposed to meet
community problems appears patently insufficient to meet significantly the community problems disclosed by the applicant's
consultations, he will be asked for an explanation by letter of
inquiry from the Commission.

32. Question: Can station editorials be used as a part of a
licensee's efforts to meet community problems?

Answer: Yes.

33. Question: Can news programming be considered as programming to
meet community problems?

Answer: Yes. However, they can not be relied upon exclusively.
Most broadcast stations, of course, carry news programs regardless
of community problems. News programs are usually considered by
the people to be a factual report of events and matters - to keep
the public informed - and, therefore, are not designed primarily to
meet community problems.

34. Question: If an applicant proposes a specialized format (all news,
rock and roll, religious, etc.), must it present broadcast
matter to meet community problems?

Answer: Yes. The broadcast matter can be fitted into the
format of the station.

35. Question: May an applicant rely upon activities other than
programming to meet community problems?

Answer: No. Many broadcasters do participate personally
in civic activities, but the Commission's concern must
be with the licensee's stewardship of his broadcast time in
serving the public interest.

36. Question: Are there any requirements as to when broadcast
matter meeting community problems should be presented?

Answer: The applicant is expected to schedule the time of
presentation on a good faith judgment as to when it could
reasonably be expected to be effective.

Appendix 4

"ACCO BROADCASTING" APPLICA-
TION FOR CHANNEL 5, DESOLAKE

FCC Form 301 January 1971 **Section I** UNITED STATES OF AMERICA FEDERAL COMMUNICATIONS COMMISSION	File No.

FCC Form 301
January 1971
Form Approved
Budget Bureau No. 52-R0014
Section I
UNITED STATES OF AMERICA
FEDERAL COMMUNICATIONS COMMISSION

Application for Authority to Construct a New Broadcast Station or Make Changes in an Existing Broadcast Station

INSTRUCTIONS

A. This form is to be used in applying for authority to construct a new standard, commercial FM, or television broadcast station, or to make changes in existing broadcast stations. This form consists of this part, Section I, and the following sections:

Section II, Legal Qualifications of Broadcast Applicant
Section III, Financial Qualifications of Broadcast Applicant
Section IV-A, Statement of Program Service of Broadcast Applicant (AM-FM)
Section IV-B, Statement of Program Service of Broadcast Applicant (TV)
Section V-A, Standard Broadcast Engineering Data
Section V-B, FM Broadcast Engineering Data
Section V-C, Television Broadcast Engineering Data
Section V-G, Antenna and Site Information
Section VI, Equal Employment Opportunity Program

B. Prepare three copies of this form and all exhibits. Sign one copy of Sections I, IV-A, and IV-B. Prepare one additional copy (a total of four) of Section V-G and associated exhibits, and one additional copy (a total of four) of Section V-C and associated exhibits. File all the above with Federal Communications Commission, Washington, D. C. 20554. A SEPARATE AND COMPLETE APPLICATION (IN TRIPLICATE) MUST BE FILED FOR EACH AM STATION, EACH FM STATION, AND EACH TV STATION.

C. Number exhibits serially in the space provided in the body of the form and list each exhibit in the space provided on page 2 of this Section. Show date of preparation of each exhibit, antenna pattern, and map, and show date when each photograph was taken.

D. The name of the applicant stated in Section I hereof shall be the exact corporate name, if a corporation; if a partnership, the names of all partners and the name under which the partnership does business; if an unincorporated association, the name of an executive officer, his office, and the name of the association. In other Sections of the form the name alone will be sufficient for identification of the applicant.

E. Information called for by this application which is already on file with the Commission (except that called for in Section III which is more than 90 days old and in Section V-G) need not be refiled in this application provided (1) the information is now on file in another application or FCC Form filed by or on behalf of this applicant; (2) the information is identified FULLY by reference to the file number (if any) the FCC form number, and the filing date of the application or other form containing the information and the page or paragraph referred to, and (3) after making the reference, the applicant states: "No change since date of filing." Any such reference will be considered to incorporate into this application all information, confidential or otherwise, contained in the application or other form referred to. The incorporated application or other form will thereafter, in its entirety, be open to the public. (See Section 1.526 of the Commission's Rules and Regulations, "Records to be maintained locally for public inspection by applicants, permittees, and licensees."

F. This application shall be personally signed by the applicant, if the applicant is an individual; by one of the partners, if the applicant is a partnership; by an officer, if the applicant is a corporation; by a member who is an officer, if the applicant is an unincorporated association; by such duly elected or appointed officials as may be competent to do so under the laws of the applicable jurisdiction, if the applicant is an eligible government entity; or by the applicant's attorney in case of the applicant's physical disability or of his absence from the United States. The attorney shall, in the event he signs for the applicant, separately set forth the reason why the application is not signed by the applicant. In addition, if any matter is stated on the basis of the attorney's belief only (rather than his knowledge), he shall separately set forth his reasons for believing that such statements are true.

G. Before filling out this application, the applicant should familiarize himself with the Communications Act of 1934, as amended, Parts 1, 2, 73 and 17 of the Commission's Rules and Regulations and the Standards of Good Engineering Practice.

H. BE SURE ALL NECESSARY INFORMATION IS FURNISHED AND ALL PARAGRAPHS ARE FULLY ANSWERED. IF ANY PORTIONS OF THE APPLICATION ARE NOT APPLICABLE, SPECIFICALLY SO STATE. DEFECTIVE OR INCOMPLETE APPLICATIONS MAY BE RETURNED WITHOUT CONSIDERATION.

File No.

1. Name of applicant (See Instruction D)

Acco Broadcasting, Inc.

Street Address

101 South Industry Blvd

City	State	ZIP Code
Desolake	Kan.	3333

2. Name and address of person to whom communications should be sent if different from item 1

Name

o/c Fred Foster, President

Street Address

City	State	ZIP Code

3(a). Purpose of application (check one)

[X] New Station   [ ] Change existing station facilities

(b). If this application is for a change in existing facilities, complete Section I plus any other Sections necessary to show all substantial changes in information previously filed with the Commission, and indicate below the Sections completed and filed with this application.

Section II	Section V-A
Section III	Section V-B
Section IV-A	Section V-C
Section IV-B	Section V-G
	Section VI

4. Requested facilities

Type of station (as Standard, FM, Television)

TV

Frequency	Call	Channel No.	Power in kilowatts		Minimum hours operation da
			Night	Day	
74-80mHz		5	100kw	100kw	18

Hours of operation

Unlimited	X	Sharing with (Specify Stations)	Other (Specify)
Daytime only			
Limited			

Station location

City	State
Desolake	Kansouri

5. In the space below refer to information already on file with the Commission which, in accordance with Instruction E, may be incorporated in this application by proper reference.

File or Form No. and Date	Section No.	Paragraph No.

FOR COMMISSION USE ONLY

THE APPLICANT hereby waives any claim to the use of any particular frequency or of the ether as against the regulatory power of the United States because of the previous use of the same, whether by license or otherwise, and requests an authorization in accordance with this application. (See Section 304 of the Communications Act of 1934).

THE APPLICANT represents that this application is not filed for the purpose of impeding, obstructing, or delaying determination on any other application with which it may be in conflict.

THE APPLICANT acknowledges that all the statements made in this application and attached exhibits are considered material representations, and that all the exhibits are a material part hereof and are incorporated herein as if set out in full in the application.

C E R T I F I C A T I O N

I certify that the statements in this application are true, complete, and correct to the best of my knowledge and belief, and are made in good faith.

Signed and dated this .... 17 .... day of ...... December ......, 19 74

(This Section should not be signed and dated until all the following Sections and Exhibits have been prepared and attached.

INCLUDE FILING FEE WITH THIS APPLICATION. SEE PART 1 OF FCC RULES FOR AMOUNT OF FEE.	Acco Broadcasting, Inc.
	(NAME OF APPLICANT)

By ....
(SIGNATURE)

WILLFUL FALSE STATEMENTS MADE ON THIS FORM ARE PUNISHABLE BY FINE AND IMPRISONMENT. U. S. CODE, TITLE 18, SECTION 1001.	

Title ...... President ......

If applicant is represented by legal or engineering counsel, state name and post office address:

EXHIBITS furnished as required by this form:

Exhibit No.	Section and Para. No. of Form	Name of officer or employee (1) by whom or (2) under whose direction exhibit was prepared (show which)	Official title
1.	IV-B, 1-A	Fred Foster (2)	President
2.	IV-B, 1-B	Fred Foster (2)	President
3.	IV-B, 1-C	Fred Foster (2)	President
4.	IV-B, 1-D	Fred Foster (2)	President
5.	IV-B, 14	Fred Foster (2)	President
6.	IV-B, 15	Fred Foster (2)	President
7.	IV-B, 20	Fred Foster (2)	President
8.	IV-B, 22	Fred Foster (2)	President
9.	IV-B, 23	Fred Foster (2)	President

FCC Form 301	FEDERAL COMMUNICATIONS COMMISSION	Section IV-B
STATEMENT OF TELEVISION PROGRAM SERVICE	Name of Applicant	
Call letters of station	City and state which station is licensed to serve	

(See Instructions, Sec. IV-B, page 7)

PART I

Ascertainment of Community Needs

1. A. State in Exhibit No. __1__ the methods used by the applicant to ascertain the needs and interests of the public served by the station. Such information shall include (1) the major communities or areas which applicant principally undertakes to serve and (2) identification of representative groups, interests and organizations which were consulted.

   B. Describe in Exhibit No. __2__ the significant needs and interests of the public which the applicant believes his station will serve during the coming license period, including those with respect to national and international matters.

   C. List in Exhibit No. __3__ typical and illustrative programs or program series (excluding Entertainment and News) that applicant plans to broadcast during the coming license period to meet those needs and interests.

   D. Describe in Exhibit No. __4__ the procedures applicant has or proposes to have for the consideration and disposition of complaints or suggestions coming from the public.

NOTE: Sufficient records shall be kept on file at the station, open for inspection by the Commission, for a period of 3 years from the date of filing of this statement (unless requested to be kept longer by the Commission) to support the representations required in answer to Question 1. A, B, and C. These records should *not* be submitted with this application and need not be available for public inspection.

PART II
Post Programming   DNA

2. A. State the total hours of operation during the composite week: _____

   B. Attach as Exhibit No. _____ one exact copy of the program logs for the composite week used as a basis for responding to questions herein. Applicants utilizing automatic program logging devices must comply with the provisions of Section 73.670(c). Automatic recordings will be returned to the applicant. Exact copies of program logs will not be returned.

   If applicant has not operated during all of the days of the composite week which would be applicable to the use of this form, applicant should so notify the Commission and request the designation of substitute day or days as required.

3. A. State the amount of time (rounded to the nearest minute) the applicant devoted in the composite week to the program types (see Definitions) listed below. Commercial matter within a program segment shall be excluded in computing time devoted to that particular program segment (e.g., a 15-minute news program containing 3 minutes' commercial matter shall be counted as a 12-minute news program).

	Hours	Minutes	% of Total Time on Air
(1) News	....	....	.... %
*(2) Public Affairs	....	....	.... %
*(3) All other programs, exclusive of Entertainment and Sports	....	....	.... %

   * Attach as Exhibit No. _____ a brief description of each program included in these categories.

   B. If in the applicant's judgment the composite week does not adequately represent the station's past programming, applicant may in addition provide in Exhibit No. _____ the same information as required in 3-A above (using the same format) for a representative period during the year preceding the filing of this application. Applicant shall identify the time period used. Applicant need not file the program logs used in responding to this question unless requested by the Commission.

4. List in Exhibit No. _____ typical and illustrative programs or program series (excluding Entertainment and News) broadcast during the year preceding the filing of this application which have served public needs and interests in applicant's judgment. Denote, by underlining the Title, those programs, if any, designed to inform the public on local, national or international problems of greatest public importance in the community served by the applicant. Use the format below. (*NOTE:* If applicant's response includes any program described in Question 3, give title of program and refer to that Question without further details.)

A. Title: E. Time broadcast & duration:

B. Source*:   F. Number of times broadcast:

C. Type*:   G. Extent, if any, to which community

D. Brief description: leaders or groups involved:

5. State below the amount of time (in hours and minutes) by source* for programs in the composite week. (The response shall be in terms of total program time, including commercial matter.)

	Local	Network	Recorded
8 a.m. - 6 p.m.	....	....	....
6 p.m. - 11 p.m.	....	....	....
All other hours	....	....	....

*See Definitions—Sec. IV-B, page 7.

FCC Form 301   STATEMENT OF TV PROGRAM SERVICE   Section IV-B, Page 2

5. Submit in Exhibit No. _____ the following information concerning the applicant's news programs:

A. The staff, news gathering facilities, news services and other sources utilized; and

B. An estimate of the percentage of news program time devoted to local and regional news during the composite week.

7. In connection with the applicant's public affairs programming, describe its policy during the past renewal period with respect to making time available for the discussion of public issues and the method of selecting subjects and participants.

DNA

8. Was the applicant affiliated with one or more national television networks during the past license period?

Yes _____ No _____

If so, give name(s) of Network(s): ....

If applicant had more than one such affiliation, which network was the principal source of network programs?

....

9. State the number of public service announcements broadcast by the applicant during the composite week: ....

10. A. In applicant's judgment, does the information supplied in this Part II adequately reflect its past programming?

Yes _____ No _____.

B. If "no," applicant may attach as Exhibit No._____ such additional information as may be necessary to describe accurately and present fairly its program service.

C. If applicant's programming practices for the period covered by this statement varied substantially from the programming representations made in applicant's last renewal application, the applicant shall submit as Exhibit No. _____ a statement explaining the variations and the reasons therefor.

PART III

Proposed Programming

1. State the proposed total hours of operation during a typical week: __126__

2. State the minimum amount of time the applicant proposes to devote normally each week to the program types (see Definitions) listed below. Commercial matter within a program segment shall be excluded in computing time devoted to that particular program segment (e.g., a fifteen-minute news program containing 3 minutes' commercial matter shall be computed as a 12-minute news program.)

	Hours	Minutes	% of Total Time on Air
(A) News	7	30	6.0 %
(B) Public Affairs	2	00	1.6 %
(C) All other programs, exclusive of Entertainment and Sports	8	30	6.7 %

3. State below the amount of time (in hours and minutes) proposed to be devoted to programs in a typical week by source*. (The response shall be in terms of total program time, including commercial matter.)

	Local	Network *	Recorded
8 a.m. - 6 p.m.	9 hr., 30 min.	38 hours	22 hr., 30 min
6 p.m. - 11 p.m.	2 ", 30 min.	24 hours	8 hr., 30 min.
All other hours	3 hours	8 hr., 30 min.	9 hr., 30 min.

4. Submit in Exhibit No. __5__ the following information concerning the applicant's proposed news programs:

A. The staff, news gathering facilities, news services and other sources to be utilized; and

B. An estimate of the percentage of news program time to be devoted to local and regional news during a typical week.

[Network affiliation is optional, but is assumed for purposes of this hypothetical application]

*See Definitions—Sec. IV-B, page 7.

15. In connection with the applicant's proposed public affairs programming, describe its policy with respect to making time available for the discussion of public issues and the method of selecting subjects and participants.

S E E   E X H I B I T   6

16. State the minimum number of public service announcements applicant proposes to present during a typical week: 135

17.* Will the applicant be affiliated with one or more national television networks during the coming license period?
Yes X No _____. If so, give name(s) of network(s): _____ABC_____

If more than one such affiliation is expected, which, if any, does applicant now expect to be the principal source of network programs? _____

PART IV

Past Commercial Practices   DNA

18. State the number of 60-minute segments of the composite week (beginning with the first full clock hour and ending with the last full clock hour of each broadcast day) containing the following amounts of commercial matter:

A. Up to and including 8 minutes .... _____
B. Over 8 and up to and including 12 minutes .... _____
C. Over 12 and up to and including 16 minutes .... _____
D. Over 16 minutes .... _____

List each segment in category (D) above, specifying the amount of commercial time in the segment, and the day and time broadcast:

*[Network affiliation is optional, but is assumed for purposes of this hypothetical application.]

19. **A.** In the applicant's judgment, does the information supplied in this Part IV for the composite week adequately reflect its commercial practices? Yes_____ No_____ .

B. If "no," applicant may attach as Exhibit No._____ such additional material as may be necessary to describe adequately and present fairly its commercial practices.

C. If applicant's commercial practices for the period covered by this statement varied substantially from the commercial representations made in applicant's last renewal application, the applicant shall explain the variations and the reasons therefor:

DNA

PART V

Proposed Commercial Practices

20. What is the maximum amount of commercial matter in any 60-minute segment which the applicant proposes normally to allow? <u>16 minutes</u>

If applicant proposes to permit this amount to be exceeded at times, state under what circumstances and how often this is expected to occur, and the limits that would then apply.

S E E   E X H I B I T   7

PART VI
General Station Policies and Procedures

21. State the name(s) and position of the person(s) who determines the day-to-day programming, makes decisions, and directs the operation of the station covered by this application and whether he is employed full-time in the operation of the station.

> Fred Foster, President of Applicant, will be employed as the full-time Station Manager and will be responsible for day-to-day matters relating to programming and station operation.

22. A. Does the applicant have established policies with respect to programming and advertising standards (whether developed by the station or contained in a code of broadcasting standards and practices) to guide the operation of the station?
     Yes__X__ No_____.

    B. If "yes," attach as Exhibit No.__8__ a brief summary of such policies. (If the station relies exclusively upon the published code of any national organization or trade association, a statement to that effect will suffice.)

23. State the methods by which applicant undertakes to keep informed of the requirements of the Communications Act and the Commission's Rules and Regulations, and a description of the procedures established to acquaint applicant's employees and agents with such requirements and to ensure their compliance.

> S E E   E X H I B I T   9

24. If, as an integral part of its station identification announcements, applicant makes or proposes to make reference to any business, profession or activity other than broadcasting in which applicant or any affiliate or stockholder is engaged or financially interested, directly or indirectly, set forth typical examples and approximate frequency of their use.

> N O N E   C O N T E M P L A T E D

25. A. State the total number of station employees:__49__.

    B. Describe in Exhibit No._____ the applicant's plans for staffing the station including the number of employees in the programming, sales, technical, and general administrative departments. Do not list the same employee in more than one category. However, if an employee performs multiple services, this may be so shown by identifying him with his various duties (e.g., if two employees are combination announcers and salesmen, the list would include an entry of "two programming-sales".

CC Form 301   STATEMENT OF TV PROGRAM SERVICE   Section IV-B, Page 6

6. State whether the applicant:

   A. Has a policy of broadcasting programs to meet public needs whether or not commercial sponsorship is available or appropriate. Yes __X__ No _____

      If ''yes'', in Exhibit No. _____ give examples to illustrate application of station's policy during the 12 months preceding the filing of this application.   DNA

   B. Has a policy of preempting time to present special programs. Yes __X__ No _____

      If ''yes'', in Exhibit No. _____ give examples to illustrate application of station's policy during the 12 months preceding the filing of this application.   DNA

PART VII

Other Matters and Certification

7. Applicant may submit as Exhibit No. _____ any additional information which, in its judgment, is necessary adequately to describe or to present fairly its services and operations in relation to the public interest.

8. The undersigned has familiarized himself with paragraph 7 of the Instructions on page 7 of Section IV-B concerning signature requirements and in light of its provisions does hereby:

   A. Acknowledge that all the statements made in this Section IV-B and the attached exhibits are considered material representations and that all the exhibits are a material part hereof and are incorporated herein as if set out in full in the application form; and

   B. Certify that the statements herein are true, complete, and correct to the best of his knowledge and belief and are made in good faith.

SIGNED AND DATED this __17__ day of __December__ .... , 19 __76__.

Acco Broadcasting, Inc.
_____
(NAME OF LICENSEE)

By: _____
(SIGNATURE)

Fred Foster
_____
(PLEASE PRINT NAME OF PERSON SIGNING)

President
_____
(TITLE)

WILLFUL FALSE STATEMENTS MADE IN THIS FORM ARE PUNISHABLE BY FINE AND IMPRISONMENT. U. S. CODE, TITLE 18, SECTION 1001.

Exhibit 1

ASCERTAINMENT

1. A detailed description of the salient characteristics
   of the Desolake Metropolitan Area has been given elsewhere. (See Market Profile -- Desolake, Kansouri.)

2. Principals of Applicant (all of whom will participate in
   the daily operations of the station) conducted personal
   interviews with seventy (70) community leaders, fifty (50)
   men and twenty (20) women. Other demographics:

White	46
Black	15
Spanish-	
Speaking	5
American Indian	2
Oriental	2

3. The leaders interviewed were from the following Desolake
   Metropolitan Area communities:

Desolake	41
Lard Cty.	6
Hathaway Cty.	6
Henry Cty.	5
Buttington Cty.	3
Caldwell Cty.	3
Morgan Cty.	2
Townsend Cty.	2
Luster Cty.	2

4. Leaders contacted represented the following groups and
   interests [detailed identification deleted in the interest
   of minimizing bulk]:

   - Agriculture
   - Business
   - Civic Improvement
   - Culture
   - Communications
   - Disadvantaged
   - Education
   - Elderly
   - Environment/Ecology
   - Government
   - Health Services
   - Industry
   - Labor
   - Law Enforcement

                                    - Minorities
                                          (a) Black
                                          (b) Spanish Speaking
                                          (c) American Indian
                                          (d) Oriental
                                          (e) Women
                                    - Professional
                                    - Recreation
                                    - Religion
                                    - Suburban Communities
                                    - Tourism
                                    - Transportation

5. Applicant also conducted its own series of telephone
   interviews with 212 members of the general public, using
   a random selection sampling technique to ensure a
   representative survey throughout the station's proposed
   service area.

                                                        Exhibit 2

COMMUNITY NEEDS, PROBLEMS AND INTERESTS ASCERTAINED BY APPLICANT

Applicant interviewed 70 leaders in the Desolake area. The Applicant

includes below all problems, needs and interests mentioned in these interviews:

A. DESOLAKE (including Metro Areas of Lard, Hathaway, and Henry Counties)

   1. Traffic
   2. Sewage
   3. Bus service
   4. The need for rejuvenation and renovation of the downtown area
   5. A broader economic base is needed for the area
   6. Unemployment is bad.

   7. More and better housing
   8. The cost of living is too high
   9. The need for better education
  10. Farm workers need to be paid better wages
  11. Crime
  12. Equality of opportunity is needed
  13. Zoning control is needed
  14. The Desolake area has to cope with the growth it is experiencing
  15. Poor city planning
  16. Poor mass transit
  17. Poor enforcement of housing codes
  18. Flooding
  19. Citizen apathy
  20. Better health care
  21. More jobs are needed for Blacks, teenagers, and retired persons
  22. Off-track betting should be allowed

23. Urban renewal is proceeding too slowly
24. The leadership of the city lacks a sense of community. There are too many distinct groups that act separately.
25. The breakdown of the family unit.
26. Inadequate drainage and storm sewers
27. Streets and sidewalks are in poor repair
28. Desolake needs programs to bring business back downtown
29. The need for better urban services
30. The need for communication and understanding among people of different classes.
31. Racial problems
32. The airport is terribly inadequate
33. The lack of natural gas
34. Organized crime
35. More recreational facilities
36. Better road netowrks
37. There is a shortage in the medical profession
38. The lack of public discipline
39. The general lowering of moral standards
40. The lack of cooperation among the churches
41. Better mental health care
42. Sanitation problems
43. Drug abuse
44. The poverty problem
45. The need to expand the public's knowledge about emergency care
46. Pollution
47. Inflation
48. Neighborhood parks are needed
49. A more representative government is needed
50. The desegregation of schools is needed
51. A convention center and a sports complex are needed
52. Add to and support the police force
53. The school board does not have the money for new facilities
54. The shortage of nurses
55. A better system for waste disposal is needed
56. Better police and community relations are needed
57. Better inner-city schools. Most of the new schools are being built outside of this area
58. More help for the handicapped
59. Better teachers are needed in the school system
60. The lack of inexpensive land and the necessary city facilities has retarded industrial growth

B.   BUTTINGTON

1. The highway into Desolake is not very safe. Guard rails are needed.
2. Recreational facilities are needed.
3. Better educational facilities are needed.
4. More parks are needed.
5. More policemen are needed.
6. Growth has been so fast that the town and county are having trouble keeping up with the services.

C.   CALDWELL

1. Shortage of doctors
2. Renovate the downtown shopping area
3. Expanded sanitation service is needed.
4. Need to increase capability of sewage treatment plant.
5. Growth is occurring very rapidly - planning is needed to cope with it.
6. Need more housing
7. More people should be involved in government.

D.   MORGAN

1. There is a need for a united community spirit.
2. The need for more housing
3. Need a four lane highway to Desolake
4. Waste disposal is getting to be a problem

E.   TOWNSEND

1. A program for sanitary storm sewers is needed
2. There is a housing shortage
3. There is a shortage of off-street parking
4. Many streets need to be widened
5. There is a water shortage problem

F.   LUSTER

1. Recreational facilities are needed
2. Juvenile delinquency
3. The need for the enlargement of sewage facilities
4. The need for the expansion of utilities

PROBLEMS IDENTIFIED BY THE GENERAL PUBLIC

Applicant interviewed more than 200 members of the general public in

the Desolake area.   Below is a listing of all problems and needs mentioned.

1. Problems related to automobile - traffic - better traffic control -
    need better roads, highways, expressways - bad railroad crossings -
    better access to shopping centers - need more parking - cars parked
    on residential streets should be required to be in driveways.

2. Downtown deterioration - implementation of urban renewal needed.

3. Bad telephone service.

4. Crime - break-ins - thefts - poor police protection.

5. Dirty streets - not enough trash receptacles - enforce litter laws.

6. Drugs and alcohol.

7. Need to work closer with police - not be afraid to get involved - watch neighbor's property - encourage police.

8. Sewers - septic tanks.

9. Need good bus system.

10. Not enough jobs.

11. Juvenile delinquency.

12. Reckless driving.

13. Need better planning and zoning - remove political interference.

14. Puddles on streets.

15. Need more recreation and parks for children - teenagers - inner city.

16. Need hospital or emergency treatment center in north end.

17. Need shopping center north of town.

18. Need bicycle paths.

19. Too much grass being paved.

20. Stop growth - too many apartments and subdivisions.

21. Fire and police underpaid.

22. Lack of communications between University and townspeople.

23. Local government should not waste money on outside consultation

24. Need more municipal child care centers - public kindergartens.

25. Run down neighborhoods.

26. Street lights needed.

27. Legal fees too high.

28. Walking policemen needed.

29. Need stiffer fine and jail sentences, higher bond fees.

30. Need moral education for children.

31. Unemployment of Blacks.

32. Need more low cost housing.

33. Pollution - ecological.

34. High taxes - inequitable taxes.

35. High food prices.

36. Schools too crowded.

37. Need additional branch libraries - library branches should be open evenings.

38. Dogs running loose.

39. Problem of finding employment if over 40.

40. Better sanitation.

41. Better city planning

42. Not enough restaurants.

43. Not enough modern shops.

44. Need more industry in the area.

45. Lack of community spirit.

46. Stricter enforcement of parking laws.

47. The cost of living is too high.

48. The mistreatment of animals.

49. Need to get the railroad tracks off the streets.

50. Need more parks.

51. Not enough activities for young people.

52. The need for a rehabilitation program for drug addicts.

53. Need more policemen on the beat downtown.

54. The need for a civic center

55. Better mass transit.

56. Racial problems

57. Zoning laws should be adhered to

58. Better training of police.

59. Better drivers.

60. School system needs to be improved.

61. Too many people are not being punished for their crimes.

62. Need a hospital on the north side of town.

63. Need to get the derelicts off the street.

64. Better street lighting.

65. Bicycle riders should obey traffic laws.

66. Too many sirens.

NEEDS AND PROBLEMS APPLICANT PROPOSES TO MEET

As a result of interviews of more than 200 members of the general public and over 70 community leaders, Applicant has decided that the following problems and needs are the ones it will attempt to meet with its programming:

1. The Problems of Growth - The Desolake area has grown very rapidly during the past two decades and all indications point to a confirmed rapid expansion. Major decisions concerning planning and zoning will have to be made in order to insure that this growth is orderly and in the best interest of the community.

2. Traffic Related Problems - There are all types of problems with traffic in Desolake. City roads were not built with the capability of handling today's flow of cars. Roads are in poor repair and in some instances the highways in and around Desolake are inadequate.

3. Sewage and drainage problems are serious in many parts of the City.

4. There is a tremendous need for low and middle income housing in the entire Desolake area.

5. The downtown urban renewal project is progressing but not as quickly as many people would like to see it progress. There are a number of vacant lots in downtown Desolake where old buildings have been torn down and new ones have not been built to replace them.

6. Although business and industry have expanded over the past decade, unemployment in Desolake recently has begun to grow. The recession has caused increasing worry about job security and the prospect of unemployment. Confidence and jobs must be restored.

7. Better relations between the police and the Community. It was apparent from the survey that a lack of understanding existed, to some degree at least, between the police and the public. Improvement is definitely needed in this area.

8. There is a real need for more doctors and nurses in the greater Desolake area. There is also a need for more and better medical facilities.

9. Recreational facilities need to be improved and expanded throughout the greater Desolake area.

10. Race relations need to be improved in Desolake as they do all over the country.

Applicant will also meet and deal with all other significant problems as they arise. Applicant is confident that the programs which it proposes in the following exhibit will be beneficial to the community in dealing with the needs and problems that now exist.

Exhibit 3

TYPICAL AND ILLUSTRATIVE PROGRAMS

The following are typical and illustrative programs and program series that the applicant plans to broadcast during the coming license period to meet the problems, needs and interests of the public:

1. Program Title: Station Editorial

    Source/Type: Local/Editorial

    Time Segment: Within regular news programs, 6:00-6:30 PM
                      and 11:00-11:30 PM.

Frequency: As often_{as} community needs and problems necessitate.

Description: Conversations with community leaders have indicated that editorials would be of great benefit in informing the public of community needs, problems, events and interests. The Station's editorials will be designed to accomplish this.

Community
Problem: Station editorials will deal with all types of community problems as they arise.

2.   Program Title: Planning and Zoning Investigation

    Source/Type: Local/Public Affairs

    Time Segment: 7:30-8:00 PM, Weeknight when report released

    Frequency: One Time

    Description: The city and county governments have formed a Planning Advisory Commission to study the community's planning and zoning activities. A report is to be made sometime during 1976. The investigation conducted and recommendations made will be discussed on this program.

    Community
    Problem: An important complaint of both community leaders and the public was inadequate planning for growth.

3.   Program Title: Big 5 Depth Report

        Source/Type: Local/Public Affairs

        Time Segment: Within regular news programs, 6:00-6:30 PM

                               and 11:00-11:30 PM, Monday through Friday,

                               and 11:00-11:30 PM Sundays.

        Frequency: Weekly, as available subject matter warrants,

                               starting upon commencement of operations.

        Description: Feature stories developing in more detail

                               the background of current hard news stories.

                               Daily segments would be approximately 3

                               minutes in length and an entire week would

                               be devoted to the treatment of an individual

                               subject. The expansion of the local Sunday

                               night news program from 15 minutes to one-

                               half hour will make possible the repeating

                               of an entire week's segments or the pre-

                               sentation of a subject that does not lend

                               itself to being divided into segments.

                               Interviews, discussions, film, slides and

                               visual aids will be employed.

        Community
          Problem: a.   Television audiences are generally

                                   small for special public affairs

                                   programs and reach mostly those who

                                   are already well-informed.

b. Present news formats do not provide
for adequate development of details
concerning community problems.

c. Probable community problems to be
studied include the following that
were named most frequently by com--
munity leaders and the general public.

   (1) Traffic, traffic control, roads
       aand highways.

   (2) Sewers, sewage treatment and
       septic tanks.

   (3) Low and moderate income housing
       shortage.

   (4) New transit authority for mass
       transportation.

   (5) Projected downtown civic center
       complex.

   (6) Reorganization of police depart-
       ment.

   (7) Enforcement of building codes and
       need for storm sewers.

   (8) Downtown urban renewal.

   (9) The impact of economic recession and
       unemployment.

d. Periodically, a week will be devoted to
presenting the problems of one of the

communities in the secondary service
area.

4. **Program Title:** Romper Room (working title)

   Source/Type: Local/Instructional

   Time Segment: 9:00–10:00 AM

   Frequency: Monday through Friday, September through May.

   Description: An educational program for pre-school children. Local children participate in learning exercises under the guidance of a trained teacher.

   Community Problem: Need for educational television service for pre-school children.

5. **Program Title:** Senior Citizens Forum (working title)

   Source/Type: Local/Public Affairs

   Time Segment: 2:00–2:30 PM

   Frequency: Alternate Sundays, September through May.

   Description: A program to discuss and publicize the needs, interests, activities and available services of/for the elderly.

   Community Problem:
   a. Medical and social needs of elderly.
   b. Programs needed for retired and aged people.
   c. Coordination of activities for senior citizens
   d. Utilize elderly.

6.   **Program Title:**   Recreation Today (working title)

     Source/Type: Local/Other

     Time Segment: 2:00–2:30 PM

     Frequency: Alternate Sundays, September through May

     Description: The Metro Government Recreation and Parks Board present a program to publicize the public recreational facilities and activities available within the community. Participants also demonstrate their various hobbies and talents.

     Community Problem: One of the most frequently mentioned problems during consultation was the need for additional recreational facilities. This program makes known all of the existing activities and facilities as well as publicizing new ones as they become available.

     Program Title: Core Soul Den (working title)

     Source/Type: Local/Public Affairs

     Time Segment: 1:00–1:30 PM

     Frequency: Alternate Sundays, September through May

     Description: Representatives of the Desolake Council on Racial Equality discuss community problems, particularly as they affect minorities, with community leaders and

candidates. The program also publicizes
the activities of Micro City Government,
an O.E.O funded program for Black youth.

Community
   Problem: a.   Improve relations between races.

                   b.   Employment for under-employed.

                   c.   Equality of opportunity.

                   d.   Juvenile crime and deliquency.

Program Title: CNO Program

Source/Type: Local/Public Affairs

Time Segment: 1:00-1:30 PM

Frequency: Alternate Sundays, September through May

Description: Representatives of the Council of Neigh
                   borhood Organizations discuss community
                   problems, particularly as they affect
                   the poor. Community leaders and candidates
                   are invited to participate.

Community
   Problem: a.   Involve poor people in government.

                   b.   Breakdown of family unit.

                   c.   Upgrade slums.

                   d.   Additional recreational facilities.

                   e.   Food, shelter, clothing and health
                        care for needy.

9. Program Title: Jerry Lewis Telethon

    Source/Type: Network-Local/Other

Time Segment: 12:00 Midnight, September 12, 1976 through
                     6:30 PM, September 13, 1976.

Description: Fund raising program anchored in New York
                     with five minute local segments each hour
                     on which local personages appear. All
                     commercial time is preempted for full
                     18-1/2 hours.

Community
Problem: Raise money for Central Kansouri Chapter
                     of Muscular Dystrophy Association.

10. Program Title   Televised Meetings
     Source/Type: Local/Public Affairs
     Time Segment: To Be Determined.
     Frequency: When appropriate.
     Description: Applicant plans to bring the regular
                         meetings of the Desolake City Commission
                         and the Lard County Commission to the
                         studios for the first live telecasts of
                         their proceedings. It is planned to re-
                         peat this after the new Metro Council is
                         elected. It is also planned to invite
                         similar bodies from the surrounding
                         counties to present typical meetings, as
                         well as other Desolake agencies, such as
                         the School Board and the Board of Health.
                         An attempt will be made to present meetings

at which controversial subjects are discussed.

The public will be invited to attend and participate.

Community
  Problem:

a. Improved communications between public and government.

b. Make governmental agencies more responsive

c. Education of public about needs of community.

d. Publicize recreational and non-commercial entertainment events.

12. Program Title: Public Service Announcements

Source/Type: Local & Recorded/PSA's

Time Segment: Various

Frequency: Daily

Description: Thirty-second announcements for non-commercial organizations.

Community
  Problem:

a. Publicity for services of government

b. and eleemosynary agencies.

b. Publicity for charitable fund drives.

c. Dissemination of public information.

Exhibit 4

PROCEDURES FOR THE CONSIDERATION OR
DISPOSITION OF COMPLAINTS OR SUGGESTIONS

Complaints, suggestions and other communications from the public will always be given careful consideration by the General Manager or, in some cases, by the appropriate department head.

If the complainant is identified, as a matter of station policy, there will be a response made, either in writing or orally.

Members of the staff will be instructed to bring significant matters to the attention of the General Manager and a written report will be made daily of complaints and suggestions received. This report will be circulated to the General Manager and other appropriate department heads. All significant matters will be investigated and appropriate action will be taken when necessary.

Exhibit 5

APPLICANT'S PROPOSED NEWS PROGRAMS

1. Applicant proposes to maintain a local   news staff including the following:

Full Time

News Director
Desolake Editor
Central Kansouri Editor
Weather Editor
Photographer

Part Time

Sports Director
Weekend Editor
Sports Editor

Other members of the staff will also be used to cover important events and elections. Stringers, who are paid on a "per story" basis, will be maintained in Central Kansouri communities outside of Desolake.

2. Applicant will operate the following   news gathering facilities:
    three motion picture cameras (one sound-on-film), one portable video
    tape recorder, three slide cameras, a Polaroid camera, audio tape recorders
    and a "beeper" telephone. There is a motion picture film processor in
    Desolake which provides fast daily service, and slides are processed at the
    station.

3.   Applicant will purchase the news wire services of the Associated
    Press, the U.S. Weather Bureau and the Desolake Metro Police Department.

4. Applicant will be affiliated with the ABC Television Network
    and will carry the weekday (6:30 - 7:00 PM) and weekend (11:00 - 11:15 PM)
    network news programs, as well as special national event news coverage.

5. It is estimated that more than 65% of non-network news program time will
    be devoted to local and regional news during the composite week.

Exhibit 6

APPLICANT'S PROPOSED PUBLIC
AFFAIRS PROGRAMMING POLICY

Applicant will provide that time be made available for the discussion
of public issues when, in the judgment of station management, the program
prospects appear worthwhile and the need or interest of the community is
apparent. ' The General Manager, the General Sales Manager,
the Operations Manager, the Production Manager and News Department personnel
will all participate in the selection of subjects and participants.

Exhibit 7

APPLICANT'S PROPOSED COMMERCIAL PRACTICES

As a general rule the Station will not exceed 16 minutes of com

mercial matter in any 60 minute segment.

However, there may be instances when the 16 minute standard

is exceeded. But, even in such instances, the maximum commercial

content will not exceed 18 minutes in any 60 minute segment. In-

stances where the 16 minute standard may be exceeded shall not

occur more than 10% of the broadcast hours in any broadcast week.

Typical possible exceptions to the standard policy are the

following instances:

1. Newspaper strikes, special local promotions, and holiday
    advertising campaigns.

2. Emergencies which interrupt the normal commercial opera-
    tion, when "make good announcements" may necessitate
    abnormal commercial loads.

3. During political campaigns, the above limit could be
    exceeded by political advertising. This is expected
    to occur no more than ten hours per week and a limit
    of 20 minutes would then apply with all of the excess
    over 18 minutes being political advertising.

Exhibit 8

PROGRAMMING AND ADVERTISING STANDARDS

Applicant will generally adhere to the NAB Code with respect to pro-

gramming and advertising standards.

All programming and advertising material will be subject to review and acceptance by the station. Programming and advertising material will be required to meet recognized standards of good taste and discretion.

News reporting and public affairs programming will be factual, fair and without bias. All commentary and analysis will be identified as such.

Exhibit 9

PROCEDURES FOR KEEPING INFORMED OF COMMISSION REQUIREMENTS

1. Applicant will maintain an up-to-date copy of pertinent Rules and Regulations.

2. Applicant's communications counsel will keep the station advised of developments of importance. Trade journals and other industry sources will be studied. Consultations will be held between Applicant's management and personnel.

3. Applicant's Program Director and Chief Engineer will notify the appropriate personnel at the station of rule changes and industry developments.

4. As required, staff meetings will be held and memoranda circulated.

5. Compliance with FCC rules will be periodically checked by supervisory personnel of Applicant.

Appendix 5

RANDOM SAMPLE SELECTION, AN EX-CERPT FROM *SUGGESTIONS FOR THE SURVEY OF THE GENERAL PUBLIC*, NAB

APPENDIX

SAMPLE SELECTION FROM TELEPHONE DIRECTORY

Before a sample of names can be drawn from a telephone directory, the number of names needed must be determined. Because not all names that are drawn will be able to be contacted -- some people won't be home when the interviewer calls, others will refuse to be interviewed -- the original sample must be larger than the intended number of completed interviews. In general, the initial sample should be between 50% larger and twice as large as the number of completed interviews that is desired. For the sake of illustration, assume that we want to complete 500 interviews, and that we will therefore select 1000 names.* These names would be selected in the following way:

---

*The figures used here are for illustrative purposes, the number of interviews will vary with the size of the community. While the FCC has specified what it considers a reasonable number of interviews for the community leader survey it has refused to specify such numbers for the general public survey.

a. Say the telephone directory has 100 white pages.
    Dividing the 1000 numbers wanted by 100 gives us
    10; so we will need to select 10 numbers per page.
    (If we wanted 200 numbers we would take 2 per page;
    if we wanted 50 we would take 1 every other page.)

b. Let's say the directory has three columns on each
    page, and we will pick one column from which to
    draw the ten names. The selection should be random;
    so we could put three slips of paper, numbered 1, 2,
    and 3 in a hat and draw one. But we have a list of
    random numbers in Figure 1. These numbers have in
    effect already been "drawn from a hat" and listed
    here. Start at the top of any of the columns of
    random numbers and go down (or start at the bottom
    and go up, or go across) until we come to a number
    between 1 and 3. For example, if we look at the
    top of the last column on the right, the first number
    is 8 (which we can't use) and the next one down is 2.
    So, use the second column on each page for the names
    needed.

c. Say each column in the directory is 10 inches deep.
    Pick a random number between 01 and 10, this time
    looking at two-digit numbers on the list of random
    numbers. For example, if we use the first two columns
    of numbers, starting with 70, notice that the first
    usable number we come to as we go down is 06, about
    half way down the table. We have now determined that
    we will start listing telephone numbers for the sample
    6 inches from the top of the second column in the
    directory.

d. On a ruled form (sheets with, say, ten lines each), we
    would then copy ten telephone numbers. We could start
    with the number nearest to the 6-inch mark from the top
    of the second column on each page, and list every fifth
    number until 10 numbers had been listed. If we reach
    the bottom of the column before listing the tenth name,
    we would simply continue the counting process at the
    top of the next column. We would use only residential
    numbers, skipping commercial or institutional listings.
    It is also desirable to copy the names so interviewers
    can use them in interviewing.

The idea behind all this is to make all decisions without our whim
entering into it and to spread the selection throughout the directory, systematically. Should we run out of numbers before we complete the survey, we would make another similar but smaller selection from throughout the book.

```
70361      41836      33098
85884      08785      41152
76390      36976      62785
48891      74601      90030
62971      40993      79767

69782      56399      55494
29927      30667      99040
06008      03027      69882
27953      69905      43592
24327      69905      45315

44017      48019      01348
33031      06081      45402
46955      16951      42276
89734      24807      23802
10331      52809      06032
```

Figure 1   Table of Random Numbers

NAB Research Department
May 1976

Appendix 6

AFFILIATION CONTRACT

UNIVERSAL BROADCASTING COMPANY, INC.

ONE BROADCASTING CENTER, NEW YORK, NY 10030

Gentlemen:

In order that your station may continue to serve the public interest, convenience and necessity, this company and your Television Station hereby mutually agree upon the following plan of network cooperation:

I.   UBC will offer to the Station for television broadcasting a variety of UBC Television Network programs. These will be furnished over interconnection facilities linking the UBC Television Network to the Station wherever UBC deems this advisable on engineering and economic grounds. UBC will pay all charges for providing interconnection facilities except that the Station will pay any non-recurring charges (whether in-

stallation or other charges) that may be assessed upon the connection of
the Station with the UBC Television Network. Where, in the opinion of
UBC, it is impractical or undesirable to furnish a program over interconnection facilities, UBC may deliver the program to the Station in the form
of motion picture film or other recorded version, as set forth in Paragraph
III below.

II.   You shall have the right of first refusal good for 72 hours, as
against any other television station located in the same community as the
Station, upon the UBC Television Network programs referred to in Paragraph
I, except that UBC may make available to any other station programs which
UBC may be legally required to make available other than through an affil-
iation agreement, or other special programs of overriding public importance.

III.   In those cases where the UBC Television Network programs
offered to the Station are not transmitted to the Station over interconnection facilities, UBC may deliver to you, transportation prepaid, a
positive print or copy of a motion picture film or other recorded version
of any such program in sufficient time for you to broadcast such program
over the Station at the time scheduled. You agree to comply with UBC's
instructions concerning the disposition to be made of each such print
or copy received by you hereunder, together with the reels and con-
tainers furnished therewith, by returning to UBC or forwarding the same
to others with transportation to be paid by you, in as good condition
as when received, ordinary wear and tear excepted, or by making such
other disposition thereof as UBC may otherwise direct. Each such print
or copy is to be returned to UBC immediately after a single television
broadcast thereof has been made over the Station, unless otherwise
specified by UBC.

IV.   With respect to programs offered or already contracted for
pursuant to this affiliation contract, nothing herein contained shall
prevent or hinder:

    (1)   The Station from:

        (a)   rejecting or refusing network programs which
the Station reasonably believes to be unsatisfactory or
unsuitable or contrary to the public interest, or

        (b)   substituting a program which, in the Station's
opinion, is of greater local or national importance, or

(2)   UBC from:

(a)   substituting one or more network sponsored
or sustaining programs in which event UBC shall offer
such substituted program or programs to Station in
accordance with the provisions of Paragraph II hereof,
or

(b)   cancelling one or more network programs.

(3)   If either party hereto shall take any action, specified
in subparagraphs (1) or (2) above, such party shall notify the
other thereof as soon as practicable.

(4)   No compensation will be paid for a cancelled program
or a substituted program unless the substituted program is commercially sponsored in which event the compensation applicable
to the substituted program will be paid for it.

V.   The following shall be the financial arrangement between UBC
and you for the UBC Television Network programs and other services which
UBC will supply to the Station and for the time which the Station will make
available for UBC Television Network programs. Settlement will be made
approximately 25 days after the close of each month.

(1)   The Network Station Rate of the Station shall be:

$_____ per hour for full-rate periods;
$_____ per hour for 50% rate periods;
$_____ per hour for 35% rate periods;
$_____ per hour for 26-1/4% rate periods; and
$_____ per hour for 20% rate periods.

Full-rate periods shall be from:

6:00 - 11:00 PM, Monday through Sunday, inclusive;

50% rate periods shall be from:

5:00 PM - 6:00 PM and from 11:00 PM - 1:00 AM,
Monday through Sunday, inclusive; and
4:00 PM - 5:00 PM, Saturdays and Sundays only;

35% rate periods shall be from:

9:00 AM - 5:00 PM, Monday through Friday,
7:00 AM - 4:00 PM, Sundays, and
2:00 PM - 4:00 PM, Saturdays.

26-1/4% rate shall apply from:

7:00 AM - 2:00 PM Saturdays;

20% rate shall apply from:

7:00 AM - 9:00 AM, Monday through Friday

The applicable Network Station Rate for programs broadcast on a delayed basis shall be the Network Station Rate in effect on the date of network origination of such programs for the rate period during which the delayed broadcast is made. The time brackets above are expressed in local time at the Station.

(2)   Compensation for UBC Television Network sponsored programs broadcast by the Station will be computed as follows except for programs covered by subparagraph (4) hereof:

(a)   The number of hours and fractions thereof of sponsored programs broadcast by the Station during the month will first be stated in terms of equivalent hours. Each hour of such programs broadcast during full-rate periods shall be equal to one equivalent hour. Each hour of programs broadcast during 50% rate periods shall be equal to half of an equivalent hour. Each hour of programs broadcast during 35% rate periods shall be equal to seven-twentieths of an equivalent hour. Each hour of programs broadcast during 26-1/4% periods shall be equal to twenty-one eightieths of an equivalent hour. Each hour of programs broadcast during 20% rate periods shall be equal to one-fifth of an equivalent hour. Fractions of an hour shall for all purposes be treated as their fractional proportions of an hour in the same rate classification.

(b)   The equivalent hour value of a network commercial announcement in programs sold to advertisers on an announcement basis shall be computed as follows:

Step 1: Determine the total amount of time available for network commercial announcements in the program period;

Step 2: Determine the fraction of this total time represented by the length of the network commercial announcement;

Step 3: Apply this fraction to the equivalent hour value of the program period.

(c)   As a means of sharing the overhead cost to UBC of providing network service, you will waive compensation on 24 equivalent hours each month.

(d)   Each equivalent hour or fraction thereof in excess of the 24 hours upon which compensation is waived will then be multiplied by the Network Station Rate of the Station for full-rate periods. UBC will pay to you 30% of the result of such multiplication.

(3)   You will pay to UBC each month, for UBC Television Network unsponsored programs on film or other recorded version which UBC delivers to the Station during the month upon your order, the price that we quote the Station. You shall have the right to cancel an order for an unsponsored program covered by this sub-paragraph (3) at any time by giving written notice thereof to UBC, provided that if such cancellation shall be for a reason other than a reason stated in clause (1) of Paragraph IV you shall reimburse UBC for the cost to it of each print of such program which has been made prior to the receipt by UBC of such cancellation notice for use by the Station.

(4)   Sports programs and special events programs (such as political conventions, election coverage, Presidential inaugurations, space shots, parades, pageants and other special events so desig-nated by UBC) shall be offered to Station in writing which will set forth the compensation terms for such programs. The compensation for all such programs accepted by the Station shall be computed in accordance with the designated terms.

(5)   Compensation for a program which was interrupted will be adjusted in accordance with any billing adjustment made to the advertisers.

(6)   If the Station for any reason excusable by law, other than a reason stated in clause (1) of Paragraph IV, fails to broadcast a sponsored UBC Television Network program which it is otherwise committed to broadcast, Station shall reimburse UBC for the cost to it of each print of such program which has been made for use by the Station and for the cost, if any, of transporting the print to and from the Station.

(7)   UBC reserves the right to change at any time the Network Station Rate of the Station   If UBC increases the Network Station Rate, such increased rate shall be used in computing the compensation due you on business actually sold by UBC at such increased rate. If UBC decreases the Network Station Rate and if such decrease is part of a general rate revision on the UBC Television Network, such decreased rate shall be used in computing the compensation due you provided UBC has given you at least 90 days' written notice of its intention so to decrease such rate.

In the event of such decrease, you may terminate this agreement as of the effective date of such decrease by giving UBC written notice within 30 days after the receipt of UBC's notice to you of such reduction.

VI.   From time to time UBC will offer to Station commercial positions within network programs available for local sale. If Station sells any such positions, it will pay UBC the cooperative program charges quoted Station in UBC's offer of the positions together with any applicable fees for performing rights.

VII.   You shall not be obligated to continue to broadcast nor shall UBC be obligated to continue to furnish, subsequent to the termination of this agreement, any programs which UBC may have offered and which you may have accepted during the term thereof.

VIII.   Your broadcast of UBC Television Network programs hereunder shall be subject to the following terms and conditions:

(1)   You will not without UBC's prior written authorization make any deletions from or additions to any program furnished to you hereunder, or broadcast any commercial or other announcements during such program.

(2)   You will not without UBC's prior written authorization sell for commercial sponsorship the UBC Television Network unsponsored programs, or unordered portions of sponsored programs which we furnish to the Station hereunder.

(3)   You will not delete any UBC Television Network identification, program promotional or production credit announcement within a Network program period, including any such announcement at the conclusion of an UBC Television Network program, except for announcements promoting a network program which is not to be broadcast by the Station. For any such deleted promotional announcements you shall substitute only other UBC Television Network or Station program promotional or public service announcements.

(4)   You will not broadcast any UBC Television Network sponsored program unless such program is offered by us to the Station and is accepted by you with notice to us.

(5)   The placement and duration of station-break periods provided for locally originated announcements between UBC Television Network programs, or segments thereof, shall be designated by UBC. The Station will broadcast each program which it has accepted from the commencement of network origination until the commencement of the terminal station break.

(6)   Nothing herein contained shall limit the rights of the Station under Paragraph IV hereof.

IX.   If the Station is unable to broadcast an UBC Television Network program at the time such program is transmitted over interconnection facilities, and if we agree on a delayed broadcast from a motion picture film or other recorded version, such delayed broadcast shall be made as follows:

(1)   At the time of each delayed broadcast, the Station will broadcast an appropriate announcement station that the program is a film or other recorded version of a program presented earlier over the UBC Television Network.

(2)   The Station will use each such film or other recorded version only for the purpose herein contemplated, will broadcast it only at the time agreed upon, and will comply with UBC's instructions concerning its disposition.

(3)   UBC reserves the right to discontinue, upon twenty-four hours' notice to you, any arrangements with you with respect to any or all delayed broadcasts of television programs.

X.   You agree to maintain for the Station such licenses, including performing rights licenses, as now are or hereafter may be in general use by television broadcasting stations and necessary for you to broadcast the programs which UBC furnishes to you hereunder. UBC will endeavor to enter into appropriate arrangements to clear at the source all music in the repertory of ASCAP and of BMI used in UBC Television Network programs thereby licensing the broadcasting of such music on such programs over the Station. In return for such clearance at the source you agree to pay UBC, at the time of settlement with you for each monthly accounting period, a sum equal to 3.59% of the compensation due you from UBC, for the broadcasting of UBC Television Network programs during such accounting period. Of such percentage rate, 2.5% is applicable to payment for use of ASCAP music and 1.09% for use of BMI music. In the event either or both of the percentage rates specified in the preceding sentence shall be increased or decreased, a corresponding increase or decrease shall be made in the percentage rate which you are required to pay UBC, effective as of the date upon which such increase or decrease becomes effective. In view of the fact that UBC pays ASCAP and BMI no royalties on certain network sponsored programs the sum which you agree to pay UBC hereunder for each month, as calculated above shall be reduced by the ratio of the number of equivalent hours broadcast by your Station of network programs on which no royalties are payable to the number of equivalent hours broadcast by your Station of all network programs for such month. It is understood that if we enter into arrangements with ASCAP or BMI, or both, for payment on a different basis than is now in effect, the Station will pay to us its prorated share of our payment to ASCAP or BMI, or both, on proportionately the same basis as it currently does.

XI.   You will submit to UBC in writing, upon forms provided by UBC, such reports as UBC may request covering the broadcast by the Station of UBC Television Network programs furnished to you hereunder.

XII.   In the event that the transmitter location, power, frequency or hours or manner of operation of the Station are changed at any time so that the station is less valuable to UBC as a network outlet than it is at the time this offer is accepted by you, UBC shall have the right to terminate this agreement by giving at least 30 days' written notice to you.

XIII.   This agreement shall become effective at 3:00AM New York City time on the   day of   19   and, unless sooner terminated as hereinabove provided, it shall remain in effect for a period of two years thereafter. It shall then be renewed on the same terms and conditions for a further period of two years and so on for successive further periods of years each, unless and until either party shall, at least   days prior to the expiration of the then current term, give the other party written notice that it does not desire to have the contract renewed for a further period.

If this is in accordance with your understanding, will you please indicate your acceptance on the copy of this letter enclosed for that purpose and return that copy to UBC.

Very truly yours,

UNIVERSAL BROADCASTING COMPANY, INC.

By_____

AGREED:

By _____

Appendix 7

NAB REVENUE AND EXPENSE YARDSTICKS

TABLE 8   REVENUE AND EXPENSE YARDSTICKS   MARKET SIZE 7 (ARB 76-100)

REVENUE AND EXPENSE ITEMS	ALL STATIONS (52)			PROFIT-ONLY STATIONS (40)			YOUR STATION	
	Typical Dollar Figures	Typical Percent Figures	Middle 50% Range	Typical Dollar Figures	Typical Percent Figures	Middle 50% Range	Dollar Figures	Percent Figures
Line No.	Col. 1	Col. 2	Col. 3	Col. 4	Col. 5	Col. 6	Col. 7	Col. 8
1. PROFIT MARGIN[a]	15.36%		2.37%-24.21%		18.64%	13.04%-28.13%		%
2. TOTAL TIME SALES	$2,298,500	100.0%	$1,765,600-$2,706,900	$2,430,000	100.0%	$1,996,300-$2,815,600		100%
From:								
3. Networks	310,300	13.5%	199,400- 354,600	328,100	13.5%	268,300- 386,900		
4. National & Regional Advertisers	951,600	41.4%	541,000- 1,186,200	1,001,200	41.2%	724,800- 1,261,800		
5. Local Advertisers	1,036,600	45.1%	764,600- 1,248,800	1,100,700	45.3%	848,200- 1,431,200		
6. TOTAL BROADCAST REVENUE[b]	$2,034,900		$1,595,100-$2,412,000	$2,121,400		$1,777,500-$2,509,100		
7. Non Broadcast Revenue	52,900		30,200- 80,400	60,000		38,600- 86,800		
8. Trade-outs & Barter	35,600		15,700- 60,500	35,600		20,700- 58,000		
9. TOTAL BROADCAST EXPENSE	$1,722,300	100.0%	$1,367,500-$2,038,300	$1,726,000	100.0%	$1,482,400-$2,056,200		100%
From:								
10. Technical	249,700	14.5%	155,800- 286,300	253,700	14.7%	183,800- 303,700		
11. Program	608,000	35.3%	408,700- 700,000	614,500	35.6%	496,600- 707,200		
12. Selling[c]	248,000	14.4%	179,600- 280,700	252,000	14.6%	195,500- 290,000		
13. General & Administrative	616,600	35.8%	475,500- 719,800	605,800	35.1%	484,300- 719,900		
SELECTED EXPENSE ITEMS								
14. Total Salaries[d]	$ 684,900	100.0%	$ 493,300-$ 801,800	$ 727,200	100.0%	$ 608,600-$ 858,100		100%
From:								
15. Technical	141,100	20.6%	98,500- 193,000	160,000	22.0%	105,000- 214,700		
16. Program	281,500	41.1%	189,900- 304,900	286,500	39.4%	233,400- 329,000		
17. Selling	158,200	23.1%	112,600- 183,500	166,500	22.9%	120,300- 194,500		
18. General & Administrative	104,100	15.2%	67,200- 132,600	114,200	15.7%	88,300- 147,700		
19. COST OF OUTSIDE NEWS SERVICE	$ 13,800		$ 10,400-$ 21,700	$ 15,600		$ 11,400-$ 22,900		
20. MUSIC LICENSE FEE	$ 41,000		$ 30,900-$ 52,300	$ 43,600		$ 34,500-$ 53,800		
21. DEPRECIATION & AMORTIZATION	$ 133,200		$ 104,900-$ 180,200	$ 139,900		$ 105,700-$ 171,900		
22. INTEREST	$ 25,200		$ 0-$ 87,700	$ 3,500		$ 0-$ 53,900		
23. FILM & TAPE RENTAL EXPENSE	$ 113,400		$ 80,000-$ 149,200	$ 116,300		$ 89,800-$ 150,900		
24. PROFIT (Before Federal income tax)	$ 312,600		$ 47,100-$ 528,800	$ 395,400		$ 231,200-$ 743,200		
25. FULLTIME EMPLOYMENT	55		45- 66	58		52	70	

[a] Derived from each station's gross profit dividend by total revenue.
[b] Time sales plus other broadcast revenues less cash discounts and commissions to agencies, representatives and brokers.
[c] Includes all promotion, excludes agency and rep. commissions.
[d] Includes salaries, wages, bonuses, and commissions paid to officers and employees.

301

INDEPENDENT STATIONS, NATIONWIDE

INCOME AND EXPENSE ITEMS	ALL STATIONS (30)			PROFIT-ONLY STATIONS (27)			YOUR STATION	
	Typical Dollar Figures	Typical Percent Figures	Middle 50% Range	Typical Dollar Figures	Typical Percent Figures	Middle 50% Range	Dollar Figures	Percent Figures
	Col. 1	Col. 2	Col. 3	Col. 4	Col. 5	Col. 6	Col. 7	Col. 8
1. PROFIT MARGIN[a]		7.57%	(3.88%)-15.47%		14.19%	7.57%-18.71%		%
2. TOTAL TIME SALES	$3,644,600	100.0%	$1,828,500-$5,540,300	$3,405,900	100.0%	$1,524,300-$5,540,300		100%
From:								
3. Networks	0	0.0%	0- 21,600	3,400	0.1%	0- 29,900		
4. National & Regional Advertisers	1,990,000	54.6%	820,500- 3,252,400	1,784,700	52.4%	461,800- 3,265,700		
5. Local Advertisers	1,654,600	45.4%	954,700- 2,134,600	1,617,800	47.5%	975,800- 2,134,600		
6. TOTAL BROADCAST REVENUE[b]	$3,104,000		$1,768,700-$4,706,100	$3,042,000		$1,411,200-$4,706,100		
7. Non Broadcast Revenue	115,700		62,200- 185,300	121,200		72,000- 178,300		
8. Trade-outs & Barter	134,200		83,400- 221,400	119,200		75,000- 160,900		
9. TOTAL BROADCAST EXPENSE	$2,869,600	100.0%	$1,503,200-$4,350,500	$2,611,000	100.0%	$1,330,700-$3,840,300		100%
From:								
10. Technical	373,100	13.0%	212,800- 541,000	318,500	12.2%	169,000- 442,500		
11. Program	1,308,500	45.6%	483,200- 1,854,800	1,182,800	45.3%	457,800- 1,819,900		
12. Selling[c]	459,100	16.0%	285,500- 591,900	451,700	17.3%	183,600- 561,400		
13. General & Administrative	728,900	25.4%	454,300- 1,226,200	658,000	25.2%	401,500- 1,019,600		
SELECTED EXPENSE ITEMS								
14. Total Salaries[d]	$ 837,900	100.0%	$ 383,500-$1,294,600	$ 731,100	100.0%	$ 356,800-$1,294,600		100%
From:								
15. Technical	246,300	29.4%	107,700- 388,600	210,600	28.8%	102,800- 278,500		
16. Program	238,800	28.5%	146,500- 414,800	223,700	30.6%	129,100- 520,500		
17. Selling	214,500	25.6%	106,000- 291,200	182,800	25.0%	65,500- 271,100		
18. General & Administrative	138,300	16.5%	84,600- 171,900	114,000	15.6%	84,400- 152,700		
19. COST OF OUTSIDE NEWS SERVICE	$ 8,800		$ 5,600-$ 26,300	$ 9,400		$ 5,900-$ 26,300		
20. MUSIC LICENSE FEE	$ 46,800		$ 19,800-$ 81,400	$ 41,800		$ 17,000-$ 81,400		
21. DEPRECIATION & AMORTIZATION	$ 160,300		$ 81,000-$ 215,500	$ 146,600		$ 77,100-$ 206,100		
22. INTEREST	$ 11,300		$ 0-$ 43,600	$ 9,300		$ 0-$ 18,600		
23. FILM & TAPE RENTAL EXPENSE	$ 552,000		$ 214,400-$ 977,800	$ 503,100		$ 148,800-$ 820,200		
24. PROFIT (Before Federal income tax)	$ 235,000		$(112,500)-$ 526,400	$ 431,800		$ 159,300-$ 678,500		
25. FULLTIME EMPLOYMENT	56		36- 81	49		32- 84		

a Derived from each station's gross profit dividend by total revenue.
b Time sales plus other broadcast revenues less cash discounts and commissions to agencies, representatives and brokers.
c Includes all promotion; excludes agency and rep. commissions.
d Includes salaries, wages, bonuses, and commissions paid to officers and employees.

REVENUE AND EXPENSE ITEMS	ALL STATIONS (6)			PROFIT-ONLY STATIONS (4)			YOUR STATION	
	Typical Dollar Figures	Typical Percent Figures	Middle 50% Range	Typical Dollar Figures	Typical Percent Figures	Middle 50% Range	Dollar Figures	Percent Figures
Line No.	Col. 1	Col. 2	Col. 3	Col. 4	Col. 5	Col. 6	Col. 7	Col. 8
1. PROFIT MARGIN[a]		6.86%						%
2. TOTAL TIME SALES	$1,269,700	100.0%						100%
From:								
3. Networks	69,800	5.5%						
4. National & Regional Advertisers	518,100	40.8%						
5. Local Advertisers	681,800	53.7%						
6. TOTAL BROADCAST REVENUE[b]	$1,411,200		SAMPLE		SAMPLE			100%
7. Non Broadcast Revenue	38,300		INSUFFICIENT		INSUFFICIENT			
8. Trade-outs & Barter	23,200		TO BE		TO BE			
9. TOTAL BROADCAST EXPENSE	$1,314,400	100.0%	MEANINGFUL		MEANINGFUL			
From:								
10. Technical	169,500	12.9%						
11. Program	347,000	26.4%						
12. Selling[c]	324,700	24.7%						
13. General & Administrative	473,200	36.0%						
SELECTED EXPENSE ITEMS								
14. Total Salaries[d]	$ 373,300	100.0%						100%
From:								
15. Technical	84,700	22.7%						
16. Program	120,600	32.3%						
17. Selling	76,900	20.6%						
18. General & Administrative	91,100	24.4%						
19. COST OF OUTSIDE NEWS SERVICE	$ 5,600							
20. MUSIC LICENSE FEE	$ 19,800							
21. DEPRECIATION & AMORTIZATION	$ 81,000							
22. INTEREST	$ 8,700							
23. FILM & TAPE RENTAL EXPENSE	$ 132,100							
24. PROFIT (Before Federal income tax)	$ 96,800							
25. FULLTIME EMPLOYMENT	34							

a Derived from each station's gross profit dividend by total revenue.

b Represents plus other broadcast revenues less cash discounts and commissions to agencies, representatives and brokers.

c Includes all promotion; excludes agency and rep. commissions.

d Includes salaries, wages, bonuses, and commissions paid to officers and employees.

TABLE 35

TABLE 35   AFFILIATED REVENUE AND EXPENSE YARDSTICKS   REVENUE SIZE 5 ($2 MILLION-$3 MILLION)

REVENUE AND EXPENSE ITEMS	ALL STATIONS (63)			PROFIT-ONLY STATIONS (56)			YOUR STATION	
	Typical Dollar Figures	Typical Percent Figures	Middle 50% Range	Typical Dollar Figures	Typical Percent Figures	Middle 50% Range	Dollar Figures	Percent Figures
Line No.	Col. 1	Col. 2	Col. 3	Col. 4	Col. 5	Col. 6	Col. 7	Col. 8
1. PROFIT MARGIN[a]		19.59%	10.31%-28.61%		20.89%	14.67%-31.04		%
2. TOTAL TIME SALES	$2,570,000	100.0%	$2,380,600-$2,818,300	$2,565,000	100.0%	$2,380,300-$2,800,600		100%
From:								
3. Networks	359,800	14.0%	306,400- 444,100	354,000	13.8%	307,400- 428,800		
4. National & Regional Advertisers	1,017,700	39.6%	824,700- 1,254,100	1,013,100	39.5%	842,900- 1,258,300		
5. Local Advertisers	1,192,500	46.4%	1,004,000- 1,412,200	1,197,900	46.7%	989,200- 1,405,500		
6. TOTAL BROADCAST REVENUE[b]	$2,312,800		$2,117,200-$2,500,000	$2,311,500		$2,118,200-$2,516,000		100%
7. Non Broadcast Revenue	68,300		32,700- 92,100	70,600		34,900- 91,900		
8. Trade-outs & Barter	53,700		29,400- 92,300	51,400		26,300- 79,900		
9. TOTAL BROADCAST EXPENSE	$1,859,700	100.0%	$1,597,000-$2,128,200	$1,828,600	100.0%	$1,567,500-$2,018,300		100%
From:								
10. Technical	241,800	13.0%	193,600- 289,900	248,700	13.6%	198,100- 294,200		
11. Program	680,700	36.6%	567,000- 751,500	662,000	36.2%	558,700- 729,500		
12. Selling[c]	249,200	13.4%	196,900- 299,300	250,500	13.7%	192,200- 298,300		
13. General & Administrative	688,000	37.0%	536,300- 821,800	667,400	36.5%	522,000- 730,500		
SELECTED EXPENSE ITEMS								
14. Total Salaries[d]	$ 743,900	100.0%	$ 640,300-$ 879,900	$ 747,900	100.0%	$ 637,800-$ 865,800		100%
From:								
15. Technical	154,700	20.8%	124,700- 185,600	154,100	20.6%	123,100- 181,400		
16. Program	305,700	41.1%	255,900- 373,900	308,900	41.3%	244,900- 374,200		
17. Selling	163,700	22.0%	125,600- 184,000	164,500	22.0%	125,100- 184,300		
18. General & Administrative	119,800	16.1%	97,600- 153,300	120,400	16.1%	97,600- 154,800		
19. COST OF OUTSIDE NEWS SERVICE	$ 18,900		$ 12,200-$ 28,200	$ 18,700		$ 11,800-$ 25,900		
20. MUSIC LICENSE FEE	$ 44,800		$ 37,700-$ 53,200	$ 45,000		$ 38,000-$ 53,000		
21. DEPRECIATION & AMORTIZATION	$ 158,000		$ 115,500-$ 224,800	$ 151,300		$ 113,700-$ 199,000		
22. INTEREST	$ 15,600		$ 0-$ 76,100	$ 6,900		$ 0-$ 52,500		
23. FILM & TAPE RENTAL EXPENSE	$ 139,300		$ 91,400-$ 209,100	$ 129,200		$ 90,800-$ 195,400		
24. PROFIT (Before Federal income tax)	$ 453,100		$ 236,300-$ 689,100	$ 482,900		$ 335,700-$ 717,500		
25. FULLTIME EMPLOYMENT	60		52 71	59		52 71		

a Derived from each station's gross profit dividend by total revenue.
b Time sales plus other broadcast revenues less cash discounts and
c Includes all promotion; excludes agency and rep. commissions.
d Includes salaries, wages, bonuses, and commissions paid to officers

REVENUE AND EXPENSE ITEMS	ALL STATIONS (17)			PROFIT-ONLY STATIONS (12)			YOUR STATION	
	Typical Dollar Figures	Typical Percent Figures	Middle 50% Range	Typical Dollar Figures	Typical Percent Figures	Middle 50% Range	Dollar Figures	Percent Figures
Line No.	Col. 1	Col. 2	Col. 3	Col. 4	Col. 5	Col. 6	Col. 7	Col. 8
1. PROFIT MARGIN[a]		9.89%	(4.57%)-18.71%		14.60%	8.32%-23.23%		%
2. TOTAL TIME SALES	$4,629,600	100.0%	$3,405,900-$5,346,200	$4,746,300	100.0%	$3,343,900-$5,561,500		100%
From:								
3. Networks	4,600	0.1%	0- 28,200	9,500	0.2%	1,400- 29,300		
4. National & Regional Advertisers	2,870,400	62.0%	1,677,900- 3,265,700	2,890,500	60.9%	1,541,700- 3,369,600		
5. Local Advertisers	1,754,600	37.9%	1,515,500- 2,041,200	1,846,300	38.9%	1,518,500- 2,282,000		
6. TOTAL BROADCAST REVENUE[b]	$3,946,600		$3,042,800-$4,518,800	$4,038,800		$2,912,400-$4,652,400		
7. Non Broadcast Revenue	115,700		72,000- 178,300	133,200		76,300- 217,200		
8. Trade-outs & Barter	161,100		126,000- 264,000	161,000		122,600- 265,700		
9. TOTAL BROADCAST EXPENSE	$3,556,300	100.0%	$2,620,300-$4,126,900	$3,449,100	100.0%	$2,392,100-$3,789,300		100%
From:								
10. Technical	519,200	14.6%	318,900- 581,900	444,900	12.9%	305,200- 510,400		
11. Program	1,579,000	44.4%	1,172,600- 1,714,700	1,603,800	46.5%	1,009,900- 1,767,300		
12. Selling[c]	572,600	16.1%	455,100- 620,700	562,200	16.3%	451,700- 582,200		
13. General & Administrative	885,500	24.9%	665,600- 1,224,800	838,200	24.3%	630,100- 974,600		
SELECTED EXPENSE ITEMS								
14. Total Salaries[d]	$1,026,300	100.0%	$759,400-$1,294,600	$1,078,500	100.0%	$724,700-$1,327,800		100%
From:								
15. Technical	300,700	29.3%	213,100- 402,900	288,000	26.7%	150,100- 421,300		
16. Program	302,800	29.5%	221,600- 410,000	347,300	32.2%	187,900- 476,800		
17. Selling	264,800	25.8%	181,000- 291,200	281,500	26.1%	177,200- 293,200		
18. General & Administrative	158,000	15.4%	123,000- 171,900	161,700	15.0%	118,300- 168,200		
19. COST OF OUTSIDE NEWS SERVICE	$ 10,400		$ 7,000-$ 29,500	$ 27,400		$ 8,200-$ 37,400		
20. MUSIC LICENSE FEE	$ 67,200		$ 42,200-$ 73,900	$ 63,400		$ 39,100-$ 77,700		
21. DEPRECIATION & AMORTIZATION	$ 165,900		$ 146,600-$ 218,200	$166,700		$ 142,600-$ 216,900		
22. INTEREST	$ 43,600		$ 3,100-$ 120,200	$ 39,600		$ 7,300-$ 127,300		
23. FILM & TAPE RENTAL EXPENSE	$ 686,900		$ 552,000-$ 977,800	$ 644,900		$ 527,500-$ 876,400		
24. PROFIT (Before Federal income tax)	$ 390,300		$(180,300)-$ 678,500	$ 589,700		$ 309,200-$ 885,000		
25. FULLTIME EMPLOYMENT	67		52 73	68		48· 86		

a Derived from each station's gross profit dividend by total revenue

b Time sales plus other broadcast revenues less cash discounts and commissions to agencies, representatives and brokers.

c Includes all promotion; excludes agency and rep. commissions.

d Includes salaries, wages, bonuses, and commissions paid to officers and employees.

TABLE 45   INDEPENDENT REVENUE AND EXPENSE YARDSTICKS   REVENUE SIZE 3 (LESS THAN $2 MILLION)

REVENUE AND EXPENSE ITEMS	ALL STATIONS (11)			PROFIT-ONLY STATIONS		
	Typical Dollar Figures	Typical Percent Figures	Middle 50% Range	Typical Dollar Figures	Typical Percent Figures	Middle 50% Range
Line No.	Col. 1	Col. 2	Col. 3	Col. 4	Col. 5	Col. 6
1. PROFIT MARGIN[a]		4.23%	(3.88%)-11.56%		10.31%	
2. TOTAL TIME SALES	$1,173,300	100.0%	$ 614,600-$1,524,300	$1,125,200	100.0%	
From:						
3. Networks	0	0.0%	0- 18,000	0	0.0%	
4. National & Regional Advertisers	364,900	31.1%	123,100- 554,500	385,900	34.3%	
5. Local Advertisers	808,400	68.9%	219,900- 927,400	739,300	65.7%	
6. TOTAL BROADCAST REVENUE[b]	$1,176,900		$ 713,700-$1,447,100	$1,022,400		
7. Non Broadcast Revenue	59,400		15,500- 111,700	38,300		
8. Trade-outs & Barter	107,700		11,500- 125,000	65,000		
9. TOTAL BROADCAST EXPENSE	$1,127,100	100.0%	$ 603,300-$1,454,500	$ 917,000	100.0%	
From:						
10. Technical	191,600	17.0%	129,700- 175,900	175,100	19.1%	SAMPLE
11. Program	368,600	32.7%	141,900- 457,800	236,600	25.8%	INSUFFICIENT
12. Selling[c]	161,200	14.3%	49,000- 276,600	112,800	12.3%	TO BE
13. General & Administrative	405,700	36.0%	229,100- 454,300	392,500	42.8%	MEANINGFUL
SELECTED EXPENSE ITEMS						
14. Total Salaries[d]	$ 354,800	100.0%	$ 191,200-$ 371,100	$ 290,000	100.0%	
From:						
15. Technical	90,100	25.4%	67,200- 107,700	85,800	29.6%	
16. Program	105,700	29.8%	69,600- 129,100	89,000	30.7%	
17. Selling	75,600	21.3%	12,500- 66,900	51,000	17.6%	
18. General & Administrative	83,400	23.5%	36,100- 85,400	64,200	22.1%	
19. COST OF OUTSIDE NEWS SERVICE	$ 3,100		$ 0-$ 5,900	$ 4,700		
20. MUSIC LICENSE FEE	$ 15,000		$ 6,900-$ 24,000	$ 13,900		
21. DEPRECIATION & AMORTIZATION	$ 77,000		$ 54,500-$ 81,000	$ 71,500		
22. INTEREST	$ 11,300		$ 600-$ 35,800	$ 9,300		
23. FILM & TAPE RENTAL EXPENSE	$ 132,100		$ 10,200-$ 214,400	$ 56,800		
24. PROFIT (Before Federal income tax)	$ 49,800		$ (56,100)-$ 110,400	$ 105,400		
25. FULLTIME EMPLOYMENT	24		22- 34	24		

a Derived from each station's gross profit dividend by total revenue.
b Time sales plus other broadcast revenues less each discount and
c Includes all promotion; excludes agency and rep. commissions.
d Includes salaries, wages, bonuses, and commissions paid to officers

306

Appendix 8

NIELSEN STATION INDEX, DESO-
LAKE KANSOURI, NOVEMBER 1975

Nielsen Station Index

DESOLAKE, KANSOURI

NOVEMBER
1975

DESOLAKE, KANSOURI

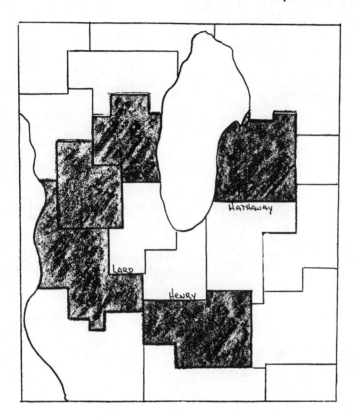

 Metro Area

 Designated Market Area (DMA) Includes Metro

 NSI Area   Includes Metro and DMA

MARKET DATA

Table I
Universe Estimates

	Total Households	TV Households
Metro	209,100	205,000
DMA	263,160	258,000
NSI	277,440	272,000

Table II
Ownership Estimates (DMA)

Color TV	69%
Multi Set	46%
UHF	92%
CATV	18%

Table III
DMA Persons Universe Estimates

Total Person 2+	673,000
Total Adults	482,000
Total Women	252,000
Women 18-49	110,000
Women 18-34	142,000
Total Men	230,000
Men 18-49	141,000
Men 18-34	91,000
Teens (12-17)	78,000
Children (2-11)	113,000

Table IV
Statistical Tolerances: DMA Households

DMA Rating	5 Day Avgs±	Individual Days±
1	0.4	0.6
5	0.8	1.2
10	1.2	1.7
15	1.4	2.0
20	1.7	2.3
35	2.1	2.7
50	2.2	2.8

Users of this report are reminded that the data reported are not precise to their mathematical value.

The chances are about 68 out of 100 that an estimate from a perfect probability sample would differ from a complete census by less than the standard error. The chances are about 95 out of 100 that the difference would be less than twice the standard error and about 99 out of 100 that it would be less than 2 1/2 times as large.

Table V
Reportable Stations

Station	Channel	Network
KNAC	3	NBC
KBGA	8	CBS

Audience data for Desolake are provided on a Designated Market Area ratings basis only - % TV households or persons within TV households. Projected households and/or persons may be calculated using the universe estimates provided in Tables I and III.

DESOLAKE, KANSOURI   NOVEMBER, 1975

MONDAY - FRIDAY START TIME / STATION / PROGRAM	HH RTG.	SHARE	WOMEN TOT	18-34	18-49	MEN TOT	18-34	18-49	TEENS TOT 12-17	CHILDREN TOT 2-11
					RATINGS					
6:30										
KNAC Off:Rural Rpt.	1									
HUT	1									
7:00										
KNAC Today Show	6	76	3	1	1	3				1
KBGA Morning News	2	20								
KIRT										
HUT	8									
7:30										
KNAC Today Show	9	74	8	2	4	6 / 1		3 / 1	2	
KBGA Morning News	3	22								
KIRT HUT	12									
8:00										
KNAC Today Show	14	59	11		4	8	1	4		
KBGA Capt. Kangaroo	8	35	2	2	1	1				21
KIRT										
HUT	22									
8:30										
KNAC Today Show	13	55	9		4	5		1		
KBGA Capt. Kangaroo	9	36	2	2	1	1				19
KIRT										
HUT	22									
9:00										
KNAC Celeb. Sweepstakes	9	42	6	2	5	4				1
KBGA Spin-Off	11	49	7	5	6					7
KIRT										
HUT	20									
9:30										
KNAC Wheel of Fortune	8	42	3		2			1		
KBGA Gambit	10	48	7	5	4	4				2
KIRT										
HUT	18									
10:00										
KNAC High Rollers	8	46	5		3	2	3	1		
KBGA Tattletales	8	43	6	5	4	2				
KIRT										
HUT	16									
10:30										
KNAC Hollywood Squares	9	44	5		2	1				
KBGA Love-Life:News	9	45	7	7	7	2				
KIRT HUT	18									

DESOLAKE, KANSOURI   NOVEMBER, 1975

MONDAY – FRIDAY	PROGRAM		WOMEN			MEN			TEENS	CHILDREN
START TIME / STATION PROGRAM	HH RTG.	SHARE	TOT	18-34	18-49	TOT	18-34	18-49	TOT 12-17	TOT 2-1
					RATINGS					
11:00										
KNAC Mag. Marble Machine	9	41	4		1	3	3	1		
KBGA Young & Restless	11	48	9	12	11	1			2	
KIRT HUT	20									
11:30										
KNAC Jackpot	9	43	6		3	3	1	1		
KBGA Search For Tomorrow	10	48	9	7	8	1				1
KIRT HUT	19									
12:00										
KNAC Noon Report	15	48	10	2	6	9	3	4		
KBGA News	14	46	11	5	7	8	3	4		
KIRT HUT	29									
12:15										
KNAC Noon Report	15	49	10	2	6	11	5	6		
KBGA Weather Woman's World	14	45	11	5	7	6	3	1		
KIRT HUT	29									
12:30										
KNAC Days of Our Lives	14	44	10	5	7	8	5	6		
KBGA As World Turns	16	50	15	12	13	5	3	3		
KIRT HUT	30									
12:45										
KNAC Days of Our Lives	14	44	11	7	8	7	5	6		
KBGA As World Turns	16	50	14	12	11	5	3	3		
KIRT HUT	30									
1:00										
KNAC Days of Our Lives	22	67	18	21	18	4	6	5		3
KBGA Guiding Light	8	25	7	10	8					
KIRT HUT	30									
1:30										
KNAC Doctors	19	64	17	19	18	1	3	2		
KBGA Edge of Night	8	26	7	10	7	1				
KIRT HUT	27									
2:00										
KNAC Another World	18	64	16	17	17	4	3	1		
KBGA Price Is Right	8	29	3	2	3					1
KIRT HUT	26									

DESOLAKE, KANSOURI   NOVEMBER, 1975

MONDAY - FRIDAY START TIME STATION / PROGRAM	PROGRAM HH RTG.	SHARE	WOMEN TOT	18-34	18-49	MEN TOT	18-34	18-49	TEENS TOT 12-17	CHILDREN TOT 2-11
2:30										
KNAC Another World	13	57	10	12	11					
KBGA Match Game '75	8	34	6	2	3	2	3	1	1	
KIRT										
HUT	22									
3:00										
KNAC Somerset	11	51	10	10	11					
KBGA Musical Chairs	8	37	6	2	4	2	3	1	2	
KIRT										
HUT	19									
3:30										
KNAC Be Our Guest	5	23	1	2	2					1
KBGA Mike Douglas	14	64	10	7	7	4	3	3	5	1
KIRT										
HUT	19									
4:00										
KNAC Huck & Yogi	15	51	1	2	1	1			14	31
KBGA Mike Douglas	11	40	9	5	6	3	3	1	3	
KIRT										
HUT	26									
4:30										
KNAC I Dream of Jeannie	16	52	3	2	4	3	3	2	21	30
KBGA Mike Douglas	11	37	9	5	6	4	3	3	2	
KIRT										
HUT	27									
5:00										
KNAC Truth Or Consequences	18	48	10	5	7	6	5	4	15	16
KBGA Dialing For $	16	42	14	7	7	6	3	3	5	4
KIRT										
HUT	34									
5:15										
KNAC Truth Or Consequences	19	49	10	7	7	6	3	4	15	16
KBGA Dialing For $	16	41	15	7	8	7	3	3	5	3
KIRT										
HUT	34									
5:30										
KNAC NBC Nitely News	24	53	16	12	13	13	5	9	5	1
KBGA CBS Evening News	17	38	13	7	8	11	3	6	4	1
KIRT										
HUT	41									
5:45										
KNAC NBC Nitely News	24	53	16	10	11	13	5	7	5	1
KBGA CBS Evening News	17	38	12	5	7	12	5	6	4	1
KIRT										
HUT	41									

RATINGS

DESOLAKE, KANSOURI   NOVEMBER, 1975

MONDAY - FRIDAY		PROGRAM		WOMEN			MEN			TEENS	CHILDREN
START TIME / STATION — PROGRAM		HH RTG.	SHARE	TOT	18-34	18-49	TOT	18-34	18-49	TOT 12-17	TOT 2-11
						RATINGS					
6:00 KNAC Eve. Report		30	59	21	12	15	19	10	15	4	1
KBGA TV Newsroom		17	33	12	5	8	11	5	7	4	1
KIRT HUT		47									
6:15 KNAC Eve. Report		30	59	20	12	15	19	10	15	4	1
KBGA TV Newsroom		17	33	12	2	8	11	5	7	4	1
KIRT HUT		47									
6:30 KNAC Various		31	56	19	17	18	19	13	16	20	18
KBGA Various		20	36	14	12	12	14	10	12	11	12
KIRT HUT		51									
7:00 KNAC Various											
KBGA Various			SEE INDIVIDUAL DAY LISTINGS								
KIRT HUT											
9:30 KNAC Various		32	56	25	21	23	24	20	19	13	12
KBGA Various		21	37	12	12	14	16	18	16	16	9
KIRT Various HUT		53									
10:00 KNAC Nite Report		35	59	29	21	24	26	15	21	5	1
KBGA News		19	32	12	10	13	14	15	15	7	3
KIRT HUT		54									
10:15 KNAC Nite Report		34	60	28	19	23	25	15	19	5	1
KBGA News		18	31	11	10	11	13	15	15	5	1
KIRT HUT		52									
10:30 KNAC Tonight Show		25	56	22	17	18	18	13	13	4	
KBGA CBS Late Movie		15	34	8	12	11	11	13	12	5	3
KIRT HUT		40									
10:45 KNAC Tonight Show		22	55	20	17	17	16	10	12	4	
KBGA CBS Late Movie		14	34	7	12	10	9	10	12	5	3
KIRT HUT		36									

DESOLAKE, KANSOURI   NOVEMBER, 1975

MONDAY - FRIDAY	PROGRAM		WOMEN			MEN			TEENS	CHIL-DREN
START TIME / STATION PROGRAM	HH RTG.	SHARE	TOT	18-34	18-49	TOT	18-34	18-49	TOT 12-17	TOT 2-11
					RATINGS					
11:00										
KNAC Tonight Show	18	54	16	14	14	12	10	9	4	
KBGA CBS Late Movie	12	36	5	10	8	8	5	9	5	3
KIRT HUT	30									
11:15										
KNAC Tonight Show	17	54	14	12	11	11	8	9	4	
KBGA CBS Late Movie	11	36	5	10	8	8	5	9	5	3
KIRT HUT	28									
11:30										
KNAC Tonight Show	14	52	9	7	7	8	3	4	2	
KBGA CBS Late Movie	10	38	4	10	7	7	5	9	4	1
KIRT HUT	24									
11:45										
KNAC Tonight Show	12	50	9	7	7	5	3	4		
KBGA CBS Late Movie	10	40	5	10	8	6	5	7	4	1
KIRT HUT	22									
12:00										
KNAC Tomorrow	6	42	4	5	4	3		1		
KBGA CBS Late Movie	6	44	4	5	7	4	5	4	4	
KIRT HUT	12									
12:15										
KNAC Tomorrow	5	41	3	5	3	3		1		
KBGA Various	5	43	3	5	6	4	5	4	2	
KIRT HUT	10									
12:30										
KNAC Tomorrow	5	100	2	5	3	2		1		
HUT	5									
12:45										
KNAC Tomorrow	5	100	2	5	3	3		1		
HUT										
1:00										

DESOLAKE, KANSOURI   NOVEMBER, 1975

MONDAY START TIME STATION — PROGRAM	HH RTG.	SHARE	WOMEN TOT	18-34	18-49	MEN TOT	18-34	18-49	TEENS TOT 12-17	CHILDREN TOT 2-11
3:30										
KNAC Be Our Guest	4	19	3	4	2	4	3	3	2	1
KBGA Mike Douglas	16	67	12	2	7					2
KIRT										
HUT	20									
4:00										
KNAC Huck & Yogi	13	48	2	5	3				11	29
KBGA Mike Douglas	12	44	9	2	4	2			2	
KIRT										
HUT	25									
4:30										
KNAC I Dream of Jeannie	16	50	3	2	3	1		1	18	30
KBGA Mike Douglas	12	39	9	2	4	4		1		
KIRT										
HUT	28									
5:00										
KNAC Truth Or Consequences	20	47	11	2	6	5		3	16	15
KBGA Dialing For $	18	44	17	7	11	9	3	3	4	6
KIRT										
HUT	38									
5:15										
KNAC Truth Or Consequences	21	48	11	2	6	6	3	4	18	15
KBGA Dialing For $	18	43	16	7	11	9	3	3	5	6
KIRT										
HUT	39									
5:30										
KNAC NBC Nitely News	29	57	18	10	11	17	10	13	13	3
KBGA CBS Evening News	17	35	15	7	10	13	5	17	2	
KIRT										
HUT	46									
5:45										
KNAC NBC Nitely News	30	59	17	7	10	14	5	9	9	3
KBGA CBS Evening News	17	35	15	7	10	13	5	7	2	
KIRT										
HUT	47									
6:00										
KNAC Eve. Report	30	57	22	14	18	19	10	15	2	
KBGA TV Newsroom	18	35	15	7	10	13	5	7	5	1
KIRT										
HUT	48									
6:15										
KNAC Eve. Report	29	56	18	14	17	16	8	12	2	1
KBGA TV Newsroom	18	35	15	7	10	13	5	7	5	1
KIRT HUT	47									

RATINGS

DESOLAKE, KANSOURI   NOVEMBER, 1975

MONDAY START TIME STATION — PROGRAM	HH RTG.	SHARE	WOMEN TOT	18-34	18-49	MEN TOT	18-34	18-49	TEENS TOT 12-17	CHILDREN TOT 2-11
					RATINGS					
6:30										
KNAC Hollywood Squares	28	49	15	15	15	12	6	7	15	16
KBGA Pop Goes Country	25	39	22	17	17	17	20	18	13	16
KIRT										
HUT	53									
7:00										
KNAC Invisible Man	26	44	15	14	15	16	16	15	16	15
KBGA Rhoda	32	47	27	21	21	25	20	22	19	20
KIRT										
HUT	58									
7:30										
KNAC Invisible Man	26	43	17	17	17	17	20	18	15	15
KBGA Phyllis	33	49	28	21	23	26	21	23	18	19
KIRT										
HUT	59									
8:00										
KNAC Mon. Nite Movie	38	64	27	25	25	25	18	19	19	23
KBGA All In Family	17	29	4	2	6	16	19	16	14	4
KIRT										
HUT	55									
8:30										
KNAC Mon. Nite Movie	37	64	25	24	24	24	18	19	18	22
KBGA Maude	18	31	5	2	6	15	18	16	14	5
KIRT										
HUT	55									
9:00										
KNAC Mon. Nite Movie	37	64	26	25	25	23	15	18	15	18
KBGA Medical Center	18	31	4	2	4	16	18	16	15	4
KIRT										
HUT	55									
9:30										
KNAC Mon. Nite Movie	36	63	26	23	25	23	15	18	16	16
KBGA Medical Center	18	32	6	5	7	15	18	16	15	3
KIRT										
HUT	54									
10:00										
KNAC Nite Report	37	61	30	24	25	27	20	22	7	3
KBGA News	19	31	8	5	7	15	20	18	13	3
KIRT										
HUT	56									
10:15										
KNAC Nite Report	36	61	29	21	24	24	18	19	5	3
KBGA News	19	32	9	5	8	16	20	19	9	1
KIRT										
HUT	55									

DESOLAKE, KANSOURI   NOVEMBER, 1975

MONDAY START TIME STATION PROGRAM	PROGRAM HH RTG.	SHARE	WOMEN TOT	18-34	18-49	MEN TOT	18-34	18-49	TEENS TOT 12-17	CHIL-DREN TOT 2-11
						RATINGS				
10:30										
KNAC Tonight Show	26	57	21	17	17	18	8	12		
KBGA CBS Late Movie	16	35	6	7	8	15	15	16	4	
KIRT										
HUT	42									
10:45										
KNAC Tonight Show	23	57	19	17	17	13	3	7	2	
KBGA CBS Late Movie	14	34	5	7	7	12	13	12	4	
KIRT										
HUT	37									
11:00										
KNAC Tonight Show	20	65	15	12	14	11	5	7	2	
KBGA CBS Late Movie	7	26	4	5	4	9	10	9		
KIRT										
HUT	27									
11:15										
KNAC Tonight Show	18	71	13	12	13	10	3	6	2	
KBGA CBS Late Movie	5	21	3	2	4	4	5	3		
KIRT										
HUT	23									
11:30										
KNAC Tonignt Show	15	79	10	7	10	7		4		
KBGA CBS Late Movie	3	15	2	2	1	3	5	3		
KIRT										
HUT	18									
11:45										
KNAC Tonignt Show	13	82	9	7	8	4		3		
KBGA CBS Late Movie	2	10	2	2	1	1				
KIRT										
HUT	15									
12:00										
KNAC Tomorrow	6	100	5	5	4	2		1		
HUT	6									
12:15										
KNAC Tomorrow	6	100	5	5	4	2		1		
HUT	6									
12:30										
KNAC Tomorrow	5	100	4	5	4	2		1		
HUT	5									

DESOLAKE, KANSOURI   NOVEMBER, 1975

MONDAY		PROGRAM		WOMEN			MEN			TEENS	CHIL-DREN
START TIME STATION	PROGRAM	HH RTG.	SHARE	TOT	18-34	18-49	TOT	18-34	18-49	TOT 12-17	TOT 2-11
				RATINGS							
12:45 KNAC Tomorrow		5	100	3	2	3	2		1		
HUT		5									
1:00											
1:15											
1:30											
1:45											

DESOLAKE, KANSOURI   NOVEMBER, 1975

TUESDAY — START TIME / STATION / PROGRAM	PROGRAM HH RTG.	SHARE	WOMEN TOT	18-34	18-49	MEN TOT	18-34	18-49	TEENS TOT 12-17	CHILDREN TOT 2-11
						RATINGS				
3:30										
KNAC Be Our Guest	5	22	2	2	3					1
KBGA Mike Douglas	13	63	10	10	8	2			5	1
KIRT										
HUT	18									
4:00										
KNAC Huck & Yogi	15	50	2	2	1				12	31
KBGA Mike Douglas	12	39	12	5	7	3	3	1	2	
KIRT										
HUT	27									
4:30										
KNAC I Dream of Jeannie	17	54	5	7	6	1			21	28
KBGA Mike Douglas	12	37	11	5	6	3	3	1	4	
KIRT										
HUT	29									
5:00										
KNAC Truth Or Consequences	19	51	13	10	10	5	3	3	16	15
KBGA Dialing For $	15	39	14	7	8	5	3	1	5	3
KIRT										
HUT	34									
5:15										
KNAC Truth Or Consequences	20	52	14	10	10	5	3	3	15	15
KBGA Dialing For $	15	39	13	5	7	7	5	3	5	3
KIRT										
HUT	35									
5:30										
KNAC NBC Nitely News	25	55	19	14	15	11	5	7	9	3
KBGA CBS Evening News	16	36	12	5	8	12	5	6	2	
KIRT										
HUT	41									
5:45										
KNAC NBC Nitely News	26	55	19	14	15	13	8	9	9	3
KBGA CBS Evening News	17	36	11	2	7	13	8	7	2	
KIRT										
HUT	43									
6:00										
KNAC Eve. Report	30	61	21	14	18	20	13	15		
KBGA TV Newsroom	16	33	11	2	7	11	8	7	4	
KIRT										
HUT	46									
6:15										
KNAC Eve. Report	31	62	21	14	17	21	15	16	2	
KBGA TV Newsroom	16	33	11	2	7	11	8	7	4	
KIRT										
HUT	47									

DESOLAKE, KANSOURI   NOVEMBER, 1975

TUESDAY START TIME / STATION PROGRAM	HH RTG.	SHARE	WOMEN TOT	18-34	18-49	MEN TOT	18-34	18-49	TEENS TOT 12-17	CHILDREN TOT 2-11
6:30										
KNAC Candid Camera	36	59	28	26	27	26	26	25	28	22
KBGA Wild Wild West	22	35	10	5	7	17	15	15	18	21
KIRT										
HUT	58									
7:00										
KNAC Movin' On	25	44	13	11	13	19	18	18	20	16
KBGA Good Times	28	47	13	15	15	20	23	19	26	25
KIRT										
HUT	53									
7:30										
KNAC Movin' On	29	51	17	13	16	21	18	19	27	19
KBGA Joe & Sons	32	55	17	18	18	24	25	23	36	26
KIRT										
HUT	61									
8:00										
KNAC Police Story	31	52	20	14	17	25	25	25	24	16
KBGA Switch	33	57	16	12	16	26	25	27	32	19
KIRT										
HUT	64									
8:30										
KNAC Police Story	30	51	20	14	17	24	23	22	23	13
KBGA Switch	31	55	15	12	15	24	23	25	30	12
KIRT										
HUT	61									
9:00										
KNAC Joe Forrester	29	47	17	18	19	24	24	26	19	9
KBGA Beacon Hill	25	42	17	17	17	18	20	19	11	13
KIRT										
HUT	54									
9:30										
KNAC Joe Forrester	29	48	19	19	20	24	25	27	18	9
KBGA Beacon Hill	26	43	19	19	20	22	20	22	11	13
KIRT										
HUT	55									
10:00										
KNAC Nite Report	36	63	28	21	24	29	23	24	4	
KBGA News	16	29	10	5	10	12	8	10	5	
KIRT										
HUT	52									
10:15										
KNAC Nite Report	34	62	25	21	21	25	20	21	4	
KBGA News	16	30	10	5	10	12	8	10	5	
KIRT										
HUT	50									

DESOLAKE, KANSOURI   NOVEMBER, 1975

TUESDAY	PROGRAM		WOMEN			MEN			TEENS	CHIL-DREN
START TIME STATION PROGRAM	HH RTG.	SHARE	TOT	18-34	18-49	TOT	18-34	18-49	TOT 12-17	TOT 2-11
						RATINGS				
10:30										
KNAC Tonight Show	25	57	20	21	20	21	20	19	4	
KBGA CBS Late Movie	15	35	9	12	13	12	10	12	2	
KIRT										
HUT	40									
10:45										
KNAC Tonight Show	23	58	20	21	20	19	18	18	4	
KBGA CBS Late Movie	13	33	8	12	11	12	10	12	2	
KIRT										
HUT	36									
11:00										
KNAC Tonight Show	19	53	14	14	13	14	15	13	2	
KBGA CBS Late Movie	14	40	9	12	12	13	10	13	2	
KIRT										
HUT	33									
11:15										
KNAC Tonight Show	18	55	13	17	14	12	13	12	2	
KBGA CBS Late Movie	12	37	9	12	11	10	5	9	2	
KIRT										
HUT	30									
11:30										
KNAC Tonight Show	14	51	10	10	10	7	8	7	2	
KBGA CBS Late Movie	11	42	9	12	11	9	5	9	2	
KIRT										
HUT	25									
11:45										
KNAC Tonight Show	12	49	10	10	10	6	5	6	2	
KBGA CBS Late Movie	11	44	9	12	11	9	5	9	2	
KIRT										
HUT	23									
12:00										
KNAC Tomorrow	5	37	5	10	7	4	3	3	2	
KBGA CBS Late Movie	8	56	7	10	10	6	5	7		
KIRT										
HUT	13									
12:15										
KNAC Tomorrow	5	42	5	10	7	4	3	3		
KBGA Various	5	46	4	5	4	4	5	4		
KIRT										
HUT	10									
12:30										
KNAC Tomorrow	5	100	4	10	7	4	3	3		
HUT	5									

DESOLAKE, KANSOURI   NOVEMBER, 1975

TUESDAY START TIME STATION PROGRAM	PROGRAM 4H RTG.	SHARE	WOMEN TOT	18-34	18-49	MEN TOT	18-34	18-49	TEENS TOT 12-17	CHIL-DREN TOT 2-11
						RATINGS				
12:45 KNAC Tomorrow	5	100	4	10	7	4	3	3		
HUT	5									
1:00										
1:15										
1:30										
1:45										

DESOLAKE, KANSOURI   NOVEMBER, 1975

| WEDNESDAY | PROGRAM | | WOMEN | | | MEN | | | TEENS | CHIL-DREN |
START TIME / STATION — PROGRAM	HH RTG.	SHARE	TOT	18-34	18-49	TOT	18-34	18-49	TOT 12-17	TOT 2-11
3:30										
KNAC Be Our Guest	4	17		1	1					1
KBGA Mike Douglas	15	69	9	7	7	4	5	3	4	1
KIRT										
HUT	19									
4:00										
KNAC Huck & Yogi	14	53	2	5	3	1	3	1	13	30
KBGA Mike Douglas	11	41	7	1	4	4	5	3	3	
KIRT										
HUT	25									
4:30										
KNAC I Dream of Jeannie	16	53	2	4	4	1	3	1	18	28
KBGA Mike Douglas	11	37	7		3	4	5	3	2	
KIRT										
HUT	27									
5:00										
KNAC Truth Or Consequences	19	49	9	7	6	7	8	4	11	18
KBGA Dialing For $	16	42	12	5	6	6	5	3	5	3
KIRT										
HUT	35									
5:15										
KNAC Truth Or Consequences	19	49	9	7	6	8	8	6	9	18
KBGA Dialing For $	16	43	13	7	7	6	5	3	5	3
KIRT										
HUT	35									
5:30										
KNAC NBC Nitely News	24	53	16	12	14	13	10	10	7	1
KBGA CBS Evening News	17	38	13	7	8	13	5	6	4	1
KIRT										
HUT	41									
5:45										
KNAC NBC Nitely News	25	54	16	14	15	13	10	10	5	1
KBGA CBS Evening News	17	38	12	5	7	13	5	7	4	
KIRT										
HUT	42									
6:00										
KNAC Eve. Report	30	60	18	12	14	18	8	13	2	3
KBGA TV Newsroom	16	32	12	5	7	12	8	9	4	
KIRT										
HUT	46									
6:15										
KNAC Eve. Report	30	59	16	7	11	19	8	15	4	3
KBGA TV Newsroom	17	33	13	5	8	12	8	9	4	
KIRT										
HUT	47									

RATINGS

DESOLAKE, KANSOURI   NOVEMBER, 1975

WEDNESDAY	PROGRAM		WOMEN			MEN			TEENS	CHIL-DREN
START TIME STATION PROGRAM	HH RTG.	SHARE	TOT	18-34	18-49	TOT	18-34	18-49	TOT 12-17	TOT 2-11
					RATINGS					
6:30										
KNAC Treasure Hunt	43	71	29	33	32	28	31	29	43	42
KBGA $25,000 Pyramid	19	32	17	12	11	13	6	7	1	2
KIRT										
HUT	62									
7:00										
KNAC House-Prairie	50	73	43	45	42	35	33	33	35	57
KBGA T. Orlando & Dawn	18	27	11	14	14	8	8	9	16	10
KIRT										
HUT	68									
7:30										
KNAC House-Prairie	50	74	41	44	42	34	34	32	36	57
KBGA T. Orlando & Dawn	17	25	9	12	11	8	8	9	15	12
KIRT										
HUT	67									
8:00										
KNAC Doctor's Hospital	34	51	27	27	27	21	15	18	29	15
KBGA Cannon	28	42	19	19	19	22	23	20	13	16
KIRT										
HUT	62									
8:30										
KNAC Doctor's Hospital	34	52	28	26	27	20	13	16	29	13
KBGA Cannon	27	42	18	19	18	21	23	19	13	15
KIRT										
HUT	61									
9:00										
KNAC Petrocelli	33	55	25	24	23	21	18	19	16	10
KBGA Kate McShane	24	40	13	14	17	18	23	19	18	10
KIRT										
HUT	57									
9:30										
KNAC Petrocelli	33	55	25	24	23	20	18	19	16	10
KBGA Kate McShane	24	40	12	15	16	19	25	21	16	9
KIRT										
HUT	57									
10:00										
KNAC Nite Report	36	60	33	21	27	26	13	21	7	1
KBGA News	20	33	13	14	14	16	15	15	4	3
KIRT										
HUT	56									
10:15										
KNAC Nite Report	36	59	29	17	23	24	13	19	7	1
KBGA News	20	33	12	12	13	15	15	16	4	3
KIRT										
HUT	56									

DESOLAKE, KANSOURI   NOVEMBER, 1975

WEDNESDAY		PROGRAM		WOMEN			MEN			TEENS	CHILDREN
START TIME STATION	PROGRAM	HH RTG.	SHARE	TOT	18-34	18-49	TOT	18-34	18-49	TOT 12-17	TOT 2-11
						RATINGS					
10:30											
KNAC	Tonight Show	25	59	22	14	17	18	10	13	5	
KBGA	CBS Late Movie	14	32	5	10	8	9	15	13	2	1
KIRT											
	HUT	39									
10:45											
KNAC	Tonight Show	23	57	22	17	18	17	10	12	5	
KBGA	CBS Late Movie	14	33	6	10	10	8	13	12	2	1
KIRT											
	HUT	37									
11:00											
KNAC	Tonight Show	17	52	16	17	15	11	10	10	4	
KBGA	CBS Late Movie	13	38	5	7	8	8	10	10	2	1
KIRT											
	HUT	30									
11:15											
KNAC	Tonight Show	16	50	14	14	13	11	10	10	2	
KBGA	CBS Late Movie	12	39	5	7	8	9	10	12	2	1
KIRT											
	HUT	28									
11:30											
KNAC	Tonight Show	13	47	11	12	11	7	5	6	2	
KBGA	CBS Late Movie	13	44	6	10	10	9	10	12	2	1
KIRT											
	HUT	26									
11:45											
KNAC	Tonight Show	12	44	9	10	8	5	5	4		
KBGA	CBS Late Movie	12	47	7	12	11	8	10	10	2	1
KIRT											
	HUT	24									
12:00											
KNAC	Tomorrow	6	47	3		3	3		1		
KBGA	CBS Late Movie	6	45	5	7	7	3	3	4	2	
KIRT											
	HUT	12									
12:15											
KNAC	Tomorrow	5	100	2		1	3		1		
	HUT	5									
12:30											
KNAC	Tomorrow	5	100	2		1	2	3	1		
	HUT	5									

DESOLAKE, KANSOURI   NOVEMBER, 1975

WEDNESDAY		PROGRAM		WOMEN			MEN			TEENS	CHIL-DREN
START TIME STATION	PROGRAM	HH RTG.	SHARE	TOT	18-34	18-49	TOT	18-34	18-49	TOT 12-17	TOT 2-11
				RATINGS							
12:45 KNAC Tomorrow		5	100	2		1	2	3	1		
HUT											
1:00											
1:15											
1:30											
1:45											

DESOLAKE, KANSOURI   NOVEMBER, 1975

THURSDAY		PROGRAM		WOMEN			MEN			TEENS	CHILDREN
START TIME STATION	PROGRAM	HH RTG.	SHARE	TOT	18-34	18-49	TOT	18-34	18-49	TOT 12-17	TOT 2-11
							RATINGS				
3:30											
KNAC	Be Our Guest	7	32	4	5	3				4	2
KBGA	Mike Douglas	13	57	12	7	8	2			5	1
KIRT	HUT	20									
4:00											
KNAC	Huck & Yogi	17	57	3	2	1	2	3	1	12	35
KBGA	Mike Douglas	11	36	9	2	4	3	3	1	7	1
KIRT	HUT	28									
4:30											
KNAC	I Dream Of Jeannie	17	55	3	2	5	1	3	1	21	35
KBGA	Mike Douglas	11	35	10	2	4	3	3	1	5	1
KIRT	HUT	28									
5:00											
KNAC	Truth Or Consequences	18	50	9	5	7	9	8	6	15	16
KBGA	Dialing For $	15	41	12	5	6	5			5	3
KIRT	HUT	33									
5:15											
KNAC	Truth Or Consequences	19	52	10	5	7	8	5	4	13	15
KBGA	Dialing For $	15	40	13	5	7	4			5	1
KIRT	HUT	34									
5:30											
KNAC	NBC Nitely News	26	55	17	10	13	14	5	10	2	3
KBGA	CBS Evening News	18	37	12	2	7	11	3	3	5	
KIRT	HUT	44									
5:45											
KNAC	NBC Nitely News	26	55	17	12	14	13	5	9	2	1
KBGA	CBS Evening News	17	36	12	2	7	12	3	3	4	
KIRT	HUT	43									
6:00											
KNAC	Eve. Report	33	61	22	12	17	22	10	16	7	1
KBGA	TV Newsroom	17	31	12	2	7	9	3	3		
KIRT	HUT	50									
6:15											
KNAC	Eve. Report	34	63	24	17	18	24	13	18	9	3
KBGA	TV Newsroom	16	30	10	2	7	9	3	3		
KIRT	HUT	50									

DESOLAKE, KANSOURI   NOVEMBER, 1975

THURSDAY	PROGRAM		WOMEN			MEN			TEENS	CHIL-DREN
START TIME STATION PROGRAM	HH RTG.	SHARE	TOT	18-34	18-49	TOT	18-34	18-49	TOT 12-17	TOT 2-11
					RATINGS					
6:30										
KNAC Hollywood Squares	31	58	22	17	18	21	14	15	15	7
KBGA Wild World of Animals	18	34	12	8	9	13	8	9	6	11
KIRT										
HUT	49									
7:00										
KNAC Montefuscos	30	47	19	13	17	21	11	16	14	18
KBGA Waltons	30	47	24	21	23	22	19	19	22	27
KIRT										
HUT	60									
7:30										
KNAC Fay	29	47	18	12	16	19	9	14	15	19
KBGA Waltons	29	47	22	20	22	21	20	19	22	25
KIRT										
HUT	58									
8:00										
KNAC Ellery Queen	29	49	21	21	20	20	15	13	5	6
KBGA Thursday Nite Movie	26	43	14	12	15	17	13	18	32	20
KIRT										
HUT	54									
8:30										
KNAC Ellery Queen	28	48	20	21	20	20	16	14	5	6
KBGA Thursday Nite Movie	25	44	14	13	16	17	13	18	31	20
KIRT										
HUT	53									
9:00										
KNAC Medical Story	32	55	24	25	23	25	26	22	11	17
KBGA Thursday Nite Movie	22	38	14	12	15	16	10	15	28	13
KIRT										
HUT	54									
9:30										
KNAC Medical Story	33	57	26	26	25	27	25	21	11	13
KBGA Thursday Nite Movie	21	37	12	10	14	15	10	15	25	13
KIRT										
HUT	54									
10:00										
KNAC Nite Report	34	57	28	14	21	25	15	19	5	1
KBGA News	21	34	17	17	18	15	13	12	5	3
KIRT										
HUT	55									
10:15										
KNAC Nite Report	34	58	26	14	20	24	10	16	7	
KBGA News	18	31	14	12	14	15	13	12		1
KIRT										
HUT	52									

DESOLAKE, KANSOURI   NOVEMBER, 1975

THURSDAY — START TIME / STATION / PROGRAM	HH RTG.	SHARE	WOMEN TOT	18-34	18-49	MEN TOT	18-34	18-49	TEENS TOT 12-17	CHILDREN TOT 2-11
10:30										
KNAC Tonight Show	26	56	23	17	18	18	10	12	7	
KBGA CBS Late Movie	18	39	15	17	14	13	18	15	7	6
KIRT										
HUT	44									
10:45										
KNAC Tonight Show	23	54	22	17	17	15	10	10	9	
KBGA CBS Late Movie	16	41	13	17	14	13	15	13	7	6
KIRT										
HUT	39									
11:00										
KNAC Tonight Show	19	53	16	10	10	14	8	9	4	
KBGA CBS Late Movie	14	41	11	14	13	10	13	10	7	3
KIRT										
HUT	33									
11:15										
KNAC Tonight Show	17	52	16	10	10	13	8	9	4	
KBGA CBS Late Movie	13	38	6	12	10	9	10	9	2	1
KIRT										
HUT	30									
11:30										
KNAC Tonight Show	15	52	13	7	7	9	5	4	4	
KBGA CBS Late Movie	11	39	7	12	10	8	8	7	2	
KIRT										
HUT	26									
11:45										
KNAC Tonight Show	13	49	13	7	7	7	5	3	4	
KBGA CBS Late Movie	11	42	7	12	10	8	8	7	2	
KIRT										
HUT	24									
12:00										
KNAC Tomorrow	6	37	3	5	4	3	3	1	2	
KBGA CBS Late Movie	9	54	6	10	8	6	8	6	2	
KIRT										
HUT	15									
12:15										
KNAC Tomorrow	4	30	2	5	3	3	3	1	2	
KBGA CBS Late Movie	8	55	3	5	6	5	8	6		
KIRT										
HUT	12									
12:30										
KNAC Tomorrow	4	46	2	5	3	3		1		
KBGA CBS Late Movie	6	49	3	5	4	3	5	3	2	
KIRT										
HUT	10									

RATINGS

DESOLAKE, KANSOURI   NOVEMBER, 1975

START TIME STATION PROGRAM	HH RTG.	SHARE	WOMEN TOT	18-34	18-49	MEN TOT	18-34	18-49	TEENS TOT 12-17	CHIL-DREN TOT 2-11
			RATINGS							
12:45 KNAC Tomorrow	4	100	2	5	3	3		1		
HUT	4									
1:00										
1:15										
1:30										
1:45										

DESOLAKE, KANSOURI   NOVEMBER, 1975

FRIDAY START TIME STATION PROGRAM	PROGRAM HH RTG.	SHARE	WOMEN TOT	18-34	18-49	MEN TOT	18-34	18-49	TEENS TOT 12-17	CHILDREN TOT 2-1
3:30										
KNAC Be Our Guest	7	29	3	5	4					4
KBGA Mike Douglas	14	65	9	10	10	6	5	4	7	1
KIRT										
HUT	21									
4:00										
KNAC Huck & Yogi	19	58	3	2	3	1	3	1	15	36
KBGA Mike Douglas	12	42	9	7	7	5	3	3	7	3
KIRT										
HUT	31									
4:30										
KNAC I Dream Of Jeannie	18	55	3	2	3	2	5	3	17	30
KBGA Mike Douglas	13	41	9	7	7	5	3	3	5	3
KIRT										
HUT	31									
5:00										
KNAC Truth Or Consequences	16	45	8	7	7	5	5	4	16	13
KBGA Dialing For $	16	45	13	10	10	6	3	3	5	6
KIRT										
HUT	32									
5:15										
KNAC Truth Or Consequences	16	45	8	5	6	5	5	4	16	13
KBGA Dialing For $	16	44	13	10	10	5	3	3	5	4
KIRT										
HUT	32									
5:30										
KNAC NBC Nitely News	21	49	16	12	13	12	8	7		1
KBGA CBS Evening News	19	45	14	7	11	11	5	6	7	4
KIRT										
HUT	40									
5:45										
KNAC NBC Nitely News	21	49	16	12	13	11	5	6		4
KBGA CBS Evening News	19	46	13	7	10	9	5	6	5	4
KIRT										
HUT	40									
6:00										
KNAC Eve. Report	25	54	16	7	11	18	8	12	4	4
KBGA TV Newsroom	17	37	13	7	11	11	3	7	7	
KIRT										
HUT	42									
6:15										
KNAC Eve. Report	26	55	16	12	14	17	5	10	4	1
KBGA TV Newsroom	17	36	12	5	10	11	3	7	7	6
KIRT										
HUT	43									

DESOLAKE, KANSOURI   NOVEMBER, 1975

FRIDAY START TIME STATION — PROGRAM	PROGRAM HH RTG.	SHARE	WOMEN TOT	18-34	18-49	MEN TOT	18-34	18-49	TEENS TOT 12-17	CHILDREN TOT 2-11
					RATINGS					
6:30										
KNAC Wild Kingdom	27	52	16	13	15	18	10	13	15	13
KBGA Jimmy Dean	24	44	16	17	18	14	18	19	26	34
KIRT										
HUT	51									
7:00										
KNAC Sanford & Son	43	68	34	31	31	34	29	29	27	30
KBGA Big Eddie	15	24	5	12	8	7	14	11	16	27
KIRT										
HUT	58									
7:30										
KNAC Chico & The Man	39	67	29	29	28	30	23	25	25	22
KBGA M*A*S*H	15	26	5	11	8	5	10	9	16	30
KIRT										
HUT	54									
8:00										
KNAC Rockford Files	30	55	20	19	20	23	21	20	17	18
KBGA Hawaii Five-O	19	34	13	12	13	12	16	16	19	10
KIRT										
HUT	49									
8:30										
KNAC Rockford Files	29	53	22	21	23	22	20	19	16	19
KBGA Hawaii Five-O	19	35	12	10	11	13	18	16	17	10
KIRT										
HUT	48									
9:00										
KNAC Police Woman	28	55	25	25	26	22	19	20	15	17
KBGA Barnaby Jones	19	34	12	14	14	14	18	18	16	9
KIRT										
HUT	47									
9:30										
KNAC Police Woman	25	57	25	26	27	23	20	20	16	18
KBGA Barnaby Jones	18	34	11	14	14	15	19	19	15	9
KIRT										
HUT	43									
10:00										
KNAC Nite Report	33	59	28	21	23	27	15	19	7	3
KBGA News	19	33	10	14	13	13	23	16	9	4
KIRT										
HUT	52									
10:15										
KNAC Nite Report	32	59	27	19	23	25	15	18	5	3
KBGA News	18	33	9	12	11	13	20	18	7	1
KIRT										
HUT	50									

DESOLAKE, KANSOURI

FRIDAY		PROGRAM		WOMEN			MEN			TEENS	CHILDREN
START TIME STATION PROGRAM		HH RTG.	SHARE	TOT	18-34	18-49	TOT	18-34	18-49	TOT 12-17	TOT 2-1
							RATINGS				
10:30											
KNAC	Tonight Show	22	53	18	14	15	16	13	13	5	1
KBGA	CBS Late Movie	17	38	10	14	13	10	15	12	18	7
KIRT											
	HUT	39									
10:45											
KNAC	Tonight Show	20	50	14	12	13	14	10	12	4	1
KBGA	CBS Late Movie	14	35	7	12	10	6	10	9	15	4
KIRT											
	HUT	34									
11:00											
KNAC	Tonight Show	17	48	13	12	13	8	8	7	5	1
KBGA	CBS Late Movie	14	40	8	12	11	6	8	9	16	6
KIRT											
	HUT	31									
11:15											
KNAC	Tonight Show	15	45	13	10	11	8	5	7	4	
KBGA	CBS Late Movie	15	43	9	14	13	6	10	10	16	7
KIRT											
	HUT	30									
11:30											
KNAC	Tonight Show	12	41	9	5	6	6	3	4	2	1
KBGA	CBS Late Movie	14	48	9	14	13	6	10	10	16	6
KIRT											
	HUT	26									
11:45											
KNAC	Tonight Show	11	39	9	5	6	5	3	4		1
KBGA	CBS Late Movie	15	51	9	14	13	7	10	10	15	6
KIRT											
	HUT	26									
12:00											
KNAC	Midnight Special	6	29	3	5	4	3	3	3	2	
KBGA	CBS Late Movie	12	58	6	12	10	5	10	9	13	4
KIRT											
	HUT	18									
12:15											
KNAC	Midnight Special	6	33	4	7	6	3	3	3	2	
KBGA	CBS Late Movie	15	71	9	17	13	10	15	13	11	9
KIRT											
	HUT	21									
12:30											
KNAC	Midnight Special	5	100	4	7	6	2	3	3		
	HUT	5									

DESOLAKE, KANSOURI   NOVEMBER, 1975

FRIDAY		PROGRAM		WOMEN			MEN			TEENS	CHILDREN
START TIME STATION	PROGRAM	HH RTG.	SHARE	TOT	18-34	18-49	TOT	18-34	18-49	TOT 12-17	TOT 2-11
							RATINGS				
12:45 KNAC	Midnight Special	6	100	4	7	6	3	5	4		1
	HUT	6									
1:00 KNAC	Midnight Special	3	100	1	2	1	1	3	1		1
	HUT	3									
1:15 KNAC	Midnight Special	2	100	1	2	1	1	3	1		1
	HUT	2									
1:30 KNAC											
1:45											

DESOLAKE, KANSOURI   NOVEMBER, 1975

SATURDAY START TIME STATION / PROGRAM	HH RTG.	SHARE	WOMEN TOT	18-34	18-49	MEN TOT	18-34	18-49	TEENS TOT 12-17	CHILDREN TOT 2-11
7:00										
KNAC Emergency +4	2	40								3
KBGA Pebbles & Bam Bam	2	47								6
KIRT										
HUT	4									
7:30										
KNAC Sigmund	3	37								9
KBGA Bugs Bunny	4	52							2	12
KIRT										
HUT	7									
8:00										
KNAC Secret Life of W. Kitty	4	32		1	1				1	13
KBGA Bugs Bunny	7	51			1				10	17
KIRT										
HUT	11									
8:30										
KNAC Pink Panther	8	42	2	2	3				7	21
KBGA Scooby-Do	9	43					1	1	5	24
KIRT										
HUT	17									
9:00										
KNAC Land of the Lost	15	60	1	2	1				6	39
KBGA Shazams/Isis Hour	8	29				1	3	1	8	16
KIRT										
HUT	23									
9:30										
KNAC Run, Joe, Run	21	77	2	5	3				11	51
KBGA Shazams/Isis Hour	4	15				1	3	1	1	7
KIRT										
HUT	25									
10:00										
KNAC Beyond Planet of Apes	22	78	1	4	2	2	3	3	20	48
KBGA Far Out Space Nuts	4	15							2	4
KIRT										
HUT	26									
10:30										
KNAC West Wind	14	57	3	7	4	1	3	1	13	29
KBGA Ghost Busters	8	31							6	12
KIRT										
HUT	22									
11:00										
KNAC Josie & Pussycats	13	63	1	4	2		1	1	18	23
KBGA Harlem Globetrotters	5	24							6	7
KIRT										
HUT	18									

RATINGS

DESOLAKE, KANSOURI   NOVEMBER, 1975

SATURDAY START TIME STATION	PROGRAM	HH RTG.	SHARE	WOMEN TOT	18-34	18-49	MEN TOT	18-34	18-49	TEENS TOT 12-17	CHILDREN TOT 2-11
11:30						RATINGS					
KNAC	Go U.S.A.	11	58	1	4	2	1	3	1	10	16
KBGA	Fat Albert & Cosby	6	28		1	1				13	9
KIRT	Kids										
HUT		17									
12:00											
KNAC	Local	12	62				1	3	1	16	25
KBGA	Children's Film Fstvl.	2	12	1	2	1	2	5	3		
KIRT											
HUT		14									
12:30											
KNAC	Indian Country	4	25				1	3	1	4	4
KBGA	Children's Film Fstvl.	5	30	1	2	1	4	8	4	2	
KIRT											
HUT		9									
1:00											
KNAC	Bible Story	4	28	1	2	1				1	7
KBGA	Death Valley Days	8	56	1	2	2	4	5	3	6	4
KIRT											
HUT		12									
1:30											
KNAC	Gilligan's	7	38	2		1	2	4	4	7	18
KBGA	High School Football	7	45	3	5	4	4	8	4	2	2
KIRT											
HUT		14									
2:00											
KNAC	Local Movie	11	58	4	2	4	3	3	3	11	9
KBGA	High School Football	6	39	3	5	4	5	10	6	4	1
KIRT											
HUT		17									
2:30											
KNAC	Local Movie	10	54	5	2	5	3	3	3	10	7
KBGA	High School Football	7	46	3	5	4	5	8	4	3	1
KIRT											
HUT		17									
3:00											
KNAC	Local Movie	11	60	6	5	7	2	3	3	11	7
KBGA	High School Football	7	46	3	5	4	5	6	5	3	2
KIRT											
HUT		18									
3:30											
KNAC	Various	6	41	1		1				5	7
KBGA	Various	8	69	3	5	4	7	10	9	5	4
KIRT											
HUT		14									

DESOLAKE, KANSOURI   NOVEMBER, 1975

SATURDAY		PROGRAM		WOMEN			MEN			TEENS	CHIL-DREN
START TIME STATION PROGRAM		HH RTG.	SHARE	TOT	18-34	18-49	TOT	18-34	18-49	TOT 12-17	TOT 2-11
							RATINGS				
3:45											
KNAC	Various	6	42	1		1				4	7
KBGA	Various	8	71	3	5	4	7	10	9	7	4
KIRT											
	HUT	14									
4:00											
KNAC	Yogi Gang	6	41	1		1	1	3	1	7	10
KBGA	Various	8	45	4	5	3	6	8	6	7	6
KIRT											
	HUT	14									
4:15											
KNAC	Yogi Gang	7	43	1		1	1	3	1	7	10
KBGA	Various	8	44	4	5	3	6	8	6	4	6
KIRT											
	HUT	15									
4:30											
KNAC	Good News	4	30	1		1	1	3	1		4
KBGA	Various	9	58	3	2	1	7	8	7	5	3
KIRT											
	HUT	13									
4:45											
KNAC	Good News	8	57	1			7	10	9	7	1
KBGA	Various	9	61	2	2	1	6	8	7	7	3
KIRT											
	HUT	17									
5:00											
KNAC	Knight Hour	8	40	6		1	3			2	4
KBGA	Various	10	44	3	2	4	9	10	10	7	1
KIRT											
	HUT	18									
5:15											
KNAC	Knight Hour	10	43	6		1	4			2	4
KBGA	Various	10	43	4	2	4	9	10	10	5	1
KIRT											
	HUT	20									
5:30											
KNAC	NBC Sat. News	18	55	14	2	7	12		4	2	1
KBGA	CBS Sat. News	13	38	7	2	7	9	8	10	4	1
KIRT											
	HUT	31									
5:45											
KNAC	NBC Sat. News	18	54	15	2	7	13	3	6	2	
KBGA	CBS Sat. News	14	41	7	2	7	9	8	10	2	1
KIRT											
	HUT	32									

DESOLAKE, KANSOURI

NOVEMBER, 1975

SATURDAY	PROGRAM		WOMEN			MEN			TEENS	CHIL-DREN
START TIME STATION PROGRAM	HH RTG.	SHARE	TOT	18-34	18-49	TOT	18-34	18-49	TOT 12-17	TOT 2-11
					RATINGS					
6:00 KNAC Lawrence Welk KBGA Hee Haw KIRT HUT	30 27 57	49 45	28 22	12 24	17 24	22 21	13 23	16 21	5 18	15 15
6:15 KNAC Lawrence Welk KBGA Hee Haw KIRT HUT	30 27 57	49 45	27 23	12 24	15 25	22 23	15 25	16 24	5 18	15 15
6:30 KNAC Lawrence Welk KBGA Hee Haw KIRT HUT	29 28 57	47 46	26 22	10 24	15 24	20 25	10 28	13 26	6 16	13 16
7:00 KNAC Emergency KBGA Jeffersons KIRT HUT	28 36 54	42 55	21 29	21 20	18 27	18 29	16 26	17 26	18 26	31 24
7:30 KNAC Emergency KBGA Doc KIRT HUT	32 21 53	58 38	27 16	29 8	28 13	23 15	23 9	24 9	25 13	44 13
8:00 KNAC Sat. Night Movie KBGA Mary T. Moore KIRT HUT	28 24 52	49 41	19 20	23 14	22 18	19 17	16 14	18 14	26 13	19 19
8:30 KNAC Sat. Night Movie KBGA Bob Newhart KIRT HUT	29 21 50	52 38	22 14	27 4	25 11	21 14	20 10	21 10	24 9	18 13
9:00 KNAC Sat. Night Movie KBGA Carol Burnett KIRT HUT	28 20 48	52 36	19 13	21 8	21 12	22 14	21 8	22 9	20 13	13 21
9:30 KNAC Sat. Night Movie KBGA Carol Burnett KIRT HUT	28 20 48	53 37	20 13	24 7	23 11	22 16	20 13	22 12	20 13	13 21

DESOLAKE, KANSOURI   NOVEMBER, 1975

RATINGS

SATURDAY START TIME / STATION PROGRAM	HH RTG.	SHARE	WOMEN TOT	WOMEN 18-34	WOMEN 18-49	MEN TOT	MEN 18-34	MEN 18-49	TEENS TOT 12-17	CHILDREN TOT 2-1
10:00										
KNAC Night Report	27	55	22	17	18	19	13	16	9	3
KBGA News	16	33	13	7	10	13	10	10	4	4
KIRT										
HUT	43									
10:15										
KNAC Night Report	26	55	21	14	17	18	13	15	7	1
KBGA News	16	34	13	7	10	13	10	10	2	4
KIRT										
HUT	42									
10:30										
KNAC Various	17	46	16	17	14	9	10	10	7	1
KBGA Star Wrestling	12	35	5	7	4	12	10	9	2	6
KIRT										
HUT	29									
10:45										
KNAC Various	16	45	15	17	14	7	10	7	9	
KBGA Star Wrestling	15	43	5	5	6	16	13	12	4	9
KIRT										
HUT	31									
11:00										
KNAC Weekend Tonight	13	51	13	14	14	6	5	6	13	1
KBGA Star Wrestling	14	48	5	7	6	12	10	9	4	7
KIRT										
HUT	27									
11:15										
KNAC Weekend Tonight	12	53	11	12	11	4	3	3	11	
KBGA Star Wrestling	13	49	5	7	6	12	10	9	4	7
KIRT										
HUT	25									
11:30										
KNAC Weekend Tonight	10	54	9	10	10	4	3	3	9	
KBGA Hank Thompson	9	42	4	7	6	7	5	6		3
KIRT										
HUT	19									
11:45										
KNAC Weekend Tonight	9	54	9	10	8	3	3	3	9	
KBGA Hank Thompson	6	36	3	5	4	4	3	4		
KIRT										
HUT	15									
12:00										

DESOLAKE, KANSOURI

NOVEMBER, 1975

SUNDAY START TIME STATION PROGRAM	PROGRAM HH RTG.	SHARE	WOMEN TOT	18-34	18-49	MEN TOT	18-34	18-49	TEENS TOT 12-17	CHILDREN TOT 2-11
7:00						RATINGS				
KNAC Local	1									1
HUT	1									
7:30										
KNAC Local	1									
KBGA Meet a Friend	1					1		1		2
KIRT										
HUT	2									
8:00										
KNAC Local	2	29	2			1				
KBGA Valley of Dinosaurs	5	64	3	2	1	3		1		1
KIRT										
HUT	7									
8:30										
KNAC Oral Roberts	4	40	2		1	2				
KBGA Cathdrl.-Tomorrow	5	53	3	2	1	3		1		1
KIRT										
HUT	9									
9:00										
KNAC Chll-Trth:Word	4	46	4		1	1		1		
KBGA Lamp Unto-Feet	4	42	3			2				
KIRT										
HUT	8									
9:30										
KNAC Day-Discovery	4	43	3			1				
KBGA Old Time Gospel	4	44	3		1	2		1	2	
KIRT										
HUT	8									
10:00										
KNAC Rex Humbard	5	42	3			2				
KBGA Old Time Gospel	5	39	3		1	3	3	3	2	
KIRT										
HUT	10									
10:30										
KNAC Rex Humbard	3	29	2			1				
KBGA Face The Nation	7	55	4		1	4		1		
KIRT										
HUT	10									
11:00										
KNAC Faith For Today	4	33	2							
KBGA Calvary Temple	6	52	4	5	4	3	3	3	2	
KIRT										
HUT	10									

DESOLAKE, KANSOURI   NOVEMBER, 1975

SUNDAY START TIME / STATION / PROGRAM	HH RTG.	SHARE	WOMEN TOT	18-34	18-49	MEN TOT	18-34	18-49	TEENS TOT 12-17	CHILDREN TOT 2-11
11:30										
KNAC Herald-Truth	3	28	2			2	3	1		
KBGA Calvary Temple	6	54	3	5	3					1
KIRT										
HUT	9									
12:00										
KNAC NBC NFL Football	11	60	4	2	4	10	8	9	6	2
KBGA NFL Today	8	40	5	2	4	7	10	7	7	3
KIRT										
HUT	19									
12:30										
KNAC NBC NFL Football	12	55	4	2	4	10	8	9	7	2
KBGA CBS NFL Football	9	40	3		3	9	13	10	5	1
KIRT										
HUT	21									
1:00										
KNAC NBC NFL Football	13	48	4	4	4	10	13	11	10	3
KBGA CBS NFL Football	13	46	3	2	4	12	13	13	9	1
KIRT										
HUT	26									
1:30										
KNAC NBC NFL Football	13	44	4	5	4	8	11	10	9	1
KBGA CBS NFL Football	13	46	3	2	4	10	10	10	13	1
KIRT										
HUT	26									
2:00										
KNAC NBC NFL Football	12	47	3	2	3	9	10	10	8	1
KBGA CBS NFL Football	11	41	3	2	4	8	8	9	9	1
KIRT										
HUT	23									
2:30										
KNAC NBC NFL Football	12	47	2	1	2	10	13	12	7	1
KBGA CBS NFL Football	10	41	4	2	4	10	8	9	10	
KIRT										
HUT	22									
3:00										
KNAC Meet The Press	13	51	3	1	2	11	13	13	5	3
KBGA CBS NFL Football	11	44	5	5	6	10	8	7	8	
KIRT										
HUT	24									
3:30										
KNAC Meet The Press	6	24	3	2	1	4	3	1		
KBGA NBA Basketball	11	46	4	5	6	10	8	9	7	
KIRT										
HUT	17									

DESOLAKE, KANSOURI   NOVEMBER, 1975

SUNDAY START TIME STATION PROGRAM	PROGRAM HH RTG.	SHARE	WOMEN TOT	18-34	18-49	MEN TOT	18-34	18-49	TEENS TOT 12-17	CHILDREN TOT 2-11
					RATINGS					
3:45										
KNAC Various	10	43	3	2	3	7	10	9	2	4
KBGA NBA Basketball	12	48	5	5	6	11	10	10	7	
KIRT HUT	22									
4:00										
KNAC Various	9	40	3	2	3	8	10	9	2	3
KBGA NBA Basketball	10	49	4	2	4	7	8	7	5	
KIRT HUT	19									
4:15										
KNAC Various	8	38	3	2	3	8	8	9	2	3
KBGA NBA Basketball	11	50	4	2	4	7	8	7	5	
KIRT HUT	19									
4:30										
KNAC Judy	8	39	3	2	3	5	8	6	2	3
KBGA NBA Basketball	10	48	2		1	8	8	9	7	
KIRT HUT	18									
4:45										
KNAC Judy	8	40	3	2	3	7	10	9	2	4
KBGA NBA Basketball	10	48	2		1	8	8	9	9	
KIRT HUT	18									
5:00										
KNAC Judy	14	59	5	2	3	7	8	7	5	7
KBGA NBA Basketball	8	34	3		4	7	8	7	5	
KIRT HUT	22									
5:15										
KNAC Judy	15	61	5	2	3	9	8	9	7	9
KBGA NBA Basketball	8	32	3		4	7	8	7	4	
KIRT HUT	23									
5:30										
KNAC NBC Sun News	22	58	17	12	15	18	5	10	13	7
KBGA NBA Basketball	8	26	3	2	3	7	8	9	5	
KIRT HUT	30									
5:45										
KNAC NBC Sun News	21	53	16	10	14	16	5	9	11	7
KBGA NBA Basketball	9	29	3	2	3	8	8	9	5	
KIRT HUT	30									

DESOLAKE, KANSOURI   NOVEMBER, 1975

SUNDAY START TIME STATION — PROGRAM	PROGRAM HH RTG.	SHARE	WOMEN TOT	18-34	18-49	MEN TOT	18-34	18-49	TEENS TOT 12-17	CHILDREN TOT 2-11
					RATINGS					
6:00 KNAC Disney	37	76	29	21	23	28	18	21	22	37
KBGA 3 For Road	5	12	4	5	6	5	5	9		1
KIRT										
HUT	42									
6:15 KNAC Disney	38	75	29	21	23	27	15	19	25	39
KBGA 3 For Road	9	17	9	7	7	7	8	9		1
KIRT										
HUT	47									
6:30 KNAC Disney	40	63	29	29	27	32	24	28	33	52
KBGA 3 For Road	18	29	12	5	10	11	13	13	22	10
KIRT										
HUT	58									
7:00 KNAC Family Holvak	38	60	29	29	27	32	25	28	31	45
KBGA Cher	19	30	11	5	10	9	13	12	24	10
KIRT										
HUT	57									
7:30 KNAC Family Holvak	37	59	25	26	26	32	26	28	37	28
KBGA Cher	21	34	17	17	17	17	18	18	16	11
KIRT										
HUT	58									
8:00 KNAC Sun. Mystery Movie	35	57	25	27	26	28	25	27	36	26
KBGA Kojak	22	36	19	18	19	19	20	19	18	9
KIRT										
HUT	57									
8:30 KNAC Sun. Mystery Movie	34	56	23	26	25	26	25	27	36	25
KBGA Kojak	22	36	15	14	15	19	18	18	10	7
KIRT										
HUT	56									
9:00 KNAC Sun Mystery Movie	35	56	24	29	27	26	24	26	35	25
KBGA Bronk	22	35	16	17	18	17	16	17	11	6
KIRT										
HUT	57									
9:30 KNAC Sun. Mystery Movie	27	45	20	24	21	20	18	19	20	12
KBGA Bronk	30	53	27	31	28	25	25	25	25	16
KIRT										
HUT	57									

DESOLAKE, KANSOURI   NOVEMBER, 1975

SUNDAY START TIME / STATION / PROGRAM	PROGRAM HH RTG.	SHARE	WOMEN TOT	18-34	18-49	MEN TOT	18-34	18-49	TEENS TOT 12-17	CHILDREN TOT 2-11
						RATINGS				
10:00 KNAC Nite Report	31	55	25	24	24	25	20	22	5	3
KBGA News, Weather	19	35	12	5	11	16	10	12	4	
KIRT										
HUT	50									
10:15 KNAC Nite Report	30	56	25	24	24	24	20	21	5	3
KBGA News, Weather	18	34	11	5	10	14	8	10	4	
KIRT										
HUT	48									
10:30 KNAC Sun. Night Movie	16	51	15	17	15	12	13	12	2	1
KBGA Movie	11	36	5	5	7	5	3	4	2	
KIRT										
HUT	27									
10:45 KNAC Sun. Night Movie	16	55	13	14	14	13	15	13	2	1
KBGA Movie	10	33	3	5	6	5	3	4	2	
KIRT										
HUT	26									
11:00 KNAC Sun. Night Movie	15	56	11	12	13	11	13	12	2	1
KBGA Movie	8	32	2	2	3	4	3	3		
KIRT										
HUT	23									
11:15 KNAC Sun. Night Movie	14	57	9	12	13	11	13	12		1
KBGA Movie	7	31	2	2	3	4	3	3		
KIRT										
HUT	21									
11:30 KNAC Sun. Night Movie	12	62	9	12	11	10	10	10		1
KBGA Goldsboro	5	24	2	2	1	3		1		
KIRT										
HUT	17									
11:45 KNAC Sun. Night Movie	12	69	9	14	13	8	5	7		1
KBGA Goldsboro	3	18	1	2	1	2				
KIRT										
HUT	15									
12:00 KNAC Sun. Night Movie	8	100	8	12	11	4	3	4		1
KBGA										
HUT	8									

DESOLAKE, KANSOURI

NOVEMBER, 1975

SUNDAY		PROGRAM		WOMEN			MEN			TEENS	CHIL-DREN
START TIME STATION / PROGRAM		HH RTG.	SHARE	TOT	18-34	18-49	TOT	18-34	18-49	TOT 12-17	TOT 2-11
							RATINGS				
12:15 KNAC Sun. Night Movie		7	100	5	5	7	2		1		1
HUT		7									
12:30 KNAC Sun. Night Movie		3	100	3	5	6	3		1		
HUT		3									
12:45											
1:00											
1:15											
1:30											
1:45											

Appendix 9

AVAILABLE FEATURE FILM
PACKAGES/MOVIE PRICING

PACKAGE: PREMIUM PACKAGE 2

DISTRIBUTOR: METROMEDIA PRODUCERS CORP.
                 485 Lexington Avenue
                 New York, New York

                 Telephone: (212) 682-9100

NO. OF PICTURES IN PACKAGE...........................12

NO. OF PICTURES IN COLOR.............................12

NO. OF OFF NET PICTURES..............................12

COMPOSITION OF PACKAGE BY RELEASE YEAR...............

                1970.......1
                1972.......4
                1973.......6
                1974.......1

FIVE PICTURES ARE AVAILABLE 9/1/75; SEVEN PICTURES ARE
AVAILABLE 9/1/76.

ALL PICTURES ARE MADE FOR TELEVISION.

COMPOSITION OF PACKAGE BY RUNNING LENGTH..............

                74........11
                78........ 1

NOTE: Distributor is unable to provide further network
        run projection. It is possible several of these
        films will have additional late night runs.

TITLE AND CAST	RELEASE YEAR	AVAIL. DATE	RUNNING LENGTH
CLASS OF '63 (C) James Brolin, Joan Hackett, Woodrow Chambliss, Cliff Gorman	1973	9/1/76	74
CONNECTION, THE (C) Charles Durning, Dana Wynter, Dennis Cole, Heather MacRae, Howard Cosell	1973	9/1/76	74
FIREHOUSE (C) Richard Roundtree, Andrew Duggan, Richard Jaeckel, Vince Edwards	1973	9/1/76	74
FOOTSTEPS (C) Richard Crenna, Joanna Pettet, Forrest Tucker, Clu Gulager	1972	9/1/75	74
GET CHRISTIE LOVE (C) Teresa Graves, Harry Guardino, Louise Sorel, Paul Stevens	1974	9/1/76	74
GO ASK ALICE (C) William Shatner, Ruth Roman, Wendell Burton, Julie Adams, Andy Griffith	1973	9/1/76	74
GREAT AMERICAN TRAGEDY, A (C) George Kennedy, Vera Miles, William Windom, Natalie Trundy, Kevin McCarthy	1972	9/1/76	74
MR. INSIDE/MR. OUTSIDE (C) Hal Linden, Tony LoBianco, Paul Benjamin, Phil Bruns	1973	9/1/75	74
NORLISS TAPES, THE (C) Roy Thinnes, Don Porter, Angie Dickinson, Claude Akins	1973	9/1/75	74
SANDCASTLES (C) Herschel Bernardi, Jan-Michael Vincent, Gary Crosby, Bonnie Bedelia	1972	9/1/75	74
SOUL SOLDIER (C) Rafer Johnson, Otis Taylor, Lincoln Kilpatrick, Robert Doqui, Isaac Fields, Cesar Romero	1970	9/1/75	78
YOUR MONEY OR YOUR WIFE (C) Ted Bessell, Elizabeth Ashley, Jack Cassidy, Betsy Von Furstenberg	1972	9/1/76	74

```
PACKAGE:              Universal 49

DISTRIBUTOR:          MCA
                      445 Park Avenue
                      New York, New York

                      Telephone: (212) 759-7500
```

NO. OF PICTURES IN PACKAGE.........................49

NO. OF PICTURES IN COLOR...........................49

NO. OF OFF NET PICTURES............................41

COMPOSITION OF PACKAGE BY RELEASE DATES............

```
     1974....... 6          1970.......6
     1973....... 5          1969.......2
     1972.......11          1967.......1
     1971.......17          1953.......1
```

COMPOSITION OF PACKAGE BY RUNNING TIMES............

```
     194    - 1           100 - 109 - 14
     145    - 1            90 -  99 - 21
   130 - 137 - 3           85 -  89 -  2
   120 - 129 - 3                    -
   110 - 119 - 4
```

COMPOSITION OF PACKAGE BY AVAILABILITIES...........

```
   20 are available in 1974
    5 will become available in 1975
    4 will become available in 1976
    8 will become available in 1977
    1 will become available in 1980
   11 are available now
```

TITLE AND CAST	RELEASE DATE	RUNNING TIME	AVAIL. DATE
CT OF THE HEART Genevieve Bujold, Donald Sutherland	1970	103	Now
AIRPORT Burt Lancaster, Dean Martin Helen Hayes	1970	137	10/80
ANDROMEDA STRAIN Arthur Hill, David Wayne, Kate Reid	1971	131	10/77
BEGUILED, THE Clint Eastwood, Geraldine Page, Elizabeth Hartman	1971	109	10/75

TITLE AND CAST	RELEASE DATE	RUNNING TIME	AVAIL DATE
BIRDMAN, THE Doug McClure, Richard Basehart, Chuck Connors	1971	94	10/74
BREEZY William Holden, Roger C. Carmel, JoAnne Hotchkis	1974	105	10/77
CASE OF RAPE, A Elizabeth Montgomery, Robert Karnes, Rosemary Murphy	1974	98	10/74
CHARLEY VARICK Walther Matthau, Felicia Farr, Sheree North	1973	111	10/77
CITY, THE Anthony Quinn, Robert Reed, Skye Aubrey, E.G. Marshall	1971	95	10/74
CODE NAME: HERACLITUS Stanley Baker, Leslie Nielsen, Jack Weston, Sheree North	1967	96	10/74
COUNTRY MUSIC Marty Robbins, Carl Smith, Barbara Mandrell	1972	90	Now
DIAL HOT LINE Vince Edwards, Kim Hunter	1970	97	10/74
DIARY OF A MADHOUSE WIFE Richard Benjamin, Carrie Snodgress, Frank Langella	1970	94	10/77
DRAGNET Jack Webb, Richard Boone, Ben Alexander, Stacy Harris	1953	89	Now
DUEL Dennis Weaver	1971	90	10/74
EXECUTION OF PRIVATE SLOVIK, THE Martin Sheen, Gary Busey	1974	122	10/74
GREAT NORTHFIELD MINNESOTA RAID, THE Cliff Robertson, Dana Elcar, Robert Duvall	1972	91	10/75

TITLE AND CAST	RELEASE DATE	RUNNING TIME	AVAIL. DATE
GOD BLESS THE CHILDREN George Peppard, Michael Sarrazin Christine Belford	1971	98	10/74
GROUNDSTAR CONSPIRACY, THE George Peppard, Christine Belford, Michael Sarrazin	1972	95	10/76
HIRED HAND, THE Peter Fonda, Warren Oates, Verna Bloom	1971	93	10/74
HOW TO FRAME A FIGG Don Knotts, Edward Andrews, Frank Walker	1971	103	3/72
I LOVE MY WIFE Elliot Gould, Angela Tompkins, Brenda Vaccaro	1970	95	10/74
INDICT & CONVICT Eli Wallach, George Grizzard, William Shatner, Myrna Loy	1974	98	10/74
JIGSAW Vera Miles, Edmond O'Brien, Richard Kiley	1972	98	10/74
LAST MOVIE, THE Dennis Hopper, Peter Fonda John Phillip Law	1971	105	Now
LAST OF THE POWERSEEKERS, THE Lana Turner, George Hamilton, Kevin McCarthy	1969	101	10/74
LONG CHASE, THE Buddy Ebsen, Frank Sinatra, Jr.	1972	95	10/74
MARCUS NELSON MURDERS, THE Telly Savalas, Jose Ferrer	1973	145	10/74
MARY, QUEEN OF SCOTS Vanessa Redgrave, Patrick McGoohan, Trevor Howard, Glenda Jackson	1972	128	10/76
MIDNIGHT MAN Burt Lancaster, Susan Clark, Cameron Mitchell	1974	117	10/77

TITLE AND CAST	RELEASE DATE	RUNNING TIME	AVAIL. DATE
NELSON AFFAIR, THE Glenda Jackson, Peter Finch, Anthony Quayle, Margaret Leighton	1973	117	10/77
ONE MORE TRAIN TO ROB George Peppard, Diana Muldaur	1971	108	5/72
PL IT AS IT LAYS Tuesday Weld, Tammy Grimes, Anthony Perkins	1972	102	Now
PUFNSTUF Jack Wild, Cass Elliott, Agnes Moorehead	1970	95	Now
PUZZLE OF A DOWNFALL CHILD Faye Dunaway, Viveca Lindfors, Roy Scheider	1971	104	Now
RAID ON ROMMEL Richard Burton, Danielle DeMetz	1971	99	4/72
RAILWAY CHILDREN Dinah Sheridan, Bernard Cribbins	1971	106	10/74
RED SKY AT MORNING Richard Thomas, Desi Arnaz, Jr., Claire Bloom, Catherine Burns	1971	111	10/75
S ENT RUNNING Bruce Dern, Ron Rifkin	1972	90	10/75
ORT WALK TO DAYLIGHT James Brolin, Abbey Lincoln	1972	91	10/74
SLAUGHTERHOUSE FIVE Michael Sachs, Valerie Perrine, Eugene Roche	1972	104	10/76
SUGARLAND EXPRESS, THE Goldie Hawn, Ben Johnson	1974	108	10/77
SUNSHINE Christina Raines, Brenda Vaccaro, Cliff DeYoung	1973	121	10/74
SWEET CHARITY Shirley MacLaine, Sammy Davis, Jr., Ricardo Montalban	1969	135	10/75

TITLE AND CAST	RELEASE DATE	RUNNING TIME	AVAIL. DATE
THEY MIGHT BE GIANTS George C. Scott, Joanne Woodward, Jack Gilford	1971	88	10/74
)-LANE BLACKTOP James Taylor, Warren Oates	1971	103	Now
TWO PEOPLE Peter Fonda, Lindsay Wagner, Estelle Parsons	1973	101	10/77
VANISHED Richard Widmark, Tom Bosley, Eleanor Parker, Robert Young, Skye Aubrey, James Farentino, William Shatner	1971	194	10/74
YOU'LL LIKE MY MOTHER Patty Duke, Richard Thomas, Rosemary Murphy	1972	92	10/76

RECAP OF FIRST RUNS

TITLE AND CAST	RELEASE DATE	RUNNING TIME	AVAIL. DATE
ACT OF THE HEART Genevieve Bujold, Donald Sutherland	1970	103	Now
COUNTRY MUSIC Marty Robbins, Carl Smith, Barbara Mandrell	1972	90	Now
DRAGNET Jack Webb, Richard Boone, Ben Alexander, Stacy Harris	1953	89	Now
LAST MOVIE, THE Dennis Hopper, Peter Fonda, John Phillip Law	1971	105	Now
PLAY IT AS IT LAYS Tuesday Weld, Tammy Grimes, thony Perkins	1972	102	Now

TITLE AND CAST	RELEASE DATE	RUNNING TIME	AVAIL. DATE
PUFNSTUF Jack Wild, Cass Elliott, Agnes Moorehead	1970	95	Now
PUZZLE OF A DOWNFALL CHILD Faye Dunaway, Viveca Lindfors, Roy Scheider	1971	104	Now
TWO-LANE BLACKTOP James Taylor, Warren Oates	1971	103	Now

PACKAGE: VOLUME 19

DISTRIBUTOR: WARNER BROS. TELEVISION
                           4000 Warner Boulevard
                           Burbank, California 91522

                           CONTACT: Al Unger
                           Telephone: (213) 843-6000

NO. OF PICTURES IN PACKAGE.........................30

NO. OF PICTURES IN COLOR..........................29

NO. OF OFF NETWORK PICTURES.......................30

COMPOSITION OF PACKAGE BY RELEASE DATE.............

          1973.......4   1969.......4
          1972.......2   1968.......8
          1971.......5   1967.......2
          1970.......3   1966.......2

COMPOSITION OF PACKAGE BY RUNNING TIME*............

          14 run 104 minutes or more
          12 run between 90 and 103 minutes
           4 run 75 minutes

COMPOSITION OF PACKAGE BY AVAILABILITIES...........

           3 are available in 1974
          12 become available in 1975
           8 become available in 1976
           7 become available in 1977

*All films will be issued for syndication as edited for
 network acceptance standards. If feature has not yet had
 its network run the timing listed here may be approximate
 pending network editing.

TITLE AND CAST	RELEASE DATE	RUNNING TIME	AVAIL. DATE
ARRANGEMENT, THE (C) Kirk Douglas, Faye Dunaway, Deborah Kerr	1969	116	10/1/75
BIG BOUNCE, THE (C) Ryan O'Neal, Leigh Taylor- Young, Van Heflin	1969	94	10/1/75
BIG HAND FOR THE LITTLE LADY, A (C) Henry Fonda, Joanne Woodward, Jason Robards	1966	95	10/1/75
CAMELOT (C) Richard Harris, Vanessa Redgrave, Franco Nero	1967	175	10/1/77
CHISUM (C) John Wayne, Forrest Tucker, Van Johnson	1970	111	12/30/77
CLIMB AN ANGRY MOUNTAIN (C) Fess Parker, Stella Stevens, Barry Nelson	1972	97	Now
COWBOYS, THE (C) John Wayne, Roscoe Lee Browne, Bruce Dern	1972	121	12/30/77
CRY RAPE! (C) Andrea Marcovicci, Peter Coffield, Gregg Mullavey	1973	75	5/26/75
DELIVER US FROM EVIL (C) George Kennedy, Jan-Michael Vincent, Bradford Dillman	1973	75	Now
DOUBLE MAN, THE (C) Yul Brynner, Britt Ekland, Lloyd Nolan	1968	105	9/30/75
FINIAN'S RAINBOW (C) Fred Astaire, Petula Clark, Tommy Steele	1968	141	10/1/77
FLAP (C) Anthony Quinn, Shelley Winters, Tony Bill	1970	97	9/15/75
GENESIS II (C) Alex Cord, Mariette Hartley, Percy Rodriques	1973	75	3/1/75
GOOD GUYS AND THE BAD GUYS, THE (C) Robert Mitchum, George Kennedy, Martin Balsam	1969	95	9/30/75
HARRY O (C) David Janssen, Martin Sheen, Margot Kidder	1973	75	5/7/75

TITLE AND CAST	RELEASE DATE	RUNNING TIME	AVAIL. DATE
HOTEL (C) Rod Taylor, Karl Malden, Catherine Spaak	1967	125	10/1/75
HOW SWEET IT IS! (C) James Garner, Debbie Reynolds, Terry-Thomas	1968	98	10/1/76
KLUTE (C) Jane Fonda, Donald Sutherland, Charles Cioffi	1971	108	10/1/77
MAN IN THE WILDERNESS (C) Richard Harris, John Huston, Henry Wilcoxon	1971	105	9/15/75
OMEGA MAN, THE (C) Charlton Heston, Anthony Zerbe, Rosalind Cash	1971	95	3/1/76
RACHEL, RACHEL (C) Joanne Woodward, James Olson, Estelle Parsons	1968	101	10/1/76
SERGEANT, THE (C) Rod Steiger, John Phillip Law, Ludmila Mikael	1968	94	Now
SKIN GAME (C) James Garner, Lou Gossett, Susan Clark	1971	102	9/15/76
STALKING MOON, THE (C) Gregory Peck, Eva Marie Saint, Robert Forster	1968	109	10/1/76
SUMMER OF '42 (C) Jennifer O'Neill, Gary Grimes, Jerry Houser	1971	100	12/30/77
SWEET NOVEMBER (C) Sandy Dennis, Anthony Newley, Theodore Bikel	1968	114	9/15/75
THERE WAS A CROOKED MAN (C) Kirk Douglas, Henry Fonda, Hume Cronyn	1970	119	10/1/76
THEY CAME TO ROB LAS VEGAS (C) Gary Lockwood, Elke Sommer, Jack Palance	1968	126	10/1/77
WHO'S AFRAID OF VIRGINIA WOOLF? (C) Elizabeth Taylor, Richard Burton, George Segal	1966	127	9/30/75
WILD BUNCH, THE (C) William Holden, Ernest Borgnine, Robert Ryan	1969	123	9/30/76

NETWORK RUNS

NBC-TV	NBC/CBS
ARRANGEMENT	CHISUM
BIG HAND FOR THE LITTLE LADY	
CAMELOT	
CLIMB AN ANGRY MOUNTAIN	
DOUBLE MAN	ABC/CBS
FINIAN'S RAINBOW	
KLUTE	COWBOYS
OMEGA MAN	
RACHEL, RACHEL	
THERE WAS A CROOKED MAN	
THEY CAME TO ROB LAS VEGAS	NBC/ABC
	HOTEL

ABC-TV

BIG BOUNCE
DELIVER US FROM EVIL
FLAP
HARRY O
MAN IN THE WILDERNESS
SUMMER OF '42
SWEET NOVEMBER

CBS-TV

CRY RAPE!
GENESIS II
GOOD GUYS & THE BAD GUYS
HOW SWEET IT IS
SERGEANT
SKIN GAME
STALKING MOON
WHO'S AFRAID OF VIRGINIA WOOLF?
WILD BUNCH

PACKAGE: VIACOM II

DISTRIBUTOR: VIACOM ENTERPRISES
                    345 Park Avenue
                    New York, New York

                    CONTACT: Bill Stynes
                    Telephone: (212) 371-5300

NO. OF PICTURES IN PACKAGE............................21

NO. OF PICTURES IN COLOR..............................19

NO. OF OFF NET PICTURES..............................15

NO. OF MADE-FOR-TELEVISION PICTURES....................11

COMPOSITION OF PACKAGE BY RELEASE DATE................

Pre 1960.......3	1972.......2
1966.......1	1973.......8
1970.......2	1974.......4
1971.......1	

COMPOSITION OF PACKAGE BY RUNNING TIME................

130-116.........1	99-90......8
115-110.........1	89-80......2
109-100........5	79-74......4

COMPOSITION OF PACKAGE BY AVAILABILITIES..............

1975.......14
1976....... 2
1977....... 2
1978....... 2
1979....... 1

DISTRIBUTOR HAS CAUTIONED US THAT THERE MAY BE ADDITIONAL
NETWORK SALES.

TITLE AND CAST	RELEASE YEAR	RUNNING TIME	AVAIL. DATE
AFRICAN QUEEN (C) Humphrey Bogart, Katherine Hepburn, Theodore Bikel	1951	105	9/1/75
*AUTOBIOGRAPHY OF MISS JANE PITTMAN, THE (C) Cicely Tyson, Odetta	1974	109	9/30/77
*BIRDS OF PREY (C) David Janssen, Ralph Meeker, Elayne Heivell	1973	81	10/1/76
*BLUE KNIGHT, THE (C) William Holden, Lee Remick	1973	104	5/1/75
*DIVORCE HERS (C) Elizabeth Taylor, Richard Burton	1973	74	Immediate
*DIVORCE HIS (C) Richard Burton, Elizabeth Taylor	1973	74	Immediate
*F. SCOTT FITZGERALD AND THE LAST OF THE BELLES (C) Richard Chamberlain, Blythe Danner, Susan Sarandon, David Hoffman	1974	98	9/78

TITLE AND COST	RELEASE YEAR	RUNNING TIME	AVAIL. DATE
*GARGOYLES (C) Cornel Wilde	1972	74	9/1/76
HITLER: THE LAST TEN DAYS (C) Alec Guinness, Diane Cilento	1974	105	5/1/78
*JANE EYRE (C) George C. Scott, Susannah York, Jack Hawkins	1971	108	Immediate
KING CREOLE (B&W) Elvis Presley, Walter Matthau, Carolyn Jones, Dolores Hart, Dean Jagger	1958	115	Immediate
LADY ICE (C) Jennifer O'Neill, Donald Sutherland, Robert Duvall	1973	93	7/77
McMASTERS, THE (C) Burl Ives, Brock Peters, David Carradine, Jack Palance, Nancy Kwan, Dane Clark	1970	97	Immediate
PARADISE HAWAIIAN STYLE (C) Elvis Presley, Suzanna Leigh	1966	91	Immediate
PERFECT FRIDAY (C) Stanley Baker, Ursula Andress	1970	95	Immediate
SAD SACK (B&W) Jerry Lewis, David Wayne, Phyllis Kirk, Peter Lorre	1957	98	Immediate
*STRANGER, THE (C) Glenn Corbett, Cameron Mitchell, Sharon Acker, Lew Ayres, Dean Jagger	1973	98	Immediate
*TELL ME WHERE IT HURTS (C) Maureen Stapleton, Paul Sorvino	1974	84	10/1/75
TERROR IN THE WAX MUSEUM (C) Ray Milland, Maurice Evans, Elsa Lanchester, Broderick Crawford	1973	94	3/1/79
WALKING TALL (C) Joe Don Baker, Elizabeth Hartman	1973	126	3/1/79
*WOMAN HUNTER, THE (C) Barbara Eden, Robert Vaughn, Stuart Whitman	1972	74	Immediate

*Made for TV

MOVIE PRICING

In general package pricing is determined by what the market
will bear. However, for purposes of this project, the following
will hold for each of the titles:

- $1,000.00 per <u>title</u>, not package, <u>but</u> title.

    A) This buys you exclusive rights in the market.

    B) Five plays per title over 5 years.

    C) Options.

- In addition to the cost per title, the distributor
  gets $100.00 per color movie each time it's telecast;
  $10.00 for B&W.

If you wish to buy the entire package from a distributor and
hold the movies at the station for your contract period, there is
a $450.00 charge per title for color; $200 for B&W.

Appendix 10

AVAILABLE SYNDICATED PROGRAMMING

AVAILABLE SYNDICATED PROGRAMMING - SERIES PRESENTLY
UNSOLD IN DESOLAKE MARKET

Program	Length (Minutes)	Price Per Telecast**	Type
Adventurer	30	$115.00	O
Animal World	30	Barter	O
Audubon Wildlife Theatre	30	90.00	O
Beat The Clock	30	65.00	S
Best of Groucho	30	35.00	S
Bobby Vinton Show	30	250.00	O
Bowery Boys	60	25.00	Movie Package
Concentration	30	70.00	O
Circus	30	100.00	O
Dealer's Choice	30	50.00	O
Diamond Head	30	55.00	O

AVAILABLE SYNDICATED PROGRAMMING – SERIES PRESENTLY
UNSOLD IN DESOLAKE MARKET (Continued)

Program	Length (Minutes)	Price Per Telecast**	Type
Dinah	60/90	25.00/40.00	S
Doctor In The House	30	125.00	O
Dusty's Trail	30	150.00	O
Evil Touch	30	75.00	O
Gilligan's Island	30	40.00	S
Great Mysteries	30	110.00	O
High Rollers*	30	140.00	O
Hollywood Screen Test	30	150.00	O
Jeopardy*	30	175.00	O
Lassie	30	15.00	S
Last of The Wild	30	Barter	O
Let's Make A Deal	30	285.00	O
Masquerade Party	30	100.00	O
Match Game*	30	115.00	O
Merv Griffin	60/90	15.00/25.00	S
Mickey Mouse Club	30	30.00	S
National Geographic	60	115.00	O
New Zoo Revue	30	20.00	S
Not For Women Only	30	15.00	S
Other People/Other Places	30	Barter	S
Ozzie's Girls	30	100.00	O
Phil Donahue	90	30.00	S
Price Is Right*	30	160.00	O
Protectors	30	Barter	O
Safari To Adventure	30	75.00	O
Sale of the Century	30	130.00	S
Salty, The Sea Lion	30	155.00	O
To Tell The Truth	30	100.00	S

AVAILABLE SYNDICATED PROGRAMMING - SERIES PRESENTLY
UNSOLD IN DESOLAKE MARKET (Continued)

Program	Length (Minutes)	Price Per Telecast**	Type
Thrillseekers	30	190.00	O
Treasure Hunt	30	175.00	O
Wait 'Til Father Gets Home	30	160.00	
What's My Line?	30	90.00	S
World of Survival	30	Barter	O

Barter - No charge for program--station receives 2 minutes and
         program, syndicator sells remaining 3 minutes nationally.

O = Once a week   S = Strip (5 per week)

*Available for scheduling in Prime Access or Prime Time periods only

**Contracts for purchase of syndicated programs are normally for 52-
weeks, firm. While the price per telecast is often negotiable, the
unit price, once agreed upon is multiplied by 52. Thus, for example,
if KIRT purchases Adventurer at the "card rate" of $115/episode, the
total annual outlay for this once-a-week series is $5,980 -- without
regard to the number of "originals" or "repeats" involved.

Appendix 11

SYNDICATED PROGRAM HISTORY, BY TYPE

<u>ADVENTURE</u>

Program Name	Women Total VPH	Women 18-49 VPH	Men Total VPH	Men 18-49 VPH	Adult Total VPH	Adult 18-49 VPH
Wild Kingdom	.74	.39	.73	.40	1.47	.79
Wild-World of Animals	.72	.36	.67	.36	1.40	.72
Animal World	.70	.34	.65	.34	1.35	.68
World of Survival	.69	.34	.68	.35	1.37	.69
Protectors	.77	.48	.68	.44	1.45	.92
Outdoors	.55	.27	.74	.41	1.29	.68
Other People-Other Places	.66	.33	.66	.36	1.31	.70
Batman	.18	.14	.17	.14	.35	.28
Tarzan	.56	.43	.49	.37	1.05	.79
Safari To Adventure	.70	.26	.68	.28	1.38	.54
Untamed World	.63	.33	.64	.33	1.27	.66
Thrillseekers	.59	.41	.73	.52	1.32	.92
Superman	.29	.25	.30	.26	.58	.50
Audubon Wildlife Threatre	.67	.29	.68	.29	1.34	.58
Flipper	.41	.27	.24	.14	.65	.41
Land of Giants	.56	.43	.46	.37	1.02	.80
Daktari	.36	.22	.34	.27	.70	.49
Lassie	.49	.29	.36	.21	.85	.50
Gentle Ben	.43	.33	.26	.20	.69	.53

Program Name	Women Total VPH	Women 18-49 VPH	Men Total VPH	Men 18-49 VPH	Adult Total VPH	Adult 18-49 VPH
Jeff's Collie	.23	.21	.15	.13	.39	.35
American Outdoorsman	.59	.39	.74	.47	1.32	.86
Call It Macaroni	.54	.37	.53	.40	1.07	.77
Rat Patrol	.46	.36	.61	.39	1.07	.76
Robin Hood	.42	.31	.36	.31	.78	.61

AUDIENCE PARTICIPATION

New Candid Camera	.79	.48	.65	.40	1.44	.89
Let's Make A Deal	.79	.40	.58	.29	1.37	.68
Truth or Consequences	.75	.38	.52	.26	1.27	.64
Dealers Choice	.72	.33	.50	.22	1.22	.56
Diamond Head Game	.70	.36	.41	.20	1.11	.56

CHILDREN

Mickey Mouse	.23	.20	.13	.11	.35	.35
Flintstones	.21	.18	.14	.11	.35	.29
Bugs Bunny	.13	.12	.13	.11	.26	.23
Little Rascals	.31	.26	.31	.26	.62	.52
3 Stooges	.22	.19	.29	.26	.51	.45
Popeye	.16	.13	.13	.12	.29	.25
Big Blue Marble	.33	.22	.27	.18	.61	.40
New Zoo Revue	.11	.09	.04	.04	.15	.13
Underdog	.11	.10	.09	.08	.21	.18
Rainbow Sundae	.58	.38	.50	.33	1.09	.72
Speed Racer	.11	.10	.07	.06	.19	.16
Huck and Yogi	.12	.11	.07	.06	.20	.17
Porky Pig	.13	.10	.10	.09	.23	.19
Banana Splits	.08	.07	.06	.05	.14	.12
Bullwinkle	.18	.14	.15	.13	.33	.27
Jabberwocky	.20	.16	.19	.14	.39	.30
Romper Room	.15	.10	.06	.03	.21	.14
Bozo	.16	.14	.07	.04	.23	.18
Mister Magoo	.11	.09	.11	.09	.22	.18
Lidsville	.15	.12	.08	.06	.23	.18
Sesame Street	.17	.15	.04	.03	.21	.18
H.R. Pufnstuf	.11	.09	.05	.04	.16	.13
Tennessee Tuxedo	.16	.13	.11	.09	.27	.22
Spiderman	.12	.11	.18	.17	.30	.28
Vision On	.27	.19	.18	.13	.45	.32
Captain Noah	.20	.15	.06	.05	.27	.20
Brother Buzz	.31	.06	.13	.01	.43	.07
Mission Magic	.19	.15	.13	.12	.32	.26
Linus The Lionhearted	.11	.08	.16	.13	.27	.21
Uncle Waldo	.20	.16	.09	.09	.29	.24

SITUATION COMEDY

Bewitched	.51	.39	.30	.22	.82	.62
Gilligan's Island	.27	.22	.19	.15	.47	.37
Hogan's Heroes	.46	.33	.54	.39	1.00	.71
Andy Griffith	.56	.42	.44	.32	1.00	.74
Beverly Hillbillies	.56	.40	.44	.32	1.00	.71

SITUATION COMEDY (continued)

Program	Women Total VPH	Women 18-49 VPH	Men Total VPH	Men 18-49 VPH	Adult Total VPH	Adult 18-49 VPH
I Dream of Jeannie	.45	33	.31	.23	.75	.56
Lucy Show	.53	.37	.30	.20	.82	.57
Partridge Family	.46	.37	.26	.20	.72	.57
Family Affair	.63	.39	.36	.22	.99	.61
I Love Lucy	.47	.39	.22	.18	.69	.57
Gomer Pyle USMC	.45	.34	.37	.28	.82	.62
Green Acres	.44	.33	.32	.23	.76	.55
That Girl	.63	.48	.34	.25	.97	.73
Dick Van Dyke	.56	.46	.35	.27	.91	.73
Leave It To Beaver	.35	.30	.23	.18	.58	.48
Best of Groucho	.69	.45	.66	.47	1.35	.92
Petticoat Junction	.44	.30	.27	.19	.70	.49
Love American Style	.61	.46	.49	.37	1.10	.82
Munsters	.28	.24	.21	.17	.50	.41
Get Smart	.35	.28	.42	.35	.76	.62
Father Knows Best	.54	.43	.24	.18	.79	.61
House of Frightenstein	.09	.08	.09	.08	.18	.16
Bowery Boys	.46	.39	.37	.31	.83	.70
F. Troop	.41	.33	.49	.39	.90	.72
Mister Ed	.15	.12	.12	.10	.27	.22
Dennis The Menace	.17	.14	.09	.08	.26	.23
Addams Family	.29	.24	.20	.16	.49	.39
Mothers In Law	.43	.35	.15	.12	.58	.47
Laurel & Hardy	.52	.36	.59	.42	1.11	.79
McHale's Navy	.42	.32	.43	.33	.85	.65
Bill Cosby	.37	.25	.31	.22	.68	.48
Nanny and the Professor	.43	.31	.18	.15	.60	.46
Hazel	.61	.45	.24	.16	.85	.61
Ozzie's Girls	.75	.53	.47	.32	1.21	.85
Mayberry RFD	.61	.42	.37	.27	.98	.69
Courtship-Eddie's Father	.57	.43	.25	.17	.82	.60
My Favorite Martian	.35	.28	.31	.23	.66	.51
Flying Nun	.34	.29	.12	.08	.46	.36
Here Come The Brides	.66	.51	.47	.33	1.13	.84
Dusty's Trail	.46	.27	.27	.11	.72	.38
Real McCoys	.45	.38	.35	.25	.81	.62
Honeymooners	.55	.45	.55	.39	1.11	.84

DOCUMENTARY

	Women Total VPH	Women 18-49 VPH	Men Total VPH	Men 18-49 VPH	Adult Total VPH	Adult 18-49 VPH
Last of the Wild	.72	.37	.68	.36	1.40	.73
World At War	.56	.34	.83	.53	1.38	.87
National Geographic	.67	.33	.71	.38	1.38	.71
Friends of Man	.65	.34	.62	.35	1.27	.69
Big Battles	.44	.28	.87	.56	1.31	.84
Lloyd Bridges Water World	.61	.39	.64	.40	1.25	.80
Secrets of the Deep	.64	.39	.61	.36	1.26	.75
Victory At Sea	.50	.32	.78	.56	1.29	.88
Journey to Adventure	.60	.16	.51	.20	1.11	.36
Changing Times	.66	.44	.46	.33	1.11	.77
Proud Country	.79	.50	.48	.21	1.28	.71

GENERAL DRAMA

Program	Women Total VPH	Women 18-49 VPH	Men Total VPH	Men 18-49 VPH	Adult Total VPH	Adult 18-49 VPH
Police Surgeon	.80	.48	.63	.38	1.42	.86
Room 222	.57	.47	.38	.30	.95	.77
Bold Ones	.75	.45	.54	.32	1.29	.77
Combat	.46	.40	.76	.66	1.23	1.05
Family Classics	.40	.35	.40	.35	.80	.69
Run For Your Life	.78	.50	.58	.36	1.36	.86

EVENING ANIMATION

Program	Women Total VPH	Women 18-49 VPH	Men Total VPH	Men 18-49 VPH	Adult Total VPH	Adult 18-49 VPH
Wait til Father Gets Home	.58	.44	.42	.31	1.01	.74

INTERVIEW

Program	Women Total VPH	Women 18-49 VPH	Men Total VPH	Men 18-49 VPH	Adult Total VPH	Adult 18-49 VPH
Mike Douglas Show-090	.80	.35	.38	.15	1.18	.50
Merv Griffin Show-090	.82	.27	.42	.13	1.23	.40
Dinah-90	.83	.36	.29	.11	1.12	.47
Dinah-60	.82	.36	.27	.11	1.09	.47
Phil Donahue Show	.83	.41	.27	.12	1.10	.53
Mike Douglas Show-060	.81	.39	.33	.15	1.14	.54
Not For Women Only	.77	.33	.18	.08	.94	.41
Merv Griffin Show-060	.79	.36	.35	.17	1.13	.53
David Susskind	.71	.38	.60	.35	1.30	.72
Reed Farrell	.57	.31	.14	.05	.71	.36
Consultation	.69	.24	.41	.16	1.10	.41
PTL Club	.69	.31	.15	.08	.85	.38

MYSTERY & SUSPENSE

Program	Women Total VPH	Women 18-49 VPH	Men Total VPH	Men 18-49 VPH	Adult Total VPH	Adult 18-49 VPH
Ironside	.76	.41	.54	.29	1.31	.70
FBI	.73	.40	.64	.35	1.37	.75
Mod Squad	.65	.45	.48	.32	1.12	.77
Dragnet	.70	.43	.63	.39	1.33	.82
Mission Impossible	.65	.45	.62	.45	1.27	.90
Untouchables	.59	.39	.74	.51	1.33	.91
Name of the Game	.76	.46	.57	.37	1.33	.83
Perry Mason	.77	.43	.49	.28	1.26	.72
It Takes a Thief	.65	.49	.61	.46	1.26	.95
My Partner The Ghost	.72	.52	.56	.42	1.28	.94
Evil Touch	.82	.61	.70	.51	1.52	1.13
Night Gallery	.68	.56	.66	.55	1.34	1.11
Avengers	.59	.48	.64	.52	1.23	.99
N.Y.P.D.	.74	.46	.70	.43	1.44	.89
Great Mysteries- O.Welles	.80	.50	.62	.41	1.42	.90
Saint	.54	.32	.52	.31	1.06	.64
I Spy	.59	.44	.56	.44	1.14	.88
Department S	.57	.37	.53	.35	1.09	.72
Alfred Hitchcock	.77	.52	.58	.39	1.35	.91
Step Beyond	.64	.45	.55	.38	1.19	.84

MYSTERY & SUSPENSE (continued)

Program Name	Women Total VPH	Women 18-49 VPH	Men Total VPH	Men 18-49 VPH	Adult Total VPH	Adult 18-49 VPH
Thriller	.63	.44	.59	.43	1.21	.86
Persuaders	.73	.52	.62	.49	1.35	1.01
Felony Squad	.68	.42	.72	.45	1.41	.87
Secret Agent	.43	.35	.57	.37	1.00	.73
Adventurer	.77	.43	.77	.47	1.53	.90

VARIETY MUSICAL

Program Name	Women Total VPH	Women 18-49 VPH	Men Total VPH	Men 18-49 VPH	Adult Total VPH	Adult 18-49 VPH
Lawrence Welk Show	.90	.27	.60	.18	1.50	.44
Hee Haw	.79	.47	.72	.42	1.52	.89
Nashville Music	.82	.42	.64	.32	1.47	.73
Bobby Goldsboro	.79	.51	.57	.36	1.36	.87
Porter Wagoner	.82	.44	.65	.33	1.46	.77
Soul Train	.76	.64	.44	.37	1.20	1.01
Pop Goes Country	.81	.50	.65	.39	1.46	.89
Jimmy Dean Show	.77	.38	.61	.31	1.38	.69
Buck Owens Show	.78	.41	.60	.28	1.38	.70
Wilburn Brothers	.82	.45	.62	.33	1.44	.77
Rock Concert	.50	.41	.60	.54	1.10	.95
Hank Thompson	.74	.40	.59	.31	1.33	.72
Arthur Smith Show	.80	.48	.53	.30	1.34	.77
Chmielewski Fun Time	.77	.24	.66	.19	1.43	.43
Party	.75	.64	.47	.38	1.22	1.02
Country Carnival	.83	.46	.61	.32	1.45	.78
Country Place	.81	.36	.59	.27	1.40	.62
Dick Rodgers	.78	.30	.69	.25	1.47	.55
Tom Jones	.82	.51	.59	.32	1.41	.83
R.F.D. Hollywood	.81	.52	.61	.26	1.42	.77
Right On	.80	.47	.53	.47	1.33	.93
George & Diane Ivey	.86	.36	.29	.14	1.14	.50

QUIZ GIVE AWAY

Program Name	Women Total VPH	Women 18-49 VPH	Men Total VPH	Men 18-49 VPH	Adult Total VPH	Adult 18-49 VPH
New Price Is Right	.83	.44	.57	.29	1.40	.73
Hollywood Squares	.84	.42	.58	.30	1.41	.72
Name That Tune	.84	.46	.55	.30	1.39	.76
New Treasure Hunt	.80	.42	.55	.29	1.34	.71
$25,000 Pyramid	.84	.47	.55	.30	1.39	.77
Celebrity Sweepstakes	.83	.51	.60	.38	1.43	.89
Jeopardy	.84	.42	.55	.29	1.39	.71
Masquerade Party	.82	.44	.56	.32	1.38	.76
Concentration	.78	.36	.44	.21	1.22	.56
Beat The Clock	.67	.39	.40	.22	1.08	.61

SPORTS EVENT & COMMENT.

Program Name	Women Total VPH	Women 18-49 VPH	Men Total VPH	Men 18-49 VPH	Adult Total VPH	Adult 18-49 VPH
Wrestling	.48	.30	.77	.49	1.25	.79
Championship Fishing	.49	.28	.80	.47	1.29	.75
Bowling For Dollars	.81	.39	.63	.30	1.44	.69
Sportsman's Friend	.47	.27	.66	.39	1.13	.66
Celebrity Bowling	.66	.35	.56	.32	1.22	.67
Facts of Fishing	.32	.16	.78	.42	1.10	.58

Program	Women Total VPH	Women 18-49 VPH	Men Total VPH	Men 18-49 VPH	Adult Total VPH	Adult 18-49 VPH
Roller Games	.58	.34	.67	.41	1.26	.74
Greatest Sports Legends	.49	.32	.67	.41	1.16	.74
Celebrity Tennis	.59	.33	.50	.35	1.09	.68
Boxing	.30	.17	.87	.41	1.17	.58
Bowling	.61	.26	.72	.33	1.32	.59
Fisherman	.59	.28	.69	.35	1.28	.64
American Ski Scene	.57	.36	.63	.42	1.21	.78
Outdoor Sportsman	.34	.17	.84	.47	1.18	.64
Lucky Jim	.50	.29	.74	.43	1.24	.72
Roller Game of Week	.56	.33	.68	.38	1.24	.71
Bill Hoffman Ski Show	.63	.38	.78	.60	1.41	.99
Fishing Hole	.53	.27	.73	.40	1.27	.67

SCIENCE FICTION

Program	Women Total VPH	Women 18-49 VPH	Men Total VPH	Men 18-49 VPH	Adult Total VPH	Adult 18-49 VPH
Star Trek	.51	.44	.57	.49	1.08	.93
Lost In Space	.32	.27	.31	.26	.63	.53
Outer Limits	.58	.47	.56	.48	1.14	.95
Twilight Zone	.57	.39	.66	.52	1.23	.91
Time Tunnel	.60	.47	.55	.43	1.15	.90
Voyage To-Bottom of-Sea	.43	.39	.48	.42	.92	.81
U F O	.40	.31	.51	.41	.91	.72

GENERAL VARIETY

Program	Women Total VPH	Women 18-49 VPH	Men Total VPH	Men 18-49 VPH	Adult Total VPH	Adult 18-49 VPH
Circus	.56	.28	.50	.28	1.06	.57

WESTERN DRAMA

Program	Women Total VPH	Women 18-49 VPH	Men Total VPH	Men 18-49 VPH	Adult Total VPH	Adult 18-49 VPH
Bonanza	.65	.37	.54	.31	1.19	.67
Big Valley	.69	.44	.46	.27	1.15	.71
Wild Wild West	.52	.36	.59	.43	1.11	.80
Daniel Boone	.60	.39	.56	.36	1.16	.75
Virginian	.74	.43	.53	.30	1.27	.73
High Chaparral	.69	.41	.56	.33	1.25	.74
Rifleman	.55	.37	.54	.35	1.09	.72
Lone Ranger	.43	.33	.53	.42	.96	.75
Death Valley	.71	.44	.63	.36	1.34	.81
Wagon Train	.78	.52	.54	.33	1.32	.85
Cisco Kid	.49	.36	.52	.42	1.01	.78
Wanted Dead or Alive	.61	.35	.58	.33	1.19	.68
Lancer	.78	.51	.53	.31	1.31	.82
Major Admas	.55	.29	.51	.29	1.06	.59
Have Gun Will Travel	.54	.33	.70	.43	1.24	.76

Appendix 12

THE ROLE OF THE CONSULTANT
Address by Philip McHugh, President, McHugh
and Hoffman, Inc., November 12, 1975

PHILIP L. MCHUGH, President, McHugh and Hoffman, Inc., has been in the radio, television, agency field since 1936, starting with a radio directing job at Notre Dame University. In 1938, he joined the CBS Radio Network in New York in the research department, but shortly shifted to becoming an associate network producer. His career was interrupted by the war, but after four years in the Navy, he returned to CBS in 1946 as a Network Program Director. During his years at CBS, he also worked with Paul White as a radio network News Director, helping to develop White's famous prototype of the daily round-up of events for CBS News.

He left CBS in 1948 to enter the radio program packaging business. In 1950, Mr. McHugh moved to the Tracey-Locke Agency in Dallas, Texas, as Radio-Television Director for four years.

From 1954 to 1962, Mr. McHugh was Vice President, Radio-Television Director of Campbell-Ewald Company in Detroit. Under his management, radio-television billings rose from $4 million to $40 million a year. He purchased and supervised a succession of outstanding wholly-sponsored commercial vehicles for Campbell-Ewald's clients, such as the *Dinah Shore* and *Bob Hope Chevy Shows, Eyewitness to History, High Adventure, My Three Sons, Route 66* and *Bonanza*. During these years, Chevrolet was also the leading sponsor of radio network newscasts, and Delco was brought in as full sponsor of Lowell Thomas' weekly newscasts. It was also during these years that Mr. McHugh and Mr. Hoffman turned to the social scientist research companies to augment and explain why ratings turned out the way they did, and develop a predictive research form to determine how programs would perform under network competition.

In February of 1962, Mr. McHugh resigned from Campbell-Ewald and formed McHugh and Hoffman, Inc., the first consulting company to examine through social research and make specific recommendations for improvement in the mass communications field, particularly television and radio. Since that time, the company's clients have included all three major networks and almost all of the key group-owned stations, as well as many of the leading independently-owned facilities.

McHugh: Four years ago we ran an ad in *Broadcasting* and the headline was: "It's news." And the first paragraph of the copy went:

> The things you've been hearing from various researchers and consultants are true. It's news, your station's news that makes the difference between being first and out of the running in your market. Local television news develops a warm, trusting and dependent relationship between the audience and the station that is essential to success, and it does it on a daily basis. The feeling that people have about the number one news station overflows into almost all the other areas of its programming. It gives you first chance at the audience for entertainment as well as information programming. If you doubt this just check how many stations are number one in total day share that don't lead in news. Very few, and almost none in the key markets . . .

News is also—and I'm really sad to say this—the last bastion of local programming. Local programming has descended hour by hour, minute by minute, to a point where there almost isn't any. Other than public affairs and news. So when you talk about what you do with the station you are devising, you must concentrate on news because of the dependent relationshp your audience has with it. The audience has made news on television their primary source for news. And there hasn't been a single study that conflicts with that statement. Therefore, the number one station for news in the market, is the number one *source* for news in that market. Interestingly enough, in most markets, even though it may be one of two, three, four or seven stations, that station's circulation—between the two newscasts—exceeds the circulation of any of the newspapers in town.

It's a very complex business, this relationship between the audience and your station in the news area. And it has become much more complicated recently with the introduction of ENG, the electronic camera which is more abused than properly used. It is being used now simply because people have it. But that's not too different from the way we used television itself when we first got it. We watched the damned picture as long as it moved and it didn't make any difference whether it was wrestling, or Mickey Mouse, or what. As long as something moved on the screen, we watched it.

The same sort of thing's going on now with ENG. ENG is a promotional tool now, more than it is a news tool. But we're learning to use it and, when we do, it will further complicate everyone's life because news directors will have to find reporters of a kind that are almost gone now. Reporters who can think on their feet. The old Bob Trouts who could ad lib for 25 minutes when all hell was breaking loose and never miss a beat, never let you know that they don't know what is going on. The newspaper has always had the advantage of being able to cover a story from an endless number of angles. The television reporter, particularly with ENG, has only one, or at most, two, and a plug in his ear through which somebody else tries to tell him what's going on else-where. His opportunity to evaluate is very limited. ENG will require, ul-timately, reporters with fantastic background, knowledge, and information. There will probably also have to be a system of relief reporters since no one man can stand up to an eight-hour shootout in the local jail. ENG is here, ENG is the coming thing, ENG will be an extremely useful tool. But ENG will put a tremendous demand on the news director and on management when it is used properly and not merely as an insert tool, it will require a new kind of journal-ism and we're only just on the threshhold.

Does ENG belong in your plans for the 75th market? Well, it's in the 96th market already so I guess it belongs in the 75th. Actually, those who have been the footdraggers with respect to ENG are in the large markets, not so much because they didn't want to get into it, but because the large markets are fraught with the kind of union problems smaller markets simply don't have.

Historically, television news started out as radio news read in front of a camera. The material was ripped off a machine and read, the same as it was on radio newscasts. And somehow that worked and people watched. It took 15 minutes—five minutes of news, five minutes of weather and five minutes of sports. And then, one day, KNXT in Los Angeles decided that it might be a pretty good idea to expand. They were the first to go to a half hour. Being pretty gutsy, they were later the first to go an hour. I remember one time sitting with Bob Wood, then the general manager of KNXT. He told me that he wanted KNXT to be the single biggest source of news west of the Mississippi River. That was his philosophy in those days and they tried very hard to make it so. But KNXT is no longer the number one station in Los Angeles.

And that brings up another interesting point which you should consider. There are only five stations in 75 markets that have remained number one all these years. There's a phenomenon I don't completely understand but I know to be predictable. It's absolute and you can count on it. With the exception of those five stations, there's something about becoming a successful news station and getting the number one figures and getting the number one money. A news department need not be the huge expense it is reported to be. It can be a profit center. If you run it well, it can be *the* profit center of the station. And if your news is number one, that means the number one money. But the difficulty is that somehow, when you become number one, the Goddamnedest atrophy the world has ever known sets in. You feel that from then on whatever you do is inherently right. The sales department knows it is right because they are out there selling. They will fight any change. The manager knows it is right because he's making good money, the bonuses are good, and he can play more golf. Everybody feels very good.

That's the beginning of the end. It occurs about a year to a year and a half or longer before the ratings begin to drop. We uncover it mostly through the use of the social scientist in in-home interviewing with open-end questionnaires. When there is a change in the market it develops in a predictable way. Things get a little sloppy and we never see our competitor the way he really is. We are never able to look at him objectively because we are too much involved in what we are doing. The changes occur very slowly; it is like a child growing up. The child is growing a little every day but you don't see it if it is your child in your house. You really only notice it when you take the annual picture or when you have to buy new shoes in order to keep up with this growing child. When things go to hell in a station, that's the way they happen—a little bit every day. You develop your own set of excuses. So the film didn't come up when the director cut to it; the reporter didn't do quite as good a job today; the film wasn't quite as well edited. So the organization of the newscast wasn't as good. But that's only today—generally we do a better job. Everybody knows that.

With in-home interviewing and open-ended questionnaires, the respondents can tell you how they are feeling as opposed to what they may have reported in a diary. This is a very important difference, and it is why there is a time lag between reality and the Nielsen and ARB ratings. When the affection of an audience begins to move from the station which has been the number one station, the home station for news, it moves the way affections begin to move in life. If a man and a woman have decided in a marriage that they are not going to make it, they don't come right out and say so. First they begin to feel. They hardly want to admit it to themselves. Over a period of time, and maybe after a lot of battles, they begin to say it to each other and then, gradually, to their close friends, maybe. Ultimately, at the point when they go to the divorce court, everybody comes to know. But that takes a long time.

When an audience moves, it starts in the same way. They have a sense of loyalty. If they are filling out a diary and they usually watch the news on station A, they say they watched station A even if they watched the competitor's news on the night before. They tend to mark the diary to be nice to a friend, to be nice to someone they've always liked. When we go in and do a study, an in-home questionaire, we find that out. We find that they actually watched the news on another station. They found something on that station that they hadn't seen before. They responded differently. But they aren't going to put that in the diary. Not yet. Not for a year or so. The change in affection takes place slowly, and is very unlike the changes that take place in prime time programming. Prime time viewing is for fun, for entertainment. The audience doesn't mind switching one way or the other. But when you go back home, as it were, to find out what happened today, you tend to go back to a specific station. If for one reason or another you are forced to watch a station you don't usually watch, you will tolerate it. More often than not the experience merely reinforces your feeling about the station you favor.

When the transition occurs, when the audience starts to move, there no longer is any lag time for correction. The first time the rating book comes in and shows the station down a point or two, you very logically say it is the margin of error. It can be; the margin of error in a rating book very often makes a station either first or third in a highly competitive market, a very interesting phenomenon that not much attention is paid to. But the change is deliberate and is a change in imagery. The audience simply says they like this new guy, they like this station, its method of presentation, whatever it was that attracted them. The change becomes very solid and the second rating book comes in. Now it is confirmed. . . . Panic.

"Do something! Whatever the hell it is, do something! Get a new act! Change the set! Nothing better than that. Give it a fresh look. Get a new anchorman! Get a new weatherman! Never did like that weatherman. The sports guy—let's change him.''

In your panic you tend to drive away what is left of your loyal fans. You multiply the error. Then you find yourself in a situation like WBBM-TV in Chicago. It's in the book for anyone to see. WBBM-TV, golden for years and years. Nobody believed it could happen, you could have gotten a bet with anyone in the industry at any odds in the world—but WBBM-TV went from first to fourth place. When the audience leaves your news they leave. And the only way you can get them back is to become so much better than the competitor in very way that the vierwer becomes unhappy with something that has become a new habit, very important to him and his primary source for finding out what happened today. You have to make him so unhappy that he'll move again. That's very hard to do.

There is a feeling generated somewhere—and we see it permeating the air when we make new business presentations—that there must be some kind of magic formula. Well, whether you open with music or open with the lead story; whether your anchorman opens or the reporter on the scene, it won't affect the ratings. Whether your set is green or blue; whether you line the people up; whether you put them in a circle, or in a row, or whatever; it hasn't a damned thing to do with your rating. What you should start with in designing the set is the kind of arrangement in the space available that will make it most comfortable for the people who have to use it, that will make it easy for them to interrelate when they have to and that will make it easy to do the electronic things that have to be done. Beyond that, what you do with it is completely unimportant.

What *is* important is what the audience reacts to when they turn the set on to find out what happened today. They did not come to the set to see anything but the news and you had better bring them the news. If everything that's on the set, if everything you are doing doesn't contribute to the development of the audience's understanding of the newscast, or what happened today and how it relates to them, then all the trimmings don't mean a thing. You can change trimmings forever; they won't change ratings for you.

Most people still look for the magic formula. There isn't any. To be successful on news for any station is rotten lousy hard work. It goes on every day. It requires thoroughness that goes beyond the news director, with all his attributes. Those attributes are many. When you think of a news director for the station you plan, think of someone who has graduated from Medill or some place like that, with a masters degree. Look for that but also look for something else. Look for a news director who is a psychologist, a baby sitter, an accountant. Look for a guy who can fight—a guy who doesn't mind being a scapegoat for almost everything that happens on the station. The news director is your first line of offensive defense. If things go well, he may get you sued for $3 or $4 million; if things don't go well, he may lose your anchorman for you. As Steve Fentress puts it, the news director has moved up from the back of the bus. He rides with top management now. He *is* top management. A good newscast starts with a good news director. He knows what he's doing and he knows where to hire the people who know what they're doing.

To be successful goes well beyond that news director. You almost can't pick out the most important person on the team. It is *the team itself*. Minimally, it is the people on the air. It is also the support team. If I had to pick out a single location where it is important to have someone who really knows what he is doing, it is the *assignment desk*. It's easy enough to get someone who will take all the handouts from the Elks' Club, who can list who will be there at lunch, who knows what meetings the City Council is going to have and the fact that the dog ran away from the fire department. All that's easy. But being perceptive, digging under, asking how the town really works, understanding the town so that he knows where to send people for stories he can't even be sure are really there is a very difficult job. If you get that kind of assignment editor it will be nearly impossible to keep him because there are about 700 other stations that are looking for him. Don't overlook the importance of the assignment editor. You can't put on the air what you don't bring into the shop. Without the assignment editor, without what he brings in, you go back to running whatever the reporters happened to pick up on their way to and fro.

The coverage of news is dependent on a very few people. A station that claims to have five news teams—they may be crews or individuals depending on the size of the market—is really operating with three-and-a-half because they have to cover seven days with people who work only five. Three-and-a-half teams or three-and-a-half individuals in a small market to cover what went on today. It makes it very complicated. We had a client in a Southern city—I won't name the market because it would embarrass them; it embarrasses me even to know about it. Our client was very powerful in the community, owns the leading newspaper, which publishes a morning and evening edition, and also a 50,000 watt radio station in addition to a television station. We presented a study to them which indicated that their television station was doing a pretty lousy job. The report caused a lot of discussion and dissension. Because this was not a huge corporate ownership but a family-owned business, the publisher was in the meeting. They had seven teams to cover their town for television. We talked about ways to get better coverage through the assignment desk, more teams, changing the work week. There was a lot of resistance; this would cost money and the news department was already eating up dollars. I simply turned to the publisher and asked "How many reporters are there on the newspaper?" "200." More people watched his newscasts, cumulatively, than read his newspaper. Yet it was very logical to him to have 200 reporters on the newspaper but to be fussing over whether there should be five, seven or eight people covering the news for television.

That kind of logic, unfortunately, is pervasive in our business. And yet, one of the things that will be happening is that the percentage of profit the television broadcaster has traditionally made will decline. No longer can the broadcaster look to increased set circulation of the kind prevalent over the last ten years. No longer can he look for anything but tougher and tougher competition. One thing the more professional news director and the consultant have brought is a higher level of acceptable news broadcasting in almost every market. The level keeps going up. That means that the coverage is better, the newscasts are better put together, they cost more money. If it costs more money you have to find a place to get the money. Some of it is going to come out of the traditional percentage of profit. Whether or not that profit is too high or too low, (and it varies from station to station), the old idea that you could buy a station and pay for it in five years is long gone. The business was founded on that idea.

There are a lot of reasons why the investment in news gathering and in news presentation will continue to increase. The business has its hands full with union problems. This year, we have gone through the greatest raiding of talent ever known. It has inflated the prices of anchormen so astronomically that you wonder how in the world a station can pay for them. But when you think that in New York City a rating point in news is worth pretty close to a million dollars a year, and when you think that the guy you are after will bring you two rating points, everybody figures "Boy, let's get him!" And that means you pay for him. I think that bubble is going to burst.

It is a very interesting set of circumstances that brought this about over the years. When we were back with our reader in the 15-minute newscast, mostly straight off the AP or INS machines, it was simply the personality of the individual who read the news to you that made you select Station A over Station B. Then, over a period of time, there developed a circumstance where content became terribly important. You began to look for electronic journalism, the news that made use of film, that made use of pictures and got away from the "pundit style," as I call it—where the attitude of the presenter, the anchorman, says to you, "Now hear this, Goddamn it! This is the news because I say it is the news." Despite *The New York Times* and its style, news is news because it is what happened today. That's what you began to look for, an intelligent presentation about what happened today. You could see it in the pictures, you could be there, you could feel how it felt. The reporter wasn't standing on the Courthouse steps saying, "There's a helluva riot going on over there . . ." He was down in there and all the sounds of the riot, the arguments and the friction were there, and you could make up your own mind about what was going on. Reporter involvement.

As that developed, it enhanced the news. Costs went up, loyalties changed, and it became obvious that somebody had been working very hard to make it happen. And what happened was that the accent went from the anchorman to the content. In one particular market—I can't tell you which—as we studied a station evolving into number one over a two or three year period, the anchorman was a two per cent favorite. The station was evolving into number one, in an extremely important market, because what happened on the newscast was important. The station became number one and it made the anchorman number one. He became the leading anchorman in the market because he was on the station where the best news was, and not because he brought the people with him, as happened back in the old days.

Now we know that there are transferable and nontransferable talents. There are guys who are number one in their markets who would lay the biggest egg there ever was if you moved them to any other market in the country. There are other people who have—I hate the word but it is the only word that works— charisma. Wherever they go, they relate to people, people relate to them. If I could define it, I'd love to, because I'd be a millionaire. They are hard to pick out, these guys, but when you find one, he can move from market to market and the audience moves with him. But the audience will not move for everybody. Somebody sees an anchorman who is number one in a certain market. He's grown up in that market, and suddenly somebody sees him and says "Boy we've got to get him. He has a 40 share! We've got to get him and get a 40 share!" When they get him, and move him to their market, they never move one single rating point. He didn't have it. Whatever that charisma is, he didn't have it and the content didn't support him.

As this shift to content continued, all news operations improved and improved significantly. In many markets, though not in all, the news is now really good on almost any station. So personalities begin to move again. The communicator becomes important because he becomes the only difference, once again. So there has been, if you will, a transition from star to content and now back to star.

The stars are getting out of hand in terms of price. But you must remember that good content and good production will, I think, support a lot of people who have not been well tried out and thoroughly seasoned as anchorpeople. The selection of those people is important. As you develop a newscast for your station, you must think about how you will promote it. What are the differences that are promotable? What have you got that no one else has? What have you got that you can talk about? Generally it is the people. Now, the selection of people is fascinating and very important but very little research is done on who is going to be put on the air. Generally, the decision is made by a group of upper-middle class people, successful in the business, who look at a guy (or, rather, now that they have tape, at 150 guys) and they say "Boy, I don't know why, but I like that guy." They do not find out what the audience thinks about him. So a lot of martini drinkers decide what beer drinkers are supposed to like. It doesn't work out that way. A martini drinker is a lousy judge of beer.

In the scramble for talent that goes on today, you will find another interesting phenomenon which is a result of the competition. The owned-and-operated stations and many of the larger groups of stations have people who do nothing but travel all over the country taping talent. You may have signed up a bright new hopeful yesterday and when he goes on the air they will begin to woo him. Their tickler file will tell them that in 18 to 24 months his contract will be up and they will woo him all during that period. When that time is up, if they want him badly enough, they will get him because they can pay more than you can. There is no security for a station any longer and that troubles me a lot. There are a few markets where they have developed a feeling that they are good places to work and pleasant places to live and there is nothing to be gained by moving around. But they are very few. I was in a market toward the bottom of the top 75 the other day where their weatherman had just been offered double what they were paying him to move to someplace else. To a 29-year old, that is a pretty attractive offer. It sure would have attracted me when I was 29. Now it so happens that he is a pretty sane guy. He took a good look at where his money would go and what it would cost him to move and he decided to stay. Management had been good to him and he liked the town and he liked the people. I don't know how to engender that into people but that's about the only holding power you have over people any more.

There is a station manager, now dead, who was an absolute expert at developing that feeling within his station. He had a magic way of seeing almost everybody in the station every day. A friendly word here—how is the baby? is so-and-so's wife out of the hospital yet? how are sales going? is he having a tough time with a new account?—You could not move anybody from that station. They have been clients of ours for 14 years now and, as a matter of fact, they have only lost one man, despite all the money that has been offered them. They have let some people go and it does not mean that they did not have any turnover. But they have lost only one man that they wanted to keep and I think that is probably because the manager is dead, and the people who are following cannot handle it in the same way he did. There were a lot of little things. I remember when the station became number one for the first time. It had been a very difficult situation. His competitor had effectively owned the market for a long time. But when they became number one he did the little things that nobody ever thinks about. In lieu of a lot of money, he simply sent the anchorman and his wife to Miami for a week or ten days, and when they got there there were flowers for her and champagne in the room. They felt wonderful and it didn't cost the manager anything like the $20,000 raise that an anchorman would expect now.

A horrible thing nowadays is that we have no place to develop talent any more. Few stations have any kind of morning show or noon newscast where people can try out. When someone steps in front of a camera these days, he has to be good, right then, that minute or else. The development of talent which used to occur in Fargo, North Dakota or in Las Vegas is now being covered by these scouts. They have tapes. I was talking with someone who is on the program here, who used to be with our company and is now with a big group, about a new person who has just gone on the air on one of our client's stations. This is his second week and that other group already has a tape of him and has made him an offer. Fortunately, it didn't work. He had the good sense to say that he just got there. But that kind of pressure is going to disrupt the loyalty the audience has. We have to be careful. It's possible to kill the goose that laid the golden egg.

We need a little more concentration on the quality of the newscast. I've made the statement, and it certainly is not original, that the audience having decided that television is its number one source of news, puts a burden on us to produce the kind of news that television is already getting credit for presenting, which for many reasons, it is not. You know all the reasons—lack of staff, lack of time to evaluate input, the compulsion to use stories once they have been filmed. But all of broadcasting did not uncover Watergate; a newspaper uncovered Watergate. Two guys who worked for a newspaper uncovered Watergate. The kind of investigative reporting that is so critical in terms of what is bothering your students, that finds out what is going on—what is really going on—and does not present the official hand-out or the official corporate position, is a complex kind of reporting. Newspapers can do it. They have the manpower. Television does a very poor job of it. We must find a way to send a guy underground for three months if we think there is something going on.

One inhibiting factor, almost insurmountable, that is terribly important, is the license. A newspaper does not have a license which can be challenged in so many ways if you are wrong. The license is more important than lawsuits. When one station, I remember, was starting a hard-hitting action line where they really did go after tough companies—companies with a lot of resources—named names and documented serious breaches of consumer relationships, they were very much afraid. I said, "Actually, if you aren't being sued for a million dollars on a pretty regular basis, you're not doing your job." A lot of suits are brought just to get publicity, just to get the chance to say they weren't doing whatever they were accused of. Then the suits are dropped. Not all are, of course, and that means that you have to be more careful. But this industry must begin to become the original source, to discover some of the things that are going on, and to justify the audience's feelings about it. We cannot just coast along forever on the reputation which was really just given to us. It is now being earned by some stations, but in the beginning it was just given to us. Nothing I say should be construed to mean that I feel there are not a lot of good newscasters. There are and the level goes up all the time. There are also a lot that are not very good. But what this medium does is to educate the audience in very subtle ways so that the audience's expectancy and its demand for a better product keeps rising every year. We can't sit on our oars any more.

That brings me back to those five stations in the 75 markets. They are the only guys—among all the owners—who haven't sat on their oars. The giants of the industry, the CBS owned stations, the NBC owned stations who at one time were thought to be golden for all time, have succumbed to this problem. The only way I can explain it is that, somehow, you don't mind the store when you're successful. You have to fight the same way when you are successful as you did when you were in third place and had everything to gain and nothing to lose. About half our clients are number one in their markets and about half are number two or number three and trying to get there. Actually, the easiest stations to work with are the stations that are second or third, because they want to get someplace. The station that is number one says: "Now wait a minute. We don't do things that way!" Also, the power-structure orientation of the station increases with success. I often say that if the manager or the owner goes out to the golf club and somebody in his foursome says "Boy, I think that was great what you did on the news last night. I thought it sure expressed our point of view," the only thing the owner can do is get the hell back to the station and turn the transmitter off because he's going to go broke. He is absolutely appealing to the wrong segment of the audience. He has to get down where the mass of the people are, where the 75 per cent of people in the middle majority of this country are because, for them, television is number one. And you have to communicate with them on their terms and in ways they can understand. For example, even news directors rebel because everybody who is in the consulting business keeps harping on the need for supers. But people, the middle majority, like to know who's on the air and where the event occurred, and without the supers they forget.

Now we have the two-hour newscasts on the West Coast and in New York—two hours plus the network—and people say: "But nobody is going to watch two hours of news!" Of course, nobody watches two hours. Nobody watches 15 minutes of news. The set is on for that period, but people's attention tunes in and out. There is no such thing as watching all the time. If you think about it enough, it makes absolutely logical sense. Because the way you go through a newspaper is that you flip the pages and certain things hit you and your attention goes there. But you're certainly not reading every page. You do the same thing with a television set but because it all happens on one screen you can't go to the sports section right away, or to the comic section. You can't flip through. You have to wait through the sequence of events to get to where you are going. And you pay attention as things occur that relate to you. When you have two or three members of a family watching, their attention is at different places. As far as the audience is concerned, there is no such thing as sitting on the edge of the chair and watching all of the newscast. It does not occur. You cannot make it occur because all you put on is not going to be interesting to them, or relevant, or even part of their lives. The set may stay there for two hours but their attention will drift in and out as things occur on the newscast that are of interest to them, that are relevant to them, that are amusing to them, or that touch them in some way.

The Question and Answer session which followed revealed more of the thinking of the professional consultant.

W. RAY MOFIELD. (Murray State University): To what extent do you think changes in public taste, such as in pop music or fashion, play a part in the ratings?

McHUGH: Changes in public taste are constant. I had a terrible communications problem with people within General Motors during the years I was responsible for Chevrolet's radio and television. In trying to get them to relate to radio broadcasting I always used to have fun with a question I think you can have fun with. I would simply take the ten bestsellers in books, the ten bestsellers in records and the ten bestsellers in three or four other categories and ask how many people had read them or heard them or been involved with them? The point was that taste changes very, very rapidly and it is always necessary to keep up with the changes in taste. But taste changes, market by market. The taste in Iowa is very different from the taste in San Francisco. I was highly amused that Mike Wallace found something to pick on, or thought he did, in the widely reported reaction to KGO's newscast.[1] But one of the things that nobody ever understood was that in San Francisco, at the time that Wallace was talking about, there were S.L.A. or pre-S.L.A. murders going on on a nightly basis. So, the local newscast in San Francisco had an entirely different look for an entirely valid set of reasons, from the newscast in Minneapolis of the same night. The critics said of KGO "all they have is sex and crime."

---

[1] *60 Minutes,* on Sunday, March 10, 1974, presented a story entitled "The Rating War" which dealt with criticisms being made of local news broadcasts. Because KGO-TV, San Francisco had one of the highest-rated late news broadcasts in the country, *60 Minutes* examined it and its competition. Mike Wallace reported that a study commissioned by *60 Minutes* and involving a week's analysis revealed: "55 per cent of all the stories on KGO's top-rated 11 P.M. news fell into the tabloid category—items on fire, crime, sex, tear-jerkers, accidents and exorcism."

That was true. But that was what was going on. The environment of San Francisco is different. That is where they discovered topless and bottomless and a whole lot of other things which have been heard about in Minneapolis, but not discovered there.

KEN GREENWOOD: Is it possible that, by now, you have isolated certain things common to many markets which result in tune-outs?

McHUGH: There are commonsense things that make you or anyone tune out—a boring, dull newscast, a newscast that is uninformative, a newscast where the presenters look as if what they have come for is just to get their checks on Friday rather than having any interest in presenting the news. All of those are common denominators. But on a market-by-market basis, they change. A common phenomenon is a station having a hard time and doing a study to discover that the anchorman on Station B is—I'll exaggerate to make the case—a 50 per cent favorite. So they hire him and get a two point jump in the first book or two and then everything goes back to normal. They do another study and they find out that he was the number one guy. He still is the number one guy, but they don't have an audience. What happened was that the environment changed. The audience that loved him, loved him in a certain environment and they like that environment enough so that they would not desert it for the individual. The environment isn't just cosmetic, though cosmetics can help. I've said before, you can change the set a hundred times but if it is not functional, if people cannot relate comforably on it, if you cannot do all the electronic things you have to do with it, if it isn't comfortable from the audience's point of view, it is not going to work. Environment, though, is not just cosmetic. It is caused by interaction, by coverage, by the feeling that the audience has. Since the first year we have been in business I've told stations "what you need to create is the feeling that if a manhole cover blows up in your town, one of your guys is going to be standing on it; you really cover the town; you are where everything happens." That is the environment you have to create.

ED GLICK: How do you feel about using services such as they are using now in Dallas in evaluating potential anchorpersons which ignore, to a large extent, the written responses of subjects, and pay more attention to their physiological responses?

McHUGH: We are about to conduct an experiment using a total polygraph for the same thing. Our feeling about it is that it is relevant only in relation to the kind of questions asked and if the analysis is done by a social scientist who really knows the impact of both the technical equipment and the kind of questions he is using, and established all that beforehand. The probing is more important than the tool and maybe if you just did the probing without the tool you would get the same answer. I think Dr. Turiki's method is wonderful for records—he's been very successful with them—but I don't think it is any way to pick an anchorman and you are going to have an example of that in Dallas.

LORIN ROBINSON: Another consultant, Frank Magid, reputedly has defined news for his clients as what people want to know, not what they need to know. How do you and your firm define news, if in fact you do, for your clients?

McHUGH: Frank and I have had many a disagreement but I couldn't totally disagree with him on that, although my reasoning may be very different from his. I back off and ask: who has the right to tell me what I need to know? I would like to know who is smart enough to tell me what I need to know except me. What I want to know comes closer because it has to do with how I am going to live my life. I think where that gets misinterpreted and the reason your question came up is asking: Do I want to know about sex? Do I want to know about who got raped and how horrible it was? If you mean all of that kind of thing, I do disagree. That is not the answer.

W. KNOX HAGOOD, (University of Alabama): Is "Happy News" just a gimmick and a fad?

McHUGH: "Happy Talk" was a phrase that was invented by a *Variety* reporter in Chicago. That's where it came from. It never came from us; it never came from Magid; it never came from anybody. It has never been used, to the best of my knowledge, in the business to describe what you want on a newscast. It has never been used other than by critics. It is a good *Variety* descriptive word. All that "Happy Talk" means is this: most news is bad. Good news doesn't travel very far or very fast, and you don't much care to hear it—unless it is 100,000 new jobs in a small town or something like that. With the impact that television has, when you present item after item of bad news you need to be concerned with the environment in which it is presented and with the relief factor. Even in one's own family, if a member of the family dies, it is interesting how somebody asks "who is going to tell mother?" They realize the gravity of what has happened requires a very special kind of communicator, somebody in whom mother has enough confidence and enough love to take the brunt of that announcement. Though obviously not in the same sense, the newscaster, anchorman or reporter, is telling something with a lot of negative shock. Therefore, the fact that these people in the newscast relate to each other comfortably, that the atmosphere in which they present the newscast is comfortable, and that they are able to laugh, or relax, or smile when it is appropriate and to be serious when that is appropriate, has a lot to do with success of the newscast. The inventor of that kind of "Happy Talk," if that is what you mean by the term, was Walter Cronkite. He and I have fought about it and he completely disagrees with me. But Cronkite was the first guy who cried when a President was killed. He was the first guy who got into a car on a one-on-one basis and would ride down the beach and talk to the astronauts in a very relaxed, easy way. If that is what you mean by "Happy Talk," fine. I call it empathy; a comfortable atmosphere so that you can take the news that is hard to take.

ROBERT KEIBER: One of the obvious advantages newspapers have with respect to investigative reporters is that they don't have to be physically or vocally attractive. How do you sell your clients on opting for journalistic talents as opposed to showbiz imagery?

McHUGH: Showbiz imagery has nothing to do with whether a newscast is good or bad. What it does mean is that the communicator of this bad news must be a certain kind of guy who can make it bearable. It is absolutely true that a good reporter may not be the kind of person who can communicate well; there are a lot of good music teachers who cannot sing or play, you know. That is life. There are people who are competent at one kind of thing, uncovering information, who are not competent at presenting it. This is not any big shocker and I don't think all the emphasis in the media on showbiz in television news is legitimate. If you look at the stations that are really successful, particularly this year, when the competition has gotten so great, you will see that they are not really presenting showbiz they are presenting television news for a mass audience.

Appendix 13

"GATEKEEPERS—WHAT THE PUBLIC GETS TO KNOW" Address by Av Westin, Executive Producer, ABC News, November 12, 1975

ON THE EVENING following their news deliberations, November 12, the Faculty-Industry Seminar heard a special address by Av Westin, the Executive Producer of ABC News. That speech and some of the questions and answers which followed, are included here because of their timelessness, their urgency, and their importance.

AV WESTIN has directed the development of the ABC News Documentary Unit since May, 1973. He assumed additional duties as the executive in charge of the *ABC Evening News With Harry Reasoner* in February, 1975.

A veteran journalist with over 25 years of experience in television news broadcasting, Mr. Westin conceived the highly acclaimed prime-time series of award-winning investigative documentaries entitled *ABC News Close-Up* in 1973. The hard-hitting and courageous investigative reports earned the series the Peabody, Emmy and Dupont Awards. Mr. Westin also conceived ABC News' *Americans All,* a series of minidocumentaries dealing with the contribution of ethnic minorities, *Adventures in America, Action Biography* and the new *Scientific Americans* series. He joined ABC News in March, 1969 as Executive Producer of the weeknight *ABC Evening News* and the weekend ABC *Weekend News*. Subsequent to the time of this address, Mr. Westin left ABC to head his own company. He has since rejoined ABC News as Vice President.

Prior to joining ABC News, Mr. Westin served as Executive Director of the Public Broadcast Laboratory (PBL) where he served as Executive Producer of its special series of Sunday evening newscasts carried over a nationally interconnected network of educational television stations. His PBL production, *Crisis in the Cities,* won Mr. Westin an Emmy Award.

Mr. Westin began his career in journalism working part-time for CBS News while earning a B.A. degree from New York University. Upon graduation, he joined CBS as a radio news writer and reporter. In 1957, he received the first CBS Foundation Fellowship to study at the Graduate Faculties of Columbia University where he earned an M.A. degree in Russian and East European studies. Mr. Westin's career at CBS spanned almost two decades and included positions in virtually every broadcast news capacity. He developed and supervised the *CBS Morning News* and produced such *CBS Reports* as "The Population Explosion" and "The Ruble War." He left CBS as Executive Producer of the CBS News Special Events and Election Units.

WESTIN: What I wanted to talk about this evening is what I described as various aspects of the subject of the public's right to know. I sat down to write this speech, and after a lot of starts, I decided to turn the subject around, and introduce you to the question of the gatekeeper. And since I'm well versed on how it works in broadcast journalism, I'll concentrate on the broadcast gatekeeper, though from time to time I'll stretch a little to either side, and include some comments about the government gatekeepers and the newspaper and wire services gatekeepers. I hope that this examination will cast a different perspective, so that the question is: what the public *gets to know,* rather than what the public *has a right to know.*

I remember standing in a cocktail party in Moscow in 1962. I was there on an assignment for CBS. Khrushchev was the boss, then, and he had just recently revealed, in a secret speech, that Joseph Stalin was really not a nice man at all. The speech was secretly delivered to government leaders of the Soviet Union, and had been obtained through channels by the C.I.A. It had been a shocker to the loyal members of the Communist Party of the Soviet Union to find out that Stalin was not the man of steel, that he had been a ruthless killer, who almost lost the war to the Nazis through inept planning, through purges, and paranoia. Stalin was a gatekeeper par excellence. Khrushchev opened the gate just as a little bit to serve his own purpose, and to launch the campaign of de-Stalinization which we have heard so much about. At the cocktail party, I was mumbling through my pidgin-Russian to the then official government representative of the Soviet Union, who was a kind of Ron Nessen and Ron Zeigler all rolled into one. I pointed out that the secret speech was bound to have an effect on the average Russian citizen, now that it had become public knowledge through the efforts of "Voice of America," and the Voice was making certain that everybody in the Soviet Union knew about it. The Russian spokesman acknowledged that it would have an effect.

"Well, why didn't you make it public?" I said, "instead of letting it leak back via the Voice of America?"

His explanation was a perfect one for the gatekeeper: "You Americans allow yourselves too much noise. We like things much quieter," he said. "We need not shout as much to be heard. We make just enough noise to be heard."

Just enough noise to be heard! That's the best euphemism for government censorship that I've heard. Keep things quiet, and the public will get to know what we want it to know.

Incidentally, to round out this Moscow anecdote, let me point out that the Russians were perfectly capable of jamming every single Voice of America broadcast. They could wipe us out. They knew the Russian people were getting the message through V.O.A., and Khrushchev's government was perfectly happy to let it happen that way. By the way, it was always easy to know how effective this Russian jamming was, or how effective V.O.A. was, because you could go to the National Hotel in Moscow, and listen to the dance band. If they played the latest American hit tunes, you knew that the jamming was intermittent, and they could note it down. But if the band kept playing old favorites, you knew the jamming was perfect that month. Just another example of gate keeping variance—very useful.

I don't want to dwell on the role of the government as a gatekeeper at this point. I'll come back to it later. But let me press on with the unique role that television news and broadcast journalism has acquired, because it has become, willingly or not, the gatekeeper for most Americans. And the individuals who exercise the decisionmaking power of determining what you see and what you hear on television and radio news broadcasts, are among the most powerful gatekeepers in the world. They are probably more powerful than newspaper editors and book publishers these days, because 65 per cent of all Americans get all or most of their information from television news broadcasts, and the percentage is rising.

Spiro Agnew called gatekeepers an unelected elite. I was one of the people he was referring to. *Time* magazine published what we all called the class yearbook, and there was a little box and a little paragraph right next to each one of our names, which gave our background. There were indeed a dozen that *Time* selected, and I was one of them. But have you ever listened or talked to a gatekeeper here in the Desolake, Kansouri? Well, what does one look like? Horned, with cloven feet? Professional and super-educated double-dull? Is she like Mary Tyler Moore, who's witty and pretty? *What criteria are used to determine what the public gets to know on the broadcasts he or she controls?*

It's my job at ABC News to have a great deal to do with determining what stories go on the air each night on the evening News, in what order they will run, or how long they will last. In addition, I oversee the production of the documentaries at ABC News, and have a great deal to do with determining the subject matter, and the adherence of those broadcasts to the principles of fairness, balance, and good journalism. And let me state—and restate—and repeat—and iterate—and reiterate—that I am *not* pleased when I hear that 65% of all Americans get all or most of their information from news broadcasts, because I know what we have to leave out every night. And if people don't read newspapers, and they don't read newsmagazines, and they don't read books, they are woefully uninformed. And tell that to your students, because that is the truth. Now, that doesn't mean that the gatekeeper in those information media—the books, the newspapers, and newsmagazines are any better than we are in television. It means simply that all sources of information are required for a citizen of this country to be fully informed.

We, in television, at the network level, take the job very, very seriously, working within a structure placed upon us by the way broadcasting is organized in the United States. Yes, it could be organized differently, and maybe it ought to be, mandating more time or more resources or more flexible schedules. But for the moment, and for the foreseeable future, broadcasting is organized in a specific way, which enables us to do some things very, very well, and gets in the way of doing other things at all.

So, if you please, let us not talk about what might be, and deal instead with the reality of the way broadcast journalism goes about its job today. What I'm about to say deals with both the network level and the local level; it deals with ABC and CBS and NBC; it deals with KIRT-TV and any other stations in real life that you listen to in your hometown community. *The primary limitation on what the public gets to know in television today is caused by time.* Now time comes in two aspects: 1) the time the broadcast goes on the air, and 2) the length of time the broadcast is to run. Unlike a newspaper, a television broadcast must begin precisely on schedule. A newspaper can hold up an edition for later developments, and the only people inconvenienced are the readers who are standing in the rain at the subway kiosk or the corner newsstand waiting for the delivery truck to show up. But a television news broadcast has to go on the air at the second it is scheduled to begin. Hundreds of affiliated stations switch to the network lines feeding the broadcast at the exact moment that the red sweep-second hand goes past the 12, and if no program is fed at that time, all those stations, and all their viewers, find themselves staring at blank screens. Since time literally means money in television, a great financial loss in commercial fees would occur. The need to begin at a fixed moment every night afects what a TV gatekeeper can put into his program, how complete the reporting can be, and where in the broadcast the story can be placed.

The other aspect of time with which a gatekeeper contends is the number of minutes and seconds he has to fill with news and information each night. It varies from network to network, but a half-hour broadcast does not have 30 minutes of broadcast time available to it. At ABC News, we have 28 minutes and 29 seconds, and some of that 28 minutes and 29 seconds is also not available for news and information content. Commercials are subtracted from that; we have 6 at ABC. CBS and NBC have 5 and one-half-minutes of commercial time, and even that time is further reduced by some mechanical factors, which have to be considered. So, at ABC, before the broadcast starts, the total air time available in a 30 minute news program is closer to *21 minutes and 50 seconds*. This is another example of how time makes television news different from newspapers. Unlike newspapers, TV cannot add a few extra pages to its regular edition, and incidentally sell a few extra department store ads, when pressure of events demands the space. On television, everything deemed newsworthy in a day has to be fitted together inside the allocated time.

Deciding how to fit the pieces together, how to divide up that 21 minutes and 50 seconds, is what a gatekeeper's job is all about. That's what he does when he makes the line-up for a show. At ABC, when the line-up is made, we start with some basic assumptions. The audience at dinnertime—which is when most network evening news programs are on the air—want to know, we believe, the answers to three very important questions: Is the world safe?—I mean that both literally and figuratively; Is my hometown and my home safe? literally and figuratively; If my wife and my children are safe, then what has happened in the past 24 hours to make them better off or to amuse them? I believe the audience wants to know the answers to these questions quickly, fairly and without distortion, and with just enough detail to satisfy an attention span which is being interrupted by clattering dishes, chattering dinner conversation, and the diminishing fatigue of a day at the office. So, a television news broadcast is based on elimination rather than inclusion. We could have enough material to fill several hours of broadcast time each night. But if we tried to include everything, we would find that our audience would be inundated. If we tried to cover everything we would find our staffs exhausted, and our budgets broken.

One of the responsibilities—and tell this to your students—of any news organization is to be *impartial* in its reporting. The gatekeeper has the job of making sure that the broadcast does not give an advantage to one set of advocates by inadvertently ignoring or down-playing the other side—inadvertently. Woe betide any of you who claim to be journalists who do it deliberately, because you are not worthy of the name. Balance cannot be achieved every day. Obviously, if the President of the United States makes a major political announcement, it will be covered that day. He will dominate that evening's program. It may so overwhelm all other viewpoints that opponents of the President's policy will feel the network news programs that night have deliberately ignored the other side. I believe balance must be achieved within a broadcast week—that is, seven broadcasts. At ABC, a deliberate effort is made to seek the other side, and present a report, or prepare an analysis for broadcast in order to achieve balance within seven days—at the outside. We try to do it on the same broadcast; at worst we try to do it the next night; but within seven days we *must* do it.

There are, of course, many thousands of details that go into the decision-making process for the gatekeeper in charge of the nightly news broadcast. I have dealt with only a few and, I admit, very briefly, but the purpose here is not to deliver a lecture on producing a television broadcast. Rather, it is to explain to you the way the public is limited in what it gets to know, even when the decision-makers are earnest professional journalists.

There are gatekeepers, of course, for documentaries as well. I presume that KIRT-TV will have a heavy documentary program. Of course you won't, but I hope you will. At ABC News, we have adopted a unique system for determining what goes into the investigative reports and the *Close-Up* series. After extensive research into a subject by reporters, researchers and producers, they are required to write a position paper which spells out what we know we can report, what we expect to be able to uncover with further investigation and what we dream we can uncover should everything break right for us. With these requirements met, we go ahead with the broadcast.

Now, I'm going to skip over the journalistic controls for accuracy, and fact checking, in order to touch on one of the special requirements that broadcast journalists face, which print journalists do not have to meet. That is *fairness and balance*. We in broadcasting are required by FCC rules to provide an opportunity for all sides in a controversial issue to be heard. Newspapers have no such requirement written into any law or governing regulation. We in broadcasting do. The FCC's Fairness Doctrine is, in my view, no impediment to good journalism. This is a controversial area among broadcasters, and I disagree with those who claim that the Fairness Doctrine has a chilling effect on investigations on television. In fact, I believe, at the network level the requirement to examine all sides of a controversial issue would be met whether there was a regulation or not.

At a local level, at KIRT-TV, I am not too sure. Not all stations are dedicated to seeking all the information that the public should have on controversial issues. Think about the stations in your own market—how many times are they likely to accede to the wishes of the incumbent? How many times are they likely not to get into something that might offend the owner of the bank, the insurance company, or the Shell Oil dealer? Think about that and what would happen if there were no Fairness Doctrine. There is evidence that some stations, like some local newspapers, would leave out the views of those with whom the station manager or the publisher disagree. The argument is advanced that local stations, anxious to avoid controversy, will not broadcast hard documentaries. There will be fewer documentaries, the argument continues, as long as this requirement to be fair exists. Well, that may be, but as a reporter, I would prefer documentaries that tell half truths or distort by omission to a plethora of shows that purport to cover the issue, but which in reality do not.

The public gets to know the truth because of the integrity of the gatekeeper. If you are hiring somebody for KIRT-TV, hire yourself a good assignment editor who has integrity and understands that he may sometimes be in an adversary position with the owner of the station, his publisher. Hire a guy with guts. That's easier to say than do. But, it doesn't hurt too much because what you find out is that the system is scared of people who will stand up and say: "Mr. Station Owner, where the hell is your integrity? And if I have to be your conscience, fire me for it, but I'm going to be it.'' You'll find that most of the time that won't happen—they won't fire you. You don't have to make their job easier. There is an adversary relationship between newsmen and publishers of newspapers, and between newsmen and owners of stations. You're not supposed to make their job easier; you're supposed to make their job tougher. Ultimately, they've got to switch. Ultimately, they've got the money. Ultimately, they can say: "We're not going to do it that way.'' And then you have another decision: "I am going to work for you, or I am not going to work for you.'' But don't make it easy for him up front; make him come to you.

Recently, a new issue for television broadcasters has arisen, and that is the question of access to broadcast time. Your local station will have it; we have it at the network. We are now challenged to allow independent documentary producers to present their shows on the air. Why, these people ask, should the networks be the only persons to determine what the public gets to know? Who says that network executives can be the only gatekeepers for the public? Who says their ideas, their productions, and their editorial controls are the only correct ones? By virtue of controlling network time, why should network broadcasts be the only ones the public gets to see? Well, they are legitimate questions, and they are troublesome—if you are honest, they are troublesome—and they are worthy of study. As a gatekeeper for a network, I am uncertain about the future. I take no rigid stand, but I seek a useful answer. I also suggest that what the public gets to know under some helter-skelter system of access will not, in my view, be worth the cost in bias, misinformation and distortion.

Let me give you some examples based on recent cases which came up. Jack Anderson interviewed President Ford recently. Frank Mankiewicz interviewed Fidel Castro recently. All network news departments turned down opportunities to broadcast those interviews as presented. Eventually, CBS brought the Mankiewicz interview, and then went back to Cuba to supplement it with their own correspondents, and Public Television eventually ran the Anderson interview with President Ford. Both Jack and Frank raised questions as to why their material could not be presented on the networks. It seemed so simple. Here were two broadcasts done by reporters of integrity, being denied access to air. Put simply, the public was being prevented from getting the information in those broadcasts.

But here is the other side. Each individual television station is, in the end, responsible for what it broadcasts. The ABC network is not the holder of the broadcast license in Desolake, Kansouri. KIRT-TV would be totally responsible for what goes on its air. If there were something libelous, or staged or inaccurate in those broadcasts, it would be KIRT-TV who would face the lawsuit, or the challenge to its license—not Frank Mankiewicz, not Jack Anderson. And the dilemma is compounded, isn't it, if the reporter had not been a man of known credentials, like Anderson or Mankiewicz, but someone else who was a self-styled journalist? It is very easy to stage a film sequence, to falsely edit a tape, to misquote a source. How does the station know that all of that broadcast is true? They put a large part of their mortgage into the pocket of the network news organizations. They know the degree of research, the standards of filming, the editorial controls that are maintained by the networks, who have the ongoing resources to spend what it takes to be absolutely accurate and to meet the requirements of the Fairness Doctrine.

Let us take another example. At *Close-Up* we have done a number of broadcasts which uncovered wrongdoing by individuals, by corporations and by government agencies. I have been visited by lawyers for people we have been investigating who have threatened me in advance with libel suits, and treat me to lectures about the pressure they can bring on my boss unless I rein in our horses. As a representative of a network news department, I am fully protected from such blackmail. ABC maintains lawyers and consultants who handle such cases. But what of the independent producer who is trying to do a similar investigative report? How many have resources to meet a lawsuit, or even the threat of one? How many would be able to withstand the pressure if it were to be brought, let's say, on the bank holding the note on their production money? How many would cut a corner here and there, making just a slight alteration in a narration to hedge just a little bit? In my view that is just like being a little bit pregnant. There is truth, or there is not; and if just one incident should occur, the credibility of all future broadcasts would be in question.

Finally, what about the pressure on the individual affiliated station not to run the broadcast? The management of any station has to protect its license. It broadcasts controversial programs produced by the network news department because it knows that the network is standing behind every single word. If a representative of a company, or of an individual, or of a government agency being investigated by an independent producer should drop in on a local station, and warn about bias or distortion, what do you suppose that a prudent station executive would probably do? If it is a network broadcast, he could call, and be reassured, even shown the evidence. I venture to guess that, in many cases, a station executive would not broadcast the independent show, because there would be a reasonable doubt about the independent producer's capacity to back-up the charges he makes, or to really prove the facts he uncovers.

This issue of access is not as simple as its advocates would have you believe. I can recognize that I can be accused of being a gatekeeper in search of the *status quo*. But suppose we did have an access system? There is a limited amount of air time available each year—even if you wiped out every single entertainment show—so who would decide which independent producer could have access to the available air time? Who would decide which independent producer could have access to prime time, and who would be stuck with the overnight? Who indeed? Just another gatekeeper—the FCC—Congress—who? It's a dilemma. It ought to be addressed, but it is clearly not the black-and-white picture that some would have you think.

I began by recalling for you a cocktail party in Moscow, and I will end by recalling a similar get-together in Peking, when I was there as part of the press group which covered President Nixon's trip in 1972. There were all these bowls filled to overflowing with fruit. We were always urged to have a tangerine, by the Chinese officials assigned to accompany us, whenever the conversation turned to politics, or to a matter of economic productivity or what happened to Lin Piao—anything other than weather. Our hosts would sit back, they would pull on their cigarettes, smile, and push the bowl of fruit at us and say: "Have a tangerine." The code name in China for evasion, for delay, for obfuscation, for denial is "have a tangerine."

Tonight, I tried to cover some of the problems we face in the decision-making processes of professional journalists when we decide what the public gets to know as they watch television news. There is as yet no government official who can make those decisions for us. We enjoy an essentially information-open-society. The First Amendment, the Freedom of Information Act, essentially keep controls on any tangerine vendors in our government. But, ladies and gentlemen, this may be changing. The role of the gatekeeper in the United States may be radically altered in the next few years.

This is no idle concern, because at this moment, before the Senate Judiciary Committee in Washington D.C., is a bill—Senate Bill 1—S-1, for short, that has built into its provisions some very interesting restrictions. The bill is 753 pages long, and it is designed to codify, revise and reform, Federal Criminal Statutes. Conservatives and Liberals alike should know what's in this bill before it becomes law. Part of it comes very close to setting up an official Secrets Act in this country. S-1 would establish for the first time the principle that the government, and not the people, own government information. Here are some of the provisions which would effect news gathering: "A reporter who obtains records and documents owned by or in the custody of the government, and who intends to appropriate them for his own use," such as writing a news story about them, could be guilty of a crime. Pentagon Papers, all of the Watergate exposé. A reporter could be prosecuted if he "conceals, removes or otherwise impairs the availability of a government record." How many reporters have taken a government document—given to them by someone who, if you will, has leaked it to them—and copied it? The reporter has in fact "removed" it and "impaired" for the period of time that he had its availability—a crime, a felony. A reporter could be prosecuted if he "reads or uses the contents of a private letter without the knowledge of the letter sender or recipient." Again, think of how many stories, even at a local level but certainly at the national level, have come because reporters have gotten a letter that somebody wrote to somebody else. *Newsweek* magazine would have had a very difficult time breaking the story of President Ford's intentions to re-alter the shape of the government. A reporter could be subjected to a fine of up to $100,000 and seven years in prison "for making unclassified national defense information public, if he knows that information may be used to prejudice the safety or interest of the United States, or to the advantage of a foreign power." How does he know that? A reporter could be guilty of a crime if he communicates unauth-

orized national defense information to unauthorized persons. That seems to me
to be legitimate. But anyone who leaks classified information to a reporter
could be guilty of a crime, even if the information was incorrectly classified in
the first place. And keep in mind that approximately 50,000 Federal bureau-
crats have the power to classify documents, and they are classifying them at the
rate of 200,000 a day! Altogether a billion government documents are now
classified.

Now, some of these provisions may be useful, and right, and others need
great study. There is concern, however, that if misapplied by government desir-
ing secrecy rather than candor, this bill, if enacted, could severely restrict the
current ability of the public to learn about government policy-making decisions,
government reports, government criminality, by establishing a form of censorship. It could mean, taken to an extreme, that the only time a reporter would
be totally free of the threat of Federal prosecution when reporting on government activities, would be when he published an official government hand-out.
Anything else would be subject to criminal proceedings under one or another
provision of this bill. Gatekeepers could turn in their keys. The decisions would
have all been made for them in advance.

So far, gatekeepers have been journalists who exercise professional judgment. They make mistakes—to be sure. But their aim is truth and information
for the public. The system has its faults—to be sure. But so far, at least, the
gatekeepers have never been forced to be fruit salesmen, offering us "another
tangerine."

QUESTIONS AND ANSWERS

ED GLICK: You talked about the right of access. What is your
feeling about the right of Presidential access to the networks?

WESTIN: If the President of the United States, whoever he may
be, says: "I have something that is of major importance to the people
of the United States," I believe we should give him time. Now, you
may not realize that there is a series of circumstances in which the
President can have air time: he can simply pass the word that he is
going to make a speech, or he can hold a news conference, or he can
request time. In recent times, we have had at least two, and possibly
three Presidents who have attempted to manipulate that. It's interesting
that Lyndon Johnson *requested* time on very few occasions, but whenever he said he was going to do something, the networks chose to give
him air time. That should not be confused with presidential requests.
Nixon began to manipulate it a little more. Ford tried it once, in our
view, shortly after he came to office. We are willing, at ABC at least,
to say that he did not know the rules at that point—he had a new team,
he himself was a new president. He issued a formal request and stated:
"I am requesting time." It turned out to be a speech that he gave in

Kansas City to the 4-H Farmers of America. He was landed on, his office was landed on, and he now understands the ground rules.

GLICK: What about the right to reply, under those circumstances?

WESTIN: This is a more recent development. I think that if, in fact, the President of the United States makes a statement that merits a reply because, let us say, he introduces a controversial point—not a political point but a controversial point—I think the right of reply should be given. This is a vast area that network executives are just entering upon and there is considerable debate. My view is that the broadcast industry and the press have no right to interpose themselves as judgmental pre-censors of what the man has to say. Comment on it all you want—there is nothing wrong with instant analysis. And the right to reply is the next step after that.

JIM COPPERSMITH: I have a few questions which I have asked of my network, CBS, and the answers which I received sounded something like "Have a tangerine." If at your network, you have so many fine stories—and I know, in fact, that you do—which do not make the 6:30 or 7:00 o'clock broadcast, why don't you either exercise a little more prejudgment and send some of them down the line earlier in the afternoon, or, perhaps, use that non-network time at 7:30 to send them down the line to the affiliates so that America might have the advantage of your good journalism in the late evening broadcast?

WESTIN: Our first feed of the *Evening News* is at 6:00; CBS and NBC's first feed is at 6:30—and most of the time the decisions about what will be included are not made until after the normal feed of what we call "DEF" or CBS calls "Syndication" or NBC calls "NTS." That is why it is not fed before the broadcast—because we really don't know.

You now come to an interesting question about 7:30. There is a half hour of air time in which the network is not feeding any programs. But what are they doing? They are feeding promotional announcements, they are feeding long lines information about how to switch the next football game, occasionally they feed down the full half-hour of a show so that you as a station manager can review the program. They are feeding other material for the network which controls those lines and the network will not give up the lines to the news division. We are prepared to feed everything we use, plus our outtakes. We have come to the conclusion that the stronger a local news operation is in its local market at any time of day—whether a fill at 7:25 in the morning, or the noon news, or a 6:00 local show, or your 11:00 o'clock show—the stronger the local station is as a conveyor of news and information in its local market, the more it will help us as a national news organization.

But what you've come at me with is just one more element of the adversary position which we, as journalists, occupy with the publisher. It is not in terms of content as well. Do you think we in the news division are delighted by the fact that our network has cut *Close-Up* in half? We fought like hell against that. Incidentally, for good old KIRT-TV, you do have some clout. Because when the network affiliates found out that *Close-Up* had been reduced from 12 to 6 broadcasts, they rose up and got the network to commit to a full schedule in 1977. It is to the credit of ABC that despite the disastrous financial position they are in—their cash position is down to zero—they stuck with 6.

Let's face it—and I want to nail this right down. The reality of this business is, it is a profit-making business, and so be it, and, in fact, God bless it. Because if it were not you wouldn't have anything on the air. You wouldn't have news on the air. You would have the old "Barbasol Sunday Nights News in Review." It was not so long ago. We all remember it.

ROBERT LaCONTO: Is there a possibility that broadcast journalism and education just do not have it put together because there is something lacking? Is that what you are getting at—the need for profits?

WESTIN: No, what I said informally before my prepared remarks and what I have said individually to a number of people here tonight is that I am concerned, as I go around the country and I lecture at reputable journalism schools which have broadcast divisions, that they are teaching the wrong things. I wish that all Journalism Schools taught the following: English (and not typewriting), Economics, History and, maybe, Logic. I have gone to leading Journalism Schools to deliver lectures to graduate students and I am appalled when instructors say "I'd like you to come to our journalism class" and I come and what I am exposed to is a young man or a young woman, sitting behind a microphone, reading. I say: "That's fine. That's a very good course in acting." "Do you think their technique is good?" I think her technique as a news reader is fine, medium, or what have you. Or are you asking me if her hair is combed right?

If you are talking about journalism, let them go and be journalists. Send that class downtown and tell them to cover City Hall and come back and tell you about it. Let them tell you what they have just experienced and never mind about the lights and cameras. Too many of these schools confuse the technique of the business with the primary thing—how to get the goddamn story and tell the truth. Woodward and Bernstein didn't get the whole Watergate scoop because they knew how to use a typewriter, or because they knew how to use a tape recorder. They did it because they knew how to ask questions, how to check sources. It is a delight to watch a professional journalist work. It is a delight to be interviewed by a professional journalist. Most of us in this business could be interviewed for six hours by many people who purport to be journalists and not tell them a damned thing. But I can always tell when a guy or a gal asks me a question which has been based on the fact that they have gotten background information some-where, and a little bit of this, a bit of that, and a bit of a document here. They have checked their facts and they ask tough questions. That is what makes good journalism. That is what made *Close-Up*. You just watch what happens when your correspondent knows more about the subject than the guy he is interviewing, and the guy goes into a stan-dard song and dance. The camera comes into a close-up and you watch that Adam's apple go when that question comes zinging him right between the eyes, and he's saying, while the eyes roll up: "That's an interesting question . . ." Damn right it is, and you know it.

GENE DYBVIG: I want you to respond to a charge made when an economist talked to us, quoting a newscast on which another network presented a deluge of percentages but nothing that would relate those figures to previous years. The basic charge was that the network news is sensationalizing.[1]

WESTIN: Sensationalism is always in the eye of the beholder, but I cannot deny that serious mistakes are made and will continue to be made. But I will claim this for broadcast journalism, particularly at the network level: We are the one industry that is not yet set in concrete, that learns from its mistakes, and that does not make too many mis-

---

[1] Jane R. Lokshin, Director and Senior Economist, RCA Economic Research, had addressed the IRTS Faculty-Industry Seminar the day before, (November 11, 1975). In her address, Ms. Lokshin had described an NBC *Evening News* broadcast of May 3, 1973, in which correspondent Jack Perkins had, in talking about the relationship of prices to profits, cited some 21 percentage fig-ures in a two-minutes, 300 word report. Ms. Lokshin's point had been that although the figures Perkins cited were all correct, without additional information they may have been misleading. In-ventory profits, Ms. Lokshin contended, were profits resulting from the fact that inventory went up in value. Inventory profits—which cannot be spent but on which taxes must be paid, accounted for 14 of the 34 percentage-point rise Perkins reported. Ms. Lokshin's point was that the spectacular number, in this case 34% rather than the more accurate 20% is "stressed out of context" in broad-cast reports. She pointed out that profits, in 1973, were not 34% but rather 5 cents of every sales dollar. This figure she compared to 15 cents per sales dollar in 1950, 10 cents in 1960, and 7½ cents in 1970.

takes twice. Think back to our initial coverage of Vietnam where the tendency was to "shoot bloody," in Mike Wallace's phrase. Think back to the days of *See It Now*. Go back and look at *See It Now* sometime and you will see things staged. Staged! Senator Somebody coming out as if walking from his office and approaching the microphones, turning, and making a statement. That is a firing offense now. If we stage anything in order to illustrate a point—recently, the police department sent a car on a simulated high-speed chase to demonstrate a story about policemen who were being killed in chases—we said, "This is a demonstration by the police department to illustrate for ABC News this and that." Years ago we would have put it on the air as if you were watching a chase. Our seven-day rule did not exist four years ago. Now it is part of the fabric at ABC.

I instituted the seven-day rule when I ran the ABC *Evening News* between 1969 and 1973. I think one of my major problems, and the problem of all broadcasters on a local or national level, is to be absolutely certain that the adversary relationship between the reporter and the outside world is not distorted into an advocacy relationship. I am opposed to advocacy journalism and I define it in the pure British legal sense. An advocate is a person who goes into court to advocate one side against the other and whose job it is to diminish the position of the other side by causing the elimination or the non-acceptance of fact, evidence or what have you, from the other side. It is not the journalist's business to eliminate anything. His business is to include, within a report, as much information as he possibly can. Too often, the unskilled, semi-skilled or occasionally forgetful journalist—print as well as television—will confuse *adversary*—which is asking and answering the tough questions—with *advocacy* journalism. That, I think, is at the core of why we are sometimes accused of having a liberal bias. Interesting enough, the fellows who publish the *Berkeley Barb* would say we are on the other side.

Appendix 14

NAB 1974 EMPLOYEE
WAGE AND SALARY DATA

TABLE 6   MARKET SIZE 5 (ARB 76-100)

JOB TITLE	GROSS WEEKLY COMPENSATION					
	Composite Wage/Salary		Lowest Reported Wage/Salary		Highest Reported Wage/Salary	
	Med.	Avg.	Med.	Avg.	Med.	Avg.
Non Supervisory Employees						
Engineering Technician	$168	$171	$138	$145	$198	$202
Studio Cameraman	I.D.*	I.D.	I.D.	I.D.	I.D.	I.D.
Floorman	109	125	98	111	144	141
Producer/Director	162	162	150	146	174	180
Technical Director	127	141	116	132	150	158
Staff Announcer	196	213	198	217	194	219
News Anchorman	203	215	180	183	215	230
News Reporter	165	166	150	148	175	180
News Film Cameraman	155	158	155	144	164	166
News Reporter-Cameraman	155	163	140	144	190	199
News Editor	I.D.	I.D.	I.D.	I.D.	I.D.	I.D.
Sportscaster	191	212	190	210	191	217
Weathercaster	206	202	200	190	206	203
Film Editor	150	144	120	140	143	148
Film Lab Technician	147	151	140	147	157	155
Traffic/Sales Clerk	110	111	102	106	114	116
Continuity/Copy Writer	114	120	101	116	120	124
Staff Artist	130	134	130	132	130	135
Time Salesman	300	301	255	251	385	365

Methods of Compensation For Sales Personnel

Supervisory Employees	Med.	Avg.		Sales Manager	Salesman
Operations Manager	$308	$340	Percent of stations using each method:		
Program Director	281	294			
Director of Engineering	269	272			
News Director	269	267			
Furn Dept. Manager	139	145			
General Sales Manager	500	505	Straight		
Local Sales Manager	460	449	Salary	0.0%	0.0%
National Sales Manager	I.D.	I.D.			
Promotion/Publicity Manager	190	181	Salary +		
Production Manager	228	226	Bonus	21.1	0.0
Business Manager	230	233			
Traffic Manager	I.D.	I.D.	Straight		
Community Affairs Director	I.D.	I.D.	Commission	0.0	14.3
Continuity Director	I.D.	I.D.			
Editorial Director	I.D.	I.D	Guaranteed		
Art Director	I.D.	I.D.	Draw against		
			Commission	5.2	28.6
Total Station Employment					
Average Number of Full time Employees		55	Salary + Commission	63.2	57.1
Average Number of Parttime Employees		5	Other	10.5	0.0

*Insufficient Data

SELECTED PLANS FOR COMPENSATING SALESMEN

In compensating salesmen, the most prevalent method used by television stations is salary plus commission (39.9%). A straight salary is received by (21%) of the salesmen, while (2.6%) of the stations combined a straight salary with a bonus. A guaranteed draw against commission is used by (37.3%) of the stations a straight commission was the method by which (17.6%) of the stations paid their salesmen. A few samples of the wide variations in plans used to compensate salesmen are listed below:

Weekly Gross		Salary		Commission

MARKET SIZE 1

$820	=			straight commission of 1.8% of local time sales
698	=	500	+	.55% override on local sales
632	=	288	+	4% commission in excess of $31,250 on net billing
530	=	250		draw against 4½% on time, talent, production
451	=	250	+	2.81% commission on gross local sales divided among 4 salesmen in proportion to their sales plus 1.275% commission on gain over the year before, divided equally among salesmen
422	=	208		draw against commission of 4.5% of net time billings

MARKET SIZE 2

$694	=	$125	+	3% agency and 7% direct sales
540	=	138		draw against 8% on net monthly billings
535	=	138	+	3.4% of monthly sales
397	=	207	+	10% commission on all billing above $10,000 for the month
385	=	184	+	commission on billings in excess of $20,000 per month 5% on $20,000 – 25,000, 6% on 25,000 to 30,000, 7% in excess of $30,000
175	=			straight commission of 8% of net sales

MARKET SIZE 3

$1120	=	$125	drawn against commissions paid only when invoices are paid

Weekly Gross		Salary		Commission
470	=	110	+	3% on sales to $15,000, 5% on sales $15,000–35,000, 7% on sales over $35,000 per month
453	=	332	+	2% of time and facilities sales
439	=	231	+	7% of local time production collections
375	=			5.5% of net time sales
270	=			12½% of sales after deducting agency commissions

MARKET SIZE 4

$432	=			straight 9¾% commission on local sales less commissions
364	=	150	+	2% commission
328	=	110	+	5% on time sales and quarter and year-end bonus
285	=	150		10% of $1,500 a week and 5% over $1,500 a week
267	=	145	+	½ of 1% of all broadcast revenue (except network)
194	=	135	+	5% on 1st 5,000 sales, 10% over 5,000 per week
125	=	125		7½% commission on local time sales

MARKET SIZE 5

$385	=	$132	+	6% on total net time and talent sales over $7,000 4% on $5,000 to $7,000
376	=	125	+	7% commission on old business & 10% on new business
346	=	192	+	Draw against 5.3% commission on time and production sales
300	=			straight commission
281	=	160	+	5% commission on collection of personal sales
194	=	100	+	20% local sales

MARKET SIZE 6

$318	=	$161	+	11½% of net local and regional sales less the guaranteed weekly draw
277	=	140		guaranteed draw against 10% commission
227	=			commission of 9% on sales to $15,000; 10% on sales over $15,000
225	=			10% commission on collections on sales.
202	=	139		guaranteed draw and 10% on net billings above quota plus 1.2% of departmental sales shared equally by salesmen if quarterly quota is met

Weekly Gross		Salary		Commission

| 190 | = | 117 | + | 4% on all net sales |
| 150 | = | 128 | + | 4.5% commission over $20,000 sales per month |

MARKET SIZE 7 & 8

$558	=		10% of all sales to 10,000 per month. If 10 − 15,000, this whole amount by 12½%, if over 15,000, whole amount at 15% commission
340	=		10% commission of own local time sales
282	=	135	guaranteed draw against 12½% time sales plus bonus of 5% over quota of 1st, 2nd and 3rd quarters, 5% over 4th quarter and 10% annual
201	=	133	guaranteed draw against 6% of all local sales
190	=	115	draw on first $2,000 in sales per month, plus 16% all sales over $2,000
173	=	92 +	7% net collections

SELECTED PLANS FOR COMPENSATING SALES MANAGERS

In compensating Sales Managers, the most prevalent method used by television stations is salary plus commission (50.8%). A straight salary is received by (11.6%) of the Sales Managers, while (24.9%) of the stations combined a straight salary with a bonus. A guaranteed draw against commission is used by (8.5%) of the stations; a straight commission was the method by which (2.6%) of the stations paid their Sales Managers. A few samples of the wide variations in plans used to compensate Sales Managers are listed below:

Weekly Gross		Salary		Commission

MARKET SIZE 1

$994	=	$692	+	½ of 1% of net billing after $1,305,000
817	=	307	+	.0035 on all time, talent, production
770	=			straight salary
757	=	461	+	½ of 1% of gross national and local sales of programs and announcements after specific deduction of $855,000 per year
707	=			straight salary plus incentives for exceptional results

Weekly Gross		Salary		Commission
704	=	481	+	.2% of gross time sales in excess of $1 million and .25% in excess of $5 million
630	=	460	+	.13% override on local and national sales

MARKET SIZE 2

S780	=	S780		straight salary only
732	=	384	+	.4% of excess of net sales for each month over monthly quotas, and .8% of excess of station's net sales for current fiscal year over net sales for past fiscal year
650	=	400	+	1% of local and national above quota
614	=	277	+	2% commission on total local sales
521	=	150	+	2½% agency and 6% direct
480	=	480		salary plus year-end bonus
345	=	195	+	3% of all time sales

MARKET SIZE 3

S752	=	S641	+	approximately 107 bonus
620	=	265	+	.75% of total cash collections over $130,000
522	=	369	+	1.5% of local, regional and national net sales over quota
476	=			commission rate is 1% of all local sales
450	=	288	+	¾ of 1% on all sales
383	=	230		against 4% net sales (excluding political)
338	=			3% of gross local and regional sales plus 1% of gross national sales

MARKET SIZE 4

$636	=	$500		or 1% of total station revenue, whichever is greater
577	=			straight salary
515	=	337	+	1% over quota
494	=	320	+	sliding scale percentage of gross national and local sales
423	=	346		drawn against 1% national and 2% local business
406	=	223	+	½ of 1% of all broadcast revenue (except network)
304	=	304		straight salary

Weekly Gross		Salary		Commission

MARKET SIZE 5

$700	=	$250	+	1% gross billing
600	=	150	+	20% local sales plus 3% override
481	=	385	+	1½% of total spot sales over 75,000 per month
479	=	190	+	1% of net local time sales
394	=	306	+	5% commission on collections of personal sales plus annual incentive bonus as an override on total local sales
340	=	213	+	5% of volume

MARKET SIZE 6

$577	=	$323	+	7% on override of 100,000, plus 15% on sales over 630,000
519	=	462	+	3,000 bonus at end of year
485	=	254	+	.8% gross local and national sales
345	=	242	+	1¾% of all non-network net billings
310	=	100	+	2% of all collections of local time sales
288	=	173	+	1% override on all local sales

MARKET SIZE 7 & 8

$661	=	$450		guaranteed draw against 2% of gross billings
600	=			straight salary
500	=	231	+	10% of personal sales and 2% of all other local sales
480	=	184	+	2% all net collections
404	=	288	+	annual percentage of volume increments
320	=	310	+	3% on yearly override of total sales quota, usually reached in last 5 weeks of year
317	=	175		guaranteed draw against 3% of all local sales

Appendix 15

Physical Properties of Television Station KIRT-TV

To gain perspective on the planning that preceded our decisions of what and where to build, to own or to lease, and equipment to buy, it should be noted that the initial proposals for transmitter equipment were submitted some three and a half years before the first air-date of our station.

The decisions were carefully weighed in terms of finances, need, quality and flexibility. It was necessary to plan for the expansion of our non-existent facilities at the same time that we planned to erect the first structure. It was necessary to plan for the addition of more diverse technical equipment within a short time after the initial equipment would be phased in. A decision

406

had to be made regarding remote equipment and its relation to our programming objectives.

We have briefly outlined our decisions in the following paragraphs.

Building

Our building was constructed adjacent to the transmitter, and was a simple to assemble, medium sized Butler building. It included a very small studio, transmitter equipment and master control. Rather than list the cost of every item in the construction, the final price of $66,665 included excavation, concrete, iron, carpentry, painting, fencing, paving, plumbing, heating, air conditioning, electrical, plans and engineering, supervision, the Butler building and miscellaneous expenses.

The cost of furninshings and telephone and telex installations are not included in this total.

Transmitter

Our decision on the selection of transmitter equipment was based purely on the financial analysis prepared in advance of receiving our CP. We had two choices available.

A.   Buy land, install a foundation and install a 1200'
     tower for our exclusive use, at a cost of about
     $500,000.

B.   Arrange with another TV station in the market to
     share a tower. This involved a build, buy-back
     and lease arrangement in which we would build a
     television tower, sell it to a financer, and then
     lease back the tower on a long-term lease.

After long deliberation, and a careful examination of the amount of capital necessary to purchase equipment and support the start-

up operation prior to receiving any income, it was decided to
exercise option B.

At the present time our balance sheet will reflect the result of
our contract for the lease-back portion of the arrangement. The
current tower lease is for $1,350 per month for 20 years. The
same rental is paid by the sharing station, enabling the purcha-
ser to realize a profit over the course of the 20 year lease.

Equipment

As with the transmitter, we had a choice of procedures available
to us when the time came to decide on the equipment which we would
need to begin studio and film/tape operation.
The choices were:

    A.   Contract with one supplier to completely equip the
         studio with equipment of his companies manufacture
         or allow them to install alternate equipment if a
         required item was not in their line.

    B.   Contract with various suppliers to deliver and in-
         stall specific items contained in their line.

On the advice of our chief engineer, we chose to follow the latter
procedure, and have ordered various equipment from RCA, General
Electric, and Ampex.
Our initial equipment package was designed to suit the needs of
our small studio and included:

    Two color cameras

    Studio lighting

    Two film chains

    Master control

    Switching

    Three video-tape machines

We are now planning to add the following equipment:

> Four color cameras in our remote equipment
>
> Two video-tape machines
>
> A slo-motion disc recorder
>
> A chiron character generator
>
> One film chain

The total cost of this equipment is approximately $1,250,000.

General Electric delivered the following equipment for our start-up:

> Automation
>
> Two live color cameras
>
> Remote Equipment
>
> Film camera
>
> Optical multiplexer
>
> Film projector
>
> Slide projector
>
> Master control switcher
>
> Sync equipment
>
> Distribution equipment
>
> Cabinetry and monitoring
>
> Audio equipment
>
> Accessory equipment

Ampex supplied:

> Three VR-1200B Low/High band video-tape recorder/reproducers
> (Specification sheet follows)

AMPEX SPECIFICATIONS

Item	Code	Qty.	Description
1	AA-11	1	Ampex VR-1200B Low/High Band Videotape* Recorder/Reproducer with Overhead Monitoring to include: (525/60 Mono Color)
		1	System Control Unit
		1	Tape Timer 60 Hz
		1	Panel-Fan Assembly
		2	Instruction Manuals
		1	System Power Supply
		1	Mechanical Parts Kit
		1	Control Panel Assembly
		1	Video Signal System
		1	Tape Transport Assembly
		1	Guide Servo Kit
		1	Misc. Maintenance Parts Kit
		1	Video Erase Drive Assembly
		1	Intersync Servo
		1	Audio System
		A/R	Blank Module
		1	Non-scratch Erase Head
		1	System Harness
		1	60 Hz Kit
		1	Color Processing Amplifier
		1	Audio Head Assembly
		1	Channel Amplifier
		1	Low Pass Filter 4.4 MHz
2	B-01	1	Video Head, 10 Mil Air Bearing
3	C-03	1	Monitor Assembly to include:
		1	Conrac 14 inch Video Monitor
		1	Tektronix RM 529 Waveform Monitor
		1	Audio Monitor and Switcher
		1	Monitor Accessory Parts Kit
		1	Stability Marker
4	D-04	1	Amtec Kit to include:
		1	Amtec 525/625
		1	Card Extension Sub-Assy
		1	Misc. Parts Kit
		2	Instruction Manuals

AMPEX

Appendix 16

RATE CARDS, KBGA AND KNAC

DESOLAKE, KANSOURI   (2 STATIONS)

KBGA Rate Card   :Effective 9/8/75
(Airdate September 26, 1954)
SUBSCRIBER TO THE NAB TELEVISION CODE.
A CBS TELEVISION NETWORK AFFILIATE
NATIONAL REPRESENTATIVES: HARRINGTON, RIGHTER & PARSONS, INC.

| MONDAY/FRIDAY | PROGRAM | 30 - SECONDS | | 10" |
		FIX	PRE	PRE
7:00-8:00AM	NEWS	$ 15	$ --	$ 10
8:00-9:00AM	CAPTAIN KANGAROO	30	25	15
9:00-12:NOON	AM ROTATION	50	40	20
12:00-3:30PM	PM ROTATION	60	50	25
3:30-5:00PM	MIKE DOUGLAS	60	50	25
5:00-5:30PM	DIALING FOR $	75	65/55	35
6:00-6:30PM	TV NEWSROOM	110	90	45
6:30-7:00PM	VARIOUS	100	85	45
10:00-10:30PM Mon/Sun	NEWS	110	90	45
10:30PM-CC	CBS LATE MOVIE	40	30	15

411

SATURDAY

7:00-1:00PM	KIDS ROTATION	60	50	25
1:30-3:30PM	HIGH SCHOOL FOOTBALL	40	30	15
6:00-7:00PM	HEE HAW	180	160	80
10:30-11:00PM	STAR WRESTLING	50	40	20
11:30-MID	HANK THOMPSON	30	--	15

SUNDAY

7:00-12:NOON	RELIGIOUS/VARIOUS	30	--	15
12:00-3:30PM	NFL FOOTBALL	175	FLAT	
3:30-6:00PM	NBA BASKETBALL	175	FLAT	

KNAC   RATE CARD   EFFECTIVE 9/8/75

(AIRDATE November 15, 1953)

SUBSCRIBER TO THE NAB TELEVISION CODE.

A NBC TELEVISION NETWORK AFFILIATE.

NATIONAL REPRESENTATIVES: BLAIR TELEVISION.

				SECTION			
			I	II	III	IV	V
BE OUR GUEST	3:30-4PM	M-F	80	70	60		
HUCK & YOGI	4-4:30PM	M-F	65	55	45		
DREAM OF JEANNIE	4:30-5PM	M-F	65	55	45		
TRUTH OR CONSEQUENCES	5-5:30PM	M-F	80	70	60		
NEWS	6-6:30PM	M-F	110	90	75		
VARIOUS	6:30-7PM	M-F	130	110	90		
LATE NEWS	10-10:30PM	Mon-Sun.	150	130	110	90	75
TONIGHT SHOW	10:30-MID	M-F	100	90	85	65	55
TOMORROW	MID-1AM	Mon-Thr.	25	20	15		
MIDNIGHT SPECIAL	MID-1:30AM	Fri.	45	35	25		
VARIOUS	10:30-CC	Sat.	55	45	35	25	15
SUNDAY MOVIE	10:30-CC	Sun.	65	55	45	35	25
L. WELK	6 - 7 PM	Sat.	65	55	45		

Appendix 17

PARTICIPANTS

IN THE FIFTH ANNUAL INTERNATIONAL RADIO AND TELEVISION SOCIETY FACULTY-INDUSTRY SEMINAR

November 10–14, 1975

IOTA GROUP

Discussion Leader: S. James Coppersmith; *Rapporteurs:* John Keshishoglou, F. Dennis Lynch; Rey L. Barnes; Walter K. Bunge; Carl Jon Denbow; Edwin L. Glick; Kenneth Harwood; Frank M. Kearns; Peter Longini; Robert K. McLaughlin; Lewis O'Donnell; Charles R. Russell; Howard L. Stevens; Sherilyn K. Ziegler.

REY L. BARNES. Dr. Barnes is Associate Professor of Journalism and Broadcasting at Oklahoma State University, Stillwater. Previously, he taught at the University of Southwestern Louisiana, the University of Utah and at Utah State University in Logan. He received his BS from Utah State and is the holder of a Certificate from Stanford, an M.S. from Utah State and his Ph.D. from the University of Iowa. Dr. Barnes is the author of numerous articles and studies and was Research Director for Beta Research from 1966 to 1973 and has been on the Publications Board of the *Journal of Broadcasting*. A member of Phi Kappa Phi, Dr. Barnes has been an NAEB Fellow and the recipient of a Westinghouse Scholarship and an NAB Research Grant.

WALTER BUNGE. Head of the Department of Journalism and Mass Communications at Kansas State University, Manhattan, Dr. Bunge was from 1963 to 1973 at the University of Wisconsin, River Falls. Earlier, he had been at the University of Idaho, Moscow. Dr. Bunge received the B.C. from the University of Wisconsin, Madison, and the M.S. from the same institution. He received his Ph.D. from the University of Minnesota in Minneapolis. Dr. Bunge served as a member of the Governor's Cable Television Commission in Wisconsin.

CARL JON DENBOW Dr. Denbow is in the Department of Journalism at Murray State University, Murray, Kentucky. He has also taught at Ohio University, Athens

413

where he served as part-time reporter, sports colorman and engineer for WOUB-AM-FM-TV, the university station. From 1964 to 1966, he served as a journalist in the United States Navy. The holder of a B.S.J. from Ohio University, he received his M.A. from Ohio State in Columbus and his Ph.D. from Ohio. Dr. Denbow's publications include "Listenability and Readibility: An Experimental Investigation" and "Daily Newspaper Subscribers and Non-subscribers: A Replication of the Ravick Multivariable Index Approach," both published in *Journalism Quarterly*.

EDWIN L. GLICK. Since 1970 the Director, Division of Radio, Television, Film at North Texas State University, Denton, Dr. Glick previously held posts at Wayne State University, Detroit, Michigan; Southern Methodist University, Dallas, Texas; Ohio University, Athens; and the University of Florida, Gainsville. From 1951 to 1953 Dr. Glick was a recording engineer for Trans Radio Productions in Boston. From 1953 to 1958 he was a studio engineer for WUOM, the University of Michigan station in Ann Arbor. From 1958 to 1959 he served as Audio Supervisor in the Motion Picture Department at WBGH-TV, Boston. It was also in Boston, at Boston University, where Dr. Glick took his first degree, a B.M. He received the M.M. and the Ph.D. from the University of Michigan. Dr. Glick's publications include "Trial by Fire: The First Ten Years of WGBH-TV," *NAEB Journal*.

KENNETH HARWOOD. Dr. Harwood is Professor and Dean of Communications at Temple University, Philadelphia, Pa., a post he has held since 1968. For the 14 years before that, he was Professor and Chairman at the University of Southern California, Los Angeles. From 1950 to 1954 he served as Professor and Chairman at the University of Alabama, Tuscaloosa. Dr. Harwood received an A.B., an A.M. and a Ph.D. from the University of Southern California. The author of more than 20 articles in scholarly journals, Dean Harwood is also co-editor of *Free and Fair,*

Readings from the Journal of Broadcasting. A former president of the Broadcast Education Association and of the International Communication Association, he has also served as a director of the Association of Educational Broadcasters and of the National Association of Broadcasters.

FRANK M. KEARNS. Mr. Kearns is Benedum Professor in the School of Journalism West Virginia University, from which he graduated in 1938. From 1953 to 1971, Mr. Kearns was a foreign correspondent for CBS News. Based at various times in Cairo, London, Paris and Rome, Mr. Kearns covered international news for radio and television in some 60 countries. He has been the recipient of the Overseas Press Club "Best Radio or Television Reporting from Abroad" award and of a citation from the same group. He has also received the George Polk Award from Long Island University, the West Virginia University P.I. Reed Achievement Award and other distinctions.

JOHN E. KESHISHOGLOU. Since 1971, Dean of the School of Communications, Ithaca College, Ithaca, New York, Dr. Keshishoglou came to Ithaca in 1965. Earlier he had been Audio-Visual Consultant at the University of Iowa, Iowa City and a part-time producer-director at KITV, the NBC affiliate in Sioux City. Prior to that he had been program director for PPC-TV, Thessaloniki, and a newspaper reporter, newsreel cameraman and a free lance photographer in Greece. Dr. Keshishoglou had received the A.A. degree from Anatolia College in Thessaloniki, the B.A. from Morningside College, Sioux City, the M.A. from the University of Iowa and the Ph.D. from Syracuse University, Syracuse, New York. He has written two books and numerous articles and is the producer-director of more than 50 instructional films and documentaries. A consultant to institutions and agencies in the United States and abroad, he has received grants from the National Endowment for the Humanities, the Exxon Education Foundation and other sources.

PETER LONGINI. Dr. Longini is Assistant Professor at Brooklyn College of the City University of New York. Prior to accepting that post, Dr. Longini had, for five years, been in a similar position at the University of Pittsburgh, Pittsburgh, Pa., from which he received his M.A. and his Ph.D. Dr. Longini had earned a B.A. at Wooster College, Wooster, Ohio. He is the author of two books, *The Television Game* and *Prime Time: The Game of Television*. His publications also include "The Night CBS Ran 'Deep Throat,' " *BEA Journal*, and "TV Access: A Pittsburgh Experiment" which appeared in the *Journal of Broadcasting*.

F. DENNIS LYNCH. From 1965 until 1968, Dr. Lynch taught at Moorhead College, Moorhead, Minnesota. He then taught at the University of Iowa, Iowa City, the University of Kansas, Lawrence and at Memphis State University. In 1975, he was appointed Associate Professor for Communications at Cleveland State University, Cleveland, Ohio. Dr. Lynch received his B.A. from Michigan State in East Lansing and both the M.A. and Ph.D. from the University of Iowa in Iowa City. The author of various publications and the producer of several educational films, Dr. Lynch is Non-Print Media Editor for the Speech Communication Association and Executive Vice President of the University Film Association.

ROBERT K. MACLAUCHLIN. Since 1969, Dr. MacLauchlin has been Associate Professor and Director of TV-Radio Instruction, Colorado State University, Fort Collins. His prior experience has included teaching at Michigan State University, East Lansing, and numerous positions in educational and commercial broadcasting. From 1962 to 1966 he served as Director of Programming for the State of Maine ETV Network. Immediately before that he had been a sportscaster for WBLZ-TV, Bangor and a writer/producer for the Horace Hildreth Stations. Graduated from the University of Massachusetts in Amherst with a B.A., he received an M.Ed. degree from Bridgewater State College, Bridgewater, Mass., and an M.S. in Radio and Television from Syracuse University. He received his Ph.D. from Michigan State University, East Lansing. Dr. MacLauchlin is the author of "International Interconnected Educational Television," in *Pacific Nations I*, and other articles.

LEWIS B. O'DONNELL. Dr. O'Donnell has been a member of the faculty of the State University of New York, Oswego, since 1971; he had served as Director of Broadcasting at SUNY, Oswego, from 1962. Before that, Dr. O'Donnell had spent 12 years in commercial broadcasting as an announcer at WGR, Buffalo and at WOLF, Syracuse, New York and as an announcer, a director, salesman, producer and program specialist at WHEN-TV, also in Syracuse. Dr. O'Donnell received a B.S., an M.S. and the Ph.D. from Syracuse University.

CHARLES G. RUSSELL. Professor of Journalism at Cornell University, Dr. Russell has been at the Ithaca, New York institution since 1959. For the three previous years, he had been at the University of Arkansas, Fayetteville. Earlier, he was a free-lance writer and a writer for the Portland Cement Association in Chicago. He was awarded the B.J. and the M.J. from the University of Texas, Austin. He received the Ph.D. from the University of Missouri in Columbus. Dr. Russell is the author of more than 30 articles and pamphlets.

HOWARD L. STEVENS. Associate Professor of Speech-Theater at Suffolk County Community College, Selden, N.Y. from 1966 to present, and earlier at Coatsville Community College, Baltimore Maryland, Mr. Stevens has also been active in commercial radio, as announcer at WALK-AM-FM, Patchogue and WRIV-AM, Riverhead, New York; as Producer-Director at WSPA-TV, Spartansburg, South Carolina; and as announcer for WPGC-AM, Prince George's County, Maryland. Mr. Stevens is the recipient of a B.A. and an M.A. from the University of Maryland, College Park.

SHERILYN K. ZEIGLER. Dr. Ziegler serves as Associate Professor of Mass Communications at the University of Tennessee, Knoxville, where she has been on the faculty since 1974. Prior to that she had been at Michigan State University, East Lansing. As a student she had worked with WKAR in East Lansing; with Foote, Cone and Belding, the advertising agency, in Chicago; and with another agency, Young and Rubicam, in Detroit. During the summer of 1972, she worked in promotion at KITV, ABC Television affiliate in Honolulu. Michigan State University awarded her a B.A., and M.A. and a Ph.D. A consultant to advertisers and broadcasters, Dr. Ziegler was the editor of *Perspectives on Advertising Education,* published by the American Academy of Advertising. She was awarded the Sigma Delta Chi award for Outstanding Teaching in 1975 and has also received the Harold Fellows Memorial Scholarship and a research grant from the National Association of Broadcasters as well as fellowships from the American Association of Adver-

tising Agencies and the American Academy of Advertising.

S. JAMES COPPERSMITH, *Industry Discussion Leader.* S. James Coppersmith has been Vice President and General Manager of WNAC-TV, Boston, Massachusetts, since May 1973. Previous to that appointment, he was Vice President and General Sales Manager of WNEW-TV, the Metromedia station in New York City. Mr. Coppersmith first joined Metromedia in 1965 as a local salesman with WTTG in Washington. In 1966, he became an account executive in New York for Metro TV Sales, the Metromedia national representative firm, and became Manager of Metro TV Sales, Los Angeles office in 1967. In 1968, he was named Vice President and West Coast Manager of Metro TV Sales, and from 1969 to 1971, he served as Vice President and general Sales Manager of KTTV in Los Angeles. Since coming to Boston, Mr. Coppersmith has been active in many community organizations. Presently, he is President of the New England Broadcasting Association. Mr. Coppersmith is a graduate of the University of Pittsburgh.

RHO GROUP

Discussion Leader: Richard P. Levy; *Rapporteurs:* Robert Schlater, Ray L. Steele; Hayes L. Anderson; Myles P. Breen; R. John DeSanto; Kenneth R. Greenwood; C. A. Kellner; Robert L. LaConto; Albert Lewis; Jeffrey Lowenhar; William Parsons; Robert L. Stevens; James L. Tungate; Wesley H. Wallace; Joseph Wetherby; Carl Windsor.

HAYES L. ANDERSON. Professor Anderson has been with the Department of Telecommunications and Film, San Diego State University, San Diego, California since 1966 after having been at Michigan State University for three years. He received his B.A. from Oregon State University, Corvallis and his M.A. from Michigan State University where he also earned a Ph.D. Dr. Anderson has been a producer-director for ITV at San Diego State; earlier he had served as an associate

producer at KOAC-TV, Oregon State University station.

MYLES P. BREEN. Dr. Breen is Associate Professor of Speech Communication at Northern Illinois University, DeKalb. He received his Ph.D. from Wayne State University, Detroit, Michigan, and an M.S. from Syracuse in 1965.

R. JOHN DE SANTO. Chairperson of the Department of Mass Communications, St.

Cloud State University, since 1972, Dr. DeSanto was earlier at Bemidji State College, Minnesota. Dr. DeSanto spent 11 years teaching journalism and English at the secondary level. A graduate of the University of Minnesota, Duluth, from which he also earned an M.A., he was granted an Ed.D. from the University of Northern Colorado, Greeley. While at St. Cloud he has served as General Manager of KVSC-FM, the University station. He was Secretary of Bunyanland ETV in Bemidji from 1971 to 1972. Among Dr. DeSanto's publications has been ''If You Can't Stand the Heat'' published in the *Minnesota Journal of Education.* He is the recipient of two Newspaper Fund Fellowships.

KENNETH R. GREENWOOD. Professor Greenwood came to the University of Tulsa in 1974 after 11 years as President of Swanco Broadcasting Co., operators of KRMG and KWEN (FM) in Tulsa, Oklahoma. From 1959 to 1963 he had been President of Dandy Broadcasting in Wichita, Kansas and Peoria, Illinois. Professor Greenwood had also worked as a salesman for Storz Broadcasting and as Program Director for KMBC-TV in Kansas City, Missouri and as Program Director for Stuart Broadcasting in Lincoln, Nebraska. He is a 1949 graduate of the University of Nebraska, Lincoln.

ALBERT L. LEWIS. Dr. Lewis has been Associate Professor of Speech at Central Washington State College, Ellensburg, since 1965 and Department Chairman since 1973. In the 1968–69 academic year, he served as Visiting Professor at the University of California, Davis. He was awarded the Ph.D. from the same institution and a B.A. from Stanford University.

JEFFREY A. LOWENHAR. Dr. Lowenhar has been Assistant Professor in the Business School of Temple University, Philadelphia, Pa.; he had been at the University of Connecticut, Storrs, at Syracuse University, Syracuse, New York, and, from 1968 until 1970, Market Planning

Manager for Burndy Corporation, Norwalk, Connecticut. Dr. Lowenhar graduated from Fairleigh Dickenson University, New Jersey. He followed his B.S. with an M.B.A. at New York University and a Ph.D. at Syracuse. Dr. Lowenhar's articles have appeared in the *Journal of Marketing Research, Journal of Advertising Research, Journal of Economic Literature, Marketing News* and *Marketing Times.* He has also delivered papers before the National Conference of the American Academy of Advertising, the American Marketing Association and the American Institute for Decision Sciences.

WILLIAM PARSONS. Chairman of Fine Arts and Communications at Northern Kentucky State College, Highland Heights, Dr. Parsons had been at Western Kentucky University, Bowling Green; at Kentucky Southern College, Louisville; and at Memphis State University. He received a B.A. from Georgetown College and an M.A. and a Ph.D. from Louisiana State University in Baton Rouge. The author of various publications, Dr. Parsons has served as President of the Kentucky Speech Communication Association and of the Kentucky Theatre Association and is currently on the Task Force for Educational Television in Kentucky.

ROBERT SCHLATER. Since 1961, Dr. Schlater has been Professor and Chairman of the Department of Telecommunications at Michigan State University, East Lansing. From 1954 to 1961 he served as Assistant General Manager of KUON-TV, the University of Nebraska station in Lincoln. Earlier he was a radio news reporter for the *Providence Journal,* Providence, R.I. He received a B.A. from the University of Nebraska, an M.A. from Columbia University and a Ph.D. at Michigan State. A Colonel in the United States Army Reserve, he serves on the Consulting Faculty of the Command and General Staff College at Fort Leavenworth, Kansas.

RAY L. STEELE. Dr. Steele has been Assistant to the Provost since 1972 and Instructor of Speech since 1973 at the University of Pittsburgh. He had been at Cornell College, Mt. Vernon, Iowa, and at Northern Illinois University, DeKalb, from which he received a B.A. and an M.A. After attendance at the University of Iowa Law School, he received his Ph.D. from the University of Pittsburgh.

ROBERT L. STEVENS. At Northern Arizona State University, Flagstaff, Dr. Stevens is Professor and Chairman of the Department of Speech and Theater, posts he has held since 1956. Dr. Stevens has also taught at Chico State College, Chico, California, and at the University of Illinois in Champaign. He received a B.S. in Ed. from Arizona State University and an M.A. from the University of Illinois from which he also received his Ph.D. He is the Co-Author of *Competence in English* and the author of several other textbooks and various articles in English education methods and in American literature.

JAMES L. TUNGATE. Dr. Tungate joined the Department of Communications at Loyola University in New Orleans in 1971; since 1973 he has been Chairman of the Department. He has also served as Director of the Institute for Religious Communication. Prior to coming to Loyola, Dr. Tungate had been at Northwestern University, Evanston, Illinois. He was an announcer/reporter at WIOK in Normal, Illinois and at WMRO-AM-FM, Aurora. Dr. Tungate did his undergraduate work at Illinois Wesleyan, Bloomington, and received an M.A. and a Ph.D. from Northwestern. Dr. Tungate has written on popular songs and their imagery and on network programming.

WESLEY H. WALLACE. Currently as Professor, Dr. Wallace has been associated with the Department of Radio, Television and Motion Pictures of the University of North Carolina, Chapel Hill, since 1952, serving during part of that time as News Director for the University's station, WUNC-TV. He came to North Carolina University after serving as General Manager, Manila Broadcasting Company from 1947 to 1950 and Officer in Charge, Armed Forces Radio Service, South West Pacific, a post he held for the previous two years. Earlier he had been Officer in Charge of Armed Forces Radio Stations in Manila and in the Solomons. Before the war, Dr. Wallace spent seven years as announcer, writer, production manager and assistant program director at WPTF Radio, Raleigh, North Carolina. In 1932 he graduated from North Carolina State University in Raleigh and received an M.A. from the University of North Carolina in 1954. His Ph.D. was awarded in 1962 by Duke University. The author of a number of publications, Dr. Wallace was honored in 1975 with the North Carolina Association of Broadcaster's Earle G. Luck Award.

JOSEPH WETHERBY. Professor Wetherby has served at Duke University, Durham, North Carolina, since 1947, after serving at Wayne State University, Detroit, Michigan and at Oklahoma State University, Stillwater. The recipient of a B.A. and M.A. from Wayne State, Professor Wetherby has also done work at the University of Florida, Gainesville.

CARL WINDSOR. Since 1971, an Assistant Professor of Broadcasting at John Brown University, Siloam Springs, Arkansas, Mr. Windsor spent the previous year as a newsman for WJIM, Lansing, Michigan. He had earlier worked as announcer at WFMK (FM), East Lansing, and as News Director at WTOM-TV, Cheboygan and at WJML (FM), Petoskey, Michigan. In 1965, he had been a writer on the national broadcast wire for United Press International in Chicago. A Doctoral Candidate in Communications at Michigan State University from which he received a B.A. and an M.A., Mr. Windsor is also the graduate of the broadcast engineer course of the Cleveland Institute of Electronics. His publications include "News Survey on Religious Stations," *International Christian Broadcasters' Bulletin.* Founder of the Intercollegiate Religious Broadcasters, he is the editor of that organization's monthly newsletter, *Campus*

Radio News. In 1973, Mr. Windsor received the Outstanding Young Educator Award from the Jaycees.

RICHARD P. LEVY—*Industry Discussion Leader.* Richard P. Levy was appointed General Sales Manager of Avco Broadcasting's Columbus, Ohio television station, WLWC, TV-4, in 1973. Mr. Levy brought 17 years of sales and sales management experience to his position. His career began as a salesman at WCAU-

TV in Philadelphia. Immediately prior to his appointment to WLWC he was Special Assistant to the President of Tele-Rep, Inc. He has held positions in sales with the Petry Company in New York, and was Eastern Sales Manager for Storer Broadcasting. Mr. Levy has also been associated with CBS Inc., and was Eastern Sales Manager with Westinghouse Broadcasting. Mr. Levy holds a bachelor's degree in radio and television from the University of North Carolina.

TAU GROUP

Discussion Leader: George J. Mitchell; *Rapporteurs:* Carol Reuss, S. P., Donald E. Agostino; Robert L. Arnold; James A. Brown, S.J.; Royal D. Colle; W. Till Curry; Louis A. Day; Homer Eugene Dybvig; W. Knox Hagood; Joseph S. Johnson; Carol Kaucic; W. Ray Mofield; Paul H. Ptacek; John L. Stanton, Jr.; Peter M. Weiner.

DONALD E. AGOSTINO. A Research Associate at the Institute for Communication Research, Bloomington, Indiana, Dr. Agostino is also Assistant Professor of Radio-Television at Indiana University. Previously he had been at Ohio University, Athens, and Writer/Producer for KCTS-TV, the University of Washington station. Dr. Agostino received his A.B. and Ph.L. degrees from Gonzaga University in Spokane, an M.A. from the University of California, and a Ph.D. from Ohio University. He is the author of various articles and reports on theoretical and applied telecommunications research.

ROBERT L. ARNOLD. For the past seven years, Dr. Arnold has been both Professor of Communications and Program Management Consultant at Florida Technological University, Orlando. From 1963 to 1968, he was at Western Illinois University, Macomb. Dr. Arnold spent 12 years in commercial broadcasting, as director and manager at WCSH and WCSH-TV, Portland, and, earlier, as announcer and newsman at WLBZ, Bangor, Maine. A graduate of the University of

Maine, he received his M.A. and his Ph.D. from the University of Ohio. Dr. Arnold has long been engaged in research and scholarly publication in the areas of subliminal perception and nontraditional learning methods. He was the writer-producer on COLLEGE CLOSE UP and the Ohio State Award winning film, "When Suzie Speaks." His series, BIOLOGY AND MAN is currently in production.

JAMES A. BROWN, S.J. Currently at Loyola University at Los Angeles, Fr. Brown had taught at the University of Southern California and at the University of Detroit. In 1971, Fr. Brown served as resident consultant to the Vice President for Program Practices of the CBS Television Network. The recipient of an A.B. from Loyola and a Ph.L. and an M.A. from the same institution, he received an S.T.L. from the Bellarmine School of Theology after being ordained as a priest in the Roman Catholic Church. In 1970, Fr. Brown received a Ph.D. from the University of Southern California, Los Angeles. He is the co-author with Ward L. Quaal of the second edition of *Broadcast Manage-*

ment: Radio, Television and has written articles on communications in the New Catholic Encyclopedia. He has also been active on communications committees of the U.S. Catholic Conference, the Broadcast Educational Association and the National Advertising Review Board.

ROYAL D. COLLE. Dr. Colle has been teaching in Ithaca, New York for the past 20 years, for the last ten at Cornell University and for the previous ten years at Ithaca College. He interrupted this stay with a year as Project Specialist for the Ford Foundation in India in 1969–1970. He has also served as consultant to the World Bank and as Consultant to the Academy for Educational Development. Dr. Colle received a B.A. from the University of Connecticut, Storrs, an M.S. from Boston University and a Ph.D. from Cornell. Dr. Colle is the author of numerous articles on the role of communications in rural development.

W. TILL CURRY. Professor Curry has been in the Speech Department of the West Virginia State College, Institute, West Virginia since 1968. Earlier, he was a counselor with the West Virginia Division of Vocational Rehabilitation at the Fairfield School, Huntington, and a speech correctionist with the Kanawha County Board of Education. From 1961 to 1963, he was with WTIP, Charleston. A graduate of Morris Harvey College in Charleston, Professor Curry received his M.A. from Marshall University, Huntington, West Virginia, and has done additional work at the University of North Carolina.

LOUIS A. DAY. A member of the faculty in the Broadcasting and Cinematic Arts Area at Central Michigan University, Dr. Day came to his post after six years as a reporter which included a tour of duty as a United States Army military correspondent in Vietnam. He also worked as reporter/photographer for WRBL-TV, Columbus, Georgia. The recipient of an A.B.J. and A.M. from the University of Georgia, Athens, Georgia, he received a Ph.D. from the University of Ohio. Dr. Day is the author of "Intelstat and the Socialist Bloc Nations' Policy on Satellite Communications", *Journal of Broadcasting,* Fall 1974. He has also delivered papers on satellite communications before various organizations including the Southern Speech Communication Association and the International Communication Association.

HOMER EUGENE DYBVIG. From 1966, to the present, Dr. Dybvig has been Associate Professor of Radio and Television at Southern Illinois University, Carbondale. For the preceding five years he had been Operations Manager for the university's station, WSIU-TV. From 1955 to 1960 he was Program Manager for WTVH-TV, now ARAU-TV, Peoria, Illinois, after serving as Assistant Professor at Bradley University, Peoria, from 1950. Dr. Dybvig holds a B.F.A. and an M.F.A. from Ohio University, Athens, and a Ph.D. from Southern Illinois University. His publications have appeared in: *Educator's Review, Political Communications Review, Feedback,* and elsewhere.

W. KNOX HAGOOD. Chairman of the Department of Broadcast and Film Communication since 1962, Professor Hagood has been teaching at the University of Alabama, Tuscaloosa, since 1948. He served as Radio-TV Combat Reporter in the United States Army's Far Eastern Command from 1950 to 1952. From 1952 to 1956 he was Chief Continuity Writer for WJRD, Tuscaloosa. Professor Hagood received his B.A. from the University of Alabama and an M.A. from Northwestern University the following year and has done additional work toward the Ph.D. at Northwestern. He has been active in numerous professional organizations among them the Speech Communication Association of America, Southern Speech Communication Association, The Broadcast Education Association, Southeastern Theatre Conference, and the Alabama Broadcasters' Association.

JOSEPH S. JOHNSON. Dr. Johnson is Associate Professor of Telecommunications and Film, at San Diego State University. Presently doing free lance appearances in film and broadcasting, he has had ten years professional experience in radio and television as announcer, program director, producer and manager. A graduate of the University of Utah, Salt Lake City, he received his Ph.D. from Michigan State University, East Lansing. Dr. Johnson is the author of *Modern Radio Station Practices,* Wadsworth Press, 1972 now being revised for its second edition, and is at work on a second book.

CAROLE KAUCIC. Ms. Kaucic is in the Humanities Department at Spalding College, Louisville, Kentucky. Her prior experience includes teaching at a variety of primary and secondary levels and posts as media specialist, librarian, vice-principal in Massachusetts, Virginia and Kentucky. A graduate of Spalding she received an M.A. from Syracuse University.

W. RAY MOFIELD. Dr. Mofield came to Murray State University, Kentucky, in 1964. Currently he is Professor of Broadcasting. Earlier Dr. Mofield had been at Southern Illinois University, Carbondale, after 13 years in commercial broadcasting. He held various jobs at WPAD-AM-FM, Paducah, Kentucky, from Chief Announcer to Manager and was also Manager of WCBL-AM-FM, Benton, Kentucky. Dr. Mofield received a B.A. from Murray State and did graduate work in Broadcasting at Northwestern. In 1958, as a CBS Foundation News Fellow, he received an M.A. from Columbia. His Ph.D. was earned at Southern Illinois. Dr. Mofield's publications include *Southern Harmony,* "History of Jackson Purchase" and "N.B. Stubblefield, Inventor of Radio" in *JPHS Journal.*

PAUL H. PTACEK. Dr. Ptacek is Professor and Chairman of the Speech Department at Case Western Reserve University, Cleveland, Ohio, where he has taught since 1957. Previously he was at the University of Minnesota, Minneapolis, at Drake University, Des Moines, Iowa, and at Texas College of Arts and Sciences, Kingsville. Dr. Ptacek received his B.A. from the University of Colorado, Boulder, his M.A. from the University of Denver and his Ph.D. from the University of Minnesota. Dr. Ptacek is the author of numerous publications in Speech, Speech-Pathology, Speech Science, and Experimental Audiology and General Semantics. He is active in and has been honored by various professional organizations.

CAROL REUSS, S.P. Dr. Reuss is Associate Professor at Loyola University, New Orleans. From 1960 to 1971 she had been at St. Mary of the Woods College, Terre Haute, Indiana, as Instructor in Journalism and Assistant to the President. From 1954 to 1960, she was with Huebner Publications as Managing Editor and Editor of trade magazines. Dr. Carol Reuss received her B.A. from St. Mary in the Woods and her M.A. from the University of Iowa, Iowa City, from which she also received her Ph.D. She is the author of articles in various professional journals.

JOHN L. STANTON, JR. Dr. Stanton is Assistant Professor of Communications at Temple University, Philadelphia, Pa. He received the B.A. from the State University of New York at Syracuse and the Ph.D. from Syracuse University. Dr. Stanton's publications have appeared in *Journal of Marketing Research, Journal of Advertising Research, Marketing News, Marketing Times,* and the *Journal of the American Institute for Decision Sciences.*

PETER M. WEINER. Professor Weiner has been at Castleton State College, Castleton, Vermont, since 1974. Before that, he had been a television director for World Plan Video in Livingston Manor, New York and Director of Educational Communications at Hawthorne, for the New York State Education Department and at WCNY-TV, the public station in Syracuse, New York. The recipient of a B.S. from Syracuse University, he received an M.A. from New York University. Professor Weiner is the author of *Making the*

Media Revolution; A Handbook for Video-tape Production, now being prepared for a fifth edition.

GEORGE J. MITCHELL, *Industry Discussion Leader.* Mr. Mitchell is presently Vice President and General Manager of WKEF-TV, Dayton, Ohio and a Director of Springfield Broadcasting Corporation. Before becoming General Manager of Channel 22, Dayton, Mr. Mitchell served as Director, Producer and Program Manager, having joined the station in 1964. Mr. Mitchell, who has spent all his adult life in television, received an A.B. from Allegheny College and both an M.A. and M.S. from Syracuse University. He serves as Adjutant Associate Professor at Wright State University and is also active in many local Dayton activities.

SIGMA GROUP

Discussion Leader: Andrew Potos; *Rapporteurs:* William Hawes, Brian R. Naughton. Bertram Barer; Rod Clefton; James E. Fletcher; James S. Harris; Robert John Keiber; Bruce A. Linton; Paul I. McLendon; John W. Phelan; Charles E. Phillips; Peter K. Pringle; Lorin Robinson; Claude Sumerlin; Mary Jean Thomas; John F. Wellman.

BERTRAM BARER. Since 1960, Dr. Barer has been Chairman of the Radio-TV Department of California State University, Northridge. A communications consultant in the Los Angeles area, he has worked with both government and industry. Professor Barer received his B.S. from Syracuse University in 1951 and his M.A. and Ph.D. from the University of Minnesota, Minneapolis. He is a member of the Cable Advisory Task Force in Los Angeles.

JAMES E. FLETCHER. Dr. Fletcher is Assistant Professor of Journalism at the University of Georgia, Athens. Earlier, he was at the University of Kentucky, Lexington, and at the University of Utah, Salt Lake City. Dr. Fletcher spent seven years, from 1959 to 1968 in various assignments as an Infantry Officer in the United States Army. He received his B.A. from the University of Arizona and his Ph.D. from the University of Utah, Salt Lake City. Dr. Fletcher is the author of numerous publications, some of which are: *Telecommunications and You,* in press, Mayfield Press; a chapter in *Education in the Allied Health Professions,* Ford and Margan, eds.; and articles in *Jewish Social Studies, Journal of Broadcasting, Western Speech, Quarterly Journal of Speech,* and *Educational Instructional Broadcasting.*

JAMES S. HARRIS. Chairman and Assistant Professor of Communications at Eastern Kentucky University, Richmond, Professor Harris was from 1958 to 1965 at Murray State University, Murray, Kentucky. Professor Harris received his A.B. from the University of Kentucky, Lexington and his M.A. from the University of Illinois, Urbana. He is a candidate for the Ph.D. at the Ohio State University, Columbus. Professor Harris is a member of the Kentucky Educational Television Advisory Council and the Governor's Efficiency Task Force and President of the Kentucky Audio Visual Association.

WILLIAM HAWES. Dr. Hawes is Head of the Radio-Television-Film Department of the University of Houston, a post he has held since 1965. Previously, he was at the University of North Carolina, at Texas Christian University, Fort Worth and At Eastern Michigan University, Ypsilanti. Dr. Hawes has also worked at WTOP-TV, Washington as a free lance. He received his A.B. from Eastern Michigan University and his M.A. from the University of Michigan from which he also received the Ph.D. A contributing author to *Radio Broadcasting: An Introduction to the Sound Medium,* and to *Television Broadcasting: An Introduction to the Visual*

Mewdium, and author of *The Performer in Mass Media,* Dr. Hawes is also an Associate Professor in Biomedical Medical Information at the School of Applied Health Sciences, at the University of Texas and Executive Producer of *Campus Workshop* over KHTV, Houston.

ROBERT JOHN KEIBER. Professor Keiber is head of the Department of Radio, TV, and Film at Shaw University, Raleigh, North Carolina. Earlier he had been Chief Consultant on Production to the North Carolina Department of Education, producer/director at WUNJ-TV, Wilmington, N.C., and at WETA, Washington, D.C. He has also been a performer on daytime dramas and specials for NBC, CBS, and PBS. His publications have appeared in *Education/Instructional Television, TV Graphics* and elsewhere. He was the director of the EMMY Award winning PBS series, *Celebrate A Book.*

BRUCE A. LINTON. Dr. Linton is currently in the Journalism Department at Shaw University, Raleigh, North Carolina. Dr. Linton worked, in the late Forties, as announcer at WHIZ, Zanesville, Ohio, as Floor Director at WMAQ-TV, Chicago and producing weekly dramatic programs at WIND, also in Chicago. He received his B.A. from Muckingham College, New Concord, Ohio and his M.A. from Northwestern University, from which he also received a Ph.D. Twice President of the Broadcast Education Association, Dr. Linton has also been the BEA International Representative and National Scholarships Chairman. The author of numerous articles in professional journals, Dr. Linton is also the author of "Self-Regulation: A Study Guide," for which he received an NAB Citation. A resource person for the National Association of Broadcasters on a number of occasions, Dr. Linton has been an industry witness before Senator Pastore's committee hearings on License Renewal.

PAUL A. MC LENDON. Dr. McLendon is Director of Telecommunications at Oral Roberts University, Tulsa, Oklahoma. Prior to coming to Oral Roberts, Dr.

McLendon had been Director of Public Relations for Harrison National Life, Indianapolis, Indiana, and on the faculty of the University of Indiana and the University of Iowa. He earned an M.A. from Northwestern University and a Ph.D. from the University of Iowa, Iowa City. Dr. McLendon is the author of numerous articles in professional journals and has been a communications consultant in the United States and abroad.

BRIAN R. NAUGHTON. Since 1974, Mr. Naughton has been an Instructor in the College of Speech, Marquette University, Milwaukee, Wisconsin. Previously he had been at the University of South Dakota, Vermillion. He received his B.S. at the State University of New York, Oneonta, and his M.A. from Ohio State University, Columbus. He is a doctoral candidate at Bowling Green State, Bowling Green, Ohio. Among his publications are articles in the *Journal of the Wisconsin Communication Association,* and in *Feedback.*

JOHN M. PHELAN. Dr. Phelan has been Chairman and Professor of Communications at Fordham University, New York, N.Y., since 1968. Since 1973 he has also been Editor and Associate at the Institute for Social Research. The recipient of both an A.B., and an M.A. from Fordham, he earned a Ph.D. from New York University. He is the author of *Communications Control.*

CHARLES E. PHILLIPS. Professor Phillips is Chairman of the Department of Mass Communications at Emerson College, Boston, Massachusetts. His earlier experience includes service at WCVS and at WTAX both in Springfield, Illinois. He holds a B.S. and an M.S. from the University of Illinois, Urbana.

PETER K. PRINGLE. Professor of Mass Communications and Director of the Caribbean Institute of Mass Communications of the University of the West Indies, Kingston, Jamaica, Dr. Pringle was previously, from 1969 to 1971, Senior Sub-Editor for the BBC in London. Before that he had been a scriptwriter for television news. From 1958 to 1968 he was a broadcast writer/editor for the Associated Press in New York. He has also been a reporter and sub-editor for the Cumberland Newspapers, Carlisle, England. Dr. Pringle received his B.A. from the University of London and an M.A. in Journalism from the University of Florida, Gainesville. His Ph.D. was awardewd by Ohio University, Athens. Dr. Pringle has had experience with radio stations in Athens, Ohio and Gainesville, Florida and was the recipient of the Frank Stanton Fellowship from the IRTS in 1974.

LORIN ROBINSON. A member of the Faculty at the University of Wisconsin, Mr. Robinson has worked in various radio stations and newspapers as Manager of WRFW, RIVER Falls, Wisconsin, a producer for KTCA-TV, St. Paul, Minnesota, staff writer for the St. Paul *Pioneer Press,* Wire Editor and Staff writer for the *Daily News Record,* Harrisonburg, Virginia, Editor for the National Eye Research Foundation, Chicago, Assistant Editor for Jefferson Publications, Chicago, and as reporter for the Lerner Newspapers Chicago. Previously, he was with radio station VOUS, St. John's, Newfoundland and with WBLT, Bedford, Virginia and KONI, Spanish Fork, Utah as an announcer and with WEAW, Evanston, Illinois, as Assistant Program Director. Mr. Robinson received his B.S. and M.S. from Northwestern and is A.B.D. at the University of Minnesota. His dissertation is entitled, *News on Public Television: An Investigation of an Alternative Format for the Presentation of TV News.*

CLAUDE SUMERLIN. Dr. Sumerlin is currently in the Department of Journalism of Henderson State College, Arkadelphis, Arkansas. Dr. Sumerlin had previously spent 11 years as a professional newspaperman and public relations practitioner, Director of Public Relations for the Quachita Baptist University, Arkadelphia, a sports writer on the San Antonio *Express* and the *Evening News,* on the Tyler Texas *Courier-Times-Telegraph,* and, while a student, a reporter and editor on the Co-

lumbia *Missourian.* He received his B.A. from Texas A and I University, Kingville, and his M.A. from Baylor University, Waco, Texas. He received his Ph.D. from the University of Missouri. Dr. Sumerlin's publications include "Let Your Editors Edit," *Photolith,* "Christopher Smart's *Song of David:* It's Influence on Robert Browning," Costerus Essays, 1972, Amsterdam, the Netherlands, and numerous articles published at the state and regional level.

MARY JEAN THOMAS. Chairman and Associate Professor of Communication Arts at Loyola University, Chicago, since 1974 Dr. Thomas was previously at Case Western Reserve University where she received the Carl F. Wittke Award for Excellence in Teaching; the University of Massachusetts, Amherst; at Penn State University, State College, Pa.; and at the University of South Dakota, Vermillion. Dr. Thomas received her B.S. from Fort Hays State College, Kansas, an M.A. from Kansas State University in Manhattan, and her Ph.D. from Penn State. With Estelle Zannes she is the Co-author of *Checkmate in Cleveland,* published in 1972 by the Case Western Reserve Press, and was co-producer of the award winning KWYC-TV, Cleveland, Ohio, documentary series, GOVERNANCE.

JOHN F. WELLMAN. Since 1973, Dr. Wellman has been in the Department of Speech Communications, Illinois University. For the preceding three years he was President of Wellman-Van Horn Productions. He is currently also President of J4 Media. Dr. Wellman was a Director at the University of Michigan TV Center at WJBK-TV, Detroit, an announcer at WTHI-AM-FM-TV and Sales Manager at WPFR-FM, both in Terre Haute, Indiana. Dr. Wellman received his B.S. and his Ph.D. from the University of Michigan. He is the recipient of various awards and grants and an active member of professional organizations.

ANDREW POTOS, *Industry Discussion Leader.* Andrew Potos has been the Vice President and General Sales Manager at

Storer Television Sales since January, 1973. STS is a television representative firm, owned and operated by the Storer Broadcasting Company. Prior to that appointment, Mr. Potos was the General Sales Manager at WITI-TV, Milwaukee, a Storer-owned station, from 1969 to 1973. From 1966 to 1969, Mr. Potos was the National Sales Manager at the station. He began his career at Storer in 1961 as a local salesman for WITI-TV. In 1963 he moved to Chicago as an STS Account Executive, a position he held for three years. Born in Milwaukee, Mr. Potos earned his B.A. and M.A. degrees in history from Marquette University. From 1954 to 1961 he taught history and English in the Milwaukee Public School System.

IRTS FACULTY-INDUSTRY SEMINAR
NOVEMBER 10–14, 1975

Seminar Committee

Co-Chairmen: Gene Accas (Leo Burnett, USA); Aaron Cohen (NBC-TV)

Engineering "Package": Robert J. Wormington (KMBA-TV)

Faculty Recruitment: Ralph Baruch (Viacom); Bill Behanna (A.C. Nielsen Co.); A. O. Knowlton (General Foods); Neil Walden (WCBS-TV)

FCC Application Abstract: Alan Kaufman (Fly, Shuebruk, Blume & Gaguine)

Financial "Package": Bill Walsh (NBC)

Industry Recruitment:

Participants: Bob Bernstein (March Five Inc.); George Dessart (WCBS-TV); Bruce Fogel (Air Time); Gerry Greenberg (Allscope); M. S. Kellner (SRA); Stan Moger (SFM); Al Shepard (Media Corp.)

Guests: Harry Francis (Meredith Broadcasting); Fred Plant (Block Drug Co.)

Logistics: Marti Stein (NBC-TV)

Market Profile: Betty Fox (Corinthian Broadcasting); Frank Tuoti (WPIX)

Network Affiliation Contract: Ray O'Connell (NBC-TV)

Problem Development: George Dessart (WCBS-TV); Dr. Robert Stanley (Hunter College, CUNY)

Program Facts/Analysis: Chuck Bachrach (Ogilvy & Mather)

Research: Charles B. Schneider (NBC-TV)

Special Fund Raising: Steve Nenno (ABC-TV)

Special Nielsen Report: Bill Behanna (A.C. Nielsen Co.); Chuch Bachrach (Ogilvy & Mather)

Special Technical Advisor: Peter Willett (UPI)

Photography: Courtesy CBS-TV and NBC-TV

Tapes: Courtesy NBC Radio Network

Tape Editing: Courtesy Faith Rogers Productions

Technical Equipment: Courtesy of UPI, ABC Owned Radio and TV Stations

Transportation: Courtesy ABC-TV, CBS Press Relations, Oldsmobile Division of General Motors Corp.

Index

427